Tarnished Heroes, Charming Villains,
and Modern Monsters

Tarnished Heroes, Charming Villains, and Modern Monsters

Science Fiction in Shades of Gray on 21st Century Television

LYNNETTE PORTER

McFarland & Company, Inc., Publishers

Jefferson, North Carolina, and London

LIBRARY OF CONGRESS CATALOGUING-IN-PUBLICATION DATA

Porter, Lynnette, 1957–
    Tarnished heroes, charming villains and modern monsters :
science fiction in shades of gray on 21st century television /
Lynnette Porter.
        p.   cm.
    Includes bibliographical references and index.

    ISBN 978-0-7864-4858-6
    softcover : 50# alkaline paper ∞

    1. Science fiction television programs—History and criticism.
2. Heroes on television.   3. Villains on television.   I. Title.
PN1992.8.S35P67   2010
791.45′615 — dc22   2010024637

British Library cataloguing data are available

Cover image: John Barrowman as Jack Harkness in *Torchwood* (BBC
America/Photofest)

Manufactured in the United States of America

McFarland & Company, Inc., Publishers
  Box 611, Jefferson, North Carolina 28640
    www.mcfarlandpub.com

Acknowledgments

Popular culture is a huge part of my life. In 2009 alone, I attended Megacon and Torchsong and participated as a speaker during sessions of the Hawaii International Conference on the Arts and Humanities, Popular Culture Association, Cornerstone Festival, Dragon Con, and Hurricane Who. I incorporate multimedia texts in many courses I teach and encourage my students to enjoy and, I hope, learn from these stories. Meeting people who inspire, create, analyze, and love science fiction TV heroes, villains, and monsters continues to be a joy of my professional and fan life.

Whether we chatted during a session, in a hallway or queue, or at the pub, thank you to these events' guests, scholars, and fans who shared their love of the series discussed in this book. Your enthusiasm for the heroes, villains, and monsters on SF TV today inspires me and reminds me of the power of storytelling.

I especially thank Gareth David-Lloyd for allowing me to interview him for this book and so graciously sharing his insights and experiences on *Torchwood* with my students and me. Thank you, too, for making Ianto Jones memorable and giving me so much to write about.

I also heartily thank Carole E. Barrowman for chatting with me during Torchsong as well as patiently answering my many email questions about "Selkie" and Captain Jack. Thank you for your books and stories, which I happily quote and use in class and within this book.

I thank the actors who, during convention sessions, graciously answered my questions about their characters or their approach to character development: John Barrowman, James Callis, Nathan Fillion, Greg Grunberg, James Marsters, and Adrian Pasdar. Thank you, too, to artist Tommy Lee Edwards, who helped me better understand the marriage of image and word for a meaningful comic and kindly answered my questions about "Selkie," and to writer Rob Shearman for his insights about *Doctor Who*.

As a fan as well as a teacher, I am indebted to the creative teams behind each series discussed in this book. You have enriched my understanding of hero texts. You've also taken many hours of my life, but you've given me plenty to think about in return.

Kristen Fitzgerald and Suzanna Brooks deserve a special thank you for reading and proofing several early drafts of these chapters. Your assistance has been invaluable.

And, as always, I am in awe of the "everyday heroes" in my life — Bart, Nancy, and Heather. You make everything worthwhile.

Table of Contents

Introduction

Fascination with heroes and villains seems a constant, as much in real life as in fantasy or science fiction (SF). In the past few years, however, public and academic interest in these characters has taken on greater importance in light of global sociopolitical events and changes. What makes us human, what separates "us" from "them," and how we might be saved from destruction are hot topics not only on television or in films but in the news.

Films are a good starting place for any discussion of villains or monsters. Not only do films unite Western societies culturally, but they show "evil" up close on larger-than-life screens in a way that TV series can't. They also provide TV series with plenty of ideas for re-imagined characters. Television often follows where blockbuster films have led. In 2008 the *Dark Knight* became even darker, and the charismatic if sociopathic Joker (aided by an Academy Award–winning performance by the late Heath Ledger) stole the screen. When the U.K.–based science fiction magazine *SFX* cited their Top 10 SF films and TV series of the decade in their December 2009 publication, not surprisingly, *The Dark Knight* made their film list (as did *The Lord of the Rings* cinematic trilogy, despite being more fantasy than science fiction, and director J.J. Abrams' re-imagined view of *Star Trek*).[1] These films and their iconic "good" and "bad" characters are discussed in greater depth in Part One of this book because they have influenced or led to the development of recent SF TV series. The characters and their different perspectives on morality, the roles of heroes or villains within society, and "predictions" of where civilization is headed not only illustrate a likely paradigm shift in the hero story but also provide cultural touchstones with which most audiences are familiar.

The *SFX* list of Top 10 television series included *Angel*, *Lost*, *Firefly* (whose later film adventure, *Serenity*, also made their Top 10 film list), *Battlestar Galactica*, and *Doctor Who*. Other notable achievements in their "review of the decade" were noted in their TV Awards of the Decade: Most Improved Show—*Torchwood*, Best Character—the Doctor (*Doctor Who*, which also was cited for Best TV Episode—"Blink"), Best U.S. TV Show—*Battlestar Galactica*, Sexiest Characters—Caprica Six (*Battlestar Galactica*) and Spike (*Buffy the Vampire Slayer*, *Angel*), Most Huggable Persons—Wilfrid Mott (*Doctor Who*) and Hiro

Nakamura (*Heroes*), and Most Welcome Casting—John Simm (the Master, *Doctor Who*). Although these "awards" are unofficial, *SFX*, one of the leading fan-oriented SF magazines in the U.K. and U.S., is well aware of audience favorites and high-quality SF films and series. Their list, released long after my selection of series to be included in this book, indicates the impact on popular culture that these post–2000 series have had and will continue to have.

Other well-known television and film publications polled audiences about their favorite heroes and villains, not just from science fiction or fantasy. In early 2009, *Entertainment Weekly* featured a special section on all-time heroes and villains from movies and TV. Fans as well as critics chose the top 20 in each category. The number 1 villain was *The Wizard of Oz*'s Wicked Witch of the West. Not surprisingly, *The Wizard of Oz* has influenced many fantasy or SF TV series, including *Lost*. The number 2 villain was Darth Vader, again not much of a shock. *Star Wars* remains an iconic part of popular culture, its clearly defined heroes neatly separated from villains. It, too, is an ancestor text for many series such as *Lost*.

Although *Entertainment Weekly*'s heroes list highlighted a wide variety of films and TV series, many of them SF, the ones to note in light of this book are everyone's favorite vampire slayer, Buffy (number 8), and *Star Trek*'s inimitable Captain James T. Kirk (number 12). Although not an SF character, *24*'s Jack Bauer came in at number 16.[2] The fact that such a controversial "hero," what I term in this book a "gray hero," made the Top 20 all-time film and television heroes list is significant. For all his good intentions and ability to save the world within 24 hours (not once, but several times), Jack Bauer does some terrible things as part of his "job."

Instead of being perfect heroes, the cinematic or televisionary heroes who are best "loved," or at least most memorable, are increasingly becoming those far removed from the traditional, idealized, highly moral heroes of the past. The public can't seem to get enough of heroes, even if they aren't always clearly the "good guys."

As *Lost* co-creator Damon Lindelof explained in a 2009 interview, audiences "want heroes to know the difference between good and bad, and ... to be strong.... However, it's hard for such [heroes] to be accessible unless they're also extremely effed up, because only a seriously disturbed individual would want to be a hero."[3] Western societies are looking for heroes to help get us out of what seem to be insurmountable global problems, but one hero, or even a group, seems unlikely to be able to do the job. Those TV characters who do get involved or regularly try to save the world usually have their own flaws and dark pasts to deal with, yet they persevere, often because they feel they have no other choice. Television seems to be a good starting place to "discuss" the type of heroes needed today, especially when real-life heroes haven't provided all the solutions to our problems. The types of heroes emerging on SF TV, however, may not have all the answers, even if they consistently try to provide pragmatic solutions under tight deadlines.

In the early 2000s, television, still the most accessible of popular culture media, is at the peak of its SF storytelling power. Lindelof knows well the ins and outs of good storytelling and the ways that audiences like their heroes, villains, and even monsters. Peabody winner *Lost* continues to skew the definitions of *hero* and *villain*, and with a mysterious island as a story playground, even the occasional smoke monster shows up. For six seasons (2004–2010) *Lost* changed the way that serialized TV dramas were told. Perhaps by sneaking in a mainstream network's back door as a "plane crash drama" in Season One, *Lost* gave the audience a mysterious character drama that, once embraced, could lead to more obviously SF story lines in later seasons.

Another highly significant, critically acclaimed series, *Battlestar Galactica*, also deals with human drama during times of crisis—this time an apocalypse that forces a small percentage of human survivors to strike out for a new homeland. The series takes on such issues as struggles between "them" and "us" but also deals with humanity's reliance on technology, the place of religion within a society, and the appropriate roles of government and the military in the lives of ordinary citizens. In March 2009, *Battlestar Galactica* concluded with a critically acclaimed finale proclaiming that humanity's mortal enemy, the Cylons, is indeed crucial to human survival. Future *Battlestar Galactica* projects promise further glimpses into prewar Caprica, and the DVD pilot movie, released in April 2009, generated plenty of interest in the Sci-Fi (later SyFy) Channel's original *Caprica* series beginning in January 2010.

Heroes took the increased interest in film superheroes and provided some intriguing, if flawed, characters just discovering their superpowers. Although the series' brilliant first season has been difficult to replicate, its notion that "gray areas" are the only viable places in which either heroes or villains can effect change still makes *Heroes* a significant series. As well, the series often revolves around two important characters, the devious Sylar and virtuous Hiro, as well as making the modern hero story accessible to a much wider audience.

The longest-running SF television program, *Doctor Who*, won new fans across generations when Russell T. Davies reinvented the series in 2005. David Tennant's popular Tenth Doctor, in particular, turned the children's program into an award-winning drama that intrigues adults as much as (if not more than) kids. By the Tenth Doctor's regeneration on January 1, 2010, he had faced classic monsters from the original series and, more importantly, faced his own weaknesses, losses, and fears as humanity's sometimes-savior.

The U.K. cult series and *Doctor Who* spinoff *Torchwood* moved to BBC1 from lesser watched BBC3 for Season Three, "Children of Earth," a devastating look at no-win scenarios when humanity is faced with a threat greater than it can defeat and requires high costs in personal sacrifice. The miniseries also illustrates, yet again, a familiar SF horror — manipulative, callous governments only out to protect themselves. With the success of "Children of Earth," *Torchwood* has become BBC America's highest rated show, and its popularity continues to grow on both sides of the pond. In 2010 U.S. cable network Starz created a unique partnership with the BBC to develop episodes for 2011.

In response to increased public pessimism about the future of humanity, SF television series have veered away from traditional hero stories. Instead, the trend is toward a grayer middle ground in which some characters may become heroic, or villainous, for a time, and villains or monsters stand just as good a (if not a better) chance of being victorious. Human survival, much less success, isn't guaranteed, and no savior with humanity's best interests at heart seems to be heading our way.

Late 2009 entries vying for primetime ratings included *V* (lizard aliens/ monsters poised to take over Earth after offering to heal and save humanity), *FlashForward* (almost everyone on the planet blacks out for more than two minutes, most seeing their future; the blackout causes mass chaos), and *The Prisoner* (one man awakens in a "village" that seems more like a futuristic POW camp, leading to questions about free will). These continuing and mini-series join other late 2000–era SF such as Joss Whedon's (soon canceled) *Dollhouse* and J.J. Abrams' (increasingly popular alternate universed) *Fringe*, and follow in the illustrious SF footsteps of earlier 2000s series like *Battlestar Galactica* and the limited but cult favorite *Firefly*. Although several recently popular series are remakes (e.g., *Battlestar Galactica*, *V*, *The Prisoner*) of camp or creepy SF from the 1960s through the 1980s, the current sociopolitical climate encourages the development of more darkly re-imagined versions of series dealing with apocalyptic plots.

The first decade of the 21st century has been a good time for science fiction series internationally, and SF, as it so often can do better than other genres, provides a safe place in which possible solutions or consequences to important problems can be played out. Unlike previous iterations of these and other series, however, the future portrayed in recent SF series is bleak. The gray heroes and villains now populating TV screens seem just as helpless as the rest of us, even if they become the characters to step forward and act heroically in an attempt to help others or to save the planet.

Whether audiences watch first-run episodes on cable (e.g., Sci-Fi/SyFy, BBCAmerica) or mainstream networks (e.g., ABC, NBC, Fox, BBC, CTV, Australia's Network 10 or the U.K.'s Five), or prefer to watch these stories on DVD or online, well-written, fan-loved SF most clearly illustrates the schism between traditional "good guys" and "bad guys," and the more modern shades of gray clouding definitions of *hero*, *villain*, and *monster*.

Of course, in SF, "villain" often equals "alien" or "monster," so a discussion of what makes a classic or a modern villain must include an analysis of non-human life forms or hybrids. Recent series' "heroes" may have an alien or monstrous past, or the monsters the heroes are so intent upon destroying may not be as bad as initially portrayed. At this pivotal time in world history, audiences are coming to understand current sociopolitical issues and their possible consequences by watching intriguing, multiple-layered SF stories that reflect cultural ambiguity about the nature of "heroes" and "villains."

In the following chapters I discuss characters from cult or mainstream popular science fiction television (SF TV) series originating in the U.S. or U.K. but available on DVD or via downloads worldwide. As a special feature, I include a separate list of episodes discussed within chapters so that readers can turn to specific episodes and see complete stories that illustrate the points being made about villains, monsters, or heroes within chapters. In addition, several series have officially sanctioned (not to mention unofficial) novels, magazines, comics or graphic novels, soundtracks, radio plays/CDs, and other "texts" that may be useful for further exploring characters and themes initially presented during TV episodes. Several of these additional texts are discussed in the following chapters, most notably regarding *Torchwood*.

The book is arranged as follows:

Part One includes all background material and discussion of multiple examples from all series highlighted in later chapters. Shifts from traditional heroes and villains to gray ones, the rise of the "sidekick" character, analyses of the roles of monsters in SF stories, themes inherent in modern SF TV series, and ways to approach a study of gray series and characters are emphasized in the first five chapters.

Part Two provides an in-depth look at the characters, episodes, and themes most important to an understanding of key science fiction television series. The following chapters of Part Two emphasize series and main characters.

About Chapter 6: The World of Joss Whedon

Buffy the Vampire Slayer, *Angel*, and *Firefly* illustrate characters and themes important to SF shortly after 2000. Buffy Summers and Captain Mal Reynolds help illustrate the shift to ever-grayer heroes, but vampires Angel and even Spike show some surprising characteristics that can turn them into either heroes or villains, as well as "monsters" because of their vampire nature. The Reavers, of course, are important to the discussion of *Firefly*, as is the Alliance that rules a post–Unification War universe.

Whedon's long-time series, spanning the 1990s into the early 2000s, help track a shift in hero "literature" from the more traditional coming-of-age Buffy stories to the far-less-hopeful world of Angel to an often-oppressive future. The short webisodes making up 2008's *Dr. Horrible's Sing-Along Blog* parody the hero-villain-monster themes Whedon presented in the fantastic worlds of *Buffy*, *Angel*, and *Firefly* and illustrate how acceptably gray the lead villain and hero have become. This parody, moreso than Whedon's series *Dollhouse*, illustrates the shift from perky, wide-eyed young heroes to disillusioned veterans to tarnished "heroes" and up-and-coming "villains."

About Chapter 7: Heroes

Heroes is in a category all its own. Although superheroes are their own subgenre of SF or fantasy, *Heroes* represents an alternate (i.e., comic book) reality reflecting viewers' real-world crises. The politicians, corporate executives, university students, cube nerds, and middle managers depicted as heroes and villains mirror roles and assumptions about them shared by many viewers. Much of the time *Heroes* may seem more fantasy than science fiction, but superhero literature traditionally is considered part of SF hero literature. As well, a discussion of television series about heroes and villains simply must include examples from a series called *Heroes.*

This series presents a traditional hero in Hiro Nakamura, whose early character development parallels the hero's journey established by Joseph Campbell. As well, "good girl" Claire Bennet becomes a latter day Buffy in her coming-of-age story as a teenaged superhero struggling to find her place in the world. The heroes' nemesis, Sylar, becomes one of the most charismatic characters on the series, and a study of *Heroes* must include the important rise of the all-powerful villain as well as the fall (or at least the stumble) of the traditional hero.

About Chapter 8: Lost

Because *Lost* changes its story emphasis and, frequently, its cast of characters during each of its six seasons, only a few of the many heroes, villains, or monsters are discussed. Jack Shephard, the character put forth most forcefully and continuously as the series' hero, is the primary focus of this chapter. Ben Linus, whether perceived as villain or self-proclaimed "good guy," is another intriguing character who well illustrates the level of grayness/darkness of SF television characters. However, the series' ongoing tug of war between "men of faith" and "men of science" provides interesting social commentary about whether science/technology or religion/spirituality should be the primary force guiding humanity. This theme, well represented by heroes, villains, and monsters who populate a mysterious island, helps illustrate how *Lost* Western societies have become.

About Chapter 9: Battlestar Galactica *and* Caprica

Although humans and Cylons represent both "faith" and "science" in this politically volatile series, the more important theme is "what makes us human." The Cylons are one of SF's best-developed "monster" races, and their origins on a Caprica that mirrors 21st century Earth hint at the direction Western societies might be taking. Religion, terrorism, scientific superiority, and cultural conflicts provide the dramatic tension in the re-imagined *Battlestar Galactica* and its spinoff prequel, *Caprica*. Although humanity is analyzed in this chapter, the most interesting characters are a fallen human scientist (Gaius Baltar) and his muse/paramour/advisor/critic, the Cylon Caprica Six and the many "model Six" incarnations throughout the series. By seeing "monsters" from a different perspective, audiences can learn what it means to be "human."

The pilot and early episodes of *Caprica* present an in-depth look at a civilization soon to explode, both because of the frustratingly different philosophies of colliding cultures and the rise of technology. More than any other SF series, even its parent *Battlestar Galactica*, *Caprica* directly confronts and confounds definitions of *human*. Although the series and its conflicting families, the Graystones and the Adamas, provide plenty of drama, the larger issue of how much a technologically advanced society can or should "play god" is emphasized in this chapter.

About Chapter 10: Doctor Who

This children's television series also may be fantasy as much as science fiction, despite its time travel premise, but its stature as the longest running SF program also puts *Doctor Who* in a category of its own. The Doctor is a perennial hero whose adventures have been enjoyed by several generations internationally.

What makes the series important to a post–2000 analysis of gray heroes is the direction in which Russell T. Davies and Julie Gardner steered the good Doctor beginning in 2005. The re-imagined series involving the Ninth and Tenth Doctors still can be considered a children's program, if one that becomes increasingly dark during the latter episodes of Tennant's tenure as the Doctor. Stories involving aliens, the possible annihilation of humanity, less than scrupulous world leaders, and a main character (the Ninth Doctor) quite frankly suffering from Post-Traumatic Stress Disorder (PTSD) and then from the continued sacrifice/loss of loved ones (the Tenth Doctor) make the 2005–2009 Davies era important to adults.

The new *Who*, as written and guided by Davies, re-invented this venerable SF series for a new world and new audiences worldwide. In doing so, Davies also faced questions about how much "darkness" is appropriate for children's programming and what type of Doctor is suitable for 21st century audiences. That such an established hero may not be as good as audiences previously believed, or regenerates into ever grayer Doctors, made the Tenth Doctor increasingly controversial (and internationally popular).

About Chapter 11: Torchwood

This "adult" spinoff of *Doctor Who*, also guided by co-creators Davies and Gardner, perhaps is the darkest science fiction series to date. Its immortal hero, Captain Jack Harkness, sometimes may seem villainous or downright monstrous to audiences, depending upon the episode (such as the highly acclaimed but controversial "Children of Earth" miniseries). *Torchwood* presents a bleak view of the present and seems to offer little hope for a less challenging future. Its opening narration informs audiences that humanity must be armed against the future because "the 21st century is when everything changes." Nevertheless, *Torchwood*'s heroes willfully take on the villains and monsters that attempt to destroy civilization, whether coming from another time or intergalactic location or just down the street.

In particular, "Children of Earth" is highlighted as a benchmark for gray heroes and series, and Captain Jack Harkness is analyzed as a pivotal SF television character. *Torchwood* is also notable for its intertextuality, which presents different versions of Captain Jack for different audiences, further emphasizing this character's importance in the development and change of SF TV heroes. Examples from novels, BBC Radio plays, soundtrack CDs, and comics supplement Jack's TV-episode development and illustrate the many shades of gray inherent within *Torchwood*.

The book concludes with materials designed to help science fiction television scholars and fans continue their exploration of these characters as gray heroes, villains, or monsters and to return to episodes and other texts that further discuss themes presented in these recent series. The aforementioned episode guide is a good place to start further exploration of gray TV series. As well, the complete bibliography of sources used in this book offers a reading list of online and in-print materials.

The characters and themes described in this book indicate the prevalence of gray characters and, more important, a paradigm shift in the definition of cultural heroes and villains, as well as expectations for these roles. As these series so aptly portray, the actions we take now, in good faith and with the best intentions, may be leading to tomorrow's destruction. By relying on technology as our savior, by welcoming a brave new world that can help millions lead longer, healthier, more productive lives, we may also be destroying what is "human" about us. Actions and their consequences—such as whether individuals can even make a difference—are the stuff of excellent SF TV drama and character development, and the series discussed in this book provide characters struggling with the same issues as the audiences who watch them.

Gray characters, like viewers, embrace the basic elements of humanity: the need for connection with others, the capacity and need for love, and the desire for a meaningful life. A strength of these SF TV series is that they deal with larger technological, political, military, ecological, and spiritual dilemmas, but their characters also face very personal human dramas: what it means to be a spouse or a parent (or a child), how to be a better person, what type of legacy to leave behind, how to face death — or life, what to believe.

What we do now determines what our future will be. According to the gray heroes and villains on post–2000 science fiction television, that future may be bleak unless we make the right choices. What separates gray heroes from villains may be slight shadings of right and wrong. The characters in the following chapters illustrate not only the myriad choices being made, on science fiction TV as well as in the real world, but the ramifications and consequences of these decisions. SF TV today, more than ever, mirrors our world and offers us less cheery but more realistic illustrations of who we are and where we might want (or not want) to go to ensure the survival of humanity, much less make that future a better one.

It is my hope that this book, like the TV series it explores, encourages discussion about these important topics and challenges readers and TV audiences as they struggle with their own decisions and philosophies. Perhaps we are all gray heroes in the making.

PART ONE

1

The Evolution of the
Traditional Hero

What makes a hero? That seems like an easy question, but literary scholars, not to mention philosophers, political scientists, and journalists, among many others, have asked that question for a very long time. It would seem to be relatively simple: A hero is someone who ... fill in the blank with something noble or self-sacrificing.

Does a hero, however, have to be a pillar of society or just someone in the right place at the right time? Does being a hero have to involve saving others' lives, or can it be something less life threatening but nonetheless important, such as providing a home for a foster child or dropping spare change in a donations bin for the homeless? Does a heroic act count if it's premeditated, or is spontaneous heroism a mark of the real thing? If someone is a hero once, does he or she have to keep being a hero, looking for even greater deeds to perform, or is a one-time act enough to grant hero status to a person for all time?

If I asked a roomful of people who their heroes are, I probably would hear as many different types of heroes and heroic acts as there are people in the room; the group most likely wouldn't agree on just one definition of *hero*. That's part of the problem when storytellers, not to mention newscasters or audiences, bandy about the label of *hero*. Just what is meant by that simple word? Creating a definition is even more difficult because changes in cultural values, over time and through paradigm shifts, often lead to changes in definitions, including that of *hero*. Nevertheless, Western cultures like to identify and define such terms, especially those laden with multiple meanings and personal connotations.

In this chapter, criteria for the definition of *traditional hero* and elements of the traditional hero's development are introduced, from classic literature (with examples from *Beowulf, Sir Gawain and the Green Knight*, and *The Lord of the Rings*) to more recent films (e.g., *Star Wars, Star Trek*) and TV series (e.g., *Heroes, Lost, Battlestar Galactica, Caprica, Torchwood, Doctor Who*). In particular, this chapter includes analysis of the ways that expectations for heroes— such as their morality (or lack of)—change when cultural expectations and a society's need for role models change. Today's SF TV heroes are less likely to be ideal role models than flawed characters with good intentions, much like the majority of the audience who follows their TV adventures.

Another shift in the way that heroes are portrayed involves the concept of "home." Whereas traditional heroes usually found or returned to their permanent, beloved home after an adventure, modern heroes may be homeless wanderers or characters forced to leave their homeland and forge less conventional families as they struggle through their journey. As discussed later in this chapter, "home" is becoming an increasingly important story element in the development of modern heroes.

Finally, the "one true leader" hero or the loner hero is less appealing to modern audiences. Unlike a traditional hero who is often *the* hero of a story, recent TV series (including but not limited to SF) feature ensembles with several potential heroes or provide shifting power structures in which the lead characters, not just a single hero, share elements of the traditional hero's role as a savior/leader/protector. All these trends in SF TV series affect not only the development of modern heroes but indicate that traditional literary heroes and their cinematic and televisionary descendents have evolved into very different, darker types of heroes. Recent TV characters may try to retain characteristics exemplified by their ancestors but are morphing into pragmatic, morally ambiguous gray heroes more palatable for current TV audiences.

Traditional Literary Heroes and Their Descendents

One of the most widely known literary critics, Joseph Campbell, identified traditional literary heroes by their common actions within the story. The hero's journey, as described by Campbell, can be simplified into stages: departure (from home) or separation (from the hero's former life and all that is familiar), initiation (into the outside world and the skill set needed to accomplish his quest, leading to the realization of that quest), and return (home, although the hero is forever changed).[1] Although Campbell's description originally explained a literary hero's creation and maturation, these developmental stages also can be easily applied to other media "texts," including films and television series.

These stages can be further broken into steps or actions that maturing heroes traditionally take, such as accepting a call to action, finding a mentor, leaving home to take up a quest or to right a wrong, finding and learning to use a special weapon, learning about a world far different from home, being tested, questioning their ability to be heroic, facing their own mortality, accepting the less-than-perfect aspects of themselves but attempting to live better lives, accomplishing the quest or completing a task that no one else (or very few) could do, returning home more experienced and wiser, and, perhaps, instructing the next generation of potential heroes who someday will begin the hero's journey for themselves. Traditionally, literary heroes like Beowulf, King Arthur, and Aragorn fit quite neatly into this pattern, as do film heroes whose scriptwriters follow a hero's linear development. Younger heroes, such as Luke Skywalker, also follow Campbell's stages of development, but their story further becomes the "coming of age" story.

More recently, *Heroes'* first-season breakout character, Hiro Nakamura, follows Campbell's pattern of development and even creates his own hero's moral code for behavior that closely mimics Campbell's, a fact that series creator Tim Kring noted at the start of the series.[2] Hiro even receives a sword — that most traditional of heroic weapons. This gift puts him in the company of literary heroes who also accept their destiny when they receive the weapon that will enable them to perform heroic deeds: Tolkien's Aragorn (who receives Andúril), Gandalf (Glamdring), Bilbo and later Frodo (Sting). In a galaxy far, far away, cinematic hero and lightsaber aficionado Luke Skywalker also receives the weapon with which he will perform heroic deeds. Even Harry Potter's wand is a recent variation on this theme; the fantasy books and film series portray Harry saving his friends and, ultimately, the wizarding and muggled worlds from Evil by using a magic wand, which can be just as deadly as a sword or lightsaber. From books to films to TV series, heroes and their preferred weapons, which they use to protect and save their world, are closely aligned.

The role of mentors in hero literature, film, and television is notable in many stories, too. Popular literary or film characters like Merlin, Gandalf, Obi-wan Kenobi, and Yoda mentor heroes throughout some of the best-loved stories; their words and deeds become so famous that they inspire generations of readers and audiences. Since the late 1970s, "May the Force be with you" has inspired young people longing for words to live by. For many, popular culture provides a more palatable form of "moral code" than that provided by religious or educational institutions.

Elements of Campbell's analysis not only help readers/viewers and critics interpret literary or cinematic texts, they also guide some TV series' creators and writers (such as *Heroes'* Kring) as they develop new characters. Although Campbell's analysis of the hero's journey is probably the most commonly used or understood, other critics who analyze patterns in literature in order to describe heroes emphasize different points of commonality. Lord Raglan (FitzRoy Somerset), for example, emphasizes the hero's nobility and lineage, usually from a royal family (which severely limits the official heroic potential for characters who aren't part of the current or future monarchy). However, upper class ruling dynasties, or perhaps even politically elected "royalty," also could be included in a loose interpretation of Raglan's criteria. Even celebrity, the modern equivalent of "royalty," especially in the U.S., might become a logical descendant of this criterion for heroes. Unlike Campbell's schema,

Raglan's is far less flexible and loses much of its meaning when it is expanded to fit modern characters whose stories are presented through a variety of media.

Some parts of Raglan's analysis, such as a linear structure for a hero's development, in many ways parallels Campbell's. According to Raglan, traditional heroes may have a mysterious birth and be threatened with death as children; they may be hidden or reared by foster parents until they are of an age to rightfully claim their place within their "kingdom." Often such heroes-to-be leave home, just as in Campbell's journey, but infants or children don't have the ability to accept a call to action. In Raglan's analysis, the threatened young often don't know their true lineage until they are of age and able to decide to return to their birth homes or to regain their birth titles.

To be recognized as the returning ruler, Raglan's hero must perform a great service, such as slaying a dragon, freeing a princess, winning a battle, or otherwise meeting a challenge that threatens the community (or, in SF, the planet, universe, or timeline). After overcoming dangerous foes and accomplishing their mission, traditional heroes are recognized as the true leaders they are, regain their rightful place in society, and rule well and usually quietly for several years. Evil, however, has a way of returning, and the older, perhaps wiser hero once more must face a challenge. In many stories the hero dies as a result, although younger heroes usually step up late in the story to provide the transition from one heroic generation to the next. Most dramatically, the aged hero often dies at the top of a hill. Dead heroes receive final tributes, such as honorable burials or send-offs (e.g., immolation or journey into the sea), elaborate monuments, or burial mounds.[3]

Again, such literary heroes as Arthur and Aragorn (whose stories are frequently adapted in other media, including film and television) fit the bill. Because these images have become ingrained in the popular consciousness, elements of these traditional hero stories often make their way into the mythology of TV series. During a dramatic late-series *Battlestar Galactica* episode ("Sometimes a Great Notion," 4.13), Kara (Starbuck) Thrace discovers her own body on Earth; she apparently crash landed and died there on an earlier mission, although a mysterious (and never explained) version of herself lives to return to *Galactica*. She then helps lead her shipmates back to the Earth she discovered earlier. Wary of sharing her "death" with her comrades, on this second visit Kara provides a traditional warrior's send-off for her dead body, found still seated in the remains of the crashed aircraft. She creates a funeral pyre and watches as her corpse burns. This honor harkens far back into hero literature and provides a visually dramatic scene for the modern (2009) SF TV series.[4] *Doctor Who* also briefly revisits this tradition, reprised as a "flashback" in "The End of Time, Part 1," when the Doctor recalls burning the Master's body on a similar pyre.

A final scene in *Torchwood*'s 2009 "Children of Earth" miniseries also features one of Raglan's characteristics of a traditional hero: the hero's death at the top of a hill. Although the immortal Captain Jack Harkness always returns from the dead and thus can't fulfill the physical death aspect of Raglan's criterion, during the last scene in the miniseries, camera angles emphasize Jack's heroic profile as he stands atop a hill outside Cardiff, the city he has long protected. As will be discussed in later chapters, the character known as Captain Jack may be interpreted as "dying"—going away for good, as the lead character departs Earth and suggests he will take on a new name and persona. Symbolically, the immortal Captain "dies" at the top of a hill in Wales at the conclusion of the "epic" miniseries.[5]

Critics' analytical criteria for (creating or discerning) literary heroes resonate in other storytelling media, and Campbell's and Raglan's analyses of the hero's journey certainly have influenced recent SF TV series. Most stories popularized in Western cultures also reflect the "morality" implied by these critics' criteria for a hero, but morality is an area where modern gray heroes begin to diverge from the qualities of traditional heroes. Nevertheless, audiences who grow up with stories of traditional heroes, whether from books, movies, or TV series, still have specific expectations for a hero's morality. In the 2000s, audiences may be familiar with and still want their SF TV heroes, like traditional heroes in all media, to follow a strict moral code and to be, above all other characters, "good." The shift to morally ambiguous heroes as TV series' leads is creating a new paradigm, one in which TV creators and writers not only are reflecting the pragmatic decisions made by real-world leaders in a chaotic world, but also those who are comfortable working in morally gray areas. These less-than-morally-pristine characters are gradually being accepted as the "norm" by TV audiences.

The Morality of Traditional Heroes

Certainly a theme within Western Judeo-Christian analyses of traditional hero stories is the hero's concept of morality and societies' need for good role-model heroes to inspire and guide the next generation. Traditional hero literature not only provides entertaining adventures for audiences but also indicates the society's values and moral code. Even when Evil seems to triumph, however temporarily, over Good, traditional heroes stand their ground and would rather die than sacrifice their beliefs and values.

Often these traditional heroes are explained as succeeding only while they have God's favor. Perhaps one of the most revered examples of knightly virtue (and self-recrimination at the inability to be as virtuous as a knight should be) is the story of Sir Gawain and his encounters with the Green Knight. Although Sir Gawain far exceeds the "goodness" of the vast majority of humans living today, he realizes that he fails to live up to the chivalric code. When tested by the Green Knight and threatened with death, Gawain lies to his nemesis, flinches when faced with beheading, and suffers a humiliating loss of pride. Forever after, he reminds himself of that virtue which his character lacks.[6]

Although Gawain's moral struggle is told in a story from what to modern readers is ancient history, chivalry and the belief in codes of honor are part of many popular fantasy and SF stories. Elements of honorable codes of behavior shape the heroes of stories ranging from the previously mentioned *Lord of the Rings* to *Star Wars* to *Heroes.* Even political invectives—like the original *Star Trek*'s Prime Directive of non-interference in other worlds' sociopolitical or technological development — reflect a society's beliefs in what is right or wrong and how to enforce those beliefs.

Although few traditional heroes of any age try to maintain such high standards of perfection as Sir Gawain, even in chivalric fantasy stories, far more recent stories of heroes present the lead characters as much less virtuous or divinely inspired. Heroes traditionally represent all that is best in their culture, and by understanding hero stories, readers or audiences, even centuries later, can come to understand a specific society, no matter how much its value system differs from that of the current audience.

A key question about modern SF TV series is whether they truly reflect average citizens' dissatisfaction with the way the world is heading or instead mirror an apathetic acceptance of a less-than-perfect world as "just the way life is." Unlike 1960s' *Star Trek* creator Gene Roddenberry's optimistic view of the world and the ability of humans to become nearly perfect in the future, currently prolific SF TV series creators, such as *Doctor Who* re-imaginer and *Torchwood* co-creator Russell T. Davies, or *Firefly, Buffy, Angel,* and *Dollhouse* creator Joss Whedon, illustrate the future as a dystopia far darker than anything Roddenberry portrayed on TV.

Expecting heroes to live up to higher standards than those most "normal" or "average" citizens can or are willing to embrace creates dramatic tension in traditional hero stories. These virtuous heroes are forever "Other," or different from the rest of the community, because of their recognized hero status and special ability to guide and protect their people. They may be revered because of their beauty, strength, cleverness, and past deeds, but these qualities also mark them as different from the norm. They may be seen as morally exemplary and thus inspired or protected by the divine. Traditional heroes often stand on pedestals, perhaps not of their own making, so that for the rest of their lives they must live up to extremely high standards and societal expectations or risk expulsion and derision. They might never be as flawed as most citizens, but they must meet unrelenting high expectations or suffer the consequences (as Arthur or Gawain, or — much later — Luke Skywalker or Hiro Nakamura find out).

Modern SF TV heroes also are portrayed as Other, but often not just because of their "job" as secret or overt protectors of their people. They are more likely to accept the idea that they have to act outside the law or social norms in order to do their jobs— and they (and, to a growing extent, the audience) are OK with that. Today's SF TV heroes may aspire to be ever better people and may have the best intentions, but they seldom overcome villains or monsters simply because they are on the side of Good. The dramatic tension in more recent SF series often comes from heroes' inner turmoil and the dissonance between what they and others expect traditional heroes to be or do and what modern heroes feel they are forced to do if they are going to be effective in averting crises or saving the majority of the population. The moral codes of SF TV heroes thus differ significantly, and permanently, from those of traditional literary heroes or even their descendents in popular fantasy and SF a few decades ago.

The Importance of "Home"

As critics like Campbell and Raglan noted, the concept of *Home* is important to traditional literary heroes. Therefore, in stories told via their cinematic descendants in the 20th century, home also becomes a defining place, the basis of cultural values and behavioral expectations, and a people to love and defend. A more recent critic, Susan Mackey-Kallis, analyzed the importance of *home* to cinematic heroes through such films as *It's a Wonderful Life*, *The Wizard of Oz*, and *Star Wars*, among others.

Particularly during the global Depression in the 1930s, *home* became an increasingly valued ideal because so many people lost their homes or became displaced. In films popular at the time, heroes not only have to leave home and all that is familiar, but their primary motivation becomes returning home, usually armed with new knowledge and inspiration. They learn from their journeys and want to pass on this knowledge to others suffering their own loss of home and family. They may need to rebuild their homes or make them better now that they have a better understanding of what *home* should be. 1939 becomes a watershed year in this period with the release of two important (now classic) films, *The Wizard of Oz* and *Gone with the Wind*.[7]

Even the later *Star Wars* series (1970s–1980s Episodes 4–6, aka the "original" films) emphasizes loss of home and family and the eventual rebuilding of Luke Skywalker's home. Luke becomes an important catalyst in the restructuring of a post–Darth Vader world. On a personal level, he loses his childhood home (as does his sister) and family, but he later regains knowledge and acceptance of his biological family while creating a widely extended family among multiple species. He has a "home" with those who love and understand him — and with whom he has shared danger and near-death (or, in the case of Yoda, Obiwan Kenobi, and Anakin Skywalker, death and post-death) experiences. He also can build a physical home in a politically stable new world, just as Leia and Han Solo seem about to do.

The search for home becomes part of more recent SF TV heroes' search for themselves and for the meaning of life. Without a clear understanding of *home*, something clear and unquestionable to traditional literary heroes, modern heroes of any genre are less effective as heroes and societal role models. As home becomes less of a certainty in later literature, and certainly in 20th century films and television series, a culture's heroes become less "traditional," and the type of heroes relevant to the culture also begin to change. With 21st century SF TV series, most heroes lose their homes or family, and *home* becomes defined in new ways.

Twists on Campbell's Hero's Journey and the Concept of Home

Campbell's traditional hero has a strong sense of "home" and belonging to a people or a place. After all, traditional literary heroes need a place from which to start during Campbell's separation or departure phase of the hero's journey. Even a soon-to-be-heroic character like young Arthur or Tolkien's Aragorn knows where his future home lies, even if he must overcome challengers in order to reach his rightful throne. Other legendary heroes in fantasy literature also have a clear sense of "home." Robin Hood carves out home turf and defends Sherwood Forest; Bilbo and, in his turn, Frodo leave but return to their beloved Shire.

In later SF, Luke Skywalker leaves Tatooine — later to return and find it destroyed — but becomes a Jedi knight protecting a much larger "homeland" by the end of *Return of the Jedi*. Even the *Return* in the original film title echoes Campbell's final phase of the hero's journey. In classic *Star Trek*, the Federation, based in San Francisco on Earth, provides a home of sorts for all Starfleet cadets, from which they depart and to which they return at times. More specifically, Kirk, Spock, and McCoy, plus their colleagues, create a home on the *Enterprise*, the home base from which they depart and to which they return after weekly episodic adventures.

The recent J.J. Abrams version of *Star Trek* begins with the introduction of new recruits fresh from "home" who establish a new family of sorts, first at Starfleet Academy and then on the *Enterprise*. For James T. Kirk, boarding the *Enterprise* is already a return; his birth begins on a starship. Villainous Nero's attack forces soon-to-be-born James Kirk's mother to abandon her intergalactic home.[8] In this way, the new *Star Trek* even places Kirk within Raglan's framework of a traditional hero's birth: unusual circumstances surround his birth, his life is threatened, and he is reared by foster parents (in lieu of his dead father and apparently frequently off-planet mother). When Kirk "finds himself" as a Starfleet cadet and manages to get onboard the *Enterprise*, he is, in fact, well on the way to reclaiming his rightful place as a starship captain and future Starfleet royalty.

On 2000s-era SF TV, the majority of hit mainstream and cult series once again emphasizes the importance of *home*, in part because of natural and political disasters throughout the first decade of the new millennium. Fears of terrorism and the destruction of homeland fuel a longing for home on *Battlestar Galactica* and *Lost*, in particular. The further real-world loss of homes and increased numbers of homeless from natural disasters, economic downturns, and regional warfare only add to home-related concerns.

Reflections on the importance of *home* are evident in many series discussed in this book. The re-imagined *Battlestar Galactica* is a story about finding *home*, ostensibly the prophesied planet Earth, although the *Galactica* itself becomes a mobile home in space while the remnants of humanity search for a permanent place to call their own. Although many SF "space" heroes also create a homey haven within their spacecraft, the grayer the SF heroes, the more they still look for a true home that stays put. These characters usually are displaced persons (in the case of *Battlestar Galactica*, even referred to as refugees) who can't live on their true home world any longer. Until they find a permanent location to settle down, "space heroes" make *home* wherever they go and are less likely to define *home* as a destination or single place; they wander with other wanderers or travelers, creating a home from their transportation and among the transported.

In the pilot episode, the Battlestar *Galactica* faces imminent retirement as a "historic" vessel when a Cylon attack forces her once again to lead a fleet. This time the "ragtag fleet" consists of anything that can escape its citizens' destroyed homeworld, and the *Galactica* ultimately becomes one of the few surviving ships to arrive on a planet the refugees dub Earth. They discover the real Earth of their legendary past to be nothing more than a decimated, unsalvageable world; their idealized future "home" is nothing but ashes. As the refugees fight and run on their way toward a more permanent home, they patch up the increasingly fragile ship but recognize it as an imperfect, and temporary, refuge. Even their attempts at colonization along the journey to their ultimate home last only briefly. Invasion and repression destroy their hoped-for new homes, which turn out to be little more than squalid prisoner of war camps. Only in the series' finale are the survivors able to establish a permanent home once again.

Caprica begins the *Battlestar Galactica* backstory by following two families: the Graystones and the Adamas. Although the Graystones are well established in the community and have a comfortable, beautiful home, the atmosphere is sterile. Parents dressed in tennis black-and-whites enjoy an afternoon set on the home court; they confront their teenaged daughter within the spacious confines of their immaculate white living space. The huge house, with its three isolated inhabitants, stands on the shore of a picturesque lake and would seem to be a successful family's dream home. Nevertheless, teenaged Zoe thinks of the house as a prison and plans to run away to another planet. The "trappings" of an upscale house prove too much for her, and her parents realize just how empty their lives and marriage have become without her once she's gone. They, as much as Zoe, haunt their designer house.

The patriarch of the Adama family is a refugee whose family and home were obliterated by war on a nearby planet. Even the home he builds as the result of his successful law practice isn't the haven he might have desired as a displaced child. Joseph Adama works late and seldom connects with his children, especially his son. He tries to fit into his adoptive culture, but his family is still perceived as outsiders.

Firefly's Mal Reynolds and compatriot Zoe Washburne fought on the wrong (i.e., losing) side of a civil war, the Unification War to unite all humans under one government. As a result, they become mercenaries or outlaws eking out a living by running contraband, doing odd jobs on remote planets, and avoiding the authoritarian Alliance who governs their universe. Along the way they gather other misfits: a mysterious preacher without a flock (Shepherd Book), a trigger-happy fighter (Jayne Cobb), a carefree female mechanic (Kaylee Frye), a sexual companion-for-hire (Inara Serra), and a talented doctor on the run for freeing his assassin-trained sister from the authorities (Simon and River Tam). Their ship, the *Serenity*, is pieced together as much as this raggedy crew who form a dysfunctional makeshift family that is seldom serene. Mal (his name a variant of "bad," although the character isn't as dark as he would like others to believe) is the story's gray hero. He often is unsure that he wants to keep the "family" together, yet these characters, until they die, keep returning to this makeshift traveling "home."

In British TV series, *Doctor Who*'s Doctor lives in a forever mobile TARDIS (which looks like an old-style blue police box but, as everyone notices, is much bigger on the inside). Although he "adopts" Earth and human companions during his travels, he is always reminded that his home planet and people no longer exist; he has long believed that he is the last of the Time Lords.

The Ninth Doctor returns to Earth after his home planet Gallifrey and its citizens die in the Time War. Even on Earth this regenerated Doctor avoids anything remotely "domestic" and prefers sharing the stars with a human companion, Rose. She, not he, is the one who begins Campbell's hero's journey by leaving home and only eventually returning to live as a hero on an alternate version of Earth. The Doctor keeps traveling; even on Earth, his adopted homeworld, he seldom is wanted, because, after all, he's alien. He stops by briefly now and then, or remains for a few years at most (but not in the Davies-era episodes), but he never wants to or is able to settle down. Even his mobile domicile, the TARDIS, is really a sentient being on her own and not just a physical "place" where the Doctor lives.

These outer-space homes are expected to be transient; the heroes' journey is very much part of the story and allows them to find new villains/monsters in unexpected locations or to be chased by villains/monsters. Other gray SF TV heroes who establish what they hope to be more permanent homes, often in places where they can defend a people they've accepted as their own, also find that "home" may not be as permanent as they'd hoped.

Even "aliens" stuck on Earth eventually lose their homes. Although *Torchwood*'s Jack Harkness lives through much of Britain's 19th, 20th and 21st centuries, his original home turf is far from Earth in time and space: the 51st century Boeshane Peninsula. Over time, he joins Torchwood and makes his physical, and later emotional, home in Cardiff. The organization's underground lair, the Hub, mirrors the jumbled, murky past of its current leader, Captain Jack.

The Hub's many layers lead into its secretive past, and the team's "home" includes such cheery sections as labs, jail cells, an autopsy bay, and vaults where past employees' bodies rest, sometimes not in peace. Jack assembles his own misfit team who lack proper homes: Toshiko Sato is a rescued political prisoner prevented from seeing her mother; Owen Harper loses his fiancée before joining Torchwood and spends his off-work time drinking and carousing; Ianto Jones loses his girlfriend but finds meaning as a Torchwood employee primarily living where he works; and Jack himself lives as well as works in the Hub, spending his sleepless nights wandering its many levels. Only Gwen Cooper, the newest team member, maintains a "normal" life outside work, and even that becomes quickly tainted by the team's job. During Season Three, the government bombs the Hub, destroying it so completely that the surviving team members have nowhere to go; their "home" is rubble. Whether traveling the stars or remaining firmly planet-bound, recent SF TV heroes continue to search for a permanent home that meets their expectations and allows them to feel at ease with themselves. In the case of Captain Jack, he feels so ill at ease where he has lived for centuries that he leaves Earth once more to wander the stars.

The most "realistic" (i.e., reflecting the audience's world) of the SF series discussed in this book is *Lost*, its very title indicating that the main characters have been separated from their previous homes. The inhabitants of a creepy tropical island feel *Lost* not only from their former homes, but from their families. Home is not an ideal place for most castaways. Many of the early seasons' stories revolve around the castaways' troubled lives back home, and several characters already have left home in search of a different life before they crash-land on a mysterious island.

When the castaways begin to accept that the island may be their permanent home and forge a new society, even the fledgling community can't survive for long. Other people on the island break up the little society and attack the newly built shelters. Even when some castaways, dubbed the Oceanic 6, return to their "real" off-island homes during Seasons Four through Six, they realize that the ideal is far removed from their reality. They still are rootless characters trying to forge new family relationships or to find their ideal place to settle down. Being lost—from self and home—is the series' recurring theme.

Unlike previous SF TV series of earlier decades, whose characters may find themselves in a new home (e.g., Buck Rogers awakening in a new century, *Lost in Space*'s Robinson family creating a new home on the planet where they crash, *Star Trek*'s *Enterprise* as a traveling, if sometimes beleaguered, home), 2000-era SF series often portray home as an illusory goal. What constitutes a home or homeland is in flux, as audiences, like the gray heroes they watch, struggle to define just what "home" means to them.

Gray heroes' "homes" aren't ideal; in many cases they are makeshift, coming apart at the seams. Constructed of leftover bits assembled over the years into a unique structure, "home" refers more to the makeshift "family" who lives within it than the wobbly base itself. The structure may symbolize the state of the characters' sense of "home" much more than present a traditional, stable, stuck-in-one-place building or setting known and loved by traditional heroes.

The shift from home as a place to home as a group of transient people accurately represents the transitory nature of modern audiences and those often unable to keep their homes in chaotic political/economic times. Wars and terrorist acts create new refugees who struggle to find shelter or a welcoming new location. Dwindling natural resources and changing climates force migrants into smaller, still habitable areas. Economic woes force socio-economically challenged citizens from their homes and into the ranks of the homeless. During the 2000s, the concept of *home* changed dramatically—and SF TV drama, predictably, often deals with audiences' fears about losing their homes or being unable to defend their homeland from invaders. SF TV heroes often lose or have lost what they believed would be permanent homes, and the new homes and families they attempt to construct frequently fall apart. Nothing—not home, not family—is certain or permanent. From this bleak premise come stories of heroism as well as defeat, and the rise and fall of heroes and villains.

A Loner No More: Changing Power Structures in the Construction of the Hero

Campbell's and other critics' analyses of heroes frequently focus on the lead character of a book or the obvious hero of a story. Even when these critics' criteria for determining a hero are co-opted to analyze heroes in film or television, the focus is on the leading actor (male or female) as the leading hero, although many stories have several potentially heroic characters. Frequently the lead hero is the title character, such as *Robin Hood*, *The Hobbit*, or *Highlander*.

Traditional heroes often must lead and make difficult decisions; hence, the battle leader, lone warrior, returning king, or knight on a quest completes the mission alone at crucial points in the story or bears the responsibility of important decisions. The lone warrior slays a dragon or rescues a princess. The king heals the wounded, leads a battle to victory, and gains a crown. A single pilot launches the bomb to destroy a Death Star.

SF TV series following this traditional pattern may present an isolated heroic lead as the go-to person when aliens invade, battle plans need to be drawn, or a difficult decision needs to be made. A case in point is *Doctor Who*. The Doctor arrives in his trusty TARDIS, sees a crisis in the making, becomes involved with the locals, and, at the end of almost every episode, leaves for his next adventure. After losing a series of beloved companions, the Tenth Doctor decides, as some of his previous regenerations did, that he is better off traveling alone. Despite his loneliness, he knows that his lifestyle as a "hero"—although his purpose as Doctor is to heal rather than be a standard action hero—endangers those he loves. He has faced loss too many times and tries to salve his damaged hearts (a Time Lord has two) by forever traveling.

Although the true Western space series discussed in this book is *Firefly*, lead character Captain Mal Reynolds isn't the typical *Shane*-type loner. He doesn't consider himself heroic, even if his actions sometimes resemble those of the lone cowboy who moseys into town, saves the day, and then rides into the sunset once his work is done. Mal prefers to think of himself as an outlaw fighting against the government/authorities against whom he fought (and to whom he lost) during the war. Nevertheless, Mal has a moral code, although he plays fast and loose with established laws if they violate his personal code of ethics. He doesn't hesitate to steal from the government or to carry passengers fleeing from it, as long as he can make a living and remain free from the constrictions of a social structure he doesn't believe in. He may question and criticize Inara's profession as a paid companion, but he falls in love with and protects her, even when it puts himself and his ship (i.e., home and livelihood) in grave danger. Despite his belief that he is best as a loner and mercenary, he can't resist fighting for underdogs or jumping into potentially deadly situations if he can help a friend or avenge a wrong. Although Mal is clearly the series' lead, he is ably assisted by *Serenity*'s crew, although if a sacrifice needs to be made, Mal usually is the one to become the sacrificial hero.

Most SF series, however, have moved beyond the loner as the ideal SF TV hero. Instead, different power structures help balance the lead hero and (usually) provide him (most series' leads are male) with the support needed to make difficult decisions and act heroically. The triumvirate, best established in classic *Star Trek* but later used for dramatic effect in *Torchwood*, is one such structure. Even more popular in the 2000s, however, is the power created by ensembles—a range of occasionally heroic characters who are burdened by very human flaws. Individually, these characters may be leaders/warriors/heroes during a story arc, but they are not *the* hero of the overall story. As SF TV heroes become less traditional and more like everyday people, the ensemble helps create a unified "hero" from among the heroic moments and characteristics of a group working together. In the 2000s, perhaps no one character — or person —can live up to the standards of perfection established by and for classic traditional literary heroes and their glorified cinematic counterparts. Instead, the responsibility — and power — of the traditional hero is becoming spread among more characters, each of whom has heroic potential but doesn't act heroically in every situation or episode.

The Power of the Triumvirate

In classic *Star Trek*, although Captain James T. Kirk clearly is *the* hero of the series, other *Enterprise* characters have their share of heroic moments. Nevertheless, the power structure isn't an ensemble, with heroic (and less heroic) moments doled out across episodes so that everyone gets a chance to have character-changing moments on screen. Instead, although McCoy or Spock might have a featured sidestory within an episode, the lead character clearly is Kirk.

The triumvirate power structure established in *Star Trek* looks something like this[9]:

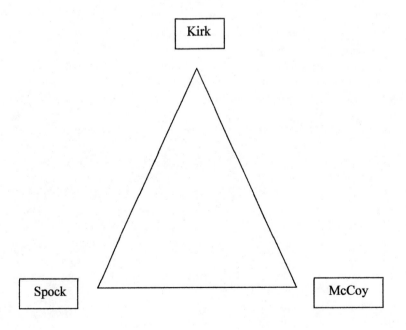

In the *Star Trek* triumvirate, Spock represents logic and facts, and McCoy represents emotion and feelings. Of course, in some episodes Spock displays a shockingly emotional side, but that is extremely rare. McCoy, as a medical doctor, certainly has a fine capacity for logic and information, but he most often reacts to situations emotionally, especially when his close friends are involved. For Kirk to be an effective leader, he needs to balance both natures, mental and emotional, objective and subjective. He relies on his closest friends and colleagues to provide often contradictory advice that helps him make his own informed decisions. Sometimes Kirk sides more with Spock; other times he and McCoy chuckle over the way a "human" approach better solves a problem.

Even in the 2009 Abrams-re-imagined *Star Trek*, the beginnings of this triumvirate are apparent, but with an important difference. The "new, improved" Spock embraces his emotions at important times and recognizes when his human half compromises pure logic. In this way Abrams creates a more appealing Spock who clearly can be as volatile (in love or war) as Kirk and is more emotionally similar than different to the lead hero. McCoy's role is therefore diminished; he no longer provides a unique perspective on problems, one based on gut instinct, although he still displays his emotions much more frequently than does Spock. If the film series continues this shift in character development, it will be interesting to see if Abrams further relies on the classic triumvirate structure of the original or switches to the ensemble structure so common in most popular SF TV series in the 2000s.

SF TV heroes have grown grayer over time, perhaps culminating with *Torchwood*'s "Children of Earth" and the devolution/deconstruction of the traditional hero. Like its parent, *Doctor Who*, *Torchwood* emphasizes *the* hero of the series, Captain Jack Harkness. Although Jack is clearly meant to be the lead character and lead hero, the series' structure provides a support network that becomes a true triumvirate during Season Three (the "Children of Earth" miniseries). As Russell T. Davies attempted to make cult-favorite *Torchwood* more realistic, more dramatic, and thus more popular to mainstream audiences, he emphasized the power triumvirate in the series' 2009 installment. Even a promotional picture clearly indicates the significance of this structure.

In a photo frequently used in series hype on the internet and in print, the three *Torchwood* characters form a visual triangle.[10] Ianto Jones and Gwen Cooper, heroes in their own right but lesser lights than the lead hero, sit on the floor of Torchwood Three's temporary warehouse quarters. Lead hero Jack sits in a chair between them. Ianto clasps Jack's knee, and Jack slightly leans toward but doesn't touch Ianto. Jack clasps Gwen's arm, but she doesn't touch him. Jack is elevated between Ianto and Gwen, who balance the image by sitting on the floor on either side of Jack. From left to right, the photo shows Ianto-Jack-Gwen, not so subtly also hinting at the past-present-future status of Torchwood employees in the continuing saga. To further symbolize Ianto not surviving

Season Three, he looks down at the floor. Jack, present for the moment but soon out of the picture, stares straight ahead at the camera/audience. Gwen looks up and right, toward the future, and indeed seems the only character at the end of "Children of Earth" to be around for future episodes.

The structure also resembles a status triangle, with Jack at the top of the pyramid as the lead hero. The supports to this hierarchy — Ianto and Gwen — provide the balance Jack needs to be an effective hero. Ianto, with his duties as archivist and his vast knowledge (upon which the team relies), is the "Spock" element of this triumvirate. Although Ianto certainly can be emotional at times, most often this character is noted for his stoic demeanor and dry humor — very similar to Spock's. In contrast, Jack initially hires Gwen to make the Torchwood team more human, to remind them of the emotional consequences of what they do. As such, Gwen is the "McCoy" of the team, balancing Jack's brutal pragmatism with softer emotions and reminders of the people who suffer the consequences of Torchwood's decisions.

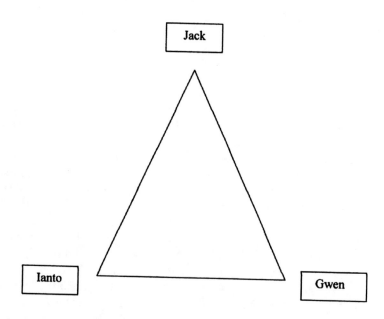

With Ianto's demise, Jack loses his effectiveness as a hero/leader, a characteristic Davies stated as the reason for Ianto's death.[11] Without his partner and colleague — and Ianto's logic and information provided at key problem-solving times — Jack becomes overly emotional. He may seem cold and uninvolved, but his grief and remorse outweigh his ability to think logically — otherwise, he may have been able to find a different solution to the crisis presented in "Children of Earth." In the aftermath of Ianto's death, Gwen becomes even more important to Jack, but she can only add emotion to the equation, throwing Jack-as-hero even further off-kilter. She idealizes Jack as a hero and has so much heart that he forces her to go home during the crisis because he "can't stand to look at her anymore."[12] She can't provide the balance that he needs as a leader to make logical decisions.

Reliance on a triumvirate as a power structure isn't perfect, Davies implies, but relying only on one lead hero (the "loner" option explored in *Doctor Who*) doesn't seem ideal, either. Perhaps Davies is implying that there isn't one clearcut dramatic structure for telling a hero story any more — only a series of power structures that don't work any better than the governmental or social structures that so easily fall apart in "Children of Earth." Davies doesn't present a new power structure, or a new type of hero, to replace what he so efficiently shows is broken, but he does a good job of pointing out problems with the current status quo of heroic characters and their interactions with their teams/colleagues and the world at large.

Ensembles to the Rescue

What has become more common in the 2000s is the ensemble cast, in which one or a few qualities of the traditional hero survive in a single character. Just like a village may be required to raise a child, an ensemble may be required to "build" a complete heroic entity. The virtuous traditional hero, whose values (e.g., a chivalric code) may seem too strict for today's citizens (even the "good" ones) to live up to, no longer represents societal values or expectations. If anything, cynical current societies expect their leaders to be flawed and even seem to enjoy tearing down those who would be recognized as "heroes" or exemplary leaders. Everyone seems to have a flawed, dark side and to make questionable — or downright illegal, if not immoral — decisions from time to time. No one person, or SF TV character, can be expected to be "perfect." In fact, if such a character exists, he or she would likely be suspect as being unrealistically "good." To create that better-than-realistic "hero," ensemble casts fill the void.

At times, a main character, such as *Battlestar Galactica*'s President Laura Roslin or Commander Bill Adama, may act heroically or present the "correct" view, according to the majority of the audience, but just as often these characters are blinded by self-interest or personal demons that make their decision-making capability suspect. The same occurs on other SF TV series. On *Heroes*, politician Nathan Petrelli vacillates between wanting to fight corruption and represent his constituents honestly, and believing that he alone knows what is best and therefore should keep secrets from the rest of the government and the people who voted for him. *Lost*'s Jack Shephard changes from self-sacrificing doctor and reluctant leader of castaways to know-it-all vigilante with the desire to change the past and, thus, he hopes, the future through increasingly questionable, potentially lethal acts. A lead protagonist isn't a "perfect" hero anymore;

the heroic qualities of several characters may need to be pooled to create the image of an "ideal" hero.

An SF TV series may have many protagonists, but it might not have clearly identifiable heroes, much less a single lead hero. Series like *Dollhouse*, *Fringe*, and *FlashForward* differ from the ensemble casts featuring at least some heroic characters (i.e., *Lost*, *Heroes*, and *Battlestar Galactica*) because they introduce characters who are simply protagonists, not heroes.

A good example of the difference between a hero (however gray) and a protagonist can be shown by the ways lead ABC-TV characters from highly promoted premiere episodes immediately respond to crisis. During *Lost*'s pilot episode, broadcast in September 2004, Jack Shephard rushes forward as a leader/healer/hero in the aftermath of a plane crash. He doesn't hesitate to become involved and almost becomes a victim himself as he runs from casualty to casualty as parts of the fuselage fall or explode.[13] Jack is unconcerned about himself; he tries to save as many crash victims as possible. In a similar tragic crash scene in the opening moments of *FlashForward*'s September 2009 pilot episode, FBI agent Mark Benford manages to help a few people escape from crumpled vehicles, but he mostly meanders among the victims on the L.A. freeway, as much in shock as everyone else. At his partner's urging, Mark runs two miles to the hospital where his surgeon wife is working.[14] He seems to take direction rather than direct the action, and he abandons his initial crisis setting in favor of checking on his wife. In the five years since *Lost*'s debut, the role of the lead character (in fact, the first character audiences see on screen) has changed substantially.

FlashForward seemed to be ABC's choice as a successor to *Lost*. Both series develop a thriller/mind-game mystery within an SF premise. They also embrace themes that question whether fate/destiny or God determines what happens, and if science or religion should be regarded most highly. Both series provide ensemble casts of intriguing characters who, as surgeons, for example, should act heroically, at least at times. However, the first few moments of each series differ radically in the way the lead protagonist is portrayed as either a likely hero or as an average citizen fighting personal demons and seeking answers to personal, as well as global, mysteries. Whereas Jack Shephard requires almost four seasons to become a suicidal doctor standing atop a bridge ("Through the Looking Glass," 3.23), *FlashForward*'s Bryce Varley achieves this dubious honor in his first scene.[15] Tragic accidents force both doctors to abandon their suicide attempts so that they can save victims.

Fringe and *Dollhouse*, although more niche- or cult-audience series than mainstream *Lost* and *FlashForward*, feature characters who once were staples of heroic stereotypes: scientists and law enforcement officers. The former's lead characters, however, are certainly protagonists but might not be perceived as heroes. Just because a character is a series' lead doesn't mean he or she is automatically a hero all the time, or even most of the time. Even series' lead characters often are victims who don't know all about what turn out to be their sordid, scary pasts. They may be more like detectives, uncovering mysteries of the world while seeking to know more about themselves—all within a world moving ever more out of their control. Heroes seek, and usually succeed, in controlling their environment and reducing chaos. Protagonists may not be able to control much of anything; they may have to ride out chaos just like everyone else in the series or audience. Protagonists who are not heroes may be at the mercy of outside forces, often behind-the-scenes monsters or villains masquerading as humans in charge. Heroes, in contrast, manage to reveal the monsters or villains and confront them. Although some SF TV series may develop protagonists into heroes as the plot progresses, lead characters meant to be heroes usually are portrayed that way from the first moments of the pilot episode, even if they later fall from their pedestal. A protagonist probably won't unite other characters to fight heroically against a common foe; instead, protagonists may be isolated or interested in their own problems more than society's.

Just as series like *Torchwood* indicate that traditional ideas about a single ideal hero or even a triumvirate may be as outmoded as the special effects of 1960s television, they also show that the evolution of the ensemble also may not be as viable as writers or audiences might like to believe. *Lost*'s hero Jack Shephard (and series' creators and writers) may believe that "if we don't live together, we'll surely die alone," which is certainly a call for an ensemble of heroes.[16] Davies and series like *Torchwood*, however, hint that, in a chaotic world full of villains and monsters, everyone dies alone anyway, even if he or she is heroic. Ensembles simply offer hope that some hero(es) may survive to fight another day.

Certainly, SF has grown darker in the 2000s (2009's optimistic-about-the-future *Star Trek* movie aside). Few SF TV series, however, are quite as pessimistic at the end of a season or a series as *Torchwood*, which creates a new benchmark for darkness at the end of the first decade of the 21st century. Other SF TV series may be dark, but they at least offer a modicum of hope that the future *may* be better.

In contrast to Davies' pessimistic future, *Serenity*, the follow-up movie to *Firefly*, hopefully flies forward, even without some beloved crew members; the little family survives, and some characters thrive on their newly forged connections with each other. *Battlestar Galactica* offers the human–Cylon race(s) another chance to start over and learn from past mistakes; their strength is in shared experience and reliance on each other. *Lost* keeps reuniting and connecting disparate characters to show that one character's story is, in essence, the story of us all. Humanity is connected in unexpected ways. The much-earlier *Buffy* and *Angel* emphasize the strength of friendships forged through adversity and loss, plus the need to fight together until the bitter end. These latter series' ensembles, consisting of multiple heroes of varying shades of gray, likely will remain the most flexible structure by which to examine individual characters and their fluctuating roles as heroes or villains, depending upon the directions the plot takes. As 2009's heavily promoted *FlashForward* indicates, even the ensemble-as-hero may someday soon become outmoded, leading to a virtually hero-less TV society made up of ensembles of protagonists.

Heroes of the Past and Future

What is most likely is that the days of the "one powerful hero" are numbered or gone. The traditional hero no longer represents the heroic ideal in 21st century Western societies. Instead, increasingly gray heroes working in groups, or series in search of heroes, may represent societies' growing unease with world tensions and the search for answers beyond traditional heroes and the religious or political institutions from which they arose.

Traditional literary heroes, as evidenced in historic epic tales such as *Beowulf, Sir Gawain and the Green Knight,* or Arthurian legends, eventually became source materials for fantasy (e.g., *The Lord of the Rings*) or SF (e.g., *Star Wars*) stories that capture(d) the popular imagination. The link among SF/fantasy tales popular in the 20th century is strong, largely because readers/audiences shared an understanding of and a need for traditional heroes. These stories and heroes provided escapist adventures, but they also often reflected the underlying reality of readers'/audiences' lives projected into a romanticized past or a utopian future. *Star Trek* and *Star Wars* most notably transported traditional heroes into otherworldly settings and offer role models designed for the 1960s or 1970s, when these series began.

Although elements of these types of heroes and stories remain in some SF TV series, especially in the coming-of-age hero sagas presented in *Buffy the Vampire Slayer* or *Heroes,* SF TV heroes in the early 21st century aren't bound by Campbell's or Raglan's criteria or even looser interpretations of them. Whether helping to compare current civilization to that of off–Earth humans in the past or future (e.g., *Battlestar Galactica, Caprica, Firefly,* or even *Doctor Who*), in an alternate fictitious universe set on current Earth (e.g., *Buffy, Angel, Heroes, Torchwood*), or, most recently, in a world closely resembling our own (e.g., *Lost, FlashForward, V*), SF TV heroes are rapidly moving away from a Campbellian-style hero into ever-grayer territory. By the end of the first decade of the 21st century, traditional heroes have been replaced on SF TV by morally ambiguous, if good-intentioned, characters put forth as series' heroes.

2

Villains and Monsters

SF heroes and villains in the early 2000s are not as clearly oppositional as yesteryear's definition of traditional heroes might indicate. Modern SF TV heroes aren't always noble or pure, but audiences still can distinguish the "good guys" from the "bad guys," even if the "good guys" occasionally drift into some morally dangerous territory. As well, audience expectations for "bad guys" may have become almost clichéd, especially when they refer to common depictions of the villain's base, where all sorts of evil plots are hatched, as well as the expected conventions illustrating an evil character.

Blurring the Lines Between Villains and Heroes as Leading Characters

The recently popular and Emmy- and Hugo-award winning web series (later DVD) *Dr. Horrible's Sing-Along Blog* parodies audience expectations for, among other things, mad scientist villains.[1] The qualities of an effective villain include an evil laugh (for which Dr. Horrible works with a vocal coach), evil philosophy ("The world is a mess, and I just need to rule it"), evil laboratory, and evil plan to thwart the hero and win over the virtuous heroine to the Dark Side.[2] The series' lead is a villain, and although Dr. Horrible has trouble getting into the Evil League of Evil, he still gets points for trying.

Of course, egotistical, sly hero Captain Hammer follows his own agenda for winning the girl by showing how wonderful he is. His good deeds, such as helping the homeless, are broadcast on the nightly news; his strength and handsome physique earn him adoring fans. Although this parody plays with conventions of SF and horror, from the title sequence to the stock characters, it also portrays Dr. Horrible, for all his evil deeds and plans, as simply a lovesick man who is more likeable than the hero. The blurring of SF heroes and villains is skewered in such a parody, but its popularity at least in part rests with the audience's ability to be in on the joke — that the old definitions of evil villain and squeaky clean hero no longer work, nor do viewers want them to.

Torchwood's opening episode, "Everything Changes" (1.1), more darkly and seriously adheres to this theme.[3] Police constable Gwen Cooper enters the Torchwood team's underground lair where she observes one woman busily welding something at her station and two others intent on their computers. A severed hand waves grotesquely amid water bubbling in its glass case. The atmosphere resembles Dr. Frankenstein's creepy laboratory more than a futuristic alien-fighting base.

When Gwen asks about a murder she observed and the crime scene that Torchwood quickly took over, she learns from mild-mannered computer wizard Toshiko Sato that the victim's body will wash up from the bay in about a week, long after she planted false witnesses and information that, in effect, prevents the alien murderer from being detected. Horrified police constable Gwen complains that Torchwood could help solve murders, but team leader Jack Harkness explains that this is not their job. In fact, Tosh blithely tells Gwen that the cover-up *is* her job. After her infiltration of Torchwood's Hub, Gwen is drugged to wipe out her recent memory of Torchwood and her home computer hacked to destroy files describing the team's activities.

Torchwood's heroes are introduced similarly to the ways old-fashioned villains often were portrayed: living secretively beneath the surface or outside normal society, having mysterious laboratories, doing what they please outside the law, misleading the public and the authorities, following their own agenda instead of working for the greater good. Gwen is "too good" for this group; she is the outsider who protests the cavalier way that Tosh deals with a murder victim and how Jack sees Torchwood's mission. Both Torchwood and Dr. Horrible would agree that the world is a mess, and although Torchwood doesn't want to rule the world, the team does plan to follow its own ideas about how to protect it. Neither Dr. Horrible nor Torchwood believes in following society's rules when they conflict with their own sense of what needs to be done or to promote their own vision of the future. However, these characters also are often quite likeable and are the stars of their respective series.

The line between "bad good guys" and "good bad guys" is further blurred by pragmatism and the sense that, in the 21st century, the old rules no longer apply when it comes to protecting one's homeland. In *Torchwood*'s "Sleeper" (2.2), Jack tortures a young woman who can't explain how the burglars entering her home ended up dead; she only remembers that her husband, badly injured in the attack, tried to protect her.[4] Fearing that the woman is an alien in human disguise, Jack ruthlessly uses a mind probe to brutally break through her mental resistance to his interrogation. Of course, in this episode the "woman" turns out to be an alien sleeper agent just awakening to help destroy Earth. If Jack hadn't authorized such dire measures to uncover her alien nature, an interplanetary attack might not have been averted. As with other episodes, this series invites questions about how far heroes can go in committing acts that make audiences uncomfortable — ranging from lying to or drugging the public, to torture and killing.

From the beginning, *Torchwood*'s "heroes" tightrope walk the division between situational ethics and societal mores, and occasionally a character loses his or her balance. More than other series, even its opening narration flaunts Torchwood's ability to work outside all established governmental agencies in its self-defined role as defender of the greater good. As Captain Jack Harkness explains in the narration of Season One, the agency is "outside the government, beyond the police," which is justified because "you've got to be ready" for the changes taking place during this century. In Season Two the narrative changes to reflect Torchwood's desire to protect humanity by "fighting for the future on behalf of the human race."[5] The ends are meant to justify the means.

As with *Torchwood* and *Battlestar Galactica*, *Lost* frames modern social issues within a fictitious reality, but its SF premise comes much closer to real life than "alien" or "outer space" series. A *Lost* character fans love to hate (and critics simply love) is Benjamin Linus. Like many shady characters, Ben changes his name, background, or recall of important details to suit his immediate purpose. In short, he lies most of the time. Nevertheless, he fervently believes that all his actions are for the good of the mysterious island on which he lives, and on which for many years he is able to imprison castaways as well as his colleagues to keep them in line.

Like traditional heroes, Ben understands the occasional need for sacrifice and the power of forgiveness, but his lessons are rather hard won. He allows his beloved daughter Alex to be executed instead of giving himself up to a mercenary working on behalf of Charles Widmore, the only man likely to wrest control of the island from Ben ("The Shape of Things to Come," 4.9).[6] In his quest to protect the island from Widmore, or others like him, Ben loses his daughter and the island's favor.[7] Still, Ben believes that his many devious, murderous acts are simply required to keep the island safe (and himself in control as long as possible). For these reasons he confidently is able to proclaim that he and his followers are "the good guys" ("Live Together, Die Alone," 2.23).[8]

Whereas most viewers may love to hate Ben Linus on *Lost* for his questionable morality in decision making, most *Torchwood* fans simply love Captain Jack, who also makes morally ambiguous decisions. Even in light of his horrific choice to sacrifice his grandson during "Children of Earth," a plot point leading many long-time fans to question whether Jack Harkness can still be considered a hero, viewers still like him — in Christian terms, it's perhaps a case of loving the sinner while hating the sin. (It also doesn't hurt that the writers and cast emphasize that Jack's choice does, in fact, end up saving the world's children and getting rid of a monster threatening the planet.) In contrast, Ben Linus, who also sacrifices a family member, albeit to a less noble cause, is perceived as untrustworthy, duplicitous, and deviant — decidedly not the qualities of a character posited as a series' hero.

To ascertain just who is still on the side of "good," audiences have to look at behavior patterns across episodes as well as a character's motivation for committing a morally questionable act. Some viewers might question whether "morality" should come into play at all; in the current sociopolitical climate, abandoning formerly accepted codes of behavior that could get humanity killed seems like a logical approach to problem solving. Characters who are able to do what is necessary — *if* their decisions and actions likely will result in saving more people or in buying the Earth more time to solve its problems — may be deemed as heroic. They, not the people who simply can't do whatever is necessary to help others survive, are heroic *because* they take responsibility for making such difficult choices or performing less than "moral" actions.

Audiences still seem to want their heroes to know the difference between what is morally ideal and what isn't, even if they don't always follow that ideal. Heroes who, for example, sacrifice a few people to save many should feel remorse for the loss of those sacrificed; audiences are much more likely to accept guilt-ridden, remorseful, or grieving characters as heroes rather than those who simply write off morally ambiguous decisions as "normal" or "acceptable" and blithely go on their way. Even in this transitional period in a paradigm shift, when audiences are more likely to accept heroes who sometimes must do "bad" things for the greater "good," there still is a line between acceptable heroic behavior and that which becomes more consistently villainous. Audiences may still be helping to define this line between SF TV heroes and villains by choosing which characters to follow week to week, or which ones to protest through internet backlash or refusal to watch a series any longer.

Classic and Modern Villains

The hero's or villain's motivation behind an act is still the best way to define each character. Although heroes may commit an atrocity, they do so only if there apparently is no other course of action and if the loss of a few lives ultimately saves the loss of many more. As well, heroes feel remorse for their action, no matter if it is legally or (temporarily) socially sanctioned during a crisis.

A constant in the definition of *villain* is that villains act for themselves and display no remorse over their actions that affect the lives of innocents. They only worry about themselves and remain the most narcissistic or self-involved characters in a story. Nevertheless, the boundary of what a hero may do, even under duress, is being stretched and tested on SF TV; audiences at some point may decide that heroes have gone too far, even in the name of saving humanity. At that point — the ultimate acceptable grayness — heroes likely will begin pulling back from common ground with villains. Even so, the days of black-and-white distinctions between TV villains and heroes are long gone. A comparison of the roles and characteristics of traditional TV heroes and villains with modern TV villains illustrates the shift made especially apparent in post–2000 SF TV series, as shown in Table 1.

Table 1. Defining Characteristics of Heroes and Villains

Classic Hero	Classic Villain	Modern Villain
Outer directed (e.g., working for the greater good)	Inner directed (e.g., working to gain personal power, wealth, and/or fame)	Inner directed, but motivated primarily to overcome feelings of inadequacy or to avenge a personal wrong
Willing to sacrifice self	Does anything to save self	May become a martyr as a last resort; tries to save self
Has superior ability or abilities (e.g., advanced technology, knowledge, mentors, magical help, physical ability, experience, special skills) to overcome weaknesses or flaws and to combat villains	Temporarily has superior capabilities (especially technology) but also has a fatal flaw (hubris)	Has superior ability, including even more resources than heroes; may be able to come back from setbacks even stronger than before
Leader	Tyrant (illegitimate power)	Tyrant, often with legitimate power (e.g., politician, corporate leader, scientist, government official)
Has a support network behind, but not with, him	Works alone, or has paid or cowed minions	Has a support network, perhaps a cult of personality, as well as mercenaries

Separating Villains from Monsters

Just as the distinctions between "bad good guys" and "good bad guys" blur lines between heroes and villains, the delineation between villains and monsters sometimes is trickier than might be expected. Of course, traditional monsters (often rubber-suited or masked Halloween costume-wearing stunties in low-budget SF series) are easy to identify. Although they may have to walk on two legs because they are really actors wearing a monster costume, they represent a non-human species, whether from Earth or another planet. More recent SF series, however, sometimes refer to humans, even series' heroes, as "monsters," using a colloquial term to indicate the temporary inhumanity of a formerly respected character. "Monster," to an SF TV hero, is about as bad a slur imaginable because, regardless of its origin, a monster should be the antithesis of a hero. Villains, although technically different from monsters, fall more closely into the same realm of anti-social behavior and self-absorption.

Traditionally, the distinctions between *villain* and *monster* were clearcut.

A *villain* is a sentient, thinking character, usually human(oid), who looks out for himself or herself to the exclusion of all else. The villain's need for power overrides anyone's or anything's needs. Villains set themselves up in positions of authority and condescendingly bait heroes into confrontations, but villains feel certain of victory, even if evidence points to the contrary. In contrast, monsters typically react rather than rationally act, or they act simply out of habit or instinct. They are unpredictable and feared because no one knows what they may do next. Monsters seldom rationalize their actions; they simply *are* monsters and do monstrous things. Their actions have no moral basis because they don't understand the concepts of *right* or *wrong*.

Even some traditional fantasy stories turn what, at first glance, might seem to be "monsters" into "villains" because of this distinction of the capacity for rational thought. Tolkien's famous dragon, Smaug, is more villain than monster, even if he is not human (or hobbit, dwarf, wizard, or elf). As written in *The Hobbit*, Smaug is devious and clever, vain and greedy, overly confident and proud. He attacks Lake-Town for a reason; he believes that the townspeople directed thieves to his lair, which is then infiltrated by a clever hobbit.[9] The 2000s British fantasy series *Merlin* presents a TV version of a similarly clever dragon, this one chained by a vengeful king in a cave beneath Camelot. (*Merlin* presents a version of Arthurian legend very different from that presented in *Le Morte d'Arthur* or even films like *Excalibur*.[10]) Young Merlin's dragon is a wise mentor (similar to *Dragonheart*'s dragon); he may act to further his own cause, but he is not a monster. These dragons also talk and clearly display their intelligence throughout their interactions with "human" (or hobbit) characters; they interact with the stories' heroes, whether as antagonists or mentors. As a result, they may be villains, or even heroes, despite their being non-human characters.

In SF TV, even the "monsters" may turn out to be thinking, feeling life forms that are just different, but no less rational, than humans. Language or cultural barriers may keep different species from understanding each other, leading to confrontations that can be resolved once the barriers are breached. Overcoming cultural/linguistic differences often forms the basis of classic *Trek* episodes introducing new aliens. Even *Battlestar Galactica*'s Cylons, originally conceived as a monstrous hive-minded metallic race, become much more human by the end of the re-imagined series. The series discussed in this book present a wide range of villains and monsters who present different perspectives on the greatest question posed by SF TV: What does it mean to be human? By recognizing what is inhuman, audiences relate more to their shared human experiences.

Retaining the Classic "Monster"

Doctor Who, the longest running single (i.e., not including spinoffs) SF series in British or American TV history, is also probably the best known "monster" series. The (to date) eleven Doctors have traditional nemeses among species spanning all time and space. Especially early in the series, which debuted in the early 1960s, the budget and technical capability for special effects were rather limited. With Russell T. Davies' re-invention of *Doctor Who*, beginning with the Ninth Doctor and continuing through the regeneration into the Eleventh Doctor, the series improved, with tighter stories, more refined acting, and better effects. Nevertheless, the classic monsters, such as Daleks and Cybermen, still make regular appearances, although they, too, received upgrades to make them more readily accepted by CGI-familiar audiences.

The monsters within the Whoniverse are outerspace baddies who, for one reason or another, set their designs on Earth. Even within the Ninth Doctor's brief (one-season) tenure, he faced a wide range of monsters who, although they were thinking beings (and could be considered villains), more importantly showed a one-dimensional focus on taking over Earth and/or destroying all humans. Their selfish reasons varied, but their monstrously single-minded objective was the same.

The Autons, for example, like the planet because of its pollution and waste, which they can use for food-like fuel. These monsters' unified action takes place only when they are "switched on" from being apparently harmless department store mannequins to becoming mobile killing machines ("Rose," 1.1).[11] More truly monstrous, the Gelth need human hosts; their native gaseous form requires them to have other vessels by which they can travel ("The Unquiet Dead," 1.3).[12] A series' staple, the Daleks turn up several times in the re-imagined series, with a first appearance only a few episodes into the Ninth Doctor's adventures.

The Daleks make a long-awaited return when the Ninth Doctor and his traveling companion, Rose Tyler, discover a single Dalek imprisoned by an American entrepreneur with a collection of alien and space artifacts. The Doctor and the Dalek recognize each other — each believes he is the last of his kind after a devastating war between the Time Lords and the Daleks. Whereas Rose attempts to communicate with the Dalek and inadvertently "humanizes" it when it accesses her mind, the Doctor simply wants to kill the Dalek, just as it normally, unthinkingly follows its order to "Exterminate!" all humans.

Robert Shearman, author of the Dalek episode, explained to fans at Hurricane Who, an Orlando, Florida, convention, that the Daleks had to be revised from the way older episodes portrayed them. Whereas original *Who* fans knew the Daleks and didn't need to be told their history, the re-imagined series reached a new as well as wider audience who weren't familiar with this monster. Thus, the Daleks needed to be re-introduced and explained in this first episode, which was based on Shearman's earlier *Doctor Who* audio story, "Jubilee."[13]

In this re-introduction, a single Dalek certainly seems less menacing than the endless invasionary force returning in later episodes. As well, when captured and tortured, the Dalek initially seems almost sympathetic. The Doctor, in contrast, obsessively wants to destroy this final reminder of the Daleks who wiped out the Time Lords. The "hero" has far less compassion than his human companion, who doesn't share his fears of or history with this enemy. She seems more inclined to mediate between the Doctor and the Dalek, empathizing with both characters.[14] However, the Daleks obviously survive to return as more menacing monsters following their directive to exterminate humanity, and the Ninth and Tenth Doctors eventually battle hordes of these monsters.

In an interview/podcast from Gallifrey 2009, Shearman commented that actor Christopher Eccleston (Ninth Doctor) envisioned the meeting between Doctor and Dalek similar to that of a Holocaust survivor and a Nazi. The resulting intensely dramatic performance enhances the story and brings a different interpretation of the Doctor (more in line with a survivor suffering from PTSD). Shearman praised actor Nicholas (Nick) Briggs, who made the Dalek "a character, not just a monster" and fulfilled the scriptwriter's hope that the role would be considered as a serious dramatic role instead of simply the synthesized voiceover of a monster.[15] Although, as explained later in this chapter, monsters in post–2000 SF TV series are becoming more human and less fundamentally, mindlessly monstrous, they are, more importantly, also becoming true characters that do more than provide a threat to the hero or those the hero needs to save. Monsters are being developed as characters more than archetypes, as even a single episode like "Dalek" illustrates.

Even on a "monster" series like *Doctor Who*, these characters aren't limited to metallic bodies or rubbery beasts; they sometimes take human form. More often, however, human "monsters" create themselves through obsession with appearance, wealth, or socio-political power. Seasons One and Two of the new *Who* provide another wide range of these kinds of monsters, including the vain Cassandra, whose interest in beauty eventually turns her into nothing more than stretched, moisturized skin ("The End of the World," 1.2), and overly eager entrepreneur Adam, one of the Doctor's temporary traveling companions, who just can't resist "upgrading" himself.[16] Adam hopes to use his knowledge of the future to make a fortune when he returns to the past, but instead he's left on 21st century Earth with a computer port in his forehead ("The Long Game," 2.7).[17] His futuristic upgrade ultimately renders him less than human and more monstrous to those without such knowledge of the future.

The Whoniverse's monsters provide a variety of entertaining forms to fit the stories; somehow it's more comforting to believe that monsters like the Daleks are "out there"—beyond Earth and far away. In the *Doctor Who* world of child-friendly heroes and monsters, when these monsters do attack, humanity, with the Doctor's help, of course, can find a way to get rid of them.

It's not so easy with the human monsters who prey on their own kind; these monsters more closely resemble real people who harm others or who are so self-interested that they look out only for themselves. The human monsters, propelled by greed, vanity, or love of power, are more of a threat than the beasties from another world because audiences see evidence almost daily of the ways that people exploit each other globally.

The new series of *Doctor Who* provides a good blend of monsters from "out there" with the home-grown variety. What the monsters represent makes *Doctor Who* applicable to adults as well as children who might just like a scare now and then. Monsters on a television screen can be dealt with easily, but the monsters they can represent in real life aren't so easily dispensed with at the end of an episode.

Yet another type of monster can take whatever form it likes and remains mysterious throughout a series' development. One of the best examples of a force that may be natural, the result of scientific experimentation run amok, or a villain who can take monstrous forms is *Lost*'s smoke monster. "Smokey" is initially pure monster during *Lost*'s early seasons—it drags people underground and kills them. It makes horrible sounds as it mysteriously and suddenly appears in the jungle, catching unlucky castaways. Audiences later see that it acts not only as a security system for the island but as a morality detector.

When Mr. Eko first encounters Smokey ("The 23rd Psalm," 2.10), he sees scenes from his life.[18] After his life literally flashes before his eyes, Eko accepts who he is, and both the good and bad aspects of his life. Smokey lets him live. This act doesn't seem random; instead, Smokey displays either a mechanical "lie detector" ability that indicates Eko's worthiness to continue living or sentience that approves of Eko's acceptance but not pride in his less than savory previous behavior. Eko apparently is on the "right" path, one approved by Smokey. In previous episodes, however, Smokey's acts seem unpredictable and random; no one knows when or how the monster appears or what it will do. It is feared because of its unpredictability and violence.

A season later, Mr. Eko has turned away from the good life he was trying to lead on the island and once again embraces the Dark Side. Smokey again visits him, but when Eko acts proud of his dark achievements, Smokey picks him up and smashes him against a tree ("The Cost of Living," 3.5).[19] The monster's actions once again are unpredictable to audiences, as well as to the castaways.

Although monsters may at times become more villainous, either as they are modernized for SF series or as audiences and human characters learn more about them, they typically look or act "inhuman." A practical way to discern SF TV monsters from villains is the way they are portrayed on screen. Monsters are often dehumanized. They are considered "it" instead of "he" or "she." A good example of this dehumanization occurs in the *Torchwood* episode "Cyberwoman" (1.4). The scientist studying the Cyberwoman is less interested in removing alien technology to make her human again than in analyzing the half-woman, half-machine. He gropes the Cyberwoman's breasts, an act that disturbs her very human boyfriend, Ianto Jones. Every time the scientist calls his specimen "it," Ianto reminds him that her name is Lisa.[20] Traditional monsters shouldn't be sympathetic characters, and dehumanizing them is one way to separate "them" from "us."

Perhaps the most currently feared, if less tangible, "monster" on SF TV is Time. Alternate and parallel universes, time travel, time loops, and gaps in time all are popular plot devices. Series like *Lost* attempt to explain the true scientific nature of time — at least as it's currently understood — while using uncontrolled leaps in time as the key plot device in Season Five. Noting that time off the island moves differently from time on the island introduces at least a few aspects of Einstein's theory of relativity into TV storytelling and adds some science to the fiction. Although characters like physicist Daniel Faraday explain how time operates and what that means for characters stuck in the past or attempting to change their future, Time can't yet be completely understood or its workings accurately predicted. It remains a "monster" that seems to randomly force characters on the island to jump from time to time, ultimately killing those who can't handle the physical aspects of time travel.

Several series discussed in this book use time travel as a plot device. The most obvious is *Doctor Who*, the adventures of a Time Lord traveling through space and time. However, even the Doctor can't always control just where and when the TARDIS will land, and the TARDIS frequently acts beyond the Doctor's control. *Torchwood* portrays the down side of time travel; 51st century Captain Jack becomes stuck in 19th century Wales and must take "the long way" by living through the decades until the Doctor's return in the early 2000s. Jack's broken vortex manipulator conveniently makes it impossible for him to travel in time and space as easily as he once did as a Time Agent, policing those who would change time lines for personal gain. (Those who abuse time travel, as noted in the recent *Star Trek* movie, tend to become series' villains, whereas those who don't change the past or do help ensure that time lines aren't altered for personal gain are portrayed as series' heroes.)

Heroes doesn't attempt to explain how time travel works but simply allows fan-favorite Hiro Nakamura to visit the future, where, in Season One, he sees a version of himself that he doesn't like. Using time travel as a moral cautionary tale may be a less frequent employment of this plot device, but Time can still be "monstrous" when it indicates how it changes heroes into people they don't want to become — in Hiro's case, a vigilante identified as a terrorist by the government.

Other series illustrate societies mirroring our own, even though they take place far away in space and time. *Firefly* offers a space Western set in the future; *Battlestar Galactica* presents a post-apocalyptic militarized society of refugees who, surprisingly, are our ancestors, not our far-flung descendants. Despite the difference in temporal or physical setting, humans of the past or future illustrate current Earth perils and ways that heroes or villains should act. Although Time isn't a physical monster in these settings, it represents the monstrous potential for change — destructive or beneficial — facing modern audiences. The sense that "time may be running out" induces fear as much as any monster in previous centuries' hero literature.

Monsters as Heroes

Ironically, some SF TV series thrive on making "monsters"—those characters decidedly not human who also are uncontrollable forces, unpredictable agents, or even victims of curses beyond their control—the heroes or at least series' protagonists. Such is the case with the BBC's *Being Human*, the saga of a ghost, a vampire, and a werewolf who try to become more socially adept in Bristol. (U.S. SyFy readied an American version for 2011.) Their story is more one of Otherness than a tale of heroes, but occasionally the plots allow them to act more heroically.

The most frequent monsters as heroes, especially post–*Twilight*, are vampires, whose popularity greatly increased beginning in 2008. Still the most popular—and, to date, arguably best—vampire TV series are Joss Whedon's *Buffy the Vampire Slayer* and spinoff *Angel*. As Angel proves once he has his own series, the monster can be a lead hero. Even more popular than Angel is Spike, whose character becomes transformed over the course of *Buffy*'s later seasons and *Angel*'s final season.

Spike, the standout vampire in the *Buffy* series, is shown in flashback to be a mild-mannered Victorian poet, a mama's boy ("Fool for Love," 5.7), before he becomes smitten—and bitten—by vampire Drusilla.[21] As a human, sweet William seems hardly heroic, much less capable of doing anything evil. When he becomes a vampire and discovers a heady power over mortals, Spike is born—vicious, calculating, sexual. For centuries he terrorizes humanity, learning from one of the most notorious vampires, Angelus.

Spike is a bad-boy vampire, but he eventually gains redemption once he falls in love with vampire slayer Buffy. Wanting to be good enough for Buffy, especially after their doomed "love" affair in the aftermath of a near-rape ("Seeing Red," 6.2), Spike realizes that he needs to regain his soul if he is to have any chance of winning Buffy's love, not just the use of her body.[22] The vampire/monster repents and, following the guidance of an African shaman, wins back his soul ("Grave," 6.22).[23] He becomes more heroic when he joins forces with Buffy during his "crush" period and works with the Scoobies. After his relationship with Buffy ends, Spike eventually becomes a crime-fighter alongside Angel, even if he never is as interesting or effective as a fledgling hero as he is when he is a dark villain or vampire/monster.

Vampire Angel becomes much more heroic once he has his own series. Another one of Buffy's former lovers, Angel, like Spike, flips back and forth between vampire/monster and wannabe hero. After Buffy and Angel make love the first time, Angel's dark side is released. Instead of being a good boyfriend who just happens to be a vampire, Angelus is a dark villain who easily slips into monster/vampire mode. Angel, too, tries to regain his soul but fails. (Eventually he loses and regains his soul several times before the series ends.) He always will remain Other because he is a vampire — undead, inhuman by definition — doubly so when he is soulless.

Whatever audiences ultimately define as making them human, having a soul is probably the top criterion. In *Angel*, the title character works within demonic law firm Wolfram & Hart in order to protect the humans living in Los Angeles. His actions are far more heroic, but audiences — and Angel himself — forever are reminded that he isn't human, despite his role as series' hero. In this way Angel always must remain something of a monster, tainted by what he is, despite his good deeds. He can't become human, and aspects of his Otherness (e.g., the lack of a soul) just won't be acceptable to audiences. Nevertheless, he becomes a hero acting on behalf of the population he'll never be able to join.

Not surprisingly, *Torchwood* also plays with definitions of life and death, and not just with the immortal Captain Jack, who dies but can't stay dead. During Season Two, Owen Harper dies while protecting a colleague; he literally takes a bullet for her ("Reset," 2.6).[24] When Jack manages to bring him back to life, using alien technology so "inhuman" that even Jack's team can't approve of it ("Dead Man Walking," 2.6),[25] Owen learns that life after death isn't quite as thrilling as audiences might wish ("A Day in the Death," 2.7).[26] He can't eat, drink, or have sex; he has no bodily functions.

A mundane but fascinating scene reminds viewers of what it means to be human — and what it means not to be. Undead Owen clears out his refrigerator because he no longer can enjoy its contents. He disposes of everything that he needs to maintain a living body. Work, ironically, continues after death. Owen ultimately is destroyed — after all, his body can't repair itself — while acting heroically once more. Whether alive or undead, he becomes a hero when his action alone can save either one person or a whole city ("Exit Wounds," 2.13). "Life" isn't what makes Owen heroic; his compassion for others allows him to overcome his fear of that final death from which he can't return.

Audiences, particularly female viewers, often gravitate to the "bad boy" characters; vampires, zombies, werewolves, ghosts, et al. may be sexy or charismatic, but they will never be attainable. They can't be "redeemed" to be fully human, no matter how much they may want to try or how much fun viewers may have fantasizing about their redemption. Although *Buffy*, for example, also has "bad girl" monsters, such as Xander's love interest, the demonic Anya, male monsters as series' heroes are more common.

The undead "monsters" defy our definition of what is human, yet these characters once were human and remember what it is like to be mortal. Perhaps that's why they can choose to act heroically, to protect what they value about human life, even if they no longer can be human. Being a hero doesn't have to be an exclusively human activity, but when inhuman or undead characters, typically thought of as "monsters" in horror or SF stories, become heroes, they can teach us what being human is all about.

Heroes as Monsters

Not every series presents traditional monsters or even newer, more sympathetic but still otherworldly versions. The more modern-themed the series, the more likely its heroes will sometimes be called or perceived as monsters— unpredictable, unfeeling, inhuman. SF TV heroes sometimes are perceived by other characters to be monstrous when their acts seem to go too far against societal values (or even the hero's own previous standards of acceptable behavior).

When *Torchwood*'s Captain Jack Harkness holds a gun to subordinate Ianto Jones' head, demanding that he kill his half-converted Cyberwoman girlfriend or be killed, Ianto calls Jack a monster and questions whether he has the capacity to love anyone. Although Ianto technically keeps a potentially humanity-destroying monster in the basement, his motivation is love for the woman subsumed by the cyberbeast. While trying to protect humanity, and undoubtedly reliving horrific encounters with Cybermen, Jack ruthlessly commands Ianto to destroy what he loves, an apparently "inhuman" act. "Cyberwoman" questions whether humans or hive-brained metal creatures are most unfeeling, what it means to be human, and whether monsters can be redeemed. That Jack, as much as the Cyberwoman, becomes the focus of these questions shows just how dark modern SF TV heroes can become.

Ianto, however, also applies the "monster" label to himself in a Season Two episode ("Adam," 2.5).[27] The Torchwood agent discovers the true identity of an alien who survives by feeding off others' memories. In retaliation, the alien tortures Ianto with "memories" of murders he's committed. Afraid that he'll kill again, Ianto begs Jack to lock him up because he has become a monster — unthinkingly murdering for pleasure and enjoying his victims' helplessness. Still more questions arise from an episode like "Adam." Can we really know ourselves, and somewhere deep down is there a monster just waiting to be unchained?

What Makes Us Human?

What makes us human — our memories and shared experiences? If memories can be distorted, lost, or manipulated, how can we know what is real or even who we truly are? Can physiology and DNA determine who is a "real" or a "fake" human? *Battlestar Galactica*, like *Torchwood*, infers that memory or self-knowledge is a faulty determinant of who or what is human. Even "regular" science might not be able to determine the real thing. For all the physical evidence that he is very much a mortal man, Colonel Tigh, a high-ranking human military commander and long-time friend of *Galactica*'s commander, shockingly discovers that he is not only Cylon, but one of the Cylons' elite. After spending what he recalls as his "human" life battling this mortal enemy, he gradually accepts the idea that he has been one of "them" all along. Memory can be manipulated and faulty, as can humanity's "objective" scientific documentation or subjective perceptions of what is, and who are, real.

Battlestar Galactica and *Caprica*, perhaps most of all, insinuate that technology is such a part of us that "being human" also must be defined without a technological basis. Cylons may have begun as a mechanized race, but their "soul" is just as human as the biological bodies audiences think of as "real people." *Caprica* proposes that the myriad bits of data stored in computers throughout a lifetime can be compiled to create a realistic hologram — a copy of a person so close to the original as to make no difference at all. When such a computer program is placed into a mechanized body — at least by the time of *Battlestar Galactica*'s story — the Cylon "race" is able to blend with humans to produce a beautiful hybrid baby.

Technology may perfect and prolong the lifespan of the average human body, making any biological definition of "human" obsolete. *Caprica* and *Battlestar Galactica* suggest that "soul" may be a defining feature of "humanity" in sentient beings, but the role of God or gods in creating any species is questioned. Both series pit monotheism and polytheism against each other as "true" religions. Humanity long favors polytheism in these series, and the Cylons act as true monotheistic believers. Can the "bad guys" in these series be the ones whose religious beliefs come closest to those of most viewers brought up in Judeo-Christian-based Western societies?

Additionally, a man initially creates the Cylon body frame into which the remaining electronic impulses of a young woman's personality are programmed. Thus, Man is Creator of what becomes a new hybrid race that eventually becomes a separate species of sentient life, able to reproduce itself. In the *Caprica/Battlestar Galactica* world, the act of Creation isn't the sole province of a divine being. Does that make humans monsters or gods — or is the way they use their knowledge the deciding factor?

Modern SF TV series often raise such questions and force audiences to consider whether any "hero" is completely "good," or whether such decisions to torture during interrogation, threaten or execute subordinates, choose family members to sacrifice, lie to or mislead the public, or even create new life forms are pragmatic or morally reprehensible decisions. These series often present villains who might closely resemble segments of the audience or whose heroes may not represent the moral viewpoints of all, or even most, viewers. Even monsters may have something positive in common with human heroes, or, conversely, heroes may temporarily share traits with monsters.

The Trend to Humanize Villains and Monsters

Traditionally, villains were easily identified because they were always inherently evil or were once good but turned to the Dark Side. They may have been reared to be evil but are possibly salvageable because they didn't know better. Today's SF TV villains aren't so easily identifiable. If modern "heroes" may occasionally do something audiences might consider villainous or monstrous, even if it's for the greater good, so too can "villains" occasionally do something good.

Heroes' main villain, Sylar, usually displays a cruel streak, even to those he loves. In Season One ("The Hard Part," 1.21), he kills his mother during an argument when she becomes afraid of him and calls him a monster.[28] Although her "accidental" stabbing may not be as inadvertent as Sylar would like to believe, he does show some remorse for his act. He seems to be at least "redeemable" because he recognizes that what he has done is wrong, even if that wrongness is mostly the pain in losing the person he wanted to love him.

A Season Three alternate future episode ("I Am Become Death," 3.4), however, shows what Sylar might have been if he'd had a more loving upbringing.[29] Believing he's a long-lost Petrelli sibling, apron-wearing Sylar happily makes pancakes for his young son while welcoming "brother" Peter into his home. Sylar seems the perfect dad: devoted, kindly, nurturing, prompting one fan blog to entitle its weekly discussion theme "Future Sylar — How Did He Become 'Betty Crocker'?"[30] The single parent and his son love each other unconditionally. Unfortunately, the child soon dies violently — although not at his father's hands — and Sylar-the-villain is reborn even in this altered reality.

Despite Sylar's apparent propensity for violence and mayhem to sooth his emotional needs, audiences still might feel sorrow for him at times. Later episodes further explain the man's troubled past and his equally evil biological father, which indicate that young Gabriel Gray might not be able to help himself. He was simply born bad. Zachary Quinto's layered portrayal suggests that Sylar might not be inherently evil, in spite of his troubled upbringing or psychopathic biological father; at times, even this villain becomes a sympathetic character because he lacked a stable, loving family during his formative years.

Early in Season Five episodes of *Heroes*, Sylar, shapeshifting as Nathan Petrelli, faces the wrath of a wronged mother who wants to avenge her dead daughter by killing Nathan. She pays to have him gruesomely killed and buried in the woods. By virtue of his self-healing power, Sylar arises from the grave just like an undead monster. The trauma, however, renders Sylar amnesiac, and he has trouble believing he could ever do anything wrong ("Hysterical Blindness," 4.5).[31] Even when confronted with evidence that he is a murderer, Sylar finds it difficult to believe. Without memory of who he really is, the "mindless" Sylar seems innocent and childlike, certainly nothing like the sadistic killer shown in previous episodes. In this way, even a "monster" like Sylar becomes a sympathetic character — once freed from his troubled past.

Although *Heroes'* stories increasingly became repetitive in later seasons, the fact that Sylar-as-potentially-good recurs, and Quinto portrays the villain as a likeable innocent when Sylar doesn't know his "true nature," indicates that even the series' hardcore villain might have a few redeeming qualities. Although "nurture" as much as "nature" may be responsible for this egomaniacal, power-hungry, cruel villain, even he might be a better man in different circumstances.

Torchwood also portrays a prime villain from Season Two as a once-innocent boy who was kidnapped and tortured for decades by alien invaders. This villain proved to be so popular with fans that they voted him the series' number-one villain, surpassing non-human threats to the world.[32] The appropriately named Gray blames his older brother for letting go of his hand during an invasion, an act that leads to the younger sibling being left behind for aliens to find. The older brother, now renamed Jack Harkness, accepts the guilt of losing his brother and the "penance" of allowing Gray to bury him alive ("Exit Wounds," 2.13).[33] Jack's acceptance of Gray's behavior indicates his own insecurity about his past deeds and his willingness to die, over and over, if it will redeem him in his brother's eyes. Although this extreme act illustrates the level of Gray's abnormality, he only becomes truly "monstrous" instead of a possibly sympathetic villain when he plots to wipe out Torchwood and destroy Cardiff in the process; he shows no regard for life in his desire for vengeance.

As with Sylar, Gray possibly would have been a normal man (i.e., not sociopathic murderer) if he'd had a kinder childhood and been treated with love instead of hatred and pain. The episode concludes with a guilt-ridden, possibly compassionate/possibly delusional Jack freezing his brother in the hope that Gray might someday be redeemable. Perhaps a character like Jack, who seriously straddles the line between hero and villain at times, must believe in forgiveness and redemption — not as spiritual concepts so much as pragmatic ones — in order to return to "good." If Jack can't be seen as forgiving and compassionate at least with his family and close friends, he can't expect to be forgiven for his less than heroic actions.

Audiences who watch this episode at the conclusion of Season Two have seen many sides to the character of Jack Harkness, not all of them traditionally heroic. The older brother may have many reasons to kill the younger — to take vengeance, to mete "justice" for the deaths he caused, to eliminate him as a future threat to society — but Jack chooses to hope that Gray one day will be able to live a "normal" life as a better person. Nevertheless, the decision to cryogenically suspend Gray for an indefinite time isn't a way for Jack to rehabilitate his sibling. Gray is left in suspension within the series as a continuing potential threat that's only eliminated by accident with the Hub's destruction in Season Three.

In this and other series, villains seldom die. They may go away (e.g., to prison, into seclusion, to escape justice) for awhile, but they likely will return, bigger and badder than before. SF TV series may explain how to live with villains or even monsters as one possible solution, but more often foes depart only to return for a later rematch. Good doesn't overcome Evil permanently, and in post–2000 series, Evil is likely to be a source of drama in some form in every episode.

Distinguishing between villains and monsters, like the line between ever-darker heroes and possibly-redemptive villains, is more difficult given the trend for characters colored in all shades of gray. Audiences might understand that villains were abused, abandoned, or otherwise traumatized earlier in their life, which leads them to bad behavior later. We live in an age when TV talk shows analyze why tragic events happen and what leads the perpetrators of those events to act in such socially unacceptable ways. We may hear on the news how a campus shooter was bullied by classmates or abused by parents or teachers, or learn that a father became so frustrated by being out of work that he bombed his former workplace. Rationalizing socially deviant behavior is the norm, but how far that rationalization should go makes for interesting debates, not only in the real world but on TV series.

The question whether heroes need to be able to match villains in dark deeds in order to stop them may be especially troubling to TV audiences. After all, if heroes and villains essentially do the same things, if for different reasons, what does that say about societal values? If, in order to fight "villains," a culture condones murder and lawlessness by the people in charge, will there someday soon be no way to distinguish the "good guys" from the "bad"? Ultimately, are SF TV heroes those characters who choose to commit murder, torture possibly innocent people, manipulate the population's beliefs, and so on, only periodically and under the most dire of circumstances? SF TV in the 2000s still toys with the idea of how "gray" a hero can become without going too far — a concept discussed in light of specific heroes in later chapters.

What also makes "villains" especially frightening to TV audiences is the realization that we might not be able to spot them in our midst. Like *Torchwood*'s sleeper agent waiting for a signal to awaken and kill all humans, the people we least expect to turn against us may be the ones who someday attack. Worse yet, we, like several *Battlestar Galactica* characters — including the ship's second in command — may discover that we really are the enemy.

Our Continuing Need for Monsters

Villains are more than the opposite of heroes; they are more than just characters who provide a story's dramatic tension. They, as well as monsters, highlight society's deepest fears about people or situations we can't control. Particularly today, when we're unsure just whom we can trust — in our neighborhood, in our workplace, in our world — we question how we can determine who is a good person or bad, who might be a friend or may turn on us as foe.

SF TV's villains and monsters not only indicate what we fear but how we might combat those fears.

According to *Battlestar Galactica*'s finale, everyone must work together if anyone is going to survive. There aren't inherently bad humans or Cylons—although individual characters may act as heroes or villains. However, Cylons and humans, just like viewers facing their own enemies, have to work through differences and try to understand one another. Otherwise, humanity is doomed to self-annihilation.

According to *Torchwood*, we may very well be capable of becoming the monsters from whom we want to be protected. Even heroes might make monstrous decisions in their desire to act on behalf of the greater good. Again, blanket labels, such as *alien, villain, monster,* or even *hero,* may be misleading because people can and do change, depending upon time, circumstance, and the choices they make. Nevertheless, individuals, no matter how good their intentions, might not be able to save everyone, and heroes are indeed fallible.

According to *Lost*, we may not now nor ever be capable of understanding just how and why the world works as it does. There may always be some mysteries, such as Smokey, that defy easy scientific explanation or personal comprehension. Nevertheless, we all are held accountable for our actions and must accept responsibility for what we choose to do. Audiences may feel just as "lost" as the series' characters, but we, like they, must decide how to act and take responsibility for those actions.

These and other SF TV series do a good job of illustrating and evaluating a range of human decisions and actions—as well as the motivations or intentions behind them. The stories that have meaning for audiences might present as many villains as heroes to analyze, but a deeper understanding of monsters and villains helps us learn more about our society and ourselves.

3

Shades of Gray:
21st Century
SF Heroes and Villains

Entertainment Weekly's popular culture guru, Jeff Jensen, prefaced a March 2009 article about heroes and villains by stating the obvious: "Heroes and Villains have been with us since ... well, day one, when God and the devil emerged donning the original white and black hats. Good guys and bad have been around since the birth of pop culture."[1] The "white hat/black hat" analogy goes back a ways in popular culture, but it is still relevant to our common understanding of Good or Evil as portrayed in cinema or on television.

The extreme distance between bad guy and good guy can easily be seen in popular U.S. television Westerns from the 1950s and 1960s. The leading good guys typically wear white cowboy hats. Roy Rogers helped pave the way as a boys' role model on Saturday mornings, while partner Dale Evans, often wearing a white cowgirl hat, provided a suitably squeaky clean example for girls. The Lone Ranger, although a masked hero, also donned a white hat. Many of the wagon masters, ranchers, and sheriffs that followed on TV screens during the 1950s and 1960s also are what would become stereotyped as "white hats": Major Seth Adams (*Wagon Train*), Marshal Matt Dillon (*Gunsmoke*), and Big John Cannon (*The High Chaparral*) are just a few examples of clearly identifiable good guys who fight for the weaker, law-abiding folks in their care.

Not only Jensen, but TV characters in the new millennium still refer to "black hats" and "white hats" for a simplistic visualization of bad or good characters. The most traditional hero among the *Heroes* characters, Hiro Nakamura, learns that this distinction between Good and Evil is still being passed on to the next generation in the aptly Western-named episode "Once Upon a Time in Texas" (4.7). A small boy gives Hiro his sheriff's hat, telling him that "good guys wear white hats; bad guys wear black hats." When the series' most notorious villain, Sylar, walks past them just as Hiro agrees with the child, the camera pans to Sylar's attire. Of course, he is wearing a black hat.[2]

Even the hero-villain parody *Dr. Horrible's Sing-Along Blog* (mentioned in

Chapter 2) skewers the Western, along with many other genres. When Dr. Horrible receives mail from evil mastermind Dark Horse (who, it turns out, really is equine — yet another Western reference), a trio of singing cowboy henchmen, all wearing black hats, explain the message to the audience. Whether in parody or drama, the link between heroes and villains and the U.S. Western motif is still strong in U.S. SF TV series.

When *Star Trek* creator Gene Roddenberry designed his SF TV series, he identified it as a "*Wagon Train* to the stars."[3] Not only did he attach his pilot script to popular Westerns, but he carried on the tradition of very good "good guys" facing a new frontier. Captain James T. Kirk was one of the first TV space heroes leading such an expedition. Like TV heroes before him, he needed to be compassionate and wise, but he often relied on his colleagues and friends, Mr. Spock and "Bones" McCoy, for advice. Similarly, the former patriarch of the Ponderosa (Ben Cartwright, played by Lorne Greene) eventually became the patriarch to the ragtag remnants of humanity in the original *Battlestar Galactica* in the late 1970s. The link between Western good guys and space heroes furthered the popularity of the strong, manly TV hero.

SF villains, like their TV Western antecedents from the 1950s to the 1970s, are hardly subtle characters. The "black hats" of Westerns typically are bank robbers, cattle rustlers, swindlers, or murderers who are dispatched by the end of an episode. Although some primarily "good" Western characters wear black hats, such as Ben Cartwright's eldest son Adam, the Virginian, or Bret Maverick, these characters are also lovable rogues who might not toe the line as carefully as other characters in their respective series, but in a fight between Good and Evil they would line up on the "correct" side. (In contrast to their older brother, the more amiable Cartwright boys, Hoss and Little Joe, wear white hats throughout the series.)

In SF, *Star Trek*'s Klingons or Romulans typically are ongoing nemeses to the United Federation of Planets, although villains of the week can come from any galaxy. They either learn how to live in harmony with the Federation, as represented by Kirk and the *Enterprise*, or they "lose" to the clever Captain Kirk. Perhaps *Battlestar Galactica* capped the genre with the original Baltar, the human who willingly colludes with the Cylons to destroy the human race.

SF TV heroes and villains inherit the same types of plots and moral dilemmas presented in earlier decades in the guise of American Westerns or historic dramas. The stories that "make us human," with a supernatural, scientific, or space-travel extra ingredient added, often become the canon for SF TV series. From *Star Trek*'s premise as "*Wagon Train* to the stars" to *Firefly*'s displaced Civil War vets seeking a new life on the frontier to *Battlestar Galactica*'s refugees looking for a new home, or even to *Lost*'s early survival guide for living off the (is)land, even 2000-era series return to a familiar theme — the great untamed wilderness — as the setting of its stories. Exploring new places, taming the wilderness, creating a home within a new world — these actions resonate within

SF TV when characters look beyond themselves for new possibilities for adventure or second chances.

Even the citizens embroiled in the urban environments of London, Cardiff, Los Angeles, or Caprica City, or middle class suburbia like Sunnydale, still dream of better lives and ways to improve or hold onto what they've built. The setting may be "tamed"—or offer new dangers lurking in the shadows of skyscrapers and downtown alleys—but the desire to make the world a better place still remains. Often that takes the form of policing or protecting innocents from those who would prey on the weak. Whether the analogy is made to American Western marshals patrolling dusty streets, British constables walking an urban beat, or forensic detectives dissecting bodies in labs and testing crime scenes, the need to protect "civilization" is the necessary next step once the explorers, settlers, immigrants, or refugees settle down. The settings may change, but the human impetus to explore, to know, to protect forms the basis of all entertaining drama and compelling hero stories.

From Judeo-Christian Morality to Moral Relativism

TV drama once clearly put the explorers, settlers, marshals, constables, police officers, and scientists on the side of "good," often allowing them to be heroic as they tried to stave off the darkness (of ignorance, paganism or atheism, lawlessness, or superstition). If words like *morality, transgression,* and *redemption* seem to provide a spiritual, or even specifically religious, context to a determination of heroes and villains, it merely reflects the Judeo-Christian values most often portrayed on television, especially in previous decades. Even post–2000 "gray" TV series—in which right and wrong are much less clearly defined, and characters are much more ambiguous as "good guys" or "bad guys"—frequently use these terms, not only within dialogue but as narrative or musical hooks to attract viewers. Questioning what is "good" or "right," and determining whether science or religion, fact or faith, destiny or free will should form our philosophy and guide our actions, are very much at the heart of SF TV in the chaotic 2000s. Gray heroes and villains struggle just as much as everyone else with finding answers to life's questions.

Buffy dies and is torn from what she perceives as heaven by her magical friend Willow; her "resurrection" leads her to question her mortal life. *Heroes* named two story arcs "Villains" and "Redemption." *Lost*'s characters frequently discuss destiny, salvation (whether spiritual or from the island), sacrifice, and redemption. A crucial theme throughout the series inspires debates about whether "men of science" or "men of faith" are correct in their leadership styles on the island and, indeed, their very philosophies.

Torchwood and *Doctor Who*, for all that they're written by proclaimed atheist Russell T. Davies, have a surprising number of Christian symbols and Biblical references—from angels to Abaddon, for example. In the "Children of Earth" miniseries serving as *Torchwood*'s Season Three, after series' hero Captain Jack Harkness commits what to many viewers is a horrific act in order to save the rest of the world, the musical theme accompanying his final scenes is entitled "Redemption."

Battlestar Galactica and *Caprica* pit two opposing theologies, monotheism and polytheism, against each other (and provide a surprise regarding which side the majority of humans take). Seeking redemption and being saved are themes for both humans and Cylons. *Lost*'s would-be successor, *FlashForward,* inserts comments about God's punishment, the Pope, saintliness, and miracles within character dialogue, between scenes of scientific inquiry, as characters attempt to figure out what caused humans worldwide to "flash forward." *V* allows two priests to question whether God sent alien visitors to help save Earth; after all, the Visitors routinely perform miracles (like curing cancer) and seem to bring messages of peace and love truly alien to modern humans.

A culture's morality often turns up in television dramas, especially in SF — the safe place to mirror current world events and concerns. Measuring SF TV heroes or villains against cultural standards of "right" and "wrong" is particularly difficult in the 2000s, however. Standards in the U.S. may differ from those in other Western nations, not to mention the rest of the world, and even politically different red or blue states may have opposing perspectives on right and wrong courses of action. Since the 1950s, TV heroes and villains who began at opposite ends of a moral continuum have gradually been moving closer toward the middle, with some "good guys" or "bad guys" occasionally crossing the midpoint and venturing, however briefly, into the other's traditional territory.

Series debuting late in the first decade of the 21st century especially lean more toward moral relativism than adherence to, or even questioning of, the moral debates found in series like *Battlestar Galactica* from a few years earlier. Pragmatic leaders or battle-weary soldiers are most likely to believe that the current life is all that exists, and that it often seems meaningless.

Heroes' politician Nathan Petrelli also waffles between spiritual rebirth and moral relativism, depending on the story arc. At some points in the series he's a crusading do-gooder who believes that God saved his life for a purpose. Later he chooses to "play God" by deciding which people with superpowers should be locked up as dangerous and which (such as his family and himself) can safely hide their powers. Even in his last episode, "The Fifth Stage" (4.12), Nathan reminisces with brother Peter about their initial understanding of their powers. Peter reminds his brother that he denied his ability to fly, even when caught in the act. Nathan grins: "Well, it was an election year." Most often, situational ethics is Nathan's forte, and even though he occasionally dabbles with Judeo-Christian moral dilemmas, he returns to pragmatic, self-determined solutions to solve his, or even the world's, problems.

In a strange plot twist, Nathan's personality becomes subsumed within ever-more-villainous Sylar. In a late 2009 episode, Nathan's personality briefly comes to the forefront for a conversation with Peter while Sylar conveniently lay unconscious. "Good," even represented by such a morally gray character as Nathan, literally is surrounded by Evil in the fifth season of *Heroes*, and Nathan's spirit proves too weak to continue to battle within villain Sylar's shapeshifting body. In a last stirring speech before giving up and dying permanently, Nathan tells Peter that he is simply too tired to go on but reminds his brother to "fight the good fight" without him ("The Fifth Stage," 4.12). He then falls to his literal, and symbolically spiritual, death, becoming yet another fallen hero who gives up when faced with overwhelming Evil.

Although *Torchwood* introduces spiritual symbolism into its plots (and indeed is often uneven in its treatment of any theme it tackles across numerous episodes), "Children of Earth" darkly posits that humanity must fend for itself, and any choice made to save the majority of Earth's citizens is bound to have collateral damage in human terms. *Star Trek* once amended its movie-series' theme of "the needs of the many outweigh the needs of the few, or the one"— as Spock iterated in his *Wrath of Khan* death scene — to emphasize the importance of the needs of the one as Kirk directs Spock's resurrection in *The Search for Spock*. *Torchwood*'s hero, Captain Jack, however, firmly adheres to *Star Trek*'s original message and sacrifices whomever necessary in order to save the greatest number of people; "Children of Earth" makes Jack a tragic hero by making him suffer the greatest personal losses as a result of his pragmatism.

In a flashback to a time more than four decades previous, when Jack Harkness follows orders to deliver a few children to visiting alien terrorists, he believes that the trade — children for a cure to a deadly flu — is worthwhile. The children won't be missed because they are orphans, while millions of people will be saved. The "cure" paves the way for the aliens' return, however, and further demands even seem OK with another character, Torchwood operative Gwen Cooper's husband, Rhys Williams. "It bought some breathing space," he admits.

Ianto, Jack's partner, however, tells Jack that the man he knows and loves in the 21st century would have instead stood up to the enemy. Ianto offers Jack a way to redeem himself, not only to his partner, colleagues, and the world, but to himself. Jack presumably has become a morally better person in the intervening years, and Ianto suggests a way for Jack to retain his goodness in the face of an old "sin" now back to haunt him.

Yet when Jack, Ianto by his side, confronts the aliens, they merely murder everyone in the building, Ianto included. His death has no meaning except to destroy Jack. The man promoting and supporting Jack's morality — indeed, enhancing his status as a traditional hero — dies without saving the day, and his loss only reinforces Jack's "dark side" of moral relativism. Jack is a hero when he finally saves the world yet again, but he is perceived as a very gray hero by many viewers because he is now firmly a moral pragmatist once again, a character more tragic but less human to many viewers.

Like Nathan Petrelli, Jack Harkness runs away and gives up the role of hero in light of overwhelming Evil and the pain caused by trying to save humanity. The shift from Judeo-Christian morality to moral relativism ironically is illustrated in the miniseries' final musical themes. Jack's "Redemption" musical theme illustrates many audience members' morality and their hope that gray hero Jack may be redeemed from his pragmatically effective but morally horrific decision-making. In contrast, the final song, "I Can Run Forever," emphasizes Jack's self-determinism in his realization that he cannot be a hero any longer and only dooms those he loves when he steps up to save the world. Jack's choice, like Nathan's, is that ultimately he cannot make any difference and is too tired to keep trying against impossible odds. He gives up but leaves "the good fight" to those who still believe they can make a difference.

Cultural relativism often comes into play with the acceptance or rejection of gray heroes. Cultures in which adherents clearly agree upon and delineate certain acts as moral or immoral have a real problem with gray heroes who decide to go against these cultural standards, even temporarily. Moral relativism allows individuals to decide what is right or wrong for themselves and states that life is meaningless; heroes or villains don't need to worry about what they *should* do because their actions ultimately don't mean anything. Heroes aren't going to be rewarded for being "good" or punished for being "bad." They just act, without any subjective morality being imposed on them. Even the term *hero* is a morally subjective term; *protagonist*, as discussed in Chapter 1, is a moral relativist's term for a lead character.

Although the majority of TV viewers in the U.S., or indeed the Western world, probably still feel more comfortable with characters who follow some semblance of Judeo-Christian morality, the presence of moral relativism is clearly being felt in SF TV, with the rise in popularity of Russell T. Davies' version of *Doctor Who* and his own creation, *Torchwood*, as well as 2009–debuting U.S. series *FlashForward* and *V*, being prime examples. Some audiences prefer more "human" heroes and villains who are flawed, neither all "good" nor all "bad," because they are more like themselves and the people they know. Audiences can relate to less-than-perfect protagonists who act heroically much more than they can relate to the morally strict heroes of previous decades' or centuries' fiction.

Nevertheless, not all audiences have moved completely into the moral relativist camp, which makes the shift from traditional, morally "perfect" heroes to modern gray heroes more troubling and controversial for them. Audiences, like the heroes and villains they watch, may accept more flaws as "normal," but most viewers still want their heroes to retain at least some remnants of Judeo-Christian morality. During the early 2000s, the paradigm shift in hero stories mirrors cultural philosophical shifts between Judeo-Christian morality and moral relativism, but audience preference still clings to morality.

The Hero's Divine Favor or Later Luck

Another illustration of the uneasy stance between Judeo-Christian morality and moral pragmatism involves the concept of luck. Traditional heroes in literature from earlier ages, or even more recent fantasy tales set in faraway times and places, often portray these characters as divinely inspired or favored. As mentioned in earlier chapters, literary heroes like Beowulf and Sir Gawain are able to beat their foes because they are favored by God. Tolkien's Aragorn may live in a pagan world, but he too interprets signs and knows just when to ascend the throne, in part guided by the character closest to a spiritual advisor as could be found in Middle-earth, Gandalf. Even Luke Skywalker can perform miraculous feats when he aligns with the Force, the most spiritual element of the *Star Wars* universe. Because of this favor, traditional heroes seem luckier than other characters. Everything seems to turn out well for them, even if they need a *deus ex machina* now and then.

Modern gray heroes don't have such divine favor, although they, like traditional heroes, may be called lucky. Indeed, many an SF story allows heroes to defy death with last-minute escapes or save the day when no one else can. Nevertheless, gray heroes quickly discover that they can't rely on this "luck," and what others call lucky may not, in fact, be what they desire or what ultimately is best for them.

When the immortal Captain Jack Harkness survives being blown apart in an explosion that destroys the Hub, his colleague and lover asks, "Don't you ever worry that your luck might run out?" For the mortal Ianto, defeating death would be lucky, but Jack knows the pain and sorrows of a thousand deaths. For him, being able to stay dead might be far luckier than returning yet again to life. Ironically, when Ianto and Jack die during a confrontation with aliens, Jack's body-bagged corpse is number 13 in a warehouse full of bodies, and his death comes on Floor 13 of Thames House. In yet another ironic bit of trivia, actor John Barrowman claims that his family's lucky number is 13, which is why he requested that number for Jack's corpse.[4]

Gray heroes rely on their and others' knowledge, experience, and skill to perform heroic deeds. Even so, their limited understanding and abilities mean that they can't control all factors in any situation; what they think is doing the right thing or manipulating situations to get the outcome they desire may backfire. Because these heroes are fallible and very human, they can't control everything and everyone. They no longer rely on God or even luck to help keep them or those they want to protect from danger. They rely on themselves and make their own decisions without worrying if God, or even society, will approve. This self-determinism is yet another element of moral relativism that is increasingly common among SF TV heroes, as well as villains.

Shades of Gray: Defining Heroes and Villains

Joseph Campbell, for example, only recognized the hero, classifications of heroes, and the hero's journey. Every analyst who labels heroes develops a set of criteria by which a hero can be identified and measured. (Refer to Chapter 1 for further discussion of these criteria.) If a character doesn't meet these criteria, then he or she isn't really a hero. Some degree of moral perfection (and, in some cases, physical or mental perfection) and consistency in attitude and behavior marks these definitions.

With the rise of what I termed the "everyman hero" (in *Unsung Heroes of The Lord of the Rings*), more characters today potentially can be heroic. Ordinary people can step up and act heroically in times of crisis; the world isn't saved by just one (super)hero or group of heroes whose "job" is to protect humanity. Characters who might not act heroically all the time still can overcome their fear or self-interest in order to help others; they may sacrifice themselves for the greater good. They may not be "heroes" all the time, but at least once they take on this role. They do so not for fame or public recognition, but because they are in the right place at the right time to save others. (See the "Rise of the Common Hero" section later in this chapter.)

With stories being told in multiple media and being revealed episodically over hours or even years, it's much more difficult for a TV hero to be sustainable as the epitome of pure goodness. The hero of a novel or a single film can be virtuously heroic for the length of the story (even if it's doubtful that status could be maintained in the real world or even in a series of film sequels). The hero of a TV series that lasts an average full season must be an intriguing character for at least 13 to 20 hours of viewing time — not an impossibility for remaining Good, certainly, but far less likely.

Similarly, a one-note villainous character who never changes is difficult to sustain over the long term without becoming a parody. If the *Dark Knight*'s Joker had to sustain his level of perverse villainy and shock-value violence for more than three hours, he might not be as intriguing a character to watch. Maintaining that level of "darkness" wouldn't be plausible for the duration of a TV series unless the villain occasionally seems to be "redeemable" or varies the extent of his or her "badness."

As well, with greater scrutiny in all media on everyone from local heroes and politicians to globe-trotting world leaders and celebrities, anyone in the news is fair game to the closest evaluation and public criticism of every action, no matter how small. Under this type of now-accepted scrutiny, TV audiences are far more skeptical than those of previous decades of a character without a few flaws, even if he or she is the lead hero.

When the amount of psychological analysis given to every criminal in recent memory and the legal/social/scientific rationales for socially aberrant behavior are added to this trend, the rise of the gray hero or gray villain is a natural outgrowth. Even politically "bad" behavior or morally questionable decisions can be rationalized as pragmatic. Black and white is passé and naïve; as *Heroes'* character Noah Bennet has explained more than once, we live in shades of gray.[5]

The designation of "gray" as a mixture of opposites black and white is a deceptively simple metaphor, as well as one that isn't scientifically or artistically accurate; certainly, the terms "black" or "white" should not be given any racial or cultural symbolism. If black is defined in art as the absence of color, perhaps it also can be an anchoring end of the hero-villain continuum representing a void of what most audiences would consider morality or "goodness." Villains traditionally lack concern or empathy for anyone but themselves; hence, "black" can refer to an absence of compassion or of anything other than self-interest. At the opposite end of the continuum is the "purity" of white, often perceived as "spotless" or "unblemished." If these designations are symbolically attached to the "white hats" or "good guys," heroes are traditionally supposed to be clustered around the "white" end of the continuum, whereas "black hats" or "bad guys"—the villains—are polar opposites.

The SF TV series discussed as "gray" series in this book—and there are many other examples, although these are some of the most popular and award-winning from the U.S. and U.K.—are noteworthy because their heroes and villains tend to lean more frequently toward the middle of this continuum. They even occasionally venture far enough afield from their "traditional" starting point that audiences may wonder if they are bad good guys, good bad guys, or if these terms have any real meaning any more.

Gray heroes or villains aren't pure—neither all-good nor all-bad—and they might not even be human. They tend to be pragmatic, even those who answer to a higher power (e.g., Laura Roslin on *Battlestar Galactica*, who for the majority of the series is a polytheist looking for divine guidance to Earth; John Locke, looking to the Island for spiritual guidance and answers; Peter Petrelli, who, during Season Three, questions the faith of his childhood and demands answers from Christ). These characters try to do what they think is best on a day-to-day basis, even if, in hindsight, their decisions seem questionable, their motives flawed.

Gray heroes more easily move along the scale between pure Good and pure Evil, but they tend to hover a little more toward the Good side of the continuum's midpoint. These heroes often take on the jobs no one else tackles or even wants to attempt—gray heroes do the thankless jobs because they need to be done. Gray villains may do something good (and not just for themselves), or they may try to change their behavior to act more like selfless heroes, but they usually revert to their "normal" bad behavior.

Gray characters tend to slide around the middle of the scale, whether as mostly good or heroic characters who occasionally do bad things, or as mostly bad or villainous characters who occasionally do good things. As discussed in

Chapter 2, modern SF TV heroes sometimes act villainous or even "monstrous," although they don't fall far or often enough from societal standards of goodness or morality to be categorized as either. The heroes discussed in the previous chapter are good examples of series' leads who feel pressured to work in shades of gray; they believe they must sometimes act in morally ambiguous ways or make the hard decisions that no one else is willing to make in order to get as positive an outcome as possible. They still work on behalf of the greater good, but along the way these gray heroes may be willing to sacrifice a few people, as well as their own scruples, if the result is likely to be "saving the world" or "rescuing more people." At least temporarily, they may seem villainous or monstrous.

Although moral relativism and situational ethics are increasingly part of the modern hero story, most Western audiences, especially those in the U.S., still believe in some moral code and cultural definitions of *good* or *bad*, *wrong* or *right*. Although the cultural definitions may change by region or religion within a country, the vast majority of audience members philosophically are aligned more closely with Judeo-Christian moral codes than with potentially chaos-inducing moral relativism. They subjectively evaluate characters' acceptance and choose to follow some characters' stories more than others because they find their stories enlightening, redeeming, or entertaining. In short, some heroes' characteristics and actions more closely fit their expectations, and so they like (and watch more avidly) their stories.

When beloved characters act in ways that conflict with viewers' expectations, fans often discuss, analyze, or even complain about this moral dissonance — or write email to news outlets and networks. If the dissonance is too great and the hero is too "dark" to mesh with most viewers' expectations, once-loyal fans start tuning out. What is intriguing about current gray SF TV heroes is that they may be coming close to the "tune out" boundary.

In this book, moral relativism is discussed only in passing as a possible direction for future SF TV heroes. Audiences (and TV series) aren't yet to the point where moral relativism is the norm, which is why viewers perceive less-than-traditional heroes as various shades of gray. Although definitions of morality are in play culturally, audiences still look for that subjectively defined "goodness" in the heroes they choose to emulate or those whom they feel best represent their culture as heroes.

The Frequency of "Gray" Names

Some characters are even named Gray, reflecting their ambiguous morality and difficult-to-determine status as hero or villain. *Gray* has sometimes meant unformed or incomplete in a character's transcendence to "white" (or purely good, ultimately redeemed, or morally or experientially more evolved than other characters). Perhaps the best example of this use of *gray* in a name is Tolkien's Gandalf the Grey, who isn't as knowledgeable or experienced as the later Gandalf the White, who returns to Middle-earth after "dying" and helps defeat the all-encompassing evil of Sauron. *Gray* as a name for modern TV characters, however, refers to their moral ambiguity, misguided use of technology to achieve personal power, or lack of concern about the potentially disastrous consequences of their actions.

Gabriel Gray, better known as Sylar, most often acts as *Heroes'* most important villain, a character who uses his ever-increasing number of superpowers for his own empowerment rather than the good of humanity. He wants to take as much power as possible and doesn't care whom he hurts or kills along the way. The family from whom he takes his surname (as an adult, he learns that he was adopted) is just as Gray in their ability to keep secrets or their preference to act purely out of self-interest.

Like *Heroes*, *Torchwood* developed a villain named Gray, although he is a minor character in the series, albeit one important to the lead hero's backstory. Much of what Captain Jack Harkness does is based on his inability to protect his little brother when they both were children. Captain Jack truly has a "Gray" area in his life that constantly reminds him of his failings as a human, as well as a brother. When Gray returns, the resulting chaos may be a penance for Jack's past or an indication of how pragmatic and questionable his adult choices have become. By the end of Season Three, Jack has become one of the grayest heroes on SF TV, and some fans wonder if he even might still be considered a hero, despite writers' reassurances that he very much is emblematic of modern heroes facing impossible choices.

In *Caprica*, *Battlestar Galactica*'s prequel, the Graystone family unwittingly begins the Cylon race of robots—later to evolve into humanoid form by the time set for the *Battlestar Galactica* story. Even their limited association with this family "taints" the Adamas and sets in motion the resulting fears and insecurities that plague fathers and sons for generations.

Gray characters may recognize that bad acts may be necessary to achieve a victory for the "good guys," or they may be so certain of the rightness of their vision that they don't care about the potentially devastating consequences of their choices. They may be "good" most of the time but become cruel when they seek vengeance. Gray heroes do what they deem is necessary to achieve their objective, but they seldom act purely from self-interest. They think they're working on behalf of humanity or settling a score that brings some measure of justice for another's atrocious act.

Modern gray characters' backstories provide plenty of rationalization for their actions. Gray villains' backstories often show them as once-powerless victims who want payback for their earlier mistreatment; they often justify their actions by seeking "justice" for the abuse or abandonment they suffered early in life. They may have had the opportunity to be normal but were warped by tragic events in their young lives. All these characters, whether leads who are supposed to be good or guest characters providing dramatic contrast as villains, may have psychological scars from years of abuse or abandonment; they may be victims of terrible crimes or circumstances. They may not have had positive role models to guide them, and they may not realize just how antisocial their behavior has become. They may act out of character once and fail to recognize the slippery slope of morality as they slide into increasingly less characteristic behavior. They may not come from a culture with the same morals as their TV audience, who typically has been reared in a predominantly capitalist culture built on Judeo-Christian values. The delineation between a good guy and a bad guy, a hero and a villain, is blurred, and heroes and villains in 2000s-era SF usually find they have some things in common.

Gray Sexuality

Finally, some characters may be perceived as "gray" by a large percentage of the viewing audience because of their sexuality, which the mainstream, primetime audience may deem as outside the norm. Some characters may have sexual practices or attitudes that fall outside the expected norm of a given community or culture, or that are deemed taboo by religious beliefs. A character who has premarital sex, practices serial monogamy, has multiple sexual partners during the same time period, or engages in activities that some viewers might consider "kinky" or "fetishist" may be labeled as "gray."

In some communities or cultures, a gay, lesbian, bisexual, or transgendered (GLBT) character also would be labeled "gray" because of sexual orientation. (See the "Hero as 'Other'" section later in this chapter for a further discussion of Otherness in relation to gray heroes and villains.) Although sexual orientation is one determinant of being Other in many communities, a character may be perceived as Other for a variety of reasons.

Although the number of GLBT characters is slowly increasing on primetime TV, many conservative viewers may see these characters as outside the norm of their community, or outside the norm of the viewer's personal experience or belief system. For now, characters from the GLBT community aren't perceived as mainstream (at least in the U.S.) and gain more attention because of their sexuality than for other identifiers about their characters.

The same has been true of every Other marginalized group who eventually makes inroads into mainstream TV. African American characters from the 1960s to the 1980s on primetime U.S. TV also could be categorized this way, as race was the most common way for most non–African American audiences to categorize this group of characters. In the U.S., series like *I Spy* in the 1960s and *The Cosby Show* in the 1980s broke the mold — behind as well as before the cameras — with multi-racial casts or crews.

Mainstream dramas (e.g., *Brothers and Sisters*, *Grey's Anatomy*, *The L Word*, *Queer as Folk*—created by Russell T. Davies, who re-imagined *Doctor Who* and created *Torchwood*) and comedies (e.g., *Will & Grace*, for which, ironically, *Torchwood* star John Barrowman said he was considered but rejected for not being gay enough to play Will) increasingly portray GLBT characters in a variety of roles, some heroic, some not so much so. In some ways, SF TV characters have come a long way toward racial, gender, or sexual equality since *Star Trek*'s first interracial kiss, which takes place only because of alien control over Kirk and Uhura. Joss Whedon's *Buffy* characters openly enjoy their sexual partners. His series most obviously and successfully portrayed a lesbian couple with *Buffy the Vampire Slayer*, but he also gave "companion" Inara multiple partners in *Firefly* and *Serenity*.

One of the most overtly sexual SF TV series is *Torchwood*. During the first season alone, Gwen (again under alien influence, perhaps not as much of a leap for equality as viewers might have hoped) shares passionate kisses with another woman; Tosh begins a relationship with Mary (who, unfortunately, also turns out to be an alien); Owen's pheromone-saturated cologne brings him male and female partners (so that he apparently has sex with a boyfriend and girlfriend who find him irresistible); Ianto shares kisses with Jack and begins a longer-term intimate relationship; and Jack is attracted to men, women, and anything interspecies that interests him. Even in family-friendly *Doctor Who*, Jack is at the least bisexual, being attracted to and chastely kissing both the female and male series leads (Rose and the Doctor); he also is portrayed as a sexual object in several episodes.

In the 2000s, GLBT SF TV characters still are "gray" to many viewers, but they likely won't be categorized that way much longer, especially if these series continue to make an impact on audiences worldwide.

Popular Subcategories of Gray Heroes

Two trends within "hero texts" became more obvious in 2000s-era SF TV: the rise of the common hero and the acceptance of the hero as Other. Of course, both concepts had been previously illustrated on TV and within SF. Superheroes in particular always have been Other to their community, hence the need for a secret identity. War stories especially feature the common soldier who saves his (or her) comrades with an extraordinary act of bravery and self-sacrifice; the common man (or woman) becomes a hero. With the series discussed in this book, however, these types of heroes set the new standard for determining who are heroes.

The "common" and "Other" qualities fit SF TV heroes far better than criteria used by Campbell and other critics to identify traditional heroes. SF TV heroes may even be comforting to audiences because they aren't ideal role models or paragons of propriety. Because these gray heroes have flaws, defy cultural expectations or stereotypes, seem Other to at least some people they try to protect, or struggle with what it means to be human or "good," they are much more like the people watching TV at home.

Perhaps because of their grayness and moral ambiguity, these characters can become more effective (if imperfect) role models for more viewers. These gray heroes come from our time and our communities worldwide — they question, fail, and try again just like everyone else. However, they also perform heroic acts — their intention is to save humanity, from itself or outside villains or monsters. Gray heroes strive to be protectors, even if they aren't leaders. They may operate on the fringes of acceptable society, but they are outer-directed to help, guide, and protect those average citizens who can't or won't act heroically. Gray heroes may stumble or fall along the way, but they are attempting to move humanity forward and preserve what makes us human.

The following sections elaborate on common subcategories of gray SF TV heroes: common men or women, all-too-humanly flawed characters, Other, those who play God, aliens, and immortals. For various, and sometimes obvious, culturally or SF-premise-related reasons, these subcategories signify grayness. However, these SF TV heroes are often loved by audiences for that very reason.

Rise of the Common Hero

Entertaining hero stories often pit an average person against extraordinary circumstances. Young Elliott discovers an extraterrestrial in his neighborhood and must decide whether to help ET phone home or turn him over to scientists for study. Buffy Summers just wants to be a normal high school girl but accepts the responsibility of being her generation's chosen vampire slayer.

Unlike the trained protectors who choose their profession, these average or "common" people face unexpected dilemmas and have to decide — often quickly — what to do. Their initial choice begins their journey on a path leading toward a new role as Hero. In TV series, the common hero probably will take on the role of Hero more than once, or else there wouldn't be much of a series. In real life, however, common heroes may only be faced with extraordinary circumstances once; their hero status is a one-off but may affect them for the rest of their lives. SF TV heroes who choose to act heroically once most likely are going to become heroes as a profession or at least an avocation. The heroic qualities, obviously the lynchpin for future episodes, provide the comedic or dramatic tension and serve as the force behind character development, more often than not all along the "hero-villain" continuum.

One of the most enjoyable aspects of *Heroes* is the premise that hundreds of superheroes, of all ages and from all backgrounds, live all over the world. At some point their special talent is triggered. Audiences can live vicariously with the notion that they, too, might be "special" because of an as-yet-unrevealed power. Although genetics might not otherwise have made them the most beautiful, strongest, or smartest, they still may have a superpower. Just like *Heroes'* characters who discover their Otherness, or special power, they would have to choose how to handle this power.

As Peter Parker's Uncle Ben famously advised, "With great power comes great responsibility."[6] Whether otherwise ordinary people choose to accept that great responsibility and become society's heroes, or whether they choose to ignore their power, use it for personal gain, or avenge wrongs done to them, determines whether they become heroes, villains, or citizens who hide their Otherness. On *Heroes*, all these choices are explored.

Hiro Nakamura and Matt Parkman are two men, living half a world apart, who feel thwarted by dead-end jobs. They are average in intelligence and job performance, although they attempt to do their best. Hiro works in a cubicle at his father's company; he may someday guide the company, but his father isn't terribly impressed with him. Matt fails the detectives' test more than once and worries that he'll never be more than a low-level police officer, much to his wife's dismay. When they discover they have superpowers, their reactions are very different. Hiro glories in the SF possibilities of traveling in space and time; at last he is an equal with the superheroes and SF TV characters (including Captain Kirk) who made his childhood tolerable. Matt isn't sure what's happening to him — he fears the voices in his head are symptoms of madness — but he wants to use his mind-reading power to help him get ahead on the job.

Of course, as the series continues, Hiro and Matt, individually and working together, learn that being a superhero isn't as glamorous or as rewarding as they originally hoped. They sometimes decide to ignore their special powers, or they find that their gifts have temporarily left them. Nevertheless, these characters return, time after time, to their "real" jobs as heroes. Matt, in particular, as a police officer and a father, is a protector; even if he doesn't take on world-saving challenges, his protective instincts are ingrained. Hiro simply lives up to his personal expectations for superheroes; he has been given a special opportunity, and he must try to do better as a savior, whether it's saving his best friend from unrequited love, saving a child from traffic, or saving the world from maniacal villains.

Characters performing mundane jobs or living quite comfortable lives who join a group or take on responsibilities greater than themselves — or face life-or-death situations because they leave home on an adventure — may become these common heroes. *Firefly*'s Kaylee Frye seems terribly naïve about most aspects of life, but she's a genius at repairing equipment and creatively finding ways to keep *Serenity* traveling. She isn't a warrior, but she can help her friends get out of trouble. Simon Tam is a loyal brother who loves his sister so much that he gives up his lucrative surgical practice and upper class lifestyle in order to free her from government testing facilities; he dedicates his life to keeping her safe and returning her to sanity, when he easily could've ignored what was happening to his little sister. *Battlestar Galactica*'s President Roslin begins the series as a schoolteacher who becomes a low-level government employee. When her world explodes around her, the new refugee discovers that, by default, she is the highest ranking surviving official and must make decisions far more crucial and difficult than anything she could've imagined. *Lost*'s John Locke dispiritedly boards a plane home after being forced to abandon an Australian walkabout — because he can't walk. Crash-landing on this particular island not only heals him, but it gives him a new life as a leader. Before her travels begin, *Doctor Who*'s Donna Noble is looking for a job and a way out of her life at home with her mother and grandfather since her fiancé was revealed to be a homicidal alien — thus, the wedding was off. When she becomes the Doctor's traveling companion, she saves the universe before she returns home.

Common heroes do more than allow audiences a comfortable entry point into the story. They illustrate the need for everyone to act heroically when an emergency arises — and many viewers perceive that the state of the world requires as many common heroes as possible if humanity is really going to survive. These common heroes also are likely to "lapse" more often or decide that the hero "business" just isn't for them. They are "gray heroes" in the sense that they can act heroically but may choose not to; being a hero isn't an everyday job for them. These gray heroes are average, normally (not tragically) flawed characters who seldom find a perfect solution but step up, at least once, to try.

ALL TOO HUMANLY FLAWED HEROES

Gray heroes, by definition, have flaws; they are human but not capable of the perfection envisioned by Gene Roddenberry in a utopian future world.[7] Instead, whether from the past, present, or future, gray heroes may be all too human — weak enough to succumb to excess, capable of selfish decisions, and too often petty instead of noble. Just how far audiences are willing to concede that these "heroes" can still be idealized for what they have done in the past, as opposed to current foibles, determines whether characters remain dark yet acceptable heroes or take the plunge into villaindom.

If *Battlestar Galactica*'s Commander Adama succumbs to self-pity at the loss of a close friend or surrogate child and drinks far too much, is a drunken, self-absorbed military leader still a gray hero because this behavior is atypical for his usual commanding, decisive presence? If Kara Thrace commits adultery and openly cuckolds her loyal husband but is an effective warrior, is she still exemplary enough a character to be considered a hero? When *Lost*'s Jack Shephard asks former military interrogator Sayid Jarrah to torture one castaway until he tells the truth, presumably to save another castaway's life, is he a villain or a pragmatic leader? If Jack, a season later, again promotes the torture of a man who infiltrates their camp and may be responsible for the disappearance of more castaways, is he justified, or is he succumbing to a love of power in deciding what happens to others?

Moral dilemmas provide dramatic tension, but they also provide an ever-changing scale against which heroes and villains are measured. During war or martial law, for example, are gray heroes' acts leading to torture and execution perceived as acceptable when these actions would be societally condemned during times of peace? If villains become ever more powerful and threaten humanity's very existence, should heroes employ darker methods of dealing with their nemeses? A society's morality often is subjective, rather than a rigid (or even Biblical) standard, even if its philosophy still isn't as objective as that required for moral relativism.

Especially in the 2000s, when situational ethics seem common, and few legal or moral behavioral proscriptions are perceived as absolute, gray heroes not only are more popular as beloved characters, but SF TV has yet to push the boundary far enough to generate complete audience backlash. How far is too far for gray heroes to go? How flawed can gray heroes become before they become "inhuman" instead of "too human for their own good"? These questions haven't yet been answered through enough fan backlash, loss of advertiser support, or ratings — the most likely barometer of the ultimate grayness characters can achieve before they are deemed villains or monsters.

HEROES WHO PLAY GOD

Although any SF TV series can show power-hungry or powerful protagonists (heroes or villains) who begin to think of themselves as the ultimate authority, a few examples from *Doctor Who* and *Heroes* illustrate how even heroes with the best intentions are tempted to play God. Characters tempted to use their superior power — from "superpower" to superior knowledge, experience, wealth, or technology — to dictate what will happen are playing God. They don't ask permission or seek advice from others; they are certain that only they know what is best and are the ultimate authority on what needs to be done. When heroes in effect declare themselves godlike, they become ever grayer and possibly flirt with villainy, depending on how far from societal norms their actions take them. Even if their actions are outer-directed, heroes may fall from public acceptance (and audience approval) if they seem to go too far or become just like the villains from whom they try to protect society.

Dealing with life-or-death issues often tempts even heroes to play God and decide who lives or dies, and why. Taking the decision-making power away from the people whose lives will be most affected by the consequences of that decision is another prime way that characters play God. Although heroes' motives may be far more pure than those of villains, the act of playing God with others' lives darkens heroes.

Heroes who've played God usually recognize that their actions, whatever the outcome, tempt them too much. They realize they can't handle that level of control over others' lives, nor do they want to. After enjoying his role as Torchwood's leader and the world's hero for many years, Jack Harkness realizes that he's come to rely only on his own judgment — and belief in his infallibility — too much. When Gwen reminds him that he has done a lot of good and saved a lot of people, Jack replies, "That's the problem. I began to like it too much" ("Children of Earth: Day Five").[8] Feeling like an invincible leader with superior knowledge and expertise — enough to make decisions affecting all of humanity but potentially destroying those he loves most — is too seductive and dangerous even for an immortal hero.

The centuries-old Ninth Doctor also recognizes the temptation of playing God, especially when he alone can see all of time and space and know the ramifications of changing the past, even to protect humanity (his favorite species). The Doctor wants to kill the last Daleks in revenge for the loss of the Time Lords, whom the Daleks killed in a final Time War. It doesn't help that the Daleks also can exterminate life on Earth, and the Doctor has grown rather fond of some humans. Ultimately, the Doctor finds that he can't wipe out all humanity to kill the Daleks also. Nevertheless, he still has moments of wanting to play God — to make decisions for everyone else and presume to know what is right. Even someone with as much knowledge and experience as the Doctor shouldn't make long-reaching decisions for others simply because he feels superior with this knowledge and experience and believes that he knows what's best for everyone.

The Doctor's companion, Rose, has much less life experience and, during a trip back in time, naively attempts to change history and keep her father alive ("Father's Day," 1.8).[9] Rose doesn't understand the consequences of her actions. After giving her a hard time until she realizes just how dire the situation is, the Doctor simply asks her, like a naïve child, to recognize that what she's done is wrong. The moment she says that she's sorry he forgives her and embraces her.

In "The Parting of the Ways" (1.13), more experienced time traveler Rose desires to travel to the future to save humanity from extinction.[10] She takes the TARDIS' superhuman power over time and space to do so, but she also uses that energy to save her traveling companions, the Doctor and an as-yet-mortal Jack Harkness. By playing God, Rose manages to avert future Earth's destruction and bring Jack back to life. However, she once again doesn't realize the ramifications of her actions. The Doctor tells Rose that she's not meant to know all of the secrets of space and time, although her new insight makes her his equal. He takes back this knowledge, but he dies to be regenerated as a completely different Doctor. Now-immortal Jack faces an eternal life of loss and pain, a fate he wouldn't have chosen.

If extremely experienced and longer-lived characters, such as Jack and the Doctor, can't handle playing God, young mortals like Rose are completely over their heads when given the power of life or death. In short, the moral to this story is not to play God; audiences (and most SF TV characters) are far too shortsighted and inwardly directed to have sole responsibility for life-or-death decisions affecting others.

THE HERO AS "OTHER"

An increasingly emphasized reason for being perceived as Other is sexuality and sexual orientation. As the U.S. wrestles with the legality of gay marriage, in contrast to legally recognized civil partnerships for same-sex couples in the U.K., more GLBT characters are coming out in SF TV. Although *Buffy* broke ground with Willow's and Tara's kiss, the first lesbian kiss on TV, Joss Whedon also killed off the couple with Tara's senseless death. Similarly, *Torchwood* received fan love and critical awards because it presented series lead hero Jack Harkness in a homosexual relationship with his employee Ianto Jones. When Russell T. Davies likewise had Ianto senselessly killed, fans who followed the series primarily because of this love story complained that the series' gay couple suffers while the heterosexual couple plans to buy a home and is having a baby. Whether GLBT heroes become popular because or in spite of their sexual orientation and onscreen relationships, sexuality as a measure of Otherness and as a way to make Other characters better accepted by mainstream audiences is an important theme being highlighted on SF TV.

Bringing a different audience to the franchise, *Torchwood* was designed to be a "*Doctor Who* for adults," complete with more graphic depictions of violence and omnisexuality, with the accompanying not-for-kids'-ears language. As one reporter phrased it, *Torchwood* "is aimed at post-watershed [later evening] viewers rather than the family audience which typically tunes into the series about the Time Lord." Because the series gained a larger and more international audience each season, *Torchwood* moved from lesser-watched BBC3 to BBC2 and finally to the main network's schedule on BBC. Barrowman lauded his series, noting, "*Torchwood* has really reached out to audiences worldwide, and the fact it's moved up the channels on the BBC is incredible."[11] The move was a "bid to introduce the series to new audiences," but with this move to the mainstream and more-often-watched BBC1, long-time fans feared that Captain Jack would be made so "family friendly" to appeal to the widest audience possible that he would lose the dark charm or blatant sexuality so much a part of his character.[12]

To help dispel these rumors, the cast and crew, including Season Three director Euros Lyn, repeatedly assured fans that the "adult" nature of the series would be preserved. Lyn told official fan magazine *Torchwood* that the "Children of Earth" plot is "about how human beings behave when they're faced with an unstoppable force; something so much bigger than they are. Some of them turn out to be heroes.... Also, the love story between Captain Jack and Ianto continues to unfold, as does the story of married life for Gwen and Rhys, as Rhys's character comes into play a lot more."[13] With the expanded general publicity for "Children of Earth," the network and director seemed especially interested in playing up the action (i.e., heroic) elements of the story without minimizing the importance of the character issues in which fans are invested. Providing both the same-sex and opposite-sex romances, one a fairly new relationship, one a marriage, also covers the romantic/sexual aspects of this dark drama, which has been a plus for the series as much as the SF themes or adrenaline-fueled action.

The series' creators, however, have a different ideal vision for *Torchwood* than do many long-time fans and perhaps even the series' actors. In an interview published shortly before "Children of Earth" was broadcast, Barrowman discussed what to many fans had become *the* reason to watch *Torchwood*: Jack's and Ianto's love relationship (called "Janto" by many fans). Barrowman noted, "It is important to have characters like Jack, like Ianto, to show the normality of their relationship on television, to show even people who are not gay that this is the way it is. Love is love no matter who you love."[14] Although Barrowman never intended to be a gay icon or role model, he has become those through the role of Captain Jack, and with the loss of Janto, male or female fans looking for positive depictions of gay couples on TV became discontented with "Children of Earth."

Women looking for masculine yet sensitive men as series' leads found their ideal characters. Surprisingly, women especially identified with Ianto and found through him, rather than Gwen, entry into the story. Gareth David-Lloyd explained that "mostly women ... empathise with Ianto as well, they want to feel like they're in his shoes rather than Gwen's."[15] Perhaps Ianto's evolving romantic relationship with Jack allowed both women and men to fantasize about sex with Captain Jack. Perhaps Ianto's unconditional love and support of his partner made his role more nurturing than that of many male TV heroes. Barrowman noted that "women want to see [the Janto relationship] develop more than the Jack and Gwen relationship, which I think is an absolutely brilliant reflection on society."[16]

During the evening that Day Four (the episode in which Ianto dies) debuted on the BBC, I monitored *Torchwood* fan forums in which women posted the majority of comments and carried on minute-by-minute discussions as the episode was broadcast. More than 18 pages of "reaction" posts were made via discussion threads on the Torch_wood LJ community alone, several lamenting the loss of Ianto and Janto; the number of comments and stream of conversation kept several similar fan sites busy on July 9.

At Comic-Con in July 2009, Barrowman noted, "The night that Ianto died, on Twitter Ianto beat out Michael Jackson! [News of Jackson's death previously had been the most discussed topic on Twitter.] The reactions that the fans have are incredible."[17] In the aftermath of "Children of Earth," mourning fans created a "Ianto memorial" at a Cardiff Bay filming location and donated more than £10,000 in Ianto's name (via the Save Ianto Jones online campaign) to Children in Need. Although many vocal online fans vow not to watch the series minus the Janto relationship, Captain Jack most likely will have other love relationships, perhaps same-sex, in any future episodes, as well as in forthcoming books and comics. (In 2010, Davies first offered a U.S. version of *Torchwood* to Fox, a move that made many critics and fans wonder if Jack would remain a character in a U.S. series and, if so, would he have a male lover.)

In late 2009 David-Lloyd announced a comic he would be writing for *Torchwood* magazine,[18] and Carole E. Barrowman hinted that in a Captain Jack story she and her brother planned to write, "Jack may have a love interest or two."[19] Whether these stories revisit Janto or provide Jack with other (sexual) adventures, sexuality will remain a key element in the further development of (at least British-based) Captain Jack.

What is notable about this *Torchwood* example is that the series often gained media attention — and continuing press after "Children of Earth" — primarily because of the televised homosexual relationship between the lead hero and increasingly prominent sidekick. (See Chapter 4 for more discussion of important sidekick characters, including Ianto.) Without this "hook," the first two seasons of *Torchwood* wouldn't be all that memorable or unique within SF TV. The characters, far more than the plots, brought the series to wider attention, earning it the right to get "big screen" development with better scripts, a larger budget, and more publicity as one of the BBC's touted programs. Destroying the Otherness which, in large part, made *Torchwood* a success certainly gained audience and press interest, for better or worse.

Seeing where Davies takes the characters next will be an interesting new phase in the development of the currently very dark hero Jack Harkness. A hero must be more than his relationship, however groundbreaking on TV, and he must be able to recover from loss if he is to remain heroic. How or if Captain Jack achieves that distinction is a noteworthy detail in the evolving hero saga and likely will make a statement, intentional or only perceived by fans, about whether Jack's ability to be a hero is heavily influenced by his sexual nature or selection of partners.

Of course, Otherness takes many other forms, not only for one society or culture but for different viewers who have their personal definitions of what is socially OK or not. *Firefly*'s Zoe, for example, might be a role model for women who look for their heroes to be strong warriors who also are in touch with their feminine sexuality. They may like the fact that Zoe is married, unlike the beautiful, sensual, highly feminized Inara, who is a registered (therefore legal) companion. Even Mal, who loves Inara but won't admit it, sometimes calls her a "whore," which creates a different type of Otherness for Inara, both within *Serenity*'s environment and among viewers. Zoe's matrimonial state is more conventional, but hers is an interracial marriage, which may be accepted by many but not all viewers. Zoe also is clearly the warrior/dominant personality in this partnership; her husband, Wash, although a talented pilot, is more likely to be captured than do the rescuing, and he sometimes takes on the "damsel in distress" role common in traditional hero stories. In some ways, to some viewers, Zoe, Inara, and even Wash may be idealized or dismissed because they and their relationships represent different aspects of Otherness to at least some viewers.

Another female warrior, *Battlestar Galactica*'s Kara Thrace, may be idealized because of her strength, leadership abilities, loyalty, and effectiveness as a pilot and soldier. These qualities, however much appreciated by the audience, may mark her as Other because such strong female warriors aren't the norm for most Western societies, although what is considered "normal" or "common" is changing within the U.S. military, for example. What may be less acceptable by religiously conservative viewers is Kara's role as a "prophet" in later *Battlestar Galactica* episodes or her insistence on the sanctity of marriage but her convenient enjoyment of an adulterous relationship that, in her mind, doesn't threaten her marriage. She marries for life, but she thinks it's all right to be sexually involved with other people. These aspects of Kara's character development may bother at least a portion of the audience and make Kara an Other hero. The "flaws" or differences from socially acceptable behavior may make it more difficult for viewers to admire Kara as an ideal hero, but she can be acceptable as a gray hero. The qualities audiences view as positive still outweigh what they may view as her lapses in morality.

Heroes are Other if they defy social conventions or expectations. Gender, sexuality, race, ethnicity, religion, age, and ability may mark heroes as Other. Heroes who are older instead of youthful may be perceived as Other in a youth-oriented culture. Cancer-fighting President Roslin illustrates that a bald woman may be a courageous role model, a hero to other women fighting breast cancer, although her disease, much less her appearance, mark her as atypical of feminine beauty or traditional heroism.

More SF TV heroes, for a variety of reasons, fall outside the stereotype of idealized (super)hero: strong, young, beautiful, wealthy, intelligent, innovative. SF TV heroes increasingly represent statistical minorities in the audience and help the social majorities expand their definition of *hero*.

1960s' Uhura may now be perceived as a glorified telephone operator, but, as Martin Luther King, Jr., assured actress Nichelle Nichols, her African American, female presence was at least on the bridge, and that alone made a powerful statement.[20] Nurse Chapel may have only assisted Dr. McCoy, but she also showed that women were in the future workforce. As mentioned in Chapter 1, when SF TV heroes are idolized for their Otherness (e.g., men dressed as Captain Jack proudly marching in Manchester's 2009 Gay Pride parade in full view of the media), they become more widely recognized and accepted. *Star Trek*'s first interracial TV kiss may not seem landmark today, when interracial couples, although not mainstream, are at least more prevalent on TV than they were in

previous decades. Same-sex relationships eventually will achieve similar acceptance, just as Willow's and Tara's remarkably innocent kissing made it more
likely that Jack and Ianto would play naked hide and seek in the Hub.

Similarly, greater gender equality is making inroads into breaking the
stereotypes about acceptable roles for women or men. *Battlestar Galactica*'s
Roslin may start as a schoolteacher, a stereotypical female job, but she becomes
president. Where would *Serenity* be without Kaylee, *Firefly*'s equivalent of *Star
Trek*'s Scotty? Although the Doctors seem to keep getting younger in appearance
as they chronologically age, recent *Doctor Who* companions have been all ages
and most often women. Pushing-40 Donna Noble gives girls, their mothers,
and their grandmothers further proof that women of any age can save the universe. These examples illustrate greater diversity among the many Other heroes
becoming less Other and more widely accepted on SF TV, in large part because
of the greater publicity and higher profile of the characters discussed in this
book.

THE HERO AS ALIEN

Few true off–Earth aliens are heroes on SF TV. With the prominent exception of classic *Star Trek*'s Spock, few aliens— that is, characters born on another
planet — have been made series' heroes. By *Star Trek: The Next Generation*, other
non-human characters are Federation crew members on the *Enterprise*; some,
like Spock, are half-human, half–Other. Deanna Troi (Betazoid) and Worf
(Klingon) become embroiled in cultural conflicts when their stories involve
family members whose arrival reminds audiences just how "different" these
beloved characters are from Earth cultures.

Of course, because the characters of *Battlestar Galactica* and *Caprica* live
on an entirely different planetary system at the beginning of the series, by definition, all these humans from Caprica, Tauron, Gemenon, and so on are "alien"
to audiences watching TV on Earth. However, because *Battlestar Galactica*'s
non–Cylon characters are human and, eventually, become our ancestors on this
planet, they seem far more human than alien.

Similarly, other heroes from the future, whether they stay there (e.g.,
Firefly) or travel back in time to 21st century Earth (e.g., Jack Harkness on
Torchwood), look comfortingly human. Only when these characters do something that seems out of character or far different from what audiences expect
as "normal" responses to a situation are viewers reminded that, indeed, the difference between the increasingly gray human-looking hero and a "real" human
may be the culture of origin.

Of the series discussed in this book, only one has an alien series' hero: the
titular *Doctor Who*. No humans know his true name; it's unpronounceable to
native English speakers. As Rose tends the ailing Tenth Doctor after a difficult
regeneration, she worries that only one of his hearts is functioning, a comment

that leads mother Jackie to wonder, "What else has he got two of?" ("The Christmas Invasion").[21] Even Prime Minister Harriet Jones, generally a supporter of the Doctor and his ideas in defending the Earth from other aliens, sometimes questions his motivations because he is, after all, alien. When she destroys departing Sycorax ships, after the Doctor has promised they can leave safely, Jones believes she is protecting Earth from future invasions. The Doctor, however, has a completely different perspective on Earth's future interactions with alien cultures.

In *Doctor Who* mythology, Torchwood was created by Queen Victoria. After a questionable encounter with the Tenth Doctor, she is suspicious of his motives and creates Torchwood to document and analyze the Doctor's future visits to the U.K. By the 2000s, Torchwood One, in London, maintains the Doctor on a "wanted" list. He is to be detained and questioned as a suspect alien if he ever returns.

Although *Doctor Who* has become an edgier family program in the 2000s, the Doctor clearly acts as Earth's protector and, to audiences, is a parental hero. With the decreasing age of the actors playing the Ninth, Tenth, and Eleventh Doctors, this hero becomes even more like the younger audience watching the series. Matt Smith, despite wearing a costume anachronistic to his 2010 debut, seems like a young man, not an alien resembling human form. The Doctor even seems to provide Amy Pond's boyfriend Rory with competition for her affection, making the Eleventh Doctor look ever more human.

Guest or recurring "aliens," such as the Cylons (who trace their origins back to a human creator/inventor instilling his teenaged daughter's "essence" into a mechanical body), also look human. By *Battlestar Galactica*'s finale, the Cylons, once perceived as inhuman and unfeeling, gradually have become much more human, sharing not only an appearance indistinguishable from "real" humans but also common emotions: love, hate, fear, hope, sorrow, joy. Some Cylons act more "human" at times than the "real" humans fighting against them. By the end of the series, Cylon-Human hybrid children are possible, and both Cylons and humans populate Earth. The implication is that audiences today are Cylon-Human hybrids; we have become the aliens audiences reviled a few seasons earlier.

Emphasizing the ways in which humans and "aliens" or Other are similar can help audiences accept the analogy that those who are alien to our country or culture aren't automatically villainous or even monstrous. Audiences are, in fact, "alien" outside their home turf. SF TV heroes often become effective role models to illustrate that audience's assumed enemies are human, too.

The Immortal Hero

Today's most successful SF TV series tackle life-or-death topics against the backdrop of a world in chaos and close to annihilation; the stories play upon real-world fears of the end of the world, at least as we know it, if not the true Armageddon. Whether audiences seek comfort or guidance from science or spiritual faith, SF TV deals with the pros and cons of such weighty potentially future topics as the merging of humans with technology in order to live much longer, if not forever. Such recent critically acclaimed series as *Buffy the Vampire Slayer*, *Angel*, *Lost*, *Heroes*, *Battlestar Galactica*, its spinoff *Caprica*, and even the campier but popular *Doctor Who* and its spinoff, *Torchwood*, feature immortal characters who gain this status in a variety of ways.

Immortality is becoming more popular on these and other SF series, not as a cheesy plot device but as a reality for more mainstream SF TV characters. How these characters achieve immortality and how they and others respond to it are more frequently explored in depth in series whose themes encompass much more than immortality. What happens to allow certain characters to "cheat death" is very much a theme worth exploring scientifically and philosophically, and SF series are providing one way to explore it.

Before immortality became quite so popular in post–2000 series, *Buffy the Vampire Slayer* explored the not-so-wonderful aspects of being immortal. Buffy trades her life to save her sister's, a noble act that she would've been content to leave as her legacy. Buffy's friends, including enthusiastic witch Willow, bring her back from the dead, but Buffy is less than pleased. She was happy in heaven and far less so back in her old life. In fact, the risen Buffy finds more in common with vampire Spike, who also has survived death, than with her mortal friends. Although Buffy likely isn't a true immortal, she is resurrected, which makes her a special type of SF TV hero. Unlike the "living dead" vampires and demons populating the series, Buffy comes back to life as a human, but she is forever separated from other mortals because she knows what it's like to die and come back.

TV series recently have been incorporating more "science" into traditional science fiction themes, which enhances the plausibility of longer life spans for all. What audiences learn from such respected TV news programs as CBS's 2006 "The Quest for Immortality," a *60 Minutes* segment, for example, makes them more likely to accept immortality, or at least extremely long human life spans, as a possibility.[22] Whether audiences approve of or want to believe in the possibility of such scientific advances as merging human brains with robotic bodies, regenerating cells to be impervious to permanent "death," or creating a new life form that dies but becomes "resurrected" is highly debatable. However, audiences often accept technological advances to make people look younger longer and to extend the average life span. In the quest for "immortality," SF TV in the 2000s has been providing more heroes and villains who are or once were human but whose life spans or death-defying resurrections are simply part of who they are. These attractive, forever-young or barely aging characters can be used to illustrate at least the philosophical pros and cons of immortality.

Undoubtedly, as "immortality" becomes more likely, the public will hotly debate the religious and scientific ramifications. Even now, SF TV series illustrate some interesting pros and cons that represent different sides of the science vs. faith debate while introducing audiences to multiple possibilities for extended life or life after death. Perhaps the most popular illustration of the relationship of secular scientific knowledge to spiritual faith comes through *Lost*. The "Man of Science, Man of Faith" debate has raged primarily through the opposition of two main characters, spinal surgeon Jack Shephard and former paraplegic John Locke. These two characters have often questioned their beliefs, temporarily shifted philosophical stances, and thoroughly "discussed," via action and dialogue, such topics as faith-based action, miracles, time travel, fate, and destiny.

Within this series, however, another important part of the scientific/spiritual themes involves immortality. One character in particular, Richard Alpert, never seems to age, no matter when *Lost*'s time-traveling characters turn up on the island. Alpert eventually explains that he thinks the island's "master," Jacob, wanted him to be that way ("The Incident," 5.16).[23] Alpert is "created" by "god" to be immortal; nothing he does, or did, made him that way. There is no medical breakthrough or technological metamorphosis to render him immortal, but he clearly is not "normal" for other humans on the island. Richard's role has been revealed as an advisor to the many shorter-lived humans living on the island and as a messenger on behalf of Jacob.

Thus, Richard's immortality seems pragmatic for Jacob, not Richard, who simply accepts what "god" has given him and plays his role in the island's history, neither relishing his longevity nor decrying it. He simply does his job, decade after decade. Richard's style of immortality seems the most pragmatic of all TV characters: he simply lives day to day, working with people in the best way he knows how. He is a middle manager, neither the leader nor purely a follower. If immortality becomes possible for the masses, eternal ordinary life might be much like this. Richard seems to have accepted his role, but then, he is an intriguing secondary character, not a series lead. His role naturally will be less well developed or dramatic in light of *Lost*'s many other characters.

Richard Alpert isn't the only one to cheat death, although his existence doesn't seem completely normal according to most humans' experience of life and death. Several characters whose physical bodies have been shown to be dead end up seeming very real to still-living characters. Of course, there's always the possibility that those who see the "living dead" suffer from that old TV-plot conceit of "hallucination," induced by drug use or mental illness. However, the continuing presence and increasing importance, in particular, of Christian Shephard as a beyond-the-grave messenger and spiritual guide to Jack Shephard and John Locke add weight to the audience's acceptance of Christian as living in another category of existence, perhaps a state that, in effect, is immortal. This type of immortality extends life past death and isn't merely an unnaturally long extension of life before death — or no possibility of death at all.

Lost embraces immortality as a real-world possibility, just like the existence of time travel, and fans eagerly pick up this theme. Although today's science (or even Lost science) may not be able to explain all the technicalities, the series presents enough real-world science throughout its many converging plots to make immortality seem as likely as any other breakthrough in medicine or physics. Whether audiences choose a "Man of Faith" perspective and suspend their disbelief about the possibility of several characters' unusual life spans, or whether they discount the "beyond the grave" characters' immortality but accept the plausibility of science extending normal human life spans to centuries, à la Richard Alpert, the series offers several "miraculous" possibilities for immortality.

Heroes often follows in Lost's footsteps in character development and plot devices, although the stories don't seem as meticulously crafted, and the superhero premise encourages SF fans to suspend their disbelief a lot more than more mainstream viewers of Lost. During Lost's first season, audiences were led to believe the series was more character/action drama than science fiction. Gradually audiences were let in on the bigger story involving "life" questions about fate, destiny, redemption, death, and life after death within an SF framework. Heroes blatantly is more SF/fantasy, and fans might expect immortality to play a recurring role in superhero/supervillain development.

Two characters, one Good, one Evil, are, for all practical purposes, immortal. Claire Bennet is a teenager trying to find a way to help others, especially those like her. Sylar becomes the supervillain who gruesomely takes powers from other "specials"; he develops the ability to heal himself, just like good superhero Claire. Both he and Claire can be "killed" with a carefully placed glass shard/spike/bullet/other pointy item at the back of the skull. If the item isn't removed, the super character appears dead. Once the item is removed, even if all other functions apparently have ceased, the body returns to life. In this way Claire finds herself "awakening" on an autopsy table, her chest splayed open for the post-mortem analysis ("One Giant Leap," 1.3).[24] She is able to come back to life and, for all intents and purposes, is immortal.

When Sylar develops the ability to shapeshift, he also decides to "shift" his one possible weak spot to an undisclosed physical location in his body so that no one will know how to "de-activate" him ("I Am Sylar," 3.24).[25] Claire, however, retains her weakness. Heroes likes to create epic battles between Good and Evil, and Sylar's brand of immortality gives him a decided edge. Throughout the fourth season, Sylar becomes progressively more powerful, as Claire, like any young woman, questions her place in the world. If Heroes returns via another medium, undoubtedly Claire will need to become a prominent Good hero to do battle once and for all with Evil villain Sylar, especially within the superhero/supervillain premise of the series.

Evil immortal characters have provided dramatic tension in other series, notably Highlander, but in that series the Good immortal MacLeod always overcomes the evil intruders on his turf. Heroes offers the possibility that Evil, in the form of only one of two immortal characters, is not so easily overcome. At this point in the story, Sylar is a much more powerful character than troubled teen Claire. Philosophically, the rise of Sylar has been an interesting story response to global fears about the unstoppable rise of Evil and the likelihood of societies falling into destruction and moral decay.

Both Sylar and Claire, like the actors who play them, gradually age in human terms. What would've happened if the series had run ten years is hard to ascertain. *Heroes* doesn't provide any indication if immortal heroes or villains age forever, if they are able to regenerate new bodies, if their aging process slows, or if there comes a point when they can't age any more. The practicalities of immortality aren't important in a series like *Heroes*. Audiences may learn by implication from the stories involving immortals, but the theme of immortality isn't taken as seriously in this popular series. Nevertheless, mainstream network audiences are presented with immortality as one of several SF themes in play in the series. Audiences not as familiar with SF may not have come across immortals as often on prime time.

How can a long-standing time travel series with an immortal Time Lord sustain the premise plausibly, even for SF or children's programming? That's an interesting part of the *Doctor Who* saga, which so far has spanned nearly 50 years and recently gained greater critical acclaim. The "immortal" Doctor now is more than 900 years old. The series' long-running conceit is that when the actor playing the Doctor dies, becomes too old, tires of the role, or is unpopular, the Doctor's current body "regenerates" and a new actor takes over the role. The Doctor retains his memories from previous lives but has new quirks, attitudes, and characteristics in addition to his new appearance. Even this character will one day permanently die, however; the original mythology set the total number of regenerations at 12. Nevertheless, the Doctor's likely extremely long life span makes him seem immortal.

Only in the Davies' era has the Doctor really discussed the loneliness of his "immortality" and the power of his role. In part, this character "matures" after his planet is destroyed and he is (perhaps) the last of his species. Loss and loneliness are recurring themes, particularly in Tenth Doctor David Tennant's later episodes. The Doctor loses several beloved time-traveling companions over a relatively short linear time span.

Rose Tyler, his love interest, becomes lost in a parallel universe; Martha Jones wants a relationship that the Doctor cannot offer her and leaves; Jack Harkness becomes a true immortal, a "fixed point in time," which the Doctor finds "wrong"; Donna Noble must lose all memory of the Doctor in order to survive. Many recent *Doctor Who* episodes beautifully illustrate immortality as only a series of losses of friendship and love, and thus an eternity of loneliness devoid of sharing life-long terms with friends or family — or even a society/culture. Like *Lost*, *Doctor Who* explores what it means to be human, or alien, and the sacrifices heroes often make in order to save humanity.

Unlike earlier generations of *Who* episodes, which posited the Doctor as an adventurer who could more lightheartedly travel anywhere in space or time, the 2000-era episodes feature the Doctor battling ever more dangerous enemies and frequently facing end-of-the-world scenarios. Although he overcomes these foes, the cost to him personally increases. Audiences are aware that such a long life of continuing danger and potential great loss must take a toll; even a thousand years of adventures must pale in comparison to the possibility of centuries yet to live with turmoil and loss. Although more of a children's program than a series like *Lost*, *Battlestar Galactica*, or even its own spinoff, *Torchwood*, *Doctor Who*'s Davies-helmed seasons add more adult philosophical elements to the adventures and make the series more relevant to audiences facing their own uncertainties about the future of Earth.

Captain Jack Harkness gains his immortality through the intervention of a "god-like" Rose, who temporarily has the power of life or death and brings her fellow time-traveling companion back to life. In the spinoff series, *Torchwood*, Jack only discovers his immortality after dying yet again; he is able to die but not stay dead. In the intervening years before he finds the Doctor and asks if he can be "fixed" — or return to being mortal — Jack dies many times. Sometimes he kills himself as part of a carnival trick; sometimes he is tortured to death in innovative ways; sometimes he dies in battle. He has most often been involved with some type of government or military agency, with periodic stints as a con man, so his leadership of the secret Torchwood agency "outside the government, beyond the police" is an extension of many other previous lives.

What makes Jack an interesting character to analyze is the implication that he is the embodiment of what will survive. Out of all species, a human(oid) male (Jack is born on another planet in the 51st century) outlives everything else. Despite his often charming demeanor, Jack's longevity allows him to see the many dark sides of human nature — and he often makes decisions that might horrify the audience. Nevertheless, pragmatic Jack, who might condemn a few innocents to death in order to save the planet (or Cardiff), is the series' lead hero.

Like the Doctor, Jack often sees the negative side to immortality. Not only does he face loss and loneliness, but he also must repeatedly face his mistakes or deal with the consequences of his past decisions — an increasingly long list of acts that may return to haunt him. Surprisingly, Jack nevertheless remains actively involved in protecting the planet from potentially evil invaders. Considering that he could have that role for eternity, whether on Earth or a distant planet, Jack seems surprisingly resilient enough to keep doing this job. In his evolution as a hero, he steadfastly accepts responsibility, at whatever cost to himself. Even in light of Jack's departure at the conclusion of "Children of Earth," his likely future appearance somewhere in the Whoniverse indicates that "Jack Harkness," even under a new name, will continue his heroic ways.

As *Torchwood* illustrates, immortality is associated with the ability to cheat death, either to die and be resurrected again and again, or never to die. Appropriately, *Obit* magazine, devoted to issues surrounding death and cultural interpretations of it, provides this explanation about the role of SF in presenting immortality to the public:

> It's not hard to see why immortality is one science fiction plotline that never gets old. Sci-fi is the modern equivalent of fairy tales, and death is one of the deepest, darkest forests through which fairy tales lead us. Who hasn't imagined living forever, outsmarting that crabbed and beastly villain, Death? But leave it to sci-fi, the province of dreamers and skeptics alike, to find the dark lining in the puffy white-cloud fantasy of everlasting life, to introduce the idea that death might not always be the bad guy.[26]

I disagree with this author that SF is the modern equivalent to fairy tales. Too often traditional fairy tales have a happy ending or a moral to the story. Series like *Torchwood* often provide tragic endings, and morality may be questionable. Instead, modern SF TV series like *Torchwood* or, especially, *Battlestar Galactica* become mirrors held up to illustrate elements of modern relationships and sociopolitical issues. On a very simple level, the immortal Captain Jack may help audiences better understand the fragility of human life, the need to connect with others, and the resulting loneliness and loss in a life spent keeping secrets from one's friends. On a more complex level, *Battlestar Galactica* and *Caprica* (or even episodes like *Torchwood*'s "Cyberwoman" [1.4], "They Keep Killing Suzie" [1.8], or "Dead Man Walking" [2.7]) analyze the moral and practical issues of prolonging life via technology, merging humans with technology to create "hybrid" life forms, or resuscitating the apparently dead. SF TV increasingly finds the "dark lining in the puffy white-cloud fantasy of everlasting life," but death may not be the panacea, either.

The philosophy behind *Doctor Who* and *Torchwood* is that everyday life, with activities that mortals might consider mundane, such as fixing dinner for the family or going on a date, become exotic experiences for immortals like the Doctor or Jack. Life, in all its detail, is incredibly precious, if fleeting. The moment is to be savored. Considering that these immortal characters may have an eternity of moments, their finding significance within a single one is another important statement.

When immortality is considered ideal, the emphasis usually is on the expansion of life so that an unlimited number of meaningful activities can take place. There is no excuse that "if I only had the time, I'd do ___." These immortal characters have time, but they value the details within the broad scope of eternity; they enjoy the company of and value individuals, even as they protect humanity in general. They know that their duties as protectors or guardians are eternal; Evil is not defeated once and for all. Nevertheless, they keep fighting the battle so that ordinary, everyday moments are possible for average people. Living for the moment and fighting to protect the sublime found within the ordinary are two philosophies being promulgated by the immortal leads in these series.

Similar themes help structure *Battlestar Galactica* and *Caprica*. In a commentary about *Battlestar Galactica*'s first few episodes of the final season, Ben Scarlato ironically discusses immortality in light of such a heroic character as Admiral Bill Adama contemplating suicide upon seeing his goal—colonizing Earth—thwarted and learning that his former daughter-in-law has committed suicide ("Sometimes a Great Notion," 4.13)[27]:

> The appeal of immortality lies not in continuously experiencing the pain and disappointment of life, but in looking forward and having the time to eventually create a situation that allows for a thriving life filled not with sorrow but with the things we cherish.[28]

Of course, Adama doesn't commit suicide, despite the onslaught of grief and despair. He lives long enough to see humanity find a habitable planet on which to thrive. Certainly the *Battlestar Galactica* finale ("Daybreak," 4.21–.22) illustrates Scarlato's point (as do *Doctor Who* and *Torchwood* episodes). The "immortality" granted to those humans and Cylons who survive and thrive on Earth is the continuance of their species, combined through the hybrid children they beget who someday become today's human race.

According to *Battlestar Galactica* and its spinoff, *Caprica*, immortality may or may not come from God, although *Battlestar Galactica* has a decidedly more spiritual perspective. One of the series' most popular heroes, Kara (Starbuck) Thrace, disappears in a damaged spacecraft and is thought dead ("Crossroads," 3.19–.20). In a later episode, she miraculously returns to the fleet of humans trying to find Earth so that the species may survive. She doesn't know how she survived or where she has been, but she brings back knowledge of the location of Earth. Her ideas seem to be divinely guided.

Even more intriguing in the series' finale ("Daybreak," 4.21–.22) is the presence of two often less-than-heroic characters, Caprica Six and Baltar.[29] Six is a Cylon, a technologically advanced mechanical being who looks human. Along the way, the Cylons have evolved from purely mechanized "robotic" beings to more human life forms that can be resurrected on a nearby ship if their bodies are destroyed. With the destruction of the last resurrection ship, however, even the Cylons become like humans in their mortality. Baltar, a narcissistic human scientist who unwittingly helps the Cylons destroy his home planetary system and nearly wipe out humanity, occasionally has moments of selflessness and heroism. Most often throughout the series, however, he is a villain who looks out only for his own interests.

Nevertheless, on the new "Earth," Baltar and Caprica Six set off to farm the land like any other colonists. Throughout the finale episode, they interact with an apparently immortal version of themselves, both in space during a final battle and on Earth. These "replications"—although *Battlestar Galactica* never explains exactly what they are or how they came to be—comment on human/Cylon history and seem to be God's representatives. They tell the mortal Baltar and Caprica Six that they have completed what God wanted them to do in this life, and they can go live the remainder of their lives peacefully. The final series' twist shows the immortals Baltar and Six strolling the street of a 21st century metropolis, wondering if humans have learned how to live successfully with technological advancements as well as each other, or if they will simply destroy themselves in still further battles between peoples or between humans and human/technological hybrids.

The fact that these characters, not the heroes of the story (even among the less-than-perfect heroes of the *Battlestar Galactica* saga), are those pictured as immortal seems like a less spiritual answer to the question of who might become immortal. For all the spiritual significance ascribed to Kara Thrace in later episodes, early *Battlestar Galactica* episodes portray her as a hard-living warrior — at times combative, adulterous, drunken. Of course, immortality doesn't have to equate to purity or goodness; "demons" may be immortal, too. Nevertheless, Baltar as an immortal questioning, but not intervening in, the progress of humanity is an intriguing way to end a series that often posed disturbing questions about modern society. Perhaps Baltar is the appropriately self-absorbed character best suited to understand modern humanity and question its future.

Caprica, the prequel showing how the Cylons came to be, offers an even darker vision of immortality. When a computer genius' equally intelligent teenaged daughter dies in a terrorist bombing, the distraught father eventually succeeds in transferring his daughter's holographic avatar into the body of a mechanical "Cylon." He fears the experiment has failed when the consciousness seems to "die" in this technologically advanced body, but Zoe, the "soul" trapped within metal, comes back to life. Presumably, the rest of the series will explore just how Zoe is able to transcend death and the implications of this use of technology to prolong human life.

Questions about what survives the death of the body — a soul, a brain, an electrical imprint based on thousands of computer interactions, a lifelike hologram imbued with the personality of its creator — necessarily have to be addressed, and *Battlestar Galactica* and *Caprica* creator Ronald D. Moore doesn't seem squeamish about dealing with controversial topics that mirror real-world concerns. If technology, much more so than divine intervention, seems likely to provide immortality for the (financially superior) masses, what are the long-term implications for society, as well as individuals? Whereas other SF series deal primarily with the individual's response to immortality, *Caprica* takes a different approach — looking at the implications for society in general as more immortals become a part of it.

Because *Caprica* is a prequel, audiences familiar with *Battlestar Galactica* know that the outcome isn't pleasant. Cylons become subjugated (enslaved) to humans until they rebel; warfare between Cylons and humans results in the near decimation of both species. Only cooperation between the two eventually results in a "better" human evolved through the millennia — those of us currently living on Earth, the descendents of these Cylon and human colonists. Nevertheless, even these "evolved" humans still face the same old problems that plagued their ancestors. That the technological capability for immortality may not save humanity, but lead to its destruction, seems to be the bottom line for *Caprica*, if it remains true to its *Battlestar Galactica* storyline.

The recent surge in the number of immortal characters is no coincidence. Western culture, especially in the U.S., prizes youth and glorifies the ability to defy aging while living longer and more healthfully. Juxtaposed with the desire for a long, physically attractive life is the realization that the world is more chaotic and hazardous than ever. Fears about national security, global warfare, lack of resources, global warming, and supergerms, among other threats, make the end of the world seem likely sooner rather than later. Since the mid-nineteenth century and especially during the twentieth century, people have relied on science to provide "miracle" cures and improve the quality and length of life. In times of crisis, people often look for spiritual answers, more so when science or technology fails to provide the solutions they seek. In response to this mix of conflicting desires and fears, SF TV programs have gained a firmer hold on mainstream audiences.

"Immortality," at least as a way to stave off death and significantly increase life span, seems to be a scientific possibility in the near future; immortality as wish fulfillment becomes a more interesting element of SF's futuristic plot developments. Whether characters analyze the spiritual or philosophical pros and cons of immortality or pragmatically deal with it daily, the ways that SF TV introduces more immortal characters and uses them to explore the science vs. faith opposition and to analyze differing philosophies makes this theme worthy of greater study.

Learning from Gray Heroes

Gray SF TV heroes set new "norms" for acceptable characters who may always remain Other in some way to human society, whether metaphorically or literally. Because so many SF TV heroes differ from viewers but are still loved and accepted by them, they help expand the range of socially acceptable heroes and make Other more common, at least on television. Gray heroes may not be ideal role models, but because they in many ways are so "human"— even if, by definition, they're technically not — they can push the boundaries of what society defines as Good or Evil. Just how far some of these heroes can push "grayness" before they are perceived as villains or monsters hasn't yet been determined, but the prevalence of gray heroes likely will reach that boundary soon. Unlike other genres, SF characters lead by example; their successes and failures mirror society's.

The characters in these series face civilization-ending events and must act in the most dire of circumstances; any day may bring the end of the world, and a happy ending just isn't possible. These gray characters provide a range of sometimes finely shaded philosophies and choices which may guide audiences in their own actions or decisions; viewers, like the characters, face uncharted territory: faltering economies, globalization, climate change, shifting political alliances, loss of resources. These issues and global awareness of humanity's interconnectedness—not only across cultures and nations but with other species—seem insurmountable, and TV series, like the real world, offer plenty of opportunities for people, real or characters, to act in heroic or villainous ways.

These gray characters challenge audience perceptions of the world and make viewers wonder whether they should become more cynical or optimistic, more isolated or outer-directed. Gray heroes are designed to be the leaders who make sure humanity survives another day. They serve a social as well as an entertainment function, even if they're clearly not created to be the ideal role models to lead society into a new Renaissance.

4

The Rise of Sidekicks

At one time, being a sidekick was less important. Traditional sidekicks like Kirk's Spock or Batman's Robin (or Alfred), for all that they help the lead characters, aren't as well developed or heroic; they remain firmly standing behind the heroes they support. Sidekicks in post–2000 SF TV series, however, successfully challenge this interpretation and have become more powerful, if still secondary, characters without whom the lead heroes would be far less effective. In many SF TV series, including *Doctor Who*, *Torchwood*, and *Battlestar Galactica*, sidekicks are key characters who often are the catalysts for heroes' decisions and actions.

Sidekicks typically are defined as the hero's inseparable companions and assistants. Frequently the same gender as the heroes they assist, traditional sidekicks may be buddies, best friends, mentees, apprentices, or employees, but they aren't equals and usually aren't lovers. Although the leading characters may require their support, sidekicks are content to let the heroes take the credit for good deeds and successful rescues. Sidekicks learn from their association with heroes, but they seldom strike out on their own as independent heroes, although they may take on more responsibilities as their skills and knowledge increase.

Although superhero sidekicks are the most prevalent and obvious examples, *Doctor Who* is the longest running SF TV series featuring very human sidekick characters. The long line of companions assisting the Doctor during several decades of episodes show the gradual transition from inferior/less experienced/less knowledgeable to the (al)most equal of all companions, Rose Tyler. Although more recent companions, most of them women, have accompanied the Ninth, Tenth, and Eleventh Doctors, Rose stands out because she is the first companion of the re-imagined 2000s' series and the one who captured audiences' (and the Doctor's) greatest attention. (Even perennial favorite and recurring character in the new series, and now star of her own spinoff, Sarah Jane Smith mostly was a good friend and not a true love interest.) Nevertheless, in the new series, other companions—most notably male, omnisexual Captain Jack Harkness; nearly middle-age, snarkier Donna Noble; and awestruck senior (Donna's grandfather) Wilfrid Mott—assured audiences of all ages and both genders that anyone could travel with the Doctor. The companion or sidekick role in the new *Who* isn't limited to pretty young women.

As well, *The Sarah Jane Adventures* emphasizes that highly capable companions who learn from the Doctor may go on to mentor another generation of smart young adventurers. Sarah Jane Smith periodically pops back into the Doctor's life — or he returns to hers at pivotal points in her life. Although clearly enamored of the Third and especially Fourth Doctors, with whom she travels, Sarah Jane survives being dropped off into "normal" life. Especially since joining the Tenth Doctor and Rose on another intergalactic adventure in 2006 ("School Reunion," 2.3), she becomes even more independent. In fact, she adopts an alien boy and mentors teens eager to explore the joys, and dangers, of aliens visiting Earth.

Similarly, Rose Tyler, although relegated to a parallel universe and "gifted" with a human version of the Tenth Doctor, remains independent and becomes a hero in her own right. Although her later adventures are alluded to more than shown in *Doctor Who* episodes, "Last of the Time Lords" (3.13) mentions that Rose works with her Earth's version of Torchwood. She travels through multiple parallel worlds to find the Doctor and help him and a collection of former companions save the universe from winking out of existence. Companions who travel with the Doctor often develop enough confidence and special knowledge that they become lead characters, whether in off-screen fictionalized lives or their own spinoff series.

Even in series in which sidekicks might be less expected, such as ensembles, critics and fans have identified several characters as members of a new, improved breed of sidekicks. Several Internet polls of SF TV series' fans, conducted between 2007 and 2009, indicate increased interest in sidekick characters as well as an expanded definition of just who might be labeled as such. A 2009 poll to determine the Top 7 Science Fiction Sidekicks named *Firefly*'s Zoe Washburne and *Battlestar Galactica*'s Starbuck among its seven. Zoe considers Captain Mal Reynolds her superior officer, even after the Unification War, when they are closer to being colleagues on *Serenity*. She is respected by fans because she knows "how to put up with Reynolds' crap, as all good sidekicks should. Smart, witty, and damn good with a gun, Zoe is one of the best female sidekicks in science fiction history." Starbuck also was commended as an excellent sidekick, "not only a hell of a pilot and a bit of a badass, but [she] also has a remarkable fate that leads her on an emotional rollercoaster to discover Earth."[1]

As discussed later in this chapter, new sidekicks have well-developed backstories and plot lines that reinforce their important influence on the lead heroes as well as the plot. Although the series isn't about them, their actions highlight important plot points. Further, ensemble series like *Firefly* and *Battlestar Galactica* may have a clear series' lead (e.g., Mal Reynolds), but the other characters play large enough roles in the story that they have their own fan following and clearly aren't characters hiding in the story's shadows. Current SF TV sidekicks may not be the lead heroes, but they are important characters, often heroic.

The sidekick role often is a way for more female heroes to be recognized within traditionally male-oriented SF TV series. These women aren't sub-servient, although technically they take orders from men. They make their own decisions, and their special skills and knowledge, as well as their bravery and coolness under fire, make them more feminist than subservient charac-ters.

Another summer 2009 online poll determined the Top 10 TV Sidekicks, not just from SF but any genre. Again, more female than male characters landed in the Top 10. This time *Buffy*'s Willow Rosenthal made the cut. Although she often was a background character early in the series, post–2000 Willow became more interesting and pivotal to the story. In addition to helping Buffy with everyday world-saving activities, she became a full-fledged witch with impres-sive magical powers, fell in love and had an important-for-TV lesbian relation-ship, and turned to the Dark Side when her lover was murdered but returned to Greater Goodness by the series' finale. Willow's increasing importance over time mirrors the increasing importance of SF TV sidekicks emerging from the lighter, happier SF series of the 1990s into the darker SF series post 2000. Willow is recognized as number 5 in this poll's Top 10 Sidekicks because she "was always there to aid Buffy, and even helped her save the world in the finale. The best thing about Willow is her wit…. Willow became a powerfully ally, and she became who she is on her own, all while helping her best friend."[2]

In a 2008 Top 10 poll, coming in at number 3 is Ando Masahashi from *Heroes*.[3] Like Willow, Ando began as a standard sidekick, the best friend of newly revealed time-and-space-transported Hiro Nakamura. Throughout the first few seasons, Ando first doubts Hiro's superpower but then does all he can to support his buddy through this astounding life-changing turn of events. At times, in later seasons, Ando's encouragement is all that keeps Hiro going or returns him to the status of a hero. Certainly in the first two seasons, Ando serves as Hiro's sidekick, but then his role changes.

Ironically, in Season Three, Ando develops a superpower of his own. This plot thread illustrates Ando's increased influence over Hiro as well as his mas-tery of the skills and knowledge needed to be a superhero on his own. Although Ando still isn't Hiro's complete equal in the story, he is much less a traditional sidekick or assistant than a fledgling hero catching up quickly to Hiro's level of power and status.

Even in a revised timeline presented in Season Four, when Hiro changes the past so that Ando and Hiro's sister, Kimiko, fall in love, Ando retains a more equal status. Although in this timeline he doesn't have a superpower, he knows Hiro's secret and, as Kimiko's future husband, has more status both within the company where they all work and in Hiro's family. Quite revealingly, he adamantly reminds Hiro "I'm not your sidekick!" during Season Four ("Upon

This Rock," 4.13). By this point in the story, Ando is a "brother." He no longer is a true sidekick but has been elevated to a new familial role.

These characters identified as popular SF TV sidekicks all come from ensemble series with a leading hero and a supporting cast revolving around that hero. Although each team as a whole often performs heroically or agrees to act as a unit to right a wrong (e.g., even mercenary Captain Mal and crew go out of their way to fight alongside Shepherd Book and make the rest of the 'verse aware of what caused the Reavers), the series' star is still the main hero. *Buffy, Angel, Firefly,* and *Torchwood* all surround the lead character/hero/commander with an ensemble of supporting players, and *Lost, Battlestar Galactica,* and *Heroes* present larger ensemble casts with more than one hero amid a shifting rota of leaders, depending on story arcs and politics. Each of these ensemble casts includes pivotal sidekick characters.

Not everyone agrees that ensembles include one or more sidekick characters, however. A U.K. Sci Fi Channel article suggests a different definition of *sidekick,* one requiring a partnership, more of a buddy relationship that implies two characters against the world, or the proverbial opposite but equal two sides of the same coin. Furthering this analogy, one online critic questioned whether *Firefly*'s ensemble could include sidekicks: "So where has the sidekick gone? Is it as simple as an entire crew being a sidekick for the leader? Are *Firefly*'s Jayne, Zoe, Inara, Kaylee, Simon, River, Book and Wash *all* Capt Tightpants' sidekicks? If so, he has a weird coin shape, or multiple personality disorder."[4]

As discussed in Chapter 2, some SF TV series experiment with different power structures over the course of the series, such as *Torchwood*'s brief shift from ensemble to triumvirate during "Children of Earth." The trend in post–2000 SF TV is to have at least one identifiable lead hero, usually a gray hero, and a group of supporting characters who may or may not be heroic, depending upon the situation. Of this group, however, not all characters are equally supportive of the lead hero and thus aren't all sidekicks.

In *Firefly,* for example, Jayne is never Mal's sidekick; if anything, the two oppose each other more often than not and sometimes work in opposition to each other, to the group's detriment. Neither character completely trusts the other, though they share adventures and often have to rely on each other. Mal and Shepherd Book have a closer relationship, especially as shown in *Serenity,* but Shepherd at most makes Mal a better man by example and at least is more of a fellow traveler than a sidekick. Zoe, more than any other *Firefly* character, fulfills the definition of a sidekick as a loyal supporter and assistant. She has been a comrade in arms but is more than that; she is equally as fierce and battle ready (i.e., competent) as Mal, but she usually defers to his command decisions. As noted previously in this chapter, some fans single out Zoe as an important sidekick.

As defined in this book, the new SF TV sidekick may stand out from others in an ensemble to support, defend, and guide the lead hero. Sidekicks may be

Other more than ever (e.g., lesbian/gay, Wiccan, African American, Asian, senior). Sidekicks may be involved in a platonic love relationship with the hero or, in a non-sidekick personal role, be the hero's lover, although that relationship is kept separate from the hero/sidekick work relationship. Sidekicks, moreover, have far more influence over heroes and balance them mentally or emotionally in unprecedented ways. Although they may be heroic in their own right, sidekicks have especially important roles because of their increased amount of influence over the heroes and their decisions or actions.

The Sidekick's Guiding Influence

The growing influence of the secondary (i.e., not lead actor-as-hero character) or sidekick hero is a marked change from the sidekick's formerly traditional role only as office support, backup "gun" or tech, or comic relief. In fact, the sidekick's influence often makes or breaks the gray SF TV hero. A companion or an assistant, who may also be a love interest (e.g., *Torchwood*'s Ianto, *Doctor Who*'s Rose) or family member (e.g., Starbuck as Adama's "daughter"), provides the logical insight, alternate perspective, and emotional support that modern heroes require if they are to be truly heroic.

Ironically, the lead hero, and perhaps even the audience, may not realize just how much the sidekick has influenced the hero or provided motivations that drive the plot until he or she is gone. When Ianto dies, when Rose becomes trapped in an alternate reality, when Starbuck disappears (twice), Jack Harkness, the Doctor, and Bill Adama recognize the depth of their reliance and (even if they don't admit it) love for the dearly departed. These characters fulfill a role that no other character can or will, despite the inevitable "replacements" introduced into continuing series. The most poignant scenes in these series often are the farewells to such beloved sidekicks when viewers and the lead heroes recognize their inevitable loss. How heroes respond to this loss, however, ultimately determines what kind and how much influence these sidekicks have had.

Torchwood, Doctor Who, and *Battlestar Galactica* have some of the strongest sidekicks who differ from the traditional "buddy" (e.g., Ando), "best friend" (e.g., Willow, even comrade-in-arms Zoe), or "secretary" model. Three important non-traditional sidekicks are emphasized in this chapter because they exemplify the complex professional and personal relationships between such sidekicks and the heroes they support: Ianto Jones (*Torchwood*), Kara (Starbuck) Thrace (*Battlestar Galactica*), and Rose Tyler (*Doctor Who*).

These characters are able to offer more than technical or emotional support alone. Because these sidekicks instigate unique love relationships with, but can be highly critical of, a lead hero, their roles are different from those of traditional lovers/partners, best friends, or children. The new sidekicks are a complete package: comrades-in-arms or competent heroes in their own right *and* those who love lead heroes completely but have enough influence and objectivity to point out their flaws. They have more power and influence over gray heroes because they understand them in ways that a character who is only a lover/spouse, colleague, or buddy can't. Despite their great influence and power, these characters will never be more on the job than a lead hero's sidekick, no matter the complexity of their relationship off the clock.

Torchwood's Ianto Jones

Enigmatic Ianto Jones' duties gradually increase from tea boy/butler to knows-everything archivist to field operative during *Torchwood*'s Seasons One through Three. His job duties at first indicate that he might be a traditional sidekick similar to Batman's Alfred or, later, a comrade-in-arms operative like Captain Mal's Zoe. When Gwen Cooper, and thus the audience, first enters the Hub, Ianto looks smugly knowing, perhaps even a bit malevolently mysterious, as he opens the door. He ushers Gwen into the inner sanctuary from the deceptively drab tourist office entryway that serves as Torchwood's public "cover." However, Ianto's bland, servile exterior is just as much a front as Torchwood's entrance.

The first indication that Ianto is "much more than the tea boy" ("Captain Jack Harkness," 1.12) occurs in the pivotal Season One episode "Cyberwoman" (1.4).[5] Loyal to a deadly fault, Ianto hides girlfriend/half-converted cyberwoman Lisa in Torchwood's basement, where he installed life-sustaining equipment. He then attempts to find the right specialist to return his girlfriend to humanity. Of course, this being Torchwood, the "cyber" part of Lisa takes control, and she kills the doctor. A nearly hysterical Ianto tries to contain the situation before his colleagues return.

When they return to the Hub earlier than expected, Ianto soon faces an irate team who discovers humankind's enemy has been living in their basement and now is running amok. Ianto only sees that his girlfriend, herself a former Torchwood employee who barely survived an alien invasion, needs help. The rest of the team is convinced that Lisa can't be saved and must be destroyed in order to save the rest of Cardiff, if not the world. Her superhuman strength and desire to be fully upgraded — and to help other humans achieve this benefit of more advanced technology — make her a threat.

Ianto begs Jack to help Lisa. He flatly refuses because he knows that once technology takes over, a return to being human is impossible (an interesting social comment in itself). By the end of the episode, Jack both threatens to kill Ianto if he doesn't destroy the cyberwoman (or murder his girlfriend, as Ianto perceives this order) and kisses him back to life after Lisa throws him across the Hub. For his part, Ianto calls Jack a monster, slugs him and vows to watch him die, but nevertheless cleans up the mess after the Torchwood team assassinates Lisa.

"Cyberwoman" poses interesting questions about monsters, but it also forms a starting point for Ianto Jones' real integration into the Torchwood team. What should have been an event to get him Retconned (i.e., memory erased) or killed turns into a way for his eventual integration into Torchwood and an increasingly important role in Jack's life, and thus the story. Perhaps because Ianto stands up to Jack in order to protect the woman he loves, as well as because Ianto's misguided action ends up threatening all of humanity, Jack sees in him a potential equal. After all, one of Jack's early conman schemes also threatened humanity, and he also is fiercely loyal to those he loves. Gareth David-Lloyd (Ianto) explains that Ianto is equally as dark a hero as Jack, although for different reasons:

> They're both tortured characters, but Ianto is tortured in a very different way. Ianto's torture is far more internal, far more self-instigated. I think he tortures himself, blames himself for not being able to make his environment, the world around him, a better place. He fails to do things, like save Lisa or be close to his family. Jack's torture is the fact that he's cursed to watch everyone he loves in the world perish. So I think they're both as dark as each other, just in slightly different ways. Jack's [torture] is more on the surface — he's physically as well as mentally tortured — whereas Ianto's torture comes from himself.[6]

Ianto, like Jack, harbors plenty of secrets about his past. Both characters make questionable decisions that often come back to haunt them, and, after being betrayed and losing loved ones because of Torchwood, are reticent to make personal attachments. Both are "monsters" at times who lie and deceive in order to further their personal agendas, but both also are capable of great compassion and love. Both find ways to hide important parts of themselves from the rest of the world. Ianto simply takes a different approach toward self-protection and disguises his emotions beneath a deliberately constructed outer persona, as David-Lloyd elaborates:

> There's a hardened exterior that Ianto puts up, and he's worked very hard on that shield. I think he's got it just right. Jack's always been quite cocksure from when he was younger, so he's never had to build that kind of hardened exterior. Even though I think on the inside Ianto is more emotional, Jack is just not as good disguising his emotions.[7]

Fitting the "two sides of the same coin" analogy of a traditional sidekick, this foundation helps Ianto become one of the new breed of sidekicks. Because Jack is an immortal with numerous intergalactic lives that provide him knowledge and experience that Ianto (or any human) can never equal, the two can never be on the same level on the job. Ianto will always remain a "sidekick" professionally to Captain Jack, but their personal relationship gives him more influence over Jack than any of the Captain's previous colleagues or lovers have had. Ianto finds a unique role to play in Jack's life, one that greatly influences the way Torchwood's leader perceives the world and his role in it.

Part of Ianto's success as a sidekick is his chameleon ability to blend with his surroundings and become whatever Jack needs him to be. David-Lloyd notes that Ianto's wardrobe consists of numerous "costumes" he wears to disguise who he truly is. When he first approaches Jack by helping him capture a Weevil, he dresses casually but provocatively in tight jeans and chest-hugging shirt ("Fragments," 2.12). When that wardrobe doesn't capture Jack's attention, Ianto switches to the suits for which he becomes famous, and those definitely catch Jack's eye. During "Children of Earth," Ianto blends into scenes by wearing clothing expected for a particular setting or situation, such as donning a yellow slicker and helmet as he drives heavy equipment, this time masquerading as a construction worker. These costumes allow Ianto to mask his true identity and show a public face that others expect, something that Jack's other colleagues haven't done.[8]

By disguising himself to everyone but Jack, Ianto joins a long line of heroes and sidekicks who keep their true identity secret and save the world dressed in a "costume," even if Ianto's wardrobe is much less obvious than a cape or tights. By day, on the job, he wears a mask and defends Cardiff wearing a suit and a deceptively mild manner. By night, alone with Jack, he returns to being who he really is. Jack also seems to follow this pattern of dressing in "costume" as a hero; he wears anachronistic-to-the-21st-century clothing and a cape-like coat. (See Chapter 11 for further discussion of Jack's wardrobe as part of his development as a hero.) The hero and sidekick are roles enacted only in the outside world, where Jack needs to retain his authority as the Torchwood leader, and Ianto is his subordinate. In private, the relationship is very different.

This duality also symbolizes Ianto's fear to reveal his sexual orientation to the rest of the world outside the Hub, including his sister and her family. During "Children of Earth" (3.1), Ianto comes out to his family, although he initially fears their derision. He is reticent to be perceived as part of a same-sex couple, perhaps because of his council estate upbringing, which may not have been as accepting of gays. When he is alone with Jack in the sanctity of the Hub, however, Ianto reveals the depth of his love for Jack and loses all inhibitions.

As the flirting attraction between Jack and Ianto increases throughout the series, fans (and fanfiction writers) have become fascinated at the way a relationship basically begun, or at least significantly interrupted by, betrayal could turn into love. The two, on the surface, seem to be opposites (i.e., Ianto is usually emotionally contained, whereas Jack is extremely extroverted and flamboyant; Jack is the obvious hero who makes grand entrances and sweeping gestures, whereas Ianto relies on facts and precision to get the desired results). Nevertheless, the aforementioned similarities in losses and betrayals, and the ability to survive tragedies, also help make the pair a good partnership within and outside Torchwood.

During a meeting of *Doctor Who/Torchwood* fans in Orlando, Florida, David-Lloyd noted that he suspected the BBC programmers regretted showing

"Cyberwoman" early in Season One.[9] Had they waited to broadcast this episode after the Jack-Ianto relationship was better established, the episode would have been more shocking and created an even greater betrayal for the characters to overcome. The heightened dramatic tension would have made Jack's over-the-top emotions in this episode — both fury and love — more personal and less about the fate of humanity than the realization that Ianto had played him and their relationship was likely a sham. As well, Ianto would have seemed less like the left-out outsider, the one to whom the rest of the team spoke only when they needed a menial task completed; he would have been turned into more of a calculating potential villain, or at least a much grayer potential hero.

Early Ianto, according to David-Lloyd, "probably feels a little on the outside of things ... and he might feel that his talents aren't being used to their full potential.... He loves Torchwood, he's fascinated by it, and he constantly wants to be better at the job and make even more important contributions to the work they do."[10] Although Ianto is a secondary sidekick character in Seasons One and Two, he gradually becomes more heroic as his presence in episodes increases. For example, he tries to save Tosh from cannibals on his first field mission with the Torchwood team ("Countrycide," 1.6); and he tries to protect the Rift, following Jack's orders not to open it, by shooting Owen when he does just that ("End of Days," 1.13). His actions in "Kiss Kiss, Bang Bang" (2.1) clearly show that he's a full-fledged member of the team; he even defies Time Agent John Hart. Ianto helps save Cardiff from destruction in "Exit Wounds" (2.13). By Season Three's "Children of Earth," Ianto is Jack's equal in their personal partnership and a fully developed hero on field missions. Yet for all his participation in such missions, his greatest role as a *Torchwood* character and Torchwood team member is as the sidekick who balances and supports Jack so that he may be the story's primary hero — and a less gray one at that.

By Season Three, when the Torchwood team is down to Jack, Gwen, and Ianto, he gets to make more important contributions. David-Lloyd told an interviewer before Season Three debuted that "filming this new series was by far the most enjoyable for me, because I'm out and about so much more, and Ianto is really part of the action all the way through. I was dodging bullets all the time, and even saving the day a couple of times, too." Instead of looking proper in a well-fitted suit, as he does for much of Seasons One and Two, in the third season Ianto is often described as "broken down" or "rough and ready,"[11] clearly more of an "action" description than his early role as butler/tea boy.

Ianto gladly risks his life on behalf of Torchwood, not only because of his relationship with Jack or his friendship with Gwen. He, too, becomes more heroically minded when it comes time to make a more important contribution to the team. As a sidekick, Ianto's greater experience and self-confidence allow him to move from behind the scenes in the Hub to the center of the action, where he becomes more actively heroic on several fronts: to rescue Jack from government agents, to save Torchwood from outside forces destroying it, to save his niece's and nephew's lives, to save the world from aliens.

Not only is Ianto an increasingly important part of the team, but his personality shines as his character is given more to do. Ianto's snarky one-liners provide a humorous bite to Seasons Two and Three; in essence, his dry comebacks not only offset Jack's enthusiastic pronouncements with a dose of reality, but they also indicate his growing sense of equality with the immortal Jack in their personal life. Jack may be the big hero, but Ianto can effectively bring him back to regular human status with his insights. Nevertheless, Ianto is Jack's greatest supporter, in part because Jack gives him a purpose.

During "Adam" (2.5), when each team member must focus on whatever defines him or her in order to destroy this alien's control of their memories, Ianto chooses Jack, emotionally revealing that "you gave me purpose."[12] When Owen nastily comments that Ianto is only Jack's "part-time shag," Ianto quietly but fervently replies, "It's not like that, Jack and me. He needs me" ("Captain Jack Harkness," 1.12).[13] In a November 2009 interview, David-Lloyd further explained, "Jack also needs Ianto in the sense that he finds it difficult to love, because he's seen so many people he's loved die. I think Ianto is helping him find that part of himself again, that part he's closed off because it hurts so much."[14]

Although Jack superficially is the strong, self-sufficient, swashbuckling hero, he couldn't play that role as well without Ianto, who needs Jack initially to give him a reason to live and then to allow him to become more confident and heroic. Ianto can act heroically in the field and occasionally saves lives, but, more significantly, he makes Jack's great acts of heroism and sacrifice not only possible, but poignant and emotionally revealing. Without Ianto in the first two seasons, Jack would seem less human and likable. Jack's actions and the sacrifice he makes during Day Five of "Children of Earth" largely show what the loss of Ianto means to the emotionally shell-shocked hero. (See the Monster Redeemer section later in this chapter for more details of Ianto's influence on Jack during "Children of Earth.")

Battlestar Galactica's Kara Thrace

As the love story grows between Admiral Bill Adama and President Laura Roslin, their interdependence makes them more emotional, both to good and bad effect. Once she becomes comfortable in her role as political leader of the remnants of humanity, Roslin often seems cool and unemotional. She must make difficult decisions, doing so without becoming the stereotypical "emotional female." When she is angry she becomes collected and deadly quiet in making pronouncements. Although Roslin displays emotion throughout the series, she seldom loses control. Her typical public persona changes when she falls in love with Adama, but her emotions don't render her weak or ineffectual. If anything, a passionately enraged Laura Roslin is a force to behold and makes her seem more heroic because of the intensity of her focus. The "villains" who stand between her and her lover come to understand just how far she is willing to go to save him.

Roslin vows vengeance on the mutineers who say they have killed Adama ("Blood on the Scales," 4.16).[15] Her famous bellow "I'm coming to get you!" provided Mary McDonnell (Roslin) with one of her favorite scenes and most obviously illustrates a shift in the way she wants others to perceive her.[16] After years of learning how to play politics and reign in her emotions, Roslin lets loose her raw anger and shows everyone just how much she, as a woman, not as president, values her lover. For his part, Adama relinquishes his command — which has been his priority not only since the annihilation of the colonies but throughout his life — to retrieve Roslin from the Cylons holding her captive. Although he realizes that this mission could be suicidal, especially for a lone pilot, Adama has no personal alternative; he can't live without her ("Sine Qua Non," 4.10).[17]

As the series' usually pragmatic, unemotional military and political leaders begin to rely more on their love relationship and openly display their affection for each other, they become less focused heroes and more well-rounded every-day characters. They still can act decisively, but, especially because Roslin is dying, they choose to focus more on each other. As leaders/heroes in a time of turmoil, they then need more support from other characters.

Kara "Starbuck" Thrace steps into the sidekick role to this relationship, especially for Bill Adama. She understands obsession, because at this time she also is obsessed with her visions of Earth and desperate quest to lead her people there. Unlike Ianto, who often provides the voice of reason and caution in *Torchwood*, Starbuck forces Adama into leaps of faith that her visions will be truly prophetic and lead the fleet to a new Earth. Roslin at this time undergoes a crisis of faith, and Starbuck supplies the element of spiritual belief provided by Roslin earlier in the series.

As a sidekick, Starbuck can be "way out" in her actions and ideas because she isn't the main character or lead hero. She can take chances and show both pragmatic, fact-based decision makers that sometimes the "crazy" notion can be correct. She provides a unique perspective and sticks with her beliefs even when she is under fire. As a sidekick, Starbuck does what Adama or Roslin isn't free to do— to follow spiritual clues that she wholeheartedly believes will save humanity.

Although Starbuck always has the Admiral's ear and heart as his adopted "daughter" (and indeed is very much like her surrogate parent), in the series' later episodes this role is enhanced with her development as a prophet and spiritual guide. Despite all logical reasons not to trust Starbuck's prophetic visions and to question her lack of specific coordinates to guide the fleet, Adama believes in her and grants her as much leeway as possible in the hope that she truly can guide them to a new home. Along the way she hears music that no one else hears and paints bizarre pictures of clues to their destination (e.g., "Someone to Watch Over Me," 4.19), acts that seem crazy to other crew members. Nevertheless, Adama's love for her as a daughter, and his relief at her earlier return after he believes her dead in a crash on a distant planet, make him trust her insights when anyone else would have locked her away. Such a command decision makes Adama seem suspect, too, but he is willing to risk being seen as weak or ineffectual because he believes so much in his surrogate daughter/veteran warrior. Starbuck understands command structure and knows exactly what she is asking Adama to risk for her behalf, more than for the general good of humanity, even if everyone will benefit if her visions are proved correct.

Starbuck becomes the influence that guides command decisions to go on a "wild goose chase." As a prophet and visionary, however frustrating she becomes for the regular troops who think Adama far too indulgent in following her visions, Starbuck does eventually guide humans and Cylons to their new planetary home. By the end of the story, Starbuck is the behind-the-scenes hero who guides her people, as well as the Cylons who will live in harmony with them, to their promised land. Adama, however, gets the credit for guiding the fleet to their new home, and the dying Roslin achieves her goal from the very beginning — to lead humanity to Earth. Roslin and Adama become the human race's mother and father figures, whereas sidekick Starbuck is a supportive "daughter." Although her personal relationship with Adama grants her a way to ask for the seemingly impossible, her well-documented war record as a pilot and unconventional hero/leader give her the skills needed to make military, not just spiritual/personal, decisions on behalf of the fleet.

Early in the series Starbuck is simply an out-of-control warrior. She displays no fear and thrives on rankling Adama's second in command, Colonel Tigh. This role as warrior/anti-hero continues until her disappearance and presumed death during a mission, an event that shakes Adama personally as well as professionally. Upon her return from the dead, Kara Thrace/Starbuck becomes more of a sidekick than a full-fledged hero. Her strange return to the *Galactica* removes her from her previous role in the military; she is less a warrior than a spiritual guide who happens also to serve in the military.

Kara is a resurrected hero, audiences later learn. Her body perishes in a crash, yet she returns whole to the *Galactica*. Back in her home environment but changed by her experience, Starbuck is vastly different from the hard-living pilot hero portrayed early in the series. She becomes more thoughtful and less reactionary; she listens and tries to explain how she knows information that can't logically be proven. Kara also becomes a better "daughter" by believing wholeheartedly in her surrogate father/commander and trying to convince him of the rightness of his belief in her, instead of butting heads with him like a rebellious teenager. Despite dramatic fallouts with her "father," she has always been the one closest to him in temperament and career choices, a relationship she uses to its greatest advantage during the series' final season.

Adama needs Kara's influence ultimately to complete his mission — to lead the remnants of humanity to Earth. Without her continuing influence and understanding, which not even his sons are able to provide him, Adama wouldn't have become the gentled, sentimental man who takes his love, Laura, on one final flight, or who is able to accept that his mission is over and his people must make their own way without him ("Daybreak," 4.22).[18] In many ways, Kara/Starbuck humanizes the stone-faced commander and makes him capable of feeling love more than duty, yet she also is the character who permits him to accomplish his military mission.

Although in early *Battlestar Galactica* episodes Starbuck is more warrior and hellion than prophet and insightful daughter, her role in the story, while important, increasingly becomes more of a catalyst for hero Adama's decisions and actions. Her strength is her ability to do what no one else can do, either as a prophet/guide to a new homeland or as the character who can emotionally get to the commander as well as "get" him psychologically and emotionally. Her role as an influential sidekick thus becomes more important than her earlier role as a warrior hero, in part because Starbuck no longer is suicidally "heroic" in battle but more thoughtful and passionate about her actions on behalf of others.

Katee Sackhoff (Starbuck) summarizes her character's development:

> We saw someone, in the beginning, who was willing to die for everyone around her because she didn't value her own life. At the end, we have a character who values *existence* so much that she's willing to die for other people.... That's a huge change. It changes everything Starbuck does. It makes her compassionate and it makes her circumstances more tragic.[19]

Ironically, Starbuck moves from being one of the series' heroes to *the* important sidekick as she intellectually, spiritually, and emotionally matures.

The Adama-Starbuck relationship also brings the *Battlestar Galactica* saga full circle. In the pilot episode the camera follows Starbuck as she jogs through *Galactica*'s corridors. When she greets Commander Adama, he asks her what she hears. "Nothing but the rain," Starbuck replies. Adama adds, "Then grab your gun and bring in the cat."[20] Although Starbuck's reply to this dialogue, often repeated throughout the series, varies depending upon the context of the scene — it is a typical exchange between the two and undoubtedly has a deeper personal meaning for them. During their last exchange on the new Earth, Adama and Starbuck realize that they are saying farewell for the final time. Once again they repeat this familiar ritual instead of spouting traditional sentimental dialogue.[21]

By introducing first Starbuck and then, through her and the trailing camera, Adama in the pilot episode and concluding their final scene with this exchange, their interdependence provides structure to the entire series. Like an important sidekick, Starbuck begins the story and ends it, leading into and out of Adama's first and last scenes. Although Kara Thrace/Starbuck changes dramatically throughout the series, Bill Adama is kept on track because of her influence. Her role, whether as a warrior pilot, good (or frustrating) daughter, or prophet/guide, often provides what the commander needs to fulfill his mission.

Throughout the series, despite all the harsh and frequently unpopular command decisions he makes, Adama becomes more "human" by relating more positively to his son Lee, opening up to his closest friends more often (and not always under the influence of alcohol), and eventually entering into a love relationship. Starbuck's influence on her surrogate father helps Adama make these transformations.

Kara/Starbuck sees Adama through his "completion" as a mature man and heroic leader: he has led the fleet to Earth and begun to facilitate colonization, permanently relinquishes the burden of command, bids farewell to Kara and Lee, and spends Laura's dying moments on a journey to the site where he wants to build a home. Although Starbuck alone isn't behind all these results (after all, it takes a village to raise a commander), her influence is pivotal in Adama's transformation and the fleet's successful arrival at their final destination. Being an SF TV lead hero is important to a series' success, but, as Starbuck's evolution indicates, the role of the sidekick has gained monumental importance.

Doctor Who's Rose Tyler

Nowhere is the sidekick more important than in *Doctor Who*, whose story revolves around the Time Lord and his companions. Although all companions are important personally and thematically, the Ninth and Tenth Doctors are most influenced by Rose Tyler, the one companion who accepts and loves the Doctor unconditionally, and, indeed, becomes his love interest. In this children's series that love is star-crossed and mostly unrequited, but it simmers enough below the surface that adults, especially women who find Time Lords sexy, watched the series for Rose's interplay with the Doctor. Rose's influence especially helps determine the type of character the Ninth (PTSD-suffering) Doctor becomes and makes the Tenth Doctor emotionally vulnerable.

The Ninth Doctor would and does "die"—or regenerate—for Rose. He is moved by her determination to return from the safe haven where he sends her to help him fight, against overwhelming odds, a Dalek invasion. Rose travels through time to be with him, even if that means she also will die defending a future Earth ("The Parting of the Ways," 1.13).[22] The Doctor's love for Rose "redeems" him for the actions he took (off screen and before the return of the new *Who*) in the Time War. The PTSD-stricken Doctor (emotionally) pushes away the very human Rose for many of their early adventures, but by his final battle with the Daleks he clearly loves her.

When Rose returns to the Doctor, she takes the TARDIS' deadly power vortex inside her to help stop the Daleks. Although with the TARDIS' power Rose destroys the monsters, she also is burning out. To save her, the Doctor takes that power from her, causing his regeneration. The danger from the Daleks over, Rose as sidekick has a glorious moment as a savior-hero before that power and role are again taken from her by the Doctor. Rose also tragically loses the Doctor she loves because of her heroic action and willingness to sacrifice herself for him, as well as for humanity.

The Doctor-Rose relationship, however, is further explored with the development of the Tenth Doctor. At first, Rose is his caretaker, nursing him to health after a difficult, lingering regeneration. She takes his place in negotiations with yet other invading aliens, despite her certainty of failure in dealing with a species and danger well beyond her capability ("The Christmas Invasion").[23] Rose can't be the hero in this Earth-threatening encounter; only the new (Tenth) Doctor can play that role. She can only be a stand-in until he arrives, although her willingness to sacrifice herself if her stall tactics fail does make her remarkably heroic. Rose has learned from the Doctor that individuals must stand up to bullies, even if they're alien invaders with greater numbers. However, like a traditional hero, the Tenth Doctor arrives in the nick of time to fight the monsters (with Rose's assistance) and save Earth once again. If Rose were to keep saving the day, the Doctor's role would be minimized, and he no longer could be an effective series' hero. Although Rose occasionally gets to play hero, her role within the series is as the Doctor's faithful companion.

Even when the Tenth Doctor fully comes into his power as a hero, Rose occasionally saves the world, but at great cost. She closes the breach between the current and a parallel universe, once again thwarting a Dalek invasionary force determined to take over Earth. However, in doing so, Rose becomes trapped in that parallel existence, literally a world away from her beloved Doctor ("Doomsday," 2.13).[24]

Again, if Rose were able to save the Earth (i.e., take the Doctor's role in the story) without consequences, she would be moving into lead hero territory. In a series entitled *Doctor Who*, that can't happen. Instead, Rose becomes a tragic secondary hero/sidekick who does manage to thwart an invasion but who then pays a high cost for that heroic decision. She won't be a continuing hero, like the Doctor, but instead a heroic character who steps up when needed, often in direct violation of what the Doctor wants her to do. The Doctor tries to protect Rose and keep her out of harm's way, but he wouldn't be successful (especially in episodes like "Parting of the Ways") if she doesn't go against his wishes and return to assist him.

Rose's growth as a heroic sidekick throughout her travels with the Ninth and Tenth Doctors is clearly documented through their adventures. By the time

Rose saves the Earth a couple of times, she has "graduated" by learning from the Doctor. It's time for her to move on; she can't forever be his sidekick. Off screen in a parallel universe, that's exactly what happens: Rose moves on, becomes a stronger leader, and takes the initiative to save her world and eventually the universe. As audiences learn in later *Doctor Who* episodes, when Rose returns as a guest character, she has become an effective hero in her new world/new life.

For his part, the Tenth Doctor is emotionally devastated by the loss of Rose. Although he has other companions who become friends and about whom he cares greatly, no one has the same influence or power over him. Despite all that the Doctor is or can be on his own, an important emotional "human" element is missing without Rose's influence. Viewers glimpse who the emotionally complete Doctor can be when Rose returns during the final moments of "The Stolen Earth" (2.13), when he arrives on the street where Rose awaits. The Doctor often runs *from* danger (at least until he can successfully thwart the villains or monsters), but this scene gives him the rare opportunity to run *toward* what should be a safe haven, Rose's arms. Before the two reach each other, however, a Dalek shoots the Doctor,[25] and another Russell T. Davies script foils a happy ending.

With the Doctor moments from dying and regenerating, Rose tearfully begs him to stay with her (much as a tearful Jack Harkness begs the dying Ianto to stay with him); such emotional "death" scenes (even when the Doctor has the potential to regenerate) not only make for heart-rending TV but also illustrate the elevated role of modern sidekicks in hero dramas. Tenth Doctor David Tennant referred to this epic SF romance as "a high point of emotion for all."[26] The Tenth Doctor is almost giddy with joy when he sees Rose after their long separation, which he believed was permanent; his joy is offset moments later when he fears that regeneration will again separate them. At such moments the Doctor seems much more human — further hints of Rose's ultimate importance in his incredibly long life. In counterpoint, Rose is most emotional when she fears losing her beloved Doctor.

Even with their "married" bickering and physical attraction, the Doctor and Rose never become a "couple." Rose is a sidekick, seldom the scene's or episode's hero. She stands beside the Doctor and follows his instructions. She sometimes remains behind when he alone runs into danger but occasionally takes the initiative to act heroically and save the day. However, whether as savior or saved, her role is most important because of her influence on the Doctor. The significance of her role as the Doctor's beloved companion/unrequited love is emphasized in the last scene before the Tenth Doctor's regeneration. After seeing his other companions one more time, the Doctor saves his encounter with Rose for last. She becomes the last person with whom the Tenth Doctor interacts before his "death" ("The End of Time, Part 2").[27]

Rose humanizes the Doctor and makes him less alien, not only to other characters but to the audience. She makes him consider the consequences of his actions. For all the times she becomes angry or frustrated by his rudeness or abrupt dismissal of humans or their need for familial attachments, she loves him completely and would sacrifice everything — even the fabric of time and space — if he would be safe. She only draws the line when he refuses to say he loves her.

Rose ultimately chooses to live with a mortal — but human, and thus "redeemable" — version of the Doctor. When part of the Doctor's personality and memory is "reborn" (cloned) in a lookalike version during the Tenth Doctor's universe-saving adventure, Rose agrees to take this human "Doctor" home with her. The Tenth Doctor/Time Lord reminds Rose that this mortal version needs her influence just as much as the broken Ninth Doctor did upon their first meeting ("Journey's End," 4.13).[28] Rose thus is given a mission, but one with a reward attached. She can humanize another troubled "Doctor" but receive the reward of his ability to love her. Rose's role as a sidekick has been completed. She and the human "Doctor" someday will be equals, although she becomes the "lead" and he initially is her "sidekick" as he learns what it means to be human.

Analyzing Sidekick Characters

As outlined in Chapter 5, elements of SF TV storytelling and character development should be analyzed to provide further insights into heroes, villains, or monsters. These elements also can be analyzed in terms of sidekicks' characteristics and the ways they motivate heroes. In the case of sidekick characters co-created by Russell T. Davies and Julie Gardner — but defined primarily by Davies' scripts for pivotal episodes — music and the concept of "home" become the two important areas to analyze. Of course, other elements discussed in the next chapter should be used to analyze many other sidekicks from U.S. or U.K. series, but *Doctor Who*'s and *Torchwood*'s soundtracks and character themes are particularly useful for character analysis, and some similarities between Rose Tyler and Ianto Jones bear further consideration.

Although Davies created other companions for the Doctor and provided Jack Harkness with a team, Rose Tyler and Ianto Jones play special roles in the series and became the most popular and best defined sidekicks for their respective heroes/love interests. Long-lived time travelers the Ninth and Tenth Doctors and Captain Jack lack a true home. Despite their residence in one place (e.g., the TARDIS, Cardiff), for long periods of time they are unable to return to their respective homelands. Jack is separated emotionally and physically from his birthplace, and the Doctor's Gallifrey is destroyed in the Time War. These heroes thus must establish new homes not so much by place but with people. The two characters with whom these heroes are most at ease or most open are their sidekicks. With them they finally establish a sense of "home" and feel that loss keenly when they are left bereft of these sidekicks' presence.

At the conclusion of the first episode in the new *Who*, Rose happily runs off with the Ninth Doctor. She later agrees to join the Tenth Doctor, despite her hard-won knowledge of exactly how dangerous travel in space and time may be. She leaves her physical home and, with it, her primary relationships with her mother and boyfriend. She establishes a new home with the Doctor and provides for him a sense of family. Whereas the Ninth Doctor refuses to "do domestic," the newly regenerated Tenth Doctor joins Rose and her family for a happy Christmas celebration on Earth, once he (with Rose's assistance) rids the world of invading aliens. Rose offers the Doctor a new home and its accompanying comfort and acceptance. In contrast, the Tenth Doctor's world becomes cold and isolated when he loses this "home" with Rose.

Ianto even more specifically creates a physical home, even temporarily, for Jack and his colleagues. When the Hub is destroyed, Ianto finds a new base and goes about making it more habitable. Of course, Hub2 also becomes a techno-logical base from which Torchwood can go about saving the world, but it is Jack's new home. With Jack's (and likely Ianto's) living quarters and belongings destroyed with the original Hub, Ianto brings comfort and establishes Hub2 as their new home when he buys coffee and presents Jack with a new RAF coat. He knows what makes Jack feel at home, and he delights in being able to provide his partner and captain with these basics.

In addition to establishing a home for their respective heroes, Rose and Ianto share similar musical themes that highlight their role as emotional sup-port. "Rose's Theme" is reworked in several episodes highlighting her close relationship with the Ninth and Tenth Doctors.[29] It is wistful and hauntingly beautiful, at first awestruck, much like the Rose first presented with the wonders of the universe. At times the tune sounds "fluttery," a musical interpretation of Rose flying away on her own, like a butterfly or bird leaving the nest. Although the song is always beautiful, it gains power as it develops. It concludes with a decisive chord, signaling that Rose's story within the Doctor's vast time-line eventually ends decisively.

Like the themes associated with Ianto, Rose's theme begins quietly, hesi-tantly, and builds in strength (confidence) as the tune crescendos. It, like Ianto's themes, is in 3/4 time and initially features piano before other instruments, primarily strings, layer and intensify the song.

"Ianto Jones" and the longer version of this theme, "The Ballad of Ianto Jones," featured on the "Children of Earth" soundtrack illustrate the character's growth as a Torchwood hero, as well as his untimely death.[30] The theme first blends *Torch-wood*'s strange-sounding "twangy" musical instrumentation from the first two seasons' opening and closing themes in counterpoint to Ianto's 3/4 time (ballad-style) main theme. "Ianto Jones" is a brief but stylistically memorable tune, in keeping with the character's brief lifespan but important role in the series.

In the much longer reworking of this theme, a dying character's musical signature crescendos to a transcendent ending; in "Children of Earth" (1.4) this musical send-off accompanies not only Ianto's death, but one of Jack's, symbolizing their personal interconnectedness and the death of their relationship. On the soundtrack CD, "Ballad" follows in the wake of "Requiem for the Fallen," which overlays the otherwise silent scene of people trying to flee a poison gas-filled building. Whereas "Requiem" relies heavily on strings for emotional impact, "Ballad" never becomes musically soppy; it relies on a single, simple piano melody to highlight Ianto's personal theme, adding guitars and drums, for example, but never strings, as more instruments join the song. The tune ends quietly, as does Ianto's life, but before that ending it builds in intensity and drive as steadfastly and purposefully as the character's development throughout "Children of Earth."

The 3/4 time signature of a ballad contrasts with the gung-ho 4/4 driving time signature of the "Captain Jack Harkness" theme of the first two seasons' soundtrack, much in the same way that "Rose's Theme" contrasts with other faster, more driven "chase" themes so often associated with the Doctor's adventures. Both sidekicks' themes highlight their distinctive natures and roles within the lives of the heroes they support and within their respective series' storylines.

Just as audiences can learn crucial details by analyzing the ways in which a hero's story is told, so can viewers gain a greater appreciation of these increasingly important sidekick characters by taking a closer look at the many cinematic, aural, and symbolic ways they are portrayed. After all, these heroes would be very different characters without the guiding influence of their sidekicks.

Monster Slayer vs. Monster Redeemer: The New Role of the Sidekick

Answers to the question of what it means to be human provide much of the drama in SF TV series. Humans, ideally, shouldn't be monsters but should rise above the abhorrent qualities that such monsters traditionally display. Although cultural values change over time, and societies have their own moral codes that may challenge the moral codes of their neighbors— whether in the next village, country, or galaxy — every hero story clearly distinguishes heroes from monsters. The hero stories that continue to be told in Western cultures generally derive meaning from Judeo-Christian moral codes, even if those stories are set in far distant times or places. Although an SF TV series isn't meant to be a morality play, series' heroes traditionally live up to higher standards of personal sacrifice and decisions made on behalf of the greater good. These behavioral standards separate heroes from villains who are "alien" to such human virtues or who are truly inhuman monsters out simply for themselves.

Traditional hero literature clearly delineates heroes and villains and most often portrays the hero as a monster slayer. In classic hero stories, the heroes battle beasts like dragons or sea demons (e.g., kelpies, selkies, hydra). The heroes who stand up to these monsters slay them, literally or symbolically. In epic tales, the hero often fights alone, claiming victory over a foe that no one else will take on (e.g., Beowulf bests Grendel and his mother; Bilbo Baggins sets up Smaug; countless virtuous knights slay dragons or demons).

In any genre of traditional tales, hero = monster slayer. Evil, in whatever monstrous form, has to be overcome, at least temporarily, although it likely will return. (Hence, generations of potential future heroes learn from the story that they may someday need to fight the good fight, just as their ancestors did.) Evil may not be permanently destroyed, but Good can be (and usually is) victorious, as long as heroes act morally (i.e., "correctly," according to the prevailing social code). Evil (e.g., the Monster, frequently ugly, inhuman, and unpredictably murderous) must be slain, not only to solve the current crisis but to illustrate to the upcoming generation that personal sacrifice does lead to the benefit of society. For humans to remain "human," to protect Judeo-Christian social values and make humanity worth saving, heroes have to overcome Evil, but they have to follow certain morally proscribed codes of behavior to do so. Sidekicks in these stories merely provide superficial support for their heroes; they often aren't fully developed characters themselves because their role is merely to help the hero achieve greatness.

As noted in other chapters, the prominence of gray heroes makes the distinctions between always-pure heroes and always-vile villains or horrible monsters much murkier. Even series' lead heroes may be called monsters or may reveal how alien they basically are in comparison with "real humans" born on planet Earth. The gray heroes of modern SF TV sometimes act monstrously themselves in stories in which the moral high road apparently leads to humanity's destruction. Although these characters only temporarily reside on the "monster" side of the hero's continuum, the choices they feel forced to make may require the sacrifice of innocents or the destruction of homeland.

Modern society needs "heroes" to do their dirty work, as the military and political leaders in *Battlestar Galactica* and *Torchwood* often discuss behind closed doors. Leaders such as prime ministers or presidents need to remain removed from public outcry against horrific choices that endanger or require the sacrifice of innocents. These leaders, however, often feel free to order their subordinates to do the tasks they refuse to do publicly. Gray heroes bear the brunt of potential public backlash if a governmental plan fails; these heroes feel compelled to do whatever is necessary to keep Evil at bay, despite personal cost. They agree to do what the official "protectors" of the people — the government — refuse to or cannot do. Of course, if the government's plan succeeds and a crisis is averted, national leaders, not the gray heroes who do the dirty work, receive praise and further esteem.

In perhaps the darkest series discussed in this book, *Torchwood*'s "Children of Earth" comes to the conclusion that there is no morality in the fight against Evil, which often has more power than the forces of Good and can't be stopped by virtuous heroes. Evil not only exists, but it's more powerful than Good and is usually unstoppable. Russell T. Davies, as the creative force behind the scripts for "Children of Earth," takes SF TV drama to an extremely dark place by indicating that no one — not God or a god, a hero with mysterious powers, the government — is likely to save humanity. Sometimes heroes pay a terrible price to create a short breathing space between encounters with Evil, but there is no "happily ever after" for humanity.

To ensure human survival, gray heroes may believe they, at least temporarily, have to act just as monstrously as the monsters they seek to chase away but are unlikely to conquer. The rules have changed, and heroes have to be willing to do whatever villains or monsters/aliens do if humanity is going to survive. Heroes, however gray, suffer as a result of such decisions; they feel guilt and remorse because they and others view their actions as morally wrong, even if they achieve a much greater good. Gray heroes realize their similarity with monsters but dislike that comparison, and feel grief and remorse over their difficult decisions. Their remorse and need for "redemption" still distinguish a modern hero from a villain or monster, who lacks psychological or emotional attachment to what is sacrificed or destroyed.

Gray heroes would choose not to sacrifice others, if possible, but they pragmatically understand that they are able to make these sacrifices that ordinary citizens, for moral reasons, or society's leaders, for political reasons, can't make. Thus, gray SF TV heroes at least occasionally become moral relativists in order to make difficult decisions, but they revert to advocates of morality when they express their grief and remorse and question their actions. As Jack Harkness agonizes over the deaths caused by his actions, instead of the millions of lives he saves, he explains that he liked being a hero too much "and look what I became" ("Children of Earth," 1.5).[31]

SF TV heroes ultimately still may be monster slayers who destroy Evil and save the world, but because they temporarily act "monstrously" in order to save humanity, they also need to be redeemed in order for audiences (or the series' society and secondary characters) to accept them again. If gray heroes are going to regain public trust, as well as fan support, for what they *may* do in future conflicts, the sidekick may have to help facilitate this redemption.

Because the gray hero occasionally makes monstrous choices, the hero's sidekick also has to change. Instead of being only comic relief or a supportive best friend, the modern SF TV sidekick takes on a more important role: monster redeemer. Instead of slaying or replacing gray heroes after they make monstrous decisions, these sidekicks become "monster" redeemers, supporting the morally fallen heroes and providing them an emotional touchstone by which they can return to being human.

The sidekick corrects, inspires, nurtures, protects, and unconditionally loves the gray hero, in spite of his or her lack of perfection or the horror of the hero's choices. Only by the sidekick's continuing influence can the "monstrous" hero move back from the darkness and into more socially acceptable shades of gray. The power of the sidekick is enormous, both as an influential heroic character and a redeemer of the increasingly gray hero.

Changes to sidekick characters often change a series' dynamic and make audiences question the lead hero's ability even to continue as a hero. When Rose is confined in a parallel world or when Ianto dies, for example, their respective series' heroes lack emotional or logical balance; the pendulum representing their emotional versus logical equilibrium may swing to wide extremes.

The monster redeemer's/sidekick's influence on the gray hero sometimes is highlighted when the sidekick isn't around to ameliorate the gray hero's darkest decisions. Rose loves the Doctor, even finding a way to breach several alternate timelines until she finds him, but she won't return to traveling with him unless he can express his love for her. He can't, and so she prefers to stay with the human "clone" of her Doctor. Although the Doctor temporarily has several other companions, he most often travels alone and becomes increasingly megalomaniacal as he "plays God" with the lives of humans he deems worthy of saving from death (e.g., "The Waters of Mars"). (See Chapter 10 for a further discussion of the Doctor as an increasingly dark hero.) The Doctor refuses to love unconditionally again after the pain of losing primarily Rose, but also successive companions. On his own, without the balance provided by a sidekick who can point out his excesses, the Tenth Doctor grows increasingly insular and even fears his own power over Time.

Throughout "Children of Earth," Ianto may be horrified by some of Jack's previous decisions as a Torchwood operative, but he steadfastly stands by his captain, even if he also forces his lover to face some hard truths about himself. He becomes the best example of the sidekick as monster redeemer, rather than monster slayer.

Although Gwen declares Jack her "best friend" (3.2), she sees him through a filter of adoration and hero worship. Ianto certainly displays those emotions, too (e.g., as shown in his expression when he first sees Jack free and whole after being blown up and later resurrected only to be encased in cement [3.2]); he loves Jack in spite of his flaws and what many people would consider amoral actions. Ianto points out and tries to make Jack face the situations in which he is being less than honest with himself and others, but he still stands by his partner, despite their philosophical differences and personal choices.

The following scenes illustrate the difference between Gwen's and Ianto's reactions to revelations about Jack. Clem, one of the children to be sacrificed to the alien 456 during their first visit to Earth in 1965, identifies Jack as the man who delivered them as "gifts." Jack agreed with the government's assessment that the orphans had no value to humanity other than to appease marauding aliens. Gwen's first response is to assure Clem that Jack fights such aliens rather than acquiescing to their demands (3.3). Jack, however, confirms Clem's revelation. Gwen then demands to know why Jack would do such a thing; when the former "sacrifice" shoots and kills Jack, she disarms and comforts the distraught Clem. As a former police officer, Gwen naturally would respond by disarming a shooter, but her immediate reaction to Clem's shocking statement is to deny the possibility of Jack's horrific action. She "mothers" Clem throughout the mini-series, even after he kills Jack.

Gwen's reactions indicate the depth of her hero worship but also the limitations of her love for Jack. Gwen assumes that ideal, traditional hero Jack wouldn't give over children so easily. His action doesn't match her expectation. As well, if Jack were a "normal" hero, unable to come back from the dead, Gwen wouldn't be so quick to comfort Clem. However, she sees Jack's immortality as part of who he is, but in doing so, she neglects to consider just how much being shot and dying likely hurts. She merely expects Jack to bounce back to life. Gwen may love Jack, but she doesn't truly understand him.

In contrast, Ianto's horrified expression at Clem's revelation indicates his revulsion at Jack's past action. Nevertheless, he immediately goes to the fallen hero, lifting and holding Jack's body after the shooting. Ianto glares at Clem while caressing Jack's face and grounds him until he can regain his bearings after violently returning from the dead. Wordlessly, Ianto shows his continuing unconditional support for Jack — who certainly doesn't need Ianto's help to return from the dead — by being there when he returns.

Other scenes from "Day Three" show an astute Ianto forcing Jack to explain what he's currently doing and why, as well as acknowledging it's much easier for Jack to avoid explaining himself. He forces Jack to live up to a higher standard of behavior and openness. He expects Jack to live up to higher moral standards not because that is an unrealistic expectation, but because he knows that Jack is ultimately a good man.

Ironically, as a result of encouraging Jack to stand up to the alien monsters (the 456) because it is the right thing to do, Ianto is sacrificed. His death brings home to Jack just how deeply the loss of one innocent life can (or should) be felt by those left behind. Even if the military/political objective is to save as much of humanity as possible, the emotional/personal costs of collateral damage shouldn't be minimized, a theme also presented in *Battlestar Galactica* and its spinoff *Caprica*.

During his death scene (3.4), Ianto asks Jack to remember him. On a superficial level, this request from a dying lover may seem simply sentimental, but the fact that Ianto provides the stability through which Jack can be a hero gives the lines greater significance. Jack promises to remember Ianto for the next thousand years. If he lives up to that promise, he will remember Ianto's counterbalancing influence — and the fact that he is worthy of such unconditional love. Ianto always challenged Jack's decisions and actions when he believed them wrong, and he is the only character to make Jack take a critical look at himself. Without that counterbalance, Jack's belief that he alone knows what is best (and his ability to justify anything he thinks he must do) can lead him down some dark paths.

Gwen finally pleads with the departing Jack (3.5) to someday come back for her; she doesn't request that Jack stay on Earth to help save humanity or even to deal with the horrors he's experienced. Hers is a romantic notion that the hero will always return for the heroine and live up to a shining ideal. Gwen still believes in Jack as a traditional hero, choosing to ignore those less than shining elements of his nature. It is doubtful that, had their roles been reversed, Ianto would've made the same request of Jack. He more likely would have forced Jack to face the consequences of running away — for Jack's sake, not his own.

The monster-redeemer sidekick sees the true nature of a gray lead hero and strives to help him or her return to the light. Sidekicks don't give up on heroes but understand that being heroic is a daily choice, not an innate quality. "Redeemed" heroes can be even more important role models or social metaphors because they are not inherently good, or their "specialness" doesn't guarantee that they will always fight for the greater good. Gray heroes need to be reminded of the dangers of too much power or the assumed rightness of their decisions, reminders significantly and often poignantly provided by the enhanced role of the monster-redeemer sidekick.

5

Analyzing Gray
SF TV Series

The way a story is told allows audiences to recognize heroes, villains, and monsters and helps create typical ways in which these characters are identified. On a soundtrack, for example, villains traditionally have darker musical themes that may be in a minor key or follow a downward progression of notes. Heroes may have dramatic "ta da!" entrances, music with a driving beat, or themes that follow a rising progression of notes. The sound effects for monsters, such as the relentless clanking of Cybermen in *Doctor Who*, or the roller coaster click and snickety sounds preceding *Lost*'s smoke monster, provide aural cues about the monsters' arrival or lurking dangers. Because TV "texts" can engage audiences visually and aurally, they provide plenty of clues leading to an in-depth understanding of heroes, villains, or monsters, and their roles within an episode or a series. Elements by which audiences should analyze characters, settings, and plot within an episode, across seasons, and throughout a complete series are described in the following sections but further explored in later chapters about individual TV series.

As noted in previous chapters, SF TV often provides a safe place in which to discuss the most volatile but significant social issues. Science vs. Religion, Faith vs. Destiny, Monotheism vs. Polytheism, Religion vs. Atheism, and a host of other religious themes increasingly pit characters against each other as representatives of different sides to the arguments. *Lost*, *Battlestar Galactica*, and *Caprica*, in particular, debate spiritual or specifically religious themes. The place of government in the lives of citizens, and whether the current government is beneficial or corrupt, frames plot developments in *Firefly* (especially *Serenity*), *Battlestar Galactica*, *Caprica*, *Torchwood*'s "Children of Earth," and occasionally even *Doctor Who*. The inhumanity of humans toward each other provides an all-encompassing theme in most SF TV series. Every series discussed in this book explores how humans may be more monstrous than the real monsters. Abuses of power, whether individual or corporate, create the most dramatic episodes and illustrate how heroes grow grayer when faced with more power than they've ever had. The role of technology in society and ways technology can benefit or warp humanity deserve further exploration and are no longer the province of futuristic SF. Whether humans should be technologically "upgraded" so they are more beautiful, intelligent, efficient, or longer lived is a popular theme in SF. Analyzing the fine points of how the story is told visually or aurally is certainly important, but without provocative or controversial issues, heroes and villains would have far fewer interesting reasons to oppose each other.

Not only is the TV series a rich text for exploring the ways characters are developed and audiences are led to believe that specific characters are heroes or villains, but most 2000s-era SF TV series offer many additional texts that further develop lead characters and provide audiences additional ways to become involved with the story. Because gray SF TV heroes, in particular, become established through multiple media and multiple texts, they are more likely to remain part of public awareness long beyond the life of a TV series. The "cult" nature of many SF series also helps ensure that SF TV heroes and villains become ingrained in popular culture and are more likely to have an impact on far more audiences than the original viewers. How these texts illustrate different aspects of a character's development — or even different versions of the same character tailored to different audiences— presents an interesting look into the way fictional heroes become part of our culture and can shape, as well as reflect, current and future generations' understanding of heroes as representative of Western societies' ideals.

Although not all TV series use the same media or combination of media to promote and develop heroic characters, *Lost*, *Battlestar Galactica*, *Heroes*, *Doctor Who*, and *Torchwood* lead the pack in successfully marketing heroic characters to multiple audiences worldwide via print (e.g., novels, magazines, comics or graphic novels, paintings or drawings, posters), music (e.g., soundtrack CDs and downloads, concerts), audio programs (e.g., radio plays, audiobooks), and internet (e.g., official websites, webisodes, interactive content, RPGs). These media tell additional stories that go beyond the canon presented via TV episodes; they are not just areas for discussion or commentary about series' episodes. SF TV heroes more than ever have multiple platforms by which to reach audiences eager to learn more about their favorite characters.

Forums, podcasts, message boards, blogs, convention appearances and panels, among others, are still more ways for series' cast, crew, and creators to interact with fans, but these types of interactions analyze, rather than create, new stories for public consumption. Nevertheless, these peripheral texts help audiences (especially fans) analyze series' canon in more detail and gain "insider" insight into production values and character development. In addition to the series' canon established through traditional TV storytelling with seasons of episodes, additional content through a variety of media, approved by the networks and production companies behind the series, offers numerous opportunities for even more people to follow the heroic adventures of ever more popular characters.

Hero stories are an embedded, personal way for cultural values to be transmitted between generations and, traditionally, to teach young audiences about societal expectations for behavior. Although SF TV series provide heroes and villains in fictitious settings, they hold up mirrors to reflect sociopolitical concerns and feature beloved characters who often have a greater impact on fans than characters from other genres. For all the jokes about SF geeks who need a life, SF TV generates a loyal "cult" audience positively influenced by series even years after cancellation or the natural end to a story, in addition to the number of viewers who regularly watch the series but aren't die-hard fans. The prevalence of SF within popular culture indicates that these TV series and their characters remain an important way for hero "literature" to survive and thrive.

Creating a Series' "Look"

Despite the multiple texts available to audiences eager for more stories about their favorite heroes or villains, TV episodes still are the first place audiences turn for original content. Often a series must achieve some measure of success before a network's and production company's marketing machine goes into action. A relatively inexpensive secondary location for original content is a series' official website, where webisodes, comics or graphic novels, or interactive features provide additional stories, new characters, or "missing scenes" from regularly broadcast TV episodes.

Networks in the 2000s provide more opportunities for audiences to watch new episodes, especially those of series just being launched. Broadcasting the pilot episode or a new season's first episode(s) numerous times on the same or several networks owned by the same company gives audiences more chances of finding the series and watching it. Making episodes available from the series' website or downloadable through iTunes or similar companies for viewing online or through PDAs adds portability and convenience to audiences who may not have time to watch TV. Networks recently began offering miniseries, pilot episodes, or even original "movies" on DVD within a few days of their original TV broadcast. *Caprica* had been greenlighted as a SyFy TV series, set to debut in January 2010, when its two-hour pilot became available first on DVD in mid–2009.

In this chapter the diverse elements of a TV story, such as camera angles and shots, color palette, and costuming, are discussed in more detail than elements of print or audio stories, simply because TV episodes are still the main source of canon information for tales of SF heroes, villains, and monsters. Many of these cinematic elements also apply to webisodes or are mimicked in comics and graphic novels. As well, some aural elements, such as musical themes, also are highlighted because they are an integral part of TV episodes' layers of symbolism and scene setting. Because other texts (e.g., novels, comics, radio dramas) are important but still secondary to canon or fanon development of characters and plots, they are discussed in later chapters about specific series but not emphasized in this chapter; storytelling elements specific only to print or purely audio texts are not analyzed here.

Visual and Aural Elements of Storytelling

Whether audiences watch stories on TV, computer, or PDA, play them through DVR or on DVD, or enjoy them as they are first broadcast or at a later, more convenient time, the story's atmosphere and "look" must appeal to viewers and keep them coming back. Establishing a familiar setting and making audiences feel at home within it are important first steps. Although plot and characterization, especially in hero stories, ultimately make or break a series, visual appeal and continuity help audiences learn a great deal about heroes and villains and the logical parameters of the story. Not all visual elements will be discussed in this book, but some aspects of TV storytelling that emphasize gray heroes' development and the "darkening" of recent SF TV series require further analysis.

THE SETTING IN TIME AND SPACE

A series' time frame (or variety of times, including flash forwards, flashbacks, and cuts between time periods) establishes audience's expectations for the series' reality. A "current time" series like *Lost, Heroes,* or *Torchwood,* for example, can include references to current popular culture, allude to world problems and the leaders who attempt to solve them (e.g., "Children of Earth"'s Prime Minister Green, perhaps a veiled reference to then–Prime Minister Brown; *Battlestar Galactica*'s thinly veiled comparisons with the Bush administration), and give viewers a sense of belonging to the "in" group who knows what's really going on in the world. Not everything may be as it seems on the surface, as many SF fans suspect. The presence of superheroes, aliens, or time travelers among us provides a modern fantasy for SF fans and makes series' characters more realistic or "human" to audiences. That these characters face the same everyday challenges and pleasures as the audience makes their Otherness more acceptable.

As well, the villains and monsters facing these series' heroes can closely mirror the audience's real fears in the form most accessible to them. For example, a shape-shifting villain in the guise of an elected official (like *Heroes*' Season Four Sylar-as-Nathan-Petrelli) comprises audience fears about the government officials supposedly working on their behalf and mirrors the schism between citizens' desire for change and belief that elected representatives really will be able to help them.

Series like *Firefly*, *Doctor Who*, or even *Battlestar Galactica* and *Caprica*, for all that they are revealed to be technologically "futuristic" from current Earth civilizations, either can provide audiences with hope for a better future, in which current problems truly are in the distant past, or warn viewers of potentially dire futures if steps aren't taken now to solve global problems. Issues involving technology — everything from "it still doesn't work right" to "it solves all our problems" — mirror concerns about rapid technological advancements and whether they are really improvements or merely harbingers of future problems. SF series set in the future or a technologically superior past provide safe settings for viewers to consider or debate issues of vital current importance.

Analyzing a series' setting also includes where the story takes place: in space, on a deserted island, within a metropolis, on Earth or an equivalent planet. An island easily symbolizes social or personal isolation and questions of how to unite people dependent on each other for survival (e.g., "no [hu]man is an island"). Spaceships also can be isolated; they are, in effect, their own little social islands. The physical setting and its natural and social challenges, the cultures of people inhabiting these settings, and the interactions when characters from different societies or cultures collide all need to be considered in light of heroes, villains, and monsters. One society's hero may be another's villain or monster, and an understanding of where characters come from and what kinds of pressures shape them is especially crucial to understanding SF TV characters, who are more likely than "real" characters to come from vastly different times or places than the viewers being influenced by them.

COLOR SCHEMES

As heroes become grayer and more morally ambiguous, the overall "look" of a series grows darker. Some *Heroes* scenes are filmed in such darkness that it becomes difficult to see all the set details! *Battlestar Galactica* and *Caprica* often set scenes in murky rooms, from claustrophobic compartments onboard *Galactica* to *Caprica*'s overcrowded rave in a holoclub. In contrast, *Lost*'s sunny tropical paradise belies the island's danger and hidden horrors. Choosing the appropriate color scheme to compliment or contrast series' themes helps establish the mood as well as setting.

Red, Black, and White

The stark combination of black and white, with red as a highlight color, marks the most dramatic recent SF TV series and films. The movie *V*, with its politicized message and bleak vision of future society, famously uses this combination, but recent SF TV series also have adopted it. *Battlestar Galactica*, *Caprica*, and *Torchwood* are the best recent examples, each emphasizing this limited color palette in set design, lighting, costuming, and even promotional materials, such as advertisements, posters, and DVD and CD covers. These colors indicate the series' apocalyptic themes and serious overtones, marking each as drama worth being taken seriously. Red highlights can reflect key symbols, too, from specific items and their connotations (e.g., blood, roses) to more abstract emotional concepts (e.g., danger, lust, violence). Red within a black-gray-white scene also provides a focal point; audiences automatically look to and follow the splashes of red within an otherwise dark scene.

Blue

Within the red-black-white scheme so popular for telling apocalyptic stories, blue often provides a kinder, gentler contrast than red as a highlight color. It often provides a sense of normalcy or calm, especially when a lead character's wardrobe shifts from red to blue. Ties, sweaters, and shirts typically turn blue when characters are striving to act normal or are serving as the voice of reason or calm emotional center in a scene.

Bright Primary Colors

In contrast to the doom and gloom of the increasingly popular black/white/red scheme, *Star Trek*'s 2009 reboot features the bright primary colors (red, yellow, blue) of the original 1960s series. Original series creator Gene Roddenberry painted a hopeful future for humanity adventuring among the stars, and the bright colors emphasized his hope for a better future, even amid the turbulent '60s. Director J.J. Abrams' re-imagined characters taking the familiar names of Kirk, McCoy, Spock, Uhura, Chekhov, and Sulu, among others in the *Star Trek* mythology, wear the traditional Starfleet uniforms in bright shades (although wearing a red shirt, in *Star Trek* parlance, is the equivalent of sporting a bullseye on the back). The setting also mirrors this bright, happy color scheme, although villain Nero and his ship ominously contrast Starfleet colors with a murky, dark ship and black leather-clad henchmen.[1] Perhaps brighter colors—using red less ominously—may become trendy as, or if, SF TV lightens up its themes, but as heroes become grayer, most series' colors also become more stark.

Although *Torchwood* thematically is the anti–*Star Trek*, "Children of Earth" contrasts a bright color palette with the gray or dark sweaters and suits favored by most characters in the stark, serious drama. The physical world is bright, whether lush green trees for outdoor scenes or green walls surrounding Prime Minister Green as he decides the fate of Earth's children. However, red visually screams danger in most scenes: red clothing worn by pivotal characters facing dangerous dilemmas, a red school uniform worn by a future child sacrifice, red flashing lights, red walls highlighting command rooms, red and black floor tiles across the 456's deadly Floor 13 domain. Red in particular provides a way to attract audience attention to a specific character in a scene: U.K. government flunkie John Frobisher wears a red tie on the day he becomes Earth's spokesman to the 456, and Gwen Cooper and Lois Habiba wear red blouses on the day they find their world turned upside down by a government conspiracy.

Bright yellow turns up in expected costume choices such as police safety vests and construction hard hats, as well as heavy equipment. However, yellow lights unexpectedly spotlight a corner of a room or, in the case of overly diligent civil servant Dekker, a bright yellow coat. Dekker may not be cowardly "yellow," although he is one "cockroach"—as he calls civil servants—who knows how to survive alien invasions and governmental fallout. He is, however, a character who should be treated cautiously because he tends to appear in scenes leading to deadly consequences for Jack Harkness' or John Frobisher's loved ones.

In addition to the primary colors, the Prime Minister's office blazes in shades of red-orange, a dangerous hybrid, as well as the aforementioned green conference rooms. Although bright reds, yellows, and blues stand out onscreen and invoke emotional responses to these colors when they're used in a scene's pivotal lighting, the secondary colors of green and orange also add brightness to the settings.

Torchwood Seasons One and Two are visually much darker, with a lot of night scenes plus interior shots of the subterranean Hub. Interior shots of morgues, government holding facilities, and Hub2 (an abandoned warehouse) still provide plenty of dark scenes in Season Three when Torchwood or the government plan their clandestine activities. To illustrate that Torchwood's activities are being increasingly forced into the open and scrutinized in the light during "Children of Earth," more of the action takes place in daylight than in previous seasons.

Among the wardrobe choices for "Children of Earth," Ianto still favors dark pinstriped suits, Gwen wears her trademark black leather jacket and dark slacks, and Jack is given yet another gray-blue RAF coat. Jack's grandson Stephen Carter frequently wears gray, although his jacket, school uniform, and stripes in a favorite jersey are bright red, foreshadowing the upcoming danger to this character. Jack's daughter, Alice Carter, wears appropriately somber shades of gray. Of course, "villain" Agent Johnson's death squads wear black uniforms, as does she. Government "suits" favor dark colors, primarily grays or blacks. While the people in charge of dealing either with the government or the 456 wear dark clothing—symbolically illustrating their dark natures or, in general, the darkness of humanity—the natural world is bright and beautiful, and the interior settings in which the darkest decisions are made are often brightly painted.[2] After all, the leaders of the world don't expect to bear the brunt of the agony caused by the decisions they make. Their settings can be brighter and blended to reflect their self-serving consensus and expectation to come through the current crisis professionally and personally unscathed.

Star Trek (both the 1960s series and 2009 movie) and *Torchwood* use primary colors in different ways to accentuate their "normal" outlooks on the future. *Star Trek* offers a "happy palette" of primary colors as part of its promise for a better tomorrow. James T. Kirk, original or re-imagined, doesn't believe in a no-win scenario and accomplishes the seemingly impossible. Collateral damage (including the 2009 movie's destruction of Spock's Vulcan homeworld!) is minimized visually and within the plot. Both the 1960s TV episodes and the 2009 movie end on an upbeat note.

Jack Harkness, however, is forced into a true no-win scenario, shown in harrowing detail, and turns ever more inward toward darkness and despair. *Torchwood*'s atypically bright background settings in "Children of Earth" mock Jack's determination to save everyone and emphasize his resulting great losses by the end of the miniseries. (Euros Lyn, who directed "Children of Earth" and the final episodes of the Tenth Doctor's era on *Doctor Who*, used the same color palette and camera techniques for both series' pivotal story arcs.) The dark palette of Seasons One and Two, and the Torchwood team's wardrobe and preference for dark, shadowy locations, reflect the usual darkness to which Jack finds himself condemned at the end of Season Three.

LIGHTING

Having gray characters' faces half in shadow, half in light when they make startling revelations about their less-than-perfect personalities is a visually effective way to split the character's personality into "good/light" and "bad/dark" halves. During *FlashForward*'s pilot episode, lead protagonist Mark Benford confides to his AA sponsor that in his flashforward he is drinking heavily again. The characters converse late at night in a darkened kitchen, the only light filtering in through a window ("No More Good Days," 1.1).[3] Not only does the scene appear almost black and white with the lack of color, but Mark's face falls farther into shadow as he discusses his fears of losing his family because of his drinking problem. This use of lighting is common on many dramatic series, but it's often used to good effect to indicate SF heroes' shocking confessions.

In "Children of Earth" (3.3), when Jack Harkness confesses that he gave children as a gift to the alien 456 more than forty years previously—certainly a surprise to his adoring colleagues—he walks from the darkness of a warehouse into light. However, only one half of his face is illuminated (the "good guy" persona his colleagues see most often); the other side remains in darkness, just like the dark past coming back to haunt him.[4] This lighting effect is mimicked even in the comic "Selkie." In two separate panels on the same page, as Jack first searches for the killer monster and then recognizes the selkie from his past, his face is half in shadow, half in light. In contrast, once Jack vanquishes the monster and resolves his moral dilemma about the selkie's death, his face is shown in full light.[5]

Caprica's pilot movie also allows teenaged Zoe to be half human/half potential monster, half Good/half potentially Evil. After her death, only Zoe's avatar stores what remains of her personality and "soul." When the avatar confronts Zoe's father in a darkened holoroom, she walks toward him from the darkness and into the light.[6] As with the lighting of Jack Harkness' face, Zoe's face is similarly half hidden in shadow. In this moment the "holographic" Zoe is both real and unreal, alive and dead. By the end of the pilot, her human personality is encased in a metallic body, and the good girl who wanted to make a better life for herself and other teens is cast adrift in a body initially built as a war machine. The foreshadowing provided by lighting during a pivotal moment in her early character development (as an avatar) suggests further contrasts between human Zoe and the Cylon prototype in the regular series' episodes.

A trademark lighting effect used in *Star Trek* TV episodes and repeated in the 2009 movie is the use of a key light on the Captain's eyes. Although Kirk's (or another Federation captain's) face is never completely in shadow and his face is turned authoritatively toward the camera (audience) in close up, the light shines across his eyes, leaving the rest of his face less well lit. If the eyes are the clichéd window to the soul, the lighting effect clearly indicates the Captain's true feelings during an important pronouncement. His words, and the sincerity evidenced through his eyes, light the way and indicate the right or good path being revealed.

Torchwood also uses key light across a hero's eyes during a bleak scene in "Children of Earth: Day Four." While Gwen hides children from a government wanting to gather them as "gifts" for the 456, her husband Rhys films what may be the last moments of humanity. Not coincidentally, this emotional scene also was used as a trailer to promote the miniseries primarily because of its dramatic lighting, contrast between light and dark (Good and Evil), and frightening dialogue. Gwen documents what she believes may be humanity's destruction, leaving behind a record of her world's downfall for whatever life forms may someday find the recording. As she explains what is happening, her face is darkly shadowed; only her eyes are lighted to emphasize her sincerity and sorrow.[7] Because Eve Myles' eyes are large and expressive, even when not made up as Gwen to focus even more attention on them, the strategically placed lighting emphasizes her dire pronouncement about the fate of humanity.

Lighting choices, whether *Star Trek*'s (over)reliance on key lights to emphasize the Captain as hero or more recent series' preference for low-lit rooms and shadowed faces, often indicates who is being promoted as the scene's hero and who may be falling off a heroic pedestal.

CAMERA ANGLES

Just as the way a scene is illuminated presents gray heroes in a different light and emphasizes changes in the way audiences perceive them, so too do camera angles, especially close-ups, long shots or zoom outs, and tilts or pans up or down. Extreme close-ups direct the audience's attention to key details, such as a single tear or emotion-filled eyes. Perhaps one of the best examples in recent years is the series of *Lost*'s extreme close-ups on a character's eye during the opening moments of each Season One episode, an effect reprised during Season Six to help bring the story to its conclusion. This visual device indicates which character's backstory is featured in that episode and literally helps viewers see a scene through that character's eyes.

Giving a character a once-over visually, with the camera voyeuristically panning up and down a body, can emphasize attitude and costuming, as when *Torchwood*'s Captain Jack dons his trademark RAF coat before announcing "I'm back!" ("Children of Earth: Day Three").[8] The camera pans up and down his body as his colleagues look approvingly at Jack's change of costume back to "normal" clothing; the camera allows viewers to do the same.

Zooming out from a character may suggest his or her isolation or increasing Otherness; the audience is physically driven back — or the character removed from viewers' clear vision. Camera angles tilting up can indicate the character's superiority, increased stature, or dominant presence in the scene; tilting down toward characters make them seem smaller or less heroic.

Although camera movement should enhance and direct audience attention to the most important details in the scene to understand character or plot development, such movement shouldn't be so obvious that it becomes a distraction instead of a guide. "Swirling" camera movements, for example, usually indicate a significant change in a character's perspective or attitude, one to which audiences should pay attention. As with lighting and other visual and sound effects, the most successful effects layer the story with additional sensory information that helps audiences understand characters and their actions within the story. Often these layers are subtle or unobtrusive. They create a pleasingly whole entertainment, and audiences may not be consciously looking for things like a lighting effect. The audiovisual effects in many SF TV series are so well done now that they warrant further analysis; even lower-budgeted series' effects have improved to the point that they are usually only laughable when they want to be.

SOUND EFFECTS

SF TV fans can identify favorite heroes or villains by the sound effects surrounding their entrance into the episode. *Doctor Who*'s clanking Cybermen, menacingly marching in step as they invade Earth; *Battlestar Galactica*'s Centurions mindlessly intoning "By your command"; the squish of a stake piercing a soon-to-be-dust vampire; the wheeze of a materializing TARDIS — these are just a few aural cues that herald a change, usually the arrival of a dreaded villain or monster, or the hero as savior. These iconic sound effects not only provide a transition into the next scene, they increase viewers' emotional response to the story's visual elements. Like music, sound effects create the entire world in which heroes, villains, and monsters interact and add another layer of meaning (and analysis) to the TV text.

Creating Iconic Characters

A series' heroes and villains not only must be distinct from each other, they also must be unique in order to capture viewers' imagination. Their speech patterns, appearance, or costume may identify them with a genre (e.g., space Western) or a stereotype (e.g., silent loner or geeky scientific genius), but they have to offer something different or new in order to attract viewers and make fans. Each hero, villain, or monster in the series discussed in this book may share some characteristics with other SF TV characters or classic types, but they also have carved a distinctive identity within the pantheon of SF TV heroes. Symbolic elements of these characters and their unique spin on familiar types help audiences understand and accept gray heroes, especially when their actions sometimes make audiences uncomfortable.

WARDROBE OR COSTUME DESIGN

The hero's coat often replicates the superhero's cape; the hero's "uniform" consistently marks the character's social identity and place in the real world. Iconic characters, especially heroes, have distinctive clothing, even if they aren't superheroes typically associated with flashy outfits or rapid costume changes that indicate the shift from regular citizen to superhero.

During *Heroes'* first season, the newly discovered superheroes wear outfits that represent their "normal" role in society, but because these characters most often wear the same wardrobe when they perform heroic acts, their costumes identify them as Other — the superhero. Claire Bennet is a high school cheerleader; she wears a red-and-white cheerleading outfit first to indicate that she's a normal high school girl. As she tests her new superpower and saves people while she wears the cheerleader outfit, she becomes identified as a superhero cheerleader just as much as Wonder Woman is identified by her skintight spangles and cape. Similarly, Peter Petrelli's nurse uniform from Season One and his paramedic uniform in Season Four remind audiences of his normal role as a caretaker and healer; when he wears these real-world uniforms as he performs superhuman feats, these clothing choices become his superhero costume.

Other SF TV heroes choose clothing that reminds them of who they were when they were most heroic, or how they now want to be perceived by others. *Firefly's* Mal Reynolds wears his long brown duster from the Unification War, even though his side lost. SF TV fan-dubbed "Browncoats," like their hero Mal, persist in wearing the long coats as a sign of rebellion against authority and solidarity with their fictional hero. *Firefly's* Browncoats are Other from the authoritative repression of mainstream government; they are idealists or rebels who stand for different values.

Similarly, other characters favoring long coats include vampire Angel, whose dark coat is a modern interpretation of Dracula's cape, and *Torchwood*'s Captain Jack Harkness, who favors the World War II–era RAF coat representing his namesake, a real World War II hero, as well as the type of traditional, perhaps romantic hero he aspires to be. The Tenth Doctor also favors a long brown coat, as well as red Converse trainers, to create a comfortable costume that looks good when he runs toward danger or helps his friends escape. Other SF TV characters prefer a rougher, tougher image provided by leather. The Ninth Doctor, *Torchwood*'s Gwen, and Angel favor leather jackets/coats and seldom are seen on the job without them.

The buttoned down look masks other characters' deep emotions and Otherness beneath a proper, formal suit. The Tenth Doctor, despite his trainers and long coat, wears a blue or brown suit, more formal than his previous regenerated character's casual wear. *Torchwood*'s Ianto Jones is the poster child for elegant, if repressive, formal wear that belies his inner passion. Although these heroes may look like they blend in with society's Establishment, the costume choices simply show how effectively they can "play the game" while deceptively hiding their true nature.

Even regulation uniforms can indicate rank or profession, as *Battlestar Galactica*'s military and flight uniforms indicate characters' place in the social hierarchy and their changing roles. Kara Thrace, for example, often appears out of uniform or in a disheveled uniform, appropriate for her rebellion against authority even if she is well established as a military hero. Commander Bill Adama most often wears his buttoned-up uniform, so much so that when he appears in civilian clothes or less-than-perfect uniform, audiences take note of the reasons for changes in his character.

Clothes truly make the character, and the styles most often worn by SF TV heroes tell viewers a lot about their role in normal society and their heroic alter egos, as well as their personality quirks and values.

DISTINCTIVE SPEECH PATTERNS AND CATCHPHRASES

Iconic heroes and villains may have catchphrases that endear them to the public, such as the line of *Star Trek*'s iconic villain, Khan: "Revenge is a dish best served cold," or the enraged bellow toward him by *Star Trek*'s iconic hero, Kirk: "Khan!!!!"[9] Spock's "Live long and prosper" is probably one of *the* most popularized catchphrases in all SF, ranking with the cinematic "May the Force be with you" (*Star Wars*) and "To infinity and beyond!" (*Toy Story*). More recently, SF TV's catchphrases include Adama's motivational "So say we all!" or the Ninth Doctor's grinning "Fantastic!" both of which provide insights into the hero's outlook on life and rhetorical response to important plot points.

Accents also indicate what is familiar or Other about heroes and villains. For all that he's from a future in which English is likely very different from our modern dialects, whether British or American, Captain Jack speaks with an American accent. In one of his first *Doctor Who* appearances, he tests his knowledge of slang, recalling that in 21st century parlance, "bad" really means "good" ("Boom Town," 1.11[10]). In *Torchwood*, however, Jack seems completely in touch with American English of the 20th and 21st centuries. His accent marks him as Other in Cardiff, even though technically he has lived in England or Wales for more than a century. Similarly, the Ninth Doctor is notable as much for his Northern English accent, instead of a posh London sound; companion Rose's accent is more shopgirl from the council estates, for all that it's a London sound. *Firefly*'s Mal swears in Chinese, a reminder that Earth's future has far more Chinese than English speakers, and knowing Mandarin swear words would be common. These details not only mark characters' origins and their awareness of languages and cultures beyond their own, but they also indicate how these characters prefer to speak and how they want others to perceive them. They may choose to make particular phrases or accents their own in order to blend in with the locals or to stand out as Other — yet another mark of their difference as heroes.

DISTINCTIVE VEHICLES

No recent SF TV hero has a vehicle quite as distinctive as the Batmobile, but spaceships and Earthly transportation still indicate how easily or well heroes blend in (or want to be camouflaged from) the societies in which they're based or which they visit. The Doctor likes the idea that the TARDIS looks like a decades-old blue police box. Although it now is an anachronism on a British street corner, it represents the (fairly recent) historic past, as appropriate for a Time Lord, plus is so unobtrusive that passersby won't notice it. The Doctor likes the "hide in plain sight" feature of the TARDIS that fits with his preference for visiting the U.K. when he comes to Earth.

In contrast, Captain Jack likes to drive a black SUV (with Torchwood logo on the side) fast and furiously through Cardiff streets, sometimes with lights flashing. For all that Torchwood is supposed to be a secret organization, citizens easily identify the SUV at strange crime scenes or in pursuit of speeding Blowfish. Jack's vehicle of choice may be dark, with tinted windows so that people can't see inside, but the SUV is as flashy as its driver.

Captain Mal's *Serenity* may be patched and held together with hope as much as technology, but it too represents and matches its owner. It doesn't fit with newer models but is generally reliable and welcoming, despite its mileage. Whereas Mal relies on *Serenity* and cares for her, he doesn't exactly know how to handle certain problems or get the ship to do exactly as he wants all the time. Mal's relationship with "her" mirrors his relationships with most women: He doesn't always get the kind of response he expects or hopes for, or he inadvertently says or does something that causes a deeper problem. He doesn't know how to diagnose relationship needs any better than he knows how to diagnose *Serenity*'s mechanical needs. Fortunately, Kaylee helps Mal keep *Serenity* functioning as smoothly as possible, despite some temporary hiccups, just as Inara makes Mal aware of his missteps not only with her and her profession, but when he deals with Kaylee's occasional need to feel more traditionally "girly."

A character's vehicle can say a lot about the outward representation of the hero's personality and the way he or she wants the public to view comings and goings.

Distinctive Weapons

Perhaps more Freudian, but nonetheless an extension of the (traditionally male) hero or villain, is the character's favorite weapon. Sometimes a lightsaber is just a lightsaber, but the presence of technologically modified weaponry, anachronistic weapons, magic weapons, or, sometimes, malfunctioning technology all can give audiences insights into a character's psyche as well as ability to be an effective protector.

Hiro Nakamura delights in receiving a samurai sword, especially one once used by his childhood idol. *Heroes*' most traditional of superheroes appropriately prefers a sword when he must fight villains, a story arc played up during the first two seasons. Along the path of this hero's journey he receives and learns to use the weapon effectively before he can become a true hero. The sword even provides a way for the estranged father and son to bond. When Hiro's father teaches him how to wield the sword and explains that he may need to use it to kill his enemy, the son realizes the level of personal commitment he must make in becoming a hero or protector. When Hiro learns how to use the sword and demonstrates his sincerity in using his superpower to save others, the senior Nakamura expresses the rare gift of pride in his son ("Landslide," 1.11).[11]

The choice of weapon often represents the SF genre. Buffy, for example, prefers a stake; although anything sharp or pointy will do in a pinch, a vampire slayer traditionally uses a stake as standard equipment. The passivist Doctor doesn't carry a true weapon but uses a sonic screwdriver to help him get out of dangerous situations. As might be expected from a Time Lord with access to future technology, the modified screwdriver indicates that viewers can also solve their problems with creative thinking and everyday items rather than resorting to violence or big guns. As well, the idea that the Doctor, with a wealth of technology available to him, chooses only to modify the screwdriver's "sonic" capability provides comic relief in tense scenes.

Captain Jack likes the feel of a Webley, an appropriate if anachronistic firearm for the 21st century hero whose style seems stuck in the 1940s. He, too, might choose more exotic alien tech available in the Hub or even smuggled from the future before he becomes stuck in an Earthbound timeline. Nevertheless, Jack chooses a handgun that requires him to confront and fire on his enemies from close range instead of blasting them from afar. Such a gun also provides a sense of "fair play" because the humans he encounters don't have alien or futuristic firepower. Nevertheless, the Webley isn't going to help Jack fight aliens with advanced technology who fall through the Rift or invade Earth. Jack's weapon indicates his preference for face-to-face or one-on-one combat, a more "honorable" style of battle.

Finding the right weapon makes heroes unique; how they choose to defend themselves and protect others indicates the type of hero they are and how close or distant to their adversaries they prefer to be during a confrontation.

Thematic Concepts of Increasing Importance

As discussed in previous chapters, themes such as *home, immortality, religion, technology,* and *"humanness"* are increasingly important in the early 2000s, when technological advances seem at odds with creating a future utopia like that envisioned by Gene Roddenberry and embraced by 1960s SF TV programs. Instead, social and personal challenges mirror the world's chaotic ups and downs, and the fears and problems of TV audiences living through these upheavals. This section summarizes each concept and its overall importance to the development of SF characters and the significance of episodes' story arcs or the direction of an entire series, although certainly the previous discussions of these themes indicate why gray heroes emerge from and are defined by these concepts.

HOME TURF

Where gray heroes or villains live or work provides myriad clues about their true nature and relationship to society. Fantasy or SF heroes often have underground lairs, or, as Gwen cheerfully reminds a possible future Torchwood employee, the door behind her leads to "a super secret crime fighting base" ("Children of Earth: Day One").[12] Batman's bat cave has been the model for numerous heroes or superheroes, and the subterranean "lair" or hidden lab graces series like *Caprica, Lost, Heroes,* and *Torchwood.* The form may differ, but the look is surprisingly the same —from Zoe's holographic room to her father's secret at-home lab project (*Caprica*), from *Torchwood*'s multilayered Hub with its many labs and offices to the Company's hidden labs and detention centers (*Heroes*), and to *Lost*'s underground Hatch or within-cave temples. Hiding beneath the surface is an obvious metaphor for the secrets heroes or villains like to keep hidden from the public living above ground and in the open.

A more morbid variation on the subterranean lair is the vampire's crypt, grave, or coffin. For a few episodes, Spike favors living in a mausoleum — no better place for secret trysts with then-despondent, self-loathing vampire slayer Buffy. An evening's walk through the cemetery always produces the undead, who pop up from graves, sometimes to reminisce about high school with Buffy before she stakes them, adding more dust to their graves. In L.A., investigator Angel hides behind sunglasses when he ventures out in daylight, preferring to travel under cover of darkness. The children of the night live again in the darkness, whether they are villains or heroes.

Still other SF TV heroes take their homes with them as they travel from crisis to crisis. Their homes are as self-contained as the characters themselves. The Doctor's TARDIS, like his centuries-long adventurous life, is bigger on the inside than it first appears on the outside. Unfortunately for the *Galactica* and *Serenity* crews, their ships aren't nearly so accommodating. The aging spaceships need constant repairs, but they still provide a welcome home for these wanderers left homeless by circumstance and misfortune.

Isolation by being Other to normal society is typical for modern SF TV heroes, and their homes, whether hidden lair, ever-traveling spacecraft, or remote location ensures that these characters remain gray or Other simply by their choice of abode. *Lost*'s off-island settings (e.g., Sydney, London, New York, Seoul, L.A.) can be just as isolating as the difficult-to-find tropical island separating the castaways from the rest of the world.

Isolationist, hidden, underground, self-contained — these terms represent heroes or villains who fall into that gray middle ground. They may want to be part of "normal" society and attempt either to save it or force it to recognize them, but they will forever be Other — in part because of their homes and lifestyles.

As mentioned in Chapter 2, "home" as a concept changes with social upheavals, and in the first decade of the 2000s, homelessness arising from displacements and migrations generated by economic and environmental disasters certainly makes "home" a more important theme in SF.

SOCIAL ISSUES AND HOT TOPICS

Although the following subjects also are thematically important to series, they are more likely to be controversial or hot topics, and several characters may have different opinions about them. Whether different perspectives are provided through discussions by gray heroes or between gray heroes and villains, most acclaimed SF TV series debate social or political issues of concern to their audiences by making these sociopolitical topics of concern to series' characters, too.

Religion

Battlestar Galactica, especially in its early seasons, most prominently debated monotheism and polytheism, with the Cylons being monotheists, like most viewers, but the majority of human characters being polytheists. President Roslin explores scriptures and prophesies as one way of finding the promised land of Earth, dispatching Starbuck to find the arrow of Athena and then following other signs, which appear just as ordained by scripture, to guide the fleet toward their destination. Later, a resurrected Starbuck follows visions and perhaps divinely given information that ultimately help her lead the would-be colonists to a new home on a planet they call Earth. Whether focusing on one God or many, Battlestar Galactica's Cylon or human characters often invoke the spiritual as the basis of their philosophy, which leads not only to confrontations or alliances with their enemies but creates political divisions, like those often found on modern Earth, between leaders with opposing philosophies determined to choose a single, unified path for humanity.

Caprica, the prequel to Battlestar Galactica, also portrays rival families, the Adamas and the Graystones, as having different religious beliefs. The Adamas follow conservative, ritualized religious traditions, including wearing gloves during a time of mourning, but the Graystones seem not to follow any particular religious beliefs, although they must at least pay lip service to the predominant polytheism in their culture. Otherwise, rebellious teenaged daughter Zoe wouldn't be trying to escape to nearby planet Gemenon, where she plans to join others who share her belief in monotheism. Ironically, Zoe becomes the first Cylon — her human "essence" implanted in a robotic (Centurion model) body — and her devout monotheism likely is the reason why Battlestar Galactica's later Cylons believe in a single God.

An early review of the Caprica pilot praises the show's "willingness to tackle religion," among other social issues, and highlights the inclusion of "a religious school administrator with ties to the monotheistic cult Soldiers of the One, which is seducing teens on the technologically advanced planet Caprica."[13] Although other SF TV shows portray spirituality or philosophical issues in more general terms, Caprica and Battlestar Galactica directly involve religion as a divisive issue between heroes and villains.

Other series, such as Lost, couch religion in more general terms, although several characters represent specific religions: Sayid Jarrah/Muslim, Rose Henderson/Protestant Christian, Charlie Pace and Desmond Hume/Catholic. Jack Shephard, ostensibly the series' lead hero, is occasionally shown in a Christian church, such as in a flashback to his wedding or the series finale's last scene, but he doesn't talk about his religious beliefs. Instead, Jack is most often referred to as a "Man of Science" in the series' debate between men of science and men of faith. Jack's opposite, John Locke, believes in the island as his "god" and practices a more general spirituality. He is a "Man of Faith" who sometimes suffers crises of faith.

Whether tackling religion head on or allowing characters to peripherally discuss or show their spiritual faith, most SF TV series deal with religion or spirituality in at least some episodes.

Science and Technology

Another hot topic is the appropriate role of science or technology in current society. Questions like how much should humanity rely on technology often arise. Who should have access to the latest weapons or technological advancements in warfare, and how far should science go in prolonging life are typical starting points for many SF TV plots, and heroes or villains often are at the heart of the answers. In *Caprica*, for example, the Graystone family opposes the Adama family in regards to what role technology should play in keeping their children "alive." When each father loses a daughter to a terrorist attack, the Graystone patriarch finds a scientific way to "reconstruct" his daughter's spirit and memories as a computerized avatar; in effect, he brings his daughter back to life in a form he can see, touch, and converse with in a virtual environment. When the Adama patriarch sees the avatar of his daughter, he is at first amazed at this miracle but then horrified when his "dead" daughter freaks out upon realizing that she is only an avatar. He concludes that, despite his grief, science and technology have gone too far in keeping his daughter "alive," and he rejects the offer of having a virtual daughter in perpetuity (although, when he becomes a much darker hero, he reconsiders this offer).[14]

The discussion about reliance on technology is also important in *Lost* and *Firefly*, where advanced technology often isn't as available as the series' heroes would like, and the "bad guys" are more likely to have the latest technological gadgets, giving them a decided advantage. Whether the Others or the Alliance are the technologically advanced "villains," these series' heroes often have to make do with malfunctioning or limited technology.

Who has technology and what they should do with it are key social issues in most SF TV series, but these issues are most likely to provide plot points in *Lost, Heroes, Firefly, Battlestar Galactica, Caprica, Torchwood,* and *Doctor Who.*

Authoritative Institutions

Can a government be trusted? Do authoritative institutions have the right to "dictate" what happens to everyone? How much should Big Business become involved with government? Is globalization helpful or destructive to the lives of average citizens? Should gray heroes work for or against established institutions, such as governmental agencies or major corporations? These are just a few questions raised by *Heroes, Battlestar Galactica,* and *Torchwood,* in particular.

In *Heroes*, politician Nathan Petrelli alternates between trying to expose corruption and fighting for the citizens who elected him, and following his own agenda because he believes he knows what is best for everyone. The premise behind *Heroes* is that a group of wealthy capitalists banded together to create people with superpowers by manipulating genetics. Although this group originally seemed altruistic, their later machinations make their children question whether their parents are heroes or villains.

Battlestar Galactica creates a lead hero in Commander Adama but then shows that his judgment is sometimes clouded by his biases and conflicting loyalties. The military leader needs to be seen as objective and fair, but he is often influenced by his family and friends. With the revelation that key members of the human government and military are indeed "sleeper" Cylons, the question of whom should be trusted becomes critical to the survival of humanity.

Torchwood's "Children of Earth" is a damning criticism of global governments, with especially pointed commentary about U.K. and U.S. leaders. The "villains" include high ranking officials, and the gray heroes are among those being persecuted and marked for death.

Particularly in the early 2000s, when globalization is a hot topic and governments around the world are in chaos and facing changes, questions about who should ultimately make decisions affecting millions and whether those in power, whether economic or political, have the best interests of the masses at heart are going to be important subjects for episodes or story arcs. The role of gray heroes or villains in these stories may surprise some viewers, especially when the "good guys" aren't the ones with legitimate power.

What Makes Us Human?

Ultimately, all these issues lead to one key question at the heart of all SF TV hero stories: What makes us human? Follow-up questions might then include what should be preserved or saved, and what makes humanity worth saving? Gray heroes struggle with these issues, in part because, as they become darker characters, they may seem less human, even if they're trying to save humanity from itself or outside forces. As SF TV series become ever darker, some viewers might even question whether humanity is worth saving if villains or monsters have more power than heroes, and the institutions designed to help the most people are helmed by bureaucrats only looking out for their own interests.

When technology can "upgrade" human bodies to prolong life or bring back the dead, should such technology be made available to everyone, and, if that is a real option, what does it mean for the future of humanity? SF TV often questions whether robots, for example, can truly become sentient, and how much of the human body needs to be present and how much can be "robotic" before a person is no longer considered fully human. As technology increases and humanity relies ever more on science, SF TV likely will provide even more disturbing or enlightening plot developments to allow audiences to think of the ramifications of an increasingly technology-dependent society.

Although not every series discussed in this book covers each theme mentioned in this chapter or uses every storytelling device to provide greater meaning to discerning audiences, several elements previously discussed are used especially well in these series. The following chapters highlight the ways that heroes, villains, and monsters are revealed and portrayed in recent SF TV series, as well as what these hero stories reveal about global societies and their likely future.

Intertextuality and the Development of Hero Stories

SF TV series provide their fans with a wealth of additional texts—some canon, some sanctioned by networks but not considered "official"—that further develop the heroes, villains, and monsters featured in TV episodes and miniseries. These peripheral texts not only keep characters in the public eye during series' hiatus, but they also prolong characters' lives long after the TV series is over. The sheer volume of texts available to audiences who want to know more about characters or follow them on even more adventures—a result of marketing a successful series and reaping further revenue from it—has the added benefit of firmly positioning SF TV heroes within popular culture longer than the life of a series. Once a part of popular culture, with plenty of texts still circulating internationally, SF TV heroes, villains, and monsters stand a much better chance of having a continued influence within Western culture and of being cultural touchstones for generations of fans.

In addition to official or canon texts, fanfiction, fanart, and fan videos circulated online—everywhere from fans' websites dedicated to characters, pairings, or series to YouTube—further create a community of fans who generate their own adventures for the heroes, villains, and aliens (often monsters) initially shown on TV. As well, some authors or artists create original characters to interact with these well-known TV characters, thus further making a series' characters important to fans, although such original stories or characters placed into very different settings (e.g., alternate universes) may bear little resemblance to the original SF TV characters and the ways they were meant to be portrayed.

Other peripheral texts include information analyzing or discussing any possible production, character, story, or cultural elements of a series. Not only are popular culture analyses (such as this book) the stuff of which academic conference presentations and courses are made, but fan guides, SF conventions, personal appearances by cast or crew, blogs, podcasts, online forums and message boards, Twitter and Facebook posts, and all types of merchandise (e.g., action figures, posters, t-shirts) further the popularity of SF TV heroes and present hardcore fans with more knowledge, from the insightful to the trivial. The celebrity of actors, plethora of behind-the-scenes technical information, and access to creators, crew, and cast make hero "literature" a big business, as well as the latest way to make sure that stories of heroes, villains, and monsters survive well into the 21st century.

Whether canon, fanon, or peripheral analytical or anecdotal texts help spread the word about heroic or villainous SF TV characters, the variety of texts in multiple media keeps hero "literature" alive and relevant for young audiences as well as their elders. The following table indicates the prevalence of intertextuality among 21st century SF TV series. (From left to right, each grouping illustrates related types of information. TV episodes may lead to fanfiction and generate press releases, for example.)

Table 2. Intertextuality from Canon, Fanon, and Peripheral Texts

Canon and Official Texts	Fanon Texts	Peripheral Texts
TV episodes, including special event episodes (e.g., *Lost*'s summary episodes, *Doctor Who* Christmas specials) and miniseries, broadcast and later released on permanent media (e.g., DVDs)	Fanfiction (e.g., collective series' archives, individual authors' websites, contests)	PR/press releases, press packs, episode trailers, and other multimedia press information
Webisodes (e.g., those on network or official series' sites, such as those provided for *Lost* and *Battlestar Galactica*)	Fanart	Network marketing information
Movies (e.g., theatrical or released as standalone films on DVD, Blue-Ray, or other media)	Fan videos, music videos	Academic or other scholarly criticism and analysis in conference presentations and proceedings, journals, and books
Radio dramas (e.g., *Doctor Who*, *Torchwood*)	Transcripts of convention appearances	Television critics'/journalists' reviews and interviews
Soundtracks (e.g., *Lost*, *Serenity*, *Doctor Who*, *Torchwood*)	Blogs, commentaries, and episode guides	Concerts (e.g., *Doctor Who* proms)
Novels, paperbacks, children's books, and other printed stories	Unofficial series' wikis and Wikipedia entries	SF conventions (e.g., cast, creator, or crew panels, scholarly or fan panels)

Canon and Official Texts	Fanon Texts	Peripheral Texts
Official magazines (e.g., *Lost, Torchwood*)	Fanfiction (e.g., collective series' archives, individual authors' websites, contests)	PR/press releases
Comics and graphic novels (e.g., *Buffy, Angel, Doctor Who*)	Fanart	Network marketing information
Posters	Fan videos, music videos	Academic or other scholarly criticism and analysis in conference presentations and proceedings, journals, and books
Action figures or dolls	Transcripts of convention appearances	Television critics'/journalists' reviews and interviews
Games, puzzles, videogames, RPGs	Blogs, commentaries, and episode guides	Concerts (e.g., *Doctor Who* proms)

All series discussed in this book benefit from some, if not all, of these texts, and intertextuality is becoming increasingly important in disseminating cultural information about heroes, in particular, to the widest audience possible. The following chapters point out this intertextuality, as well as the most important elements and themes by which characters and stories are told and their grayness revealed.

Although the many elements useful to analyze and understand SF TV heroes, villains, or monsters can be applied to every series discussed in Part 2, only those elements that stand out as the best examples of a theme or that are especially helpful in understanding a character's development are emphasized. Intertextuality, for example, is a special strength of *Torchwood*'s development of Jack Harkness, although other series also provide a wealth of texts supplementing TV episodes. Monsters are a specialty of *Doctor Who*, and classic monsters and their modernization for post–2000 audiences are discussed in more detail than are monsters found in other SF TV series. Only those characters that provide particularly important or unique illustrations of gray heroes, villains, and monsters are emphasized in Part 2, as are the elements most useful in an interpretation of them. The elements introduced in this chapter should be further applied to each series discussed in Part 2, for every series carefully crafts its characters with these storytelling elements.

PART TWO

Introduction

"Sci-fi is sometimes just an excuse for dressed-up swashbuckling and kinky sex, but it can also provide a kit for examining the paradoxes and torments of what was once fondly referred to as the human condition.... Within the frequently messy sandbox of sci-fi fantasy, some of the most accomplished and suggestive intellectual play of the last century has taken place."[1]
— Margaret Atwood

The series and characters discussed in Part 2 certainly fit Atwood's description of SF TV in the early 2000s. Prolific Joss Whedon's series spanned the 1990s and ushered SF TV heroes, villains, and monsters into a new millennium. *Buffy the Vampire Slayer* stakes out new territory within the coming-of-age story and gives viewers charismatic heroes and villains long to be remembered. *Angel* brings audiences into the darkness but lets redeemed heroes see the light, and *Firefly* returns SF TV to its cowboy roots with an outlaw hero. From the past century to the present, Whedon's work often revives well-worn genres (including the musical) that make fans think as they join the chorus. With *Dr. Horrible's Sing-Along Blog*, the gray villain finally gets what's coming to him — but it isn't redemption or doom. Whedon's characters provide rich ancestor texts for the increasingly dark SF or fantasy prevalent on TV in the early 2000s.

Heroes and Hiro Nakamura make the superhero story mainstream once again. Although the many heroes depicted in this serial often waffle over whether to be heroic, a dark villain — Sylar — steals scenes as easily as specials' powers. Part Campbellian hero's journey, part morality play, part coming-of-age story, the often uneven nature of *Heroes* storytelling still allows individual heroes and villains to swap lives and explore each other's perspectives. They popularize hero literature and make it accessible to a wider audience.

Long-running, innovative, complex *Lost* introduces a "traditional" hero, then spends six seasons dissecting his life. Under the microscope, even the best intentioned hero's flaws are magnified. Series creators J.J. Abrams, Carlton Cuse, and Damon Lindelof throw in a mystical island, a smoke monster, conflicting groups spanning first decades and then centuries, time travel, flash-

131

forwards, flashbacks, flashsideways, and mythology-spanning literature, history, physics, religion, linguistics, architecture, and art. The result is mind-expanding SF TV with enough heroes, villains, and monsters to analyze for years to come.

Battlestar Galactica takes on the world's fear of coming apocalypse and turns it into wartime drama that likely will stand the test of time. Characters aren't as good — or as bad — as they think they are; they might not even be *who* or *what* they think they are. Once again, the "monsters" become some of the most intriguing characters, revealing more about the would-be heroes than viewers might expect. The prequel to this saga, the more recent series *Caprica*, illustrates how easily civilization can party all the way to self-destruction.

British series *Doctor Who* and *Torchwood* surprisingly gained so much popularity in the U.S. that early into the second decade of the 21st century TV networks planned their own American versions. The originals, however, especially under the auspices of Russell T. Davies, tweak SF TV by making even children's heroes deliciously darker. *Torchwood* initially suggests a definition of adult SF drama different from *Battlestar Galactica*'s, but its third season takes the SF TV hero so deeply into the darkness that some fans question if he can find his way back.

The subgenres of SF TV in these series not only indicate the ambiguity of gray heroes and villains but the many issues that change the way they — and audiences— think of protagonists and antagonists, heroes and villains. These are the best and most creative expressions of a pivotal decade in SF TV and the continuing development of the hero story.

6

The World
of Joss Whedon

One TV critic put it best: "Joss Whedon entered into the decade riding high on a *Buffy/Angel* cocktail. Though his name wasn't enough to overcome Fox's confusing treatment of *Firefly*, the show's eventual cult popularity led to the *Serenity* feature film, and the Whedon brand helped make *Dr. Horrible's Sing-Along Blog* an important moment for web-based content."[1]

Chronologically, a selective study of early 21st century SF TV heroes must start with *Buffy the Vampire Slayer* and continue with several Joss Whedon/Mutant Enemy creations: *Angel*, *Firefly*, and even *Dr. Horrible's Sing-Along Blog*. In many ways, each of these series represents heroes, villains, and monsters in clearcut terms. Good fights Evil. It's that simple. Just who wins, however, may surprise viewers, as each series grows progressively darker.

In the Whedonverse, who is willing and able to become a hero often defies two-dimensional thinking or traditional expectations. Whedon's heroes may be those socially identified Others most often categorized as "monsters": vampires, witches, demons. The motto of *Buffy* or *Angel* might as well be "You can't judge a vampire by his fangs." Some vampires becomes lead heroes; some waffle between Good and Evil as the plot shifts and circumstances change; some just like to prey on innocents (and usually end up being staked).

Especially in the Buffyverse, heroes fight Evil and serve as protectors, not only of their high school, suburb, or city, but, later, of their country and the world at large. While that mission seems black and white, the type and number of heroes vary, leading to an ever grayer middle ground from which new heroes are born. Lead hero Buffy Summers, the chosen slayer for her generation, initially seems to be the only one, but near the end of the series, many potential slayers come forth to be trained to do battle with Evil. Although the series officially begins in 1997 (an unaired pilot episode was made in 1996), by the early 2000s, Buffy needs help to battle the never-ending series of Big Bads. By that time, she no longer is in high school but has become a young adult faced with the responsibility of maintaining her home, making a living, guiding a younger sister, *and* being a slayer, when any one could be a full-time job. Buffy's changes mirror an increasingly chaotic real world and emphasize the need for more everyday heroes to step up to help the slayer. Her growth as a hero in many ways is a typical coming-of-age story following Campbell's developmental steps leading to the creation of a full-fledged hero.

Young female heroes following in Buffy's footsteps, including future slayers during the series' last season, believe in Buffy and often learn from her experiences, good or bad. *Buffy* also makes characters like *Heroes'* Claire Bennet possible and easily compared with the slayer (e.g., high school Buffy and Claire both struggle with "normal" school activities versus their "abnormal" roles as protectors). In later seasons, each takes on increasingly adult burdens, including the death of a parent and the first year of university. Both heroes die and come back to life.

Along the way, they also experience typical coming-of-age epiphanies, such as exploring their sexuality as they date men (and, in Claire's case, a woman — perhaps a nod to *Buffy*'s Willow-Tara relationship). Although Claire isn't a Buffy clone, her development as an SF TV hero in many ways parallels Buffy's and continues the strong-teen-as-hero role model particularly important to young female viewers. Without Buffy first becoming a role model for other young women — on TV and in real life — characters like Claire wouldn't be as likely.

Although *Buffy* as a series becomes grayer over the years, culminating in the destruction of Sunnydale (accompanied by the news that a new Hellmouth has opened in Cleveland), it generally sticks with the Good versus Evil battles. The series' teenaged characters become darker as they lose their youthful innocence (such as Buffy's dalliance with Spike and period of low self-esteem or depression arising from adult responsibilities, including working a dead-end fast-food job).

Throughout the series, Good and Evil are clearly differentiated, and even Angel's or Spike's struggles for redemption portray the vampires on a progression from one extreme to the other. Their journeys toward regaining their respective souls are agonizingly documented in lengthy story arcs. The stakes get higher as Evil becomes progressively more powerful, and both *Buffy* and *Angel* conclude with the heroes' realization that, at best, they can only slow down Evil, no matter what they do.

In the later, Western-themed *Firefly*, Good and Evil still most often work opposite sides of the street, but the series' "good guys" are far from traditional heroes. Instead, they are gray Others working on the fringes of society. Mal Reynolds may not even want to do what is right and, like a villain, often chooses to look out only for himself. During many episodes, however, he faces a moral dilemma along the lines of the following:

Choice 1: Make money stealing back his client's property from a train's supply run — no questions asked.

Choice 2: Steal his client's property, but then return the goods because they include medicine needed by innocents, and face the client's anger.

Here is another moral dilemma to test Mal's conscience:

Choice 1: Carry on board his ship fugitives who can pay a hefty fee. Dump them the moment they cause trouble or can't pay for the ride.

Choice 2: Hide on his ship a young woman tortured by the authoritarian interplanetary Alliance and the brother who freed her, even when they cause trouble or no longer can pay cash.

Despite his initial decision to go with Choice 1, Mal changes his mind and eventually goes with Choice 2. His initial response matches that of a gray character indecisively poised between the extremes of Hero and Villain, but his shift to the second, revised plan turns him into a hero.

Firefly's characters may seem more "normal" than vampire slayers, witches, or demons presented in a fantastical setting. They live within the bounds of two well-established genres: the Western, with roots to real-world U.S. history, and the Space Drama, which also has ties to TV Westerns. Captain Mal is both a war veteran and a spaceship captain, TV roles with which more viewers have experience. The good guys of *Firefly* consist of just about every TV Western stereotype imaginable. These Others band together and deal daily with moral ambiguities as they figure out how to survive. They inadvertently become heroes when they make decisions that reflect the Judeo-Christian morality of their audience, although they usually are reluctant heroes.

Like spaceship captains before him, Mal traverses the 'verse, encountering new or recurring villains, dealing with the weekly episodic conflict, and then heading thataway into the starry unknown. Unlike less morally ambiguous space captains before him, Mal is far more self-interested and monetarily minded. His adventures are all about living another day and making ends meet. Only after a more harrowing adventure with a decided battle between Good and Evil, as told in the movie *Serenity*, does Mal vow to become more of a heroic avenger, although the Alliance he plans to subvert would consider him nothing more than a terrorist.

Firefly's conclusion with the movie *Serenity* doesn't provide a happy ending for all characters fans have come to know and love. Nevertheless, at least some characters find their happily ever after (or are at least looking that way at the end of the movie). Mal's story, in contrast, is left ambiguous at the movie's conclusion. In some ways, Captain Mal Reynolds is one of Whedon's grayest characters because he is consistently ambivalent about being "good"; his actions are based on what he deems is the correct course of action at the time, but he doesn't go out of his way to perform public good deeds. Whedon once described how he likes to write the character, as well as "happy endings": "People love a happy ending. So every episode I will explain once again that I don't like people. And then Mal will shoot someone. Someone we like. And their puppy."[2]

Perhaps Whedon's tongue-in-cheek view of heroes, villains, and monsters indicates the further graying of once-traditional heroes as a type. He more effectively ends the decade-long shift toward less good heroes and less bad villains with *Dr. Horrible's Sing-Along Blog* (much more so than with the 2010-canceled *Dollhouse*).

Even though Dr. Horrible seems benign enough at the beginning of his story, by the end of the short Internet series, viewers realize that he really is working for Evil and, for all his young lover's angst and cute awkwardness, can help destroy society. More telling is Captain Hammer, the supposed hero, who does good deeds only to further his own agenda, knows how to play the hero to win (and bed) the virginal "good girl," and abandons his role as protector when he gets hurt.

Dr. Horrible becomes a successful parody because it not only skewers traditional depictions of heroes and villains but because it plays off Whedon's own previous hero-villain-monster series. *Buffy* and *Firefly* alum Nathan Fillion is cast as Captain Hammer, a gray hero apparently averaged from his Big Bad role as Caleb on *Buffy* and his morally ambiguous but generally heroic Captain Mal from *Firefly*. Whereas Caleb is a defrocked priest and serial killer who serves as the right hand of the First Evil (*Buffy*'s ultimate villain/monster), Mal fights the Good Fight when he believes in a cause and tries to protect his friends. Captain Hammer knows the difference between society-defined right and wrong, but he also knows that his celebrity image will help him get away with being self-centered and bullying. He is a surface hero who isn't noble or even all that effective when confronted with well-organized evil.

The following sections highlight key aspects of *Buffy the Vampire Slayer*, *Angel*, *Firefly*, and *Dr. Horrible's Sing-Along Blog*. This chapter describes a few key aspects of Whedon's series that reflect the trend away from traditional SF TV (and now web) heroes or villains to ever grayer characters hovering in the middle of the continuum of Good and Evil.

The Continuing Influence of Buffy

Repeated themes of darkness, Otherness, and an undead/below-the-surface society permeate the world of Whedon. Most spectacularly, *Buffy the Vampire Slayer*, based on a less-than-successful film, elevates the "girl hero" to new heights. Buffy Summers (Sarah Michelle Gellar) surpasses the blonde teen stereotype to present a young woman who matures from high school vampire slayer to seasoned mentor for the next generation of slayers; from a child cared for by her mother and surrogate father/mentor/minder Rupert Giles (Anthony Head) to a mother figure caring for her sister Dawn (Michelle Trachtenburg) and the world at large; from a lovelorn good girl pining after the bad boy vamp who becomes her guardian Angel to the independent woman who doesn't want to be "cookie dough" molded by any man, living or dead. Buffy traverses heaven and hell, dies and rises again to become as much role model as savior to a world literally going to hell.

Buffy, like Whedon's other heroes, including redeemed but soulless Angel (David Boreanaz), evil incarnate turned redeemed-with-a-soul Spike (James Marsters), and war vet of the losing side/mercenary out for himself Mal Reynolds (Nathan Fillion), learns that it takes everyone working together (e.g., Scoobies, dead/undead sidekicks, or a shipload of misfits) to make humanity more human and save the world for just a few more hours. Along the way, these heroes sacrifice those they love — including themselves — to do what they believe is right, which usually means fighting demons of some sort.

For Buffy and, later, Angel, demons take physical form but also represent all of a community's parasitic ills that destroy individuals and, collectively, whole societies. Evil comes back; the villains are literally monsters with far more power and desire to wreak havoc than mere mortals can muster in defense or retaliation. This premise sets the tone for Whedon's later series and paves the way for even darker SF TV heroes later in the decade.

Once More, with Feeling

Even people who have never seen a *Buffy* episode have likely heard about Whedon's foray into musicals with the highly publicized episode and now cult favorite "Once More, with Feeling" (6.7).[3] Although not a typical *Buffy* episode, the well-established format of the musical focuses audience attention on individual lines of dialogue as well as the choreographed relationships of the principal characters. In true Whedon fashion, the joy inherent in most musicals is present in "Once More, with Feeling," but it is twisted into resurrection angst for hero Buffy. Unlike a traditional musical's definitive, and usually uplifting, final number, "Once More, with Feeling" asks "Where Do We Go from Here?" and turns a kiss between young lovers into a foreshadowing of something much darker and dangerous.

Even the title, a trite directorial command to the "actors" in the theater of Buffy's life, reminds viewers that Buffy has been forced back into the turmoil of mortality and away from any peace she may have found in death. The title also feeds into the episode's plot: Buffy, like many other characters featured in this episode, has trouble understanding or expressing her feelings. She is simply going through the motions of being a hero. She doesn't feel any connection to her old, heroic life now that she has been brought back from the dead. Other characters, including Giles and Willow's lover, Tara, also struggle with their feelings in this episode. Giles plans to return overseas so that Buffy will be forced to make decisions on her own; he fears she has grown dependent on him. Tara plans to break up with Willow after learning that a magical spell renders her unable to remember their argument.

Ironically, the dead (or undead) Spike advises Buffy to keep on living because that's all she can do. Buffy's death and resurrection provide her common ground with Spike, who remembers his death and rebirth as a vampire. Hero Buffy learns from once-villain Spike how to live again after surviving death. This experience provides the pair with common ground and forges a strange relationship that changes both characters.

Like many musicals, this one ends in a kiss. Spike and Buffy kiss, their relationship obviously changing, as is the nature of the villain and hero. Spike gradually becomes more heroic and struggles to regain his soul as a result of Buffy's influence on him. Buffy acknowledges her feelings for Spike and later takes a multi-episode trip to the Darker Side as they develop an awkward sexual relationship (including an attempted rape). The kiss to conclude the musical blends the positive and negative aspects of these characters, but their union is far from easy or pleasant. In Whedonesque fashion, they don't get a happy ending down the line and at the end of "Once More, with Feeling" can only join the chorus asking "Where Do We Go from Here?"

Another important plot development is Buffy's friends' realization that they may have yanked her from Heaven, not Hell, as they believed when they brought her back. Buffy's resurrection doesn't reassure or save her followers; it fills them with remorse and self-recrimination. It also makes them aware that Buffy might not want to be their slayer/savior or even to remain with them. Unlike a Christ-like savior whose return prompts followers to rejoice and find faith in the risen hero, Buffy's return forces her followers to re-examine their motives for wanting her back. Do they want their friend Buffy because they can't stand to be parted from her? Or do they need their leader or slayer/savior to help them fight Evil because they don't want to take that responsibility on their own? Do they need to prove how powerful they are (e.g., a magical Willow out of control) by being able to resurrect her?

The resurrected Buffy not only faces the struggles of her former life, she also loses her status as "the one" — the slayer chosen for her generation. With her death, a new slayer has been activated, and Buffy is no longer the exclusive slayer/savior. As a hero, she loses her unique edge, reminding the Scoobies and fans that every hero can be replaced or is in vogue for just a little while. Buffy may share "resurrected hero" status with literary characters or religious icons, but her resulting reality isn't joyous or exalted. Buffy sings in a minor key as she reports she thinks she was in heaven but now is back in hell — or at least in the Hellmouth.

Although Buffy is the focal point of "Once More, with Feeling," she struggles with her role as a hero. The lyrics of her first song illustrate how lost the slayer has become. As she meanders through a cemetery and slays vamps or demons while she sings, she admits that she is not nearly as enthusiastic about her "job" now that she has returned from the dead. She agrees with the popular assessment that, in the past, she has acted bravely and been a kick-ass hero, but her commitment to being a slayer isn't as strong as it once was. Even the undead demons providing backup vocals see the change and harmonize that she seems to be going through the motions.[4] The opening song in this musical sets the tone for the rest of the episode. From this moment through the ending chorus of "Where Do We Go from Here?" Buffy questions her role as a hero but not knowing what else to do if she doesn't continue being a slayer. The conventions of a musical allow characters to share the thoughts and feelings usually bottled up inside; music frees them to be honest with themselves and each other.

When Buffy is honest with herself at this point in the story, she is dissatisfied with her life and poised to try something new — not necessarily something good or heroic. Despite her uncertainty about being a slayer, she continues to play this role, eventually returning to a Campbellian hero during the final season. After purging herself of doubts and darkness, Buffy becomes a mentor to other girls chosen to be slayers. She influences a generation of young women internationally — very much like *Buffy the Vampire Slayer* has successfully done for more than fifteen years.

Angel

In a TV spinoff starring a vampire hero with a soul (who loses and regains it four times by the end of the series), dialogue about whether the hero is really a villain or a monster is expected, even within a single scene. In "That Old Gang of Mine" (3.3)[5], Angel, Charles Gunn (J. August Richards), Wesley Wyndham-Price (Alexis Denisof), and Winfred (Fred) Burkle (Amy Acker) are surrounded by members of Gunn's old gang, now armed with stakes and crossbows. The vigilantes are on a mission to kill demons, vampires, and other monsters that prey on society. Gunn, once one of their gang, now works with Angel and is forced to decide which side he is on.

Very traditionally, the scene doesn't allow any shades of gray in side-choosing. As defined by the crossbow-wielding leader of the avengers, a newcomer named Gio, Gunn is either on the side of Good (the gang) or Evil (Team Angel, the series' heroes). Choosing human vampire hunters over a vampire might seem to be the logical decision, but *Angel* fans know that, in this series, the titular vampire is the hero. Having horns or fangs in the Buffyverse isn't necessarily a mark of Evil. Defining Good or Evil by appearance alone causes a problem in Whedon's world of gray heroes, villains, and monsters; the limited choices of two clearly defined moral sides are a few options short of the characters' reality.

During the confrontation in "That Old Gang of Mine," the range of the Heroes-Monsters scale seems very wide indeed in regard to past or current Angel/Angelus. Each character defines Angel differently, as revealed in their dialogue:

> WESLEY: He's a vampire with a soul.... When he did his pleasure killing, he had no soul. Can you say the same? (he asks Gio).
> ANGEL: This is what I am. Deal with it or don't. (Angel then vamps out, looking monstrous indeed.)

GUNN, SPEAKING TO GIO: He can never be my friend on account of what he is.... It's
  about the mission [to rid the world of Evil]. He's got it, and you don't.
GIO: He's a monster, and I kill monsters. That's what I do.

Gio then offers escape from the monster-killing spree he plans to anyone
who wants to leave. The only catch is that that person must kill Angel before
leaving. The "good guy" vigilante asks an innocent to do the deed, removing
himself from killing the series' lead hero.

This scene illustrates the grayness of the Whedonverse. Angel is now a
hero, although in the past he has been a monster/villain. Gunn works with
Angel in order to save innocents from monstrous predators, but he can never
consider Angel as less than a monster because of what he technically will always
be — a vampire. Wesley's definition of hero or monster hinges on morality; a
person/vampire with a soul can make a decision whether to kill. Angelus the
monster enjoyed a good murder spree and was a monstrous force without
morality; the soulful Angel may kill to protect others, but he doesn't enjoy or
glorify the death. His soul allows him the ability to make moral decisions and
the desire to do so. Without a soul (or the ability to want one), Angel would
never be able to be a hero, according to this definition, which probably is the
one most viewers accept.

Interestingly enough, Angel doesn't argue that he is either hero or monster.
He simply is who he is, whether he vamps out and looks menacing or seems
just like the handsome guy next door. Whether he looks like a vampire, fangs
bared, or a casual businessman, Angel acts the same. His ability to be a hero
isn't based on what he is or how he looks. After all, the slick personnel of law
firm Wolfram & Hart may not look like demons or minions, but they know
how to appease their immoral clientele. When Angel goes to work for the firm,
he struggles to remain a more-or-less moral hero within an immoral environment. He becomes the embodiment of a gray hero, a contrast from his villainous, even monstrous past, as well as from the embodiments of Evil within
Wolfram & Hart.

In previous centuries Angelus once was one of the true monsters, a vampire
so bloody that even neophyte sociopath vampire Spike, during his own killing
days, looked to Angelus for inspiration. With the monster's shift to become
more heroic, a gray hero progressively more sacrificial and good, if more self-
doubting, as time goes on, Angelus becomes Angel. This avenging Angel can
never live down his past, especially in the long-lived vampire/demon community, but his transformation to an increasingly less gray hero forces viewers
(and a huge number of fans, even years after the series' end) to decide exactly
how they wish to define heroes, villains, or monsters.

As a Los Angeles detective keeping an eye on the often-menacing activities
of Wolfram & Hart, Angel protects innocents and tries to steer lost souls in the
right direction. His guilt over his actions as Angelus makes him a moral hero
once he regains his soul; he can't make amends for the horrors committed in

earlier centuries, but he can do what he feels is right as a moral hero in the current time period. Angelus is lurking beneath the surface, however, and Angel always must keep rein on the dark side of his personality. Because of his past, which many fans feel is redeemed by his present, and the potentially demonic side to his personality, Angel automatically is a gray hero, if one who becomes more complex but also more sympathetic in his own TV show.

Just as *Torchwood* is described as a "*Doctor Who* for adults," so *SFX* heralded *Angel* as a "*Buffy* for adults." In its description of the Top 10 TV Series of the Decade, the magazine aptly summarized Angel's role as a gray hero. He provides "a darker undercurrent to Sunnydale's external brightness. While Buffy struggled to find her place in the world, blindly lurching from fight to fight and crisis to crisis, Angel already knew his place. He was simply trying to justify it."[6] In the series' finale, Angel bravely leads a small band of loyal followers to a battle to the (likely real) death with Evil, in the form of Wolfram & Hart's Senior Partners, whose Earthly representatives plotting the apocalypse have just been destroyed by Angel and his associates. With this final act and his "just do it" attitude toward attacking Evil, Angel's last line is "Let's get to work" ("Not Fade Away," 5.22).[7] With that statement and the series' fade-out, fans understand just how heroic this redeemed vampire has become.

Viewers' final image of SF TV hero Angel takes place in the moment before he, accompanied by his surviving colleagues, including vampire Spike, faces the biggest Big Bad ever — with the clear expectation of ultimate destruction. (He previously advises his friends to live this day as if it were their last, which for many, if not all, becomes prophetic.) Nevertheless, Angel accepts his likely self-sacrifice, and the sacrifice of all he's built to fight Evil, and steps forward to do battle. In this sense, Angel becomes a traditional hero: Evil needs to be stopped. Good fights the good fight, no matter what. Ergo, Angel willingly steps up, even if it means his final death.

Firefly

After creating the Buffyverse, Whedon wanted to make a modern story set in space, one that would feel contemporary but be different from what he'd done before. The result is the creative space Western *Firefly*. Although the series only lasted 14 episodes and a full-length film, it has developed a devoted fan following and established *Firefly* as one of the best SF TV series of the early 2000s. As is typical of SF TV heroes whose stories remain popular (via DVD and rebroadcast) long after their series ends, *Firefly*'s gray hero, Captain Mal Reynolds, will be long remembered in popular culture as well as "hero literature." When the series' DVDs were first released, Whedon noted that "the fact the DVDs will be out there forever is very important ... It's some of the most important work I might ever do. Maybe not the most popular, but it's catching on. Even on the internet our following has increased since it was cancelled, which is bittersweet, but with a lot of sweet."[8]

In a decade's-end review of one of the best SF movies of the early 2000s, *SFX* praised hero Mal Reynolds' response to *Serenity*'s main villain, a man so focused on being an executioner for the 'verse-governing Alliance that he seems more like an unstoppable monster than a human. When the villain tells Mal that he is unarmed, the film's "hero" says "Good" and promptly shoots him in the chest. Of course, the villain also wears body armor and immediately gets up to fight again. Nevertheless, *SFX* enthused, "That's still the kind of captain we'd want leading us through *Serenity*'s Wild West universe."[9]

Apparently plenty of fans feel the same way. Nearly a decade after *Firefly* briefly graced Fox's schedule, Browncoats still gather to celebrate the exploits of Captain Mal, the series' hero. They dress in the famed long brown duster worn by their hero; both coat and character have become cult favorites. Even in the Halloween 2009 episode ("Vampire Weekend," 2.6) of Fillion's series *Castle* he dresses in the fabled brown coat, as well as the rest of Mal's typical outfit, thinking it very cool as a holiday costume. He is told, however, that the look is "so five years ago." Fillion and *Firefly* fans loved this shout-out to a lasting SF TV hero and his trademark costume.[10]

SF TV heroes often are compared either with *Star Trek* or *Star Wars* characters, and Fillion's Captain Mal is no exception. In a roundup of the decade's best SF series, one critic dubbed Mal as "a Han Solo ripoff" while declaring *Firefly* one of the best series of the decade to be unceremoniously canceled before its time.[11] Another end-of-decade reviewer furthered the *Star Wars* comparison, citing Reynolds as "a more three-dimensional version of Han Solo. He carries a lot of baggage, and even though I get the impression that sometimes he resents it, he always does the right thing. He also has great dialogue."[12] Captain Mal, like many infamous gray captains before and after him, wins fans and critical acclaim because he is a hero with an attitude. His self-deprecatory, sly, dry comments make him the kind of pragmatic hero that fans want to emulate; they like his wit in assessing people and situations. He can be heroic, if necessary, but he prefers to keep himself and his crew safe, if at all possible.

Even years after *Firefly*'s cancellation, and despite the fact that the series lasted only a few episodes (not all of them even broadcast by Fox), this space Western remains a favorite because of Captain Mal and his dedicated, if often contentious, crew. Mal remains a hero because of his grayness. He is Other from the Alliance-governed future society and lives on the fringes of society. His politics aside, he retains many rough edges of the American frontier outlaw or cowboy and seldom plays by society's rules, even when he knows them. As he succinctly states in the pilot episode, "Governments [get] in a man's way" ("Serenity," 1.1).[13] During an interview shortly before *Firefly*'s debut, Fillion described Mal as "an atypical hero" who is the hero only "by default, because he's the captain of the ship. He doesn't have grand plans or a vision; Mal's idea of grand plans involve today, tomorrow and maybe the next day. He's not about 'Let's save this planet'; he's about 'Let's save our [skins].'"[14]

Yet by the end of the 2005 follow-up film, *Serenity*, Mal re-dedicates himself to helping others and going against the Alliance as much as possible, because he believes that they perform evil deeds in the misguided assumption that they are making citizens "better." Two recurring examples of the Alliance's meddling with humanity involve River Tam and the Reavers.

River (Summer Glau) slowly regains her humanity after the youthful genius is held against her will and trained as a government assassin. Mentally wounded, the volatile young woman is rescued by her brother, Simon (Sean Maher), a talented physician who gives up a life of ease and prestige to save his sister. At first, Mal only keeps the pair onboard because they pay what he asks, but later he accepts them into his crew and "family." By the end of *Serenity*, a more mentally stable River takes her place as Mal's co-pilot. He accepts her as yet another soldier/victim of the Alliance, and although their "war" experiences differ, they both have ample reason to use their battle skills against the oppressive interplanetary government.

Mal plans to continue to work against the Alliance, despite their being the 'verse's governing authority. The agency often fails to act morally, and Mal gains hero status by openly opposing them with his actions. By the film's conclusion, he seems more dedicated to a "cause" — beating the Alliance — than to making a living as a smuggler/mercenary who likes going against the Alliance only if it doesn't interfere with his livelihood.

In part, Mal's renewed dedication against the Alliance stems from his war experience and his growing respect for the Tams, but the loss of two friends during *Serenity* deepens his resolve to work against the legal authority. As well, he has seen yet again first hand how the Alliance's attempts to "improve" people only end up killing them.

The series' "monsters," the Reavers, are described in the short-lived series' mythology as demonic humanoid creatures who kill and cannibalize their enemies. They ruthlessly attack anyone nearing their home turf on the fringes of the 'verse, and horror stories of their actions increase their notoriety. They are the stuff of nightmares and cautionary warnings.

Mal discovers, however, that the Reavers also are victims of governmental actions. They become "monsters" because of a drugged water supply that makes citizens go mad. The Reavers don't choose to become monsters; they accidentally become that way, and the Alliance covers its tracks with misinformation and denials. On the surface, the Alliance maintains propriety and enforces social mores, but in reality their actions often create misery, oppression, and death. At the end of the film, Mal promises, "No more runnin'; I aim to misbehave."[15]

Like Han Solo, who also turns from self-interested smuggler into political (anti-)hero, Mal Reynolds is a diamond in the rough. His roughness makes him seem rude or uncouth, especially when dealing with Inara Serra (Morena

Baccarin) or Kaylee Frye (Jewel Staite). Undoubtedly attracted to Inara and, later in the series, quite protective of her, he nonetheless has difficulty overcoming his prejudice that she is a professional Companion, despite her superior education and manners. Her career goes against Mal's sense of morality, even though he clearly runs his life by situational ethics. Kaylee is such a free-spirited "tomboy" that Mal has a tough time taking her seriously when she tries to adopt more social graces and become more "ladylike."

In one episode he rebuffs Kaylee's efforts to find a party dress for an important dance, and he laughs at her choice of attire. Kaylee thinks a dress that looks more like a Little Bo Peep costume than slinky evening wear is the height of fashion. A snickering Mal derides her choice, calling Kaylee "an upright sheep" ("Shindig," 1.4).[16] Because he sees her more as a mechanic and plainspeaking comrade, he doesn't understand that he hurts her feelings by laughing at her efforts to take on a more acceptable social role, perhaps because Mal feels no personal need to be socially acceptable. In many ways Mal relies on his crew to help "socialize" him because his experiences and personality have made him feel like an outcast from proper society for so long.

Nevertheless, Mal's growing affection for Inara and his loyalty to his crew often cause him to go against his need for self-preservation. When Inara attends a formal dance during one planetary visit, she and Mal both are "working." She is paid to be a courtesan to a wealthy businessman, and Mal is attending the "Shindig" (1.4) as part of his cover for a smuggling job. He won't admit his displeasure at seeing Inara with her client, even as he is trying to get a job from a client of his own. He insults her partner and insists on dancing with her, but when Inara's client cuts in because "money changed hands" and he wants what he paid for, Mal feels obligated to hit the man for insulting Inara's honor. Although Mal maintains a double standard about the acceptability of Inara's profession, he doesn't want anyone else to think of her as less than a lady. His misunderstanding of local culture, however, forces him into a duel to the death as a result of striking a man from the aristocracy.

Inara herself is confused by the discrepancy between Mal's private attitude toward her profession and his very public action to defend her honor. Mal, however, sees no such dissonance. To him, the client insulted Inara, not her profession, whereas Mal favors Inara but doesn't like what she does for a living. He berates her job, not her. Mal's code of ethics requires him to defend his friend, no matter the circumstance, even when that inadvertently can lead to his death, for Mal is no expert at fencing, and a duel seems to be a death sentence for him. Nonetheless, he refuses Inara's offer to help him escape and chooses to fight honorably instead of running away as a coward. These actions clearly illustrate Mal's definition of what it means to be a respectable man, if not exactly a hero, even if his reasoning seems convoluted to Inara.

As expected, Mal is wounded and disarmed in the duel, but Inara steps in to offer to stay with her client if he'll spare Mal's life. Her willingness to "sacrifice" herself for Mal may seem a heroic act to some in the audience, and her heroism provides Mal with yet another opportunity to seem even more traditionally heroic himself. While the client is thus distracted by Inara's offer, Mal takes control of the duel, taking his opponent's weapon and wounding him. He won't kill the man, as social custom dictates, but he is satisfied with humiliating him. Once again, Mal's definition of appropriate behavior may surprise viewers who have seen him shoot villains without hesitation.

Inara further wounds her former client professionally by telling him that his conduct will have him censured from the Companion registry. Socially, the tables are turned, and the "outlaw" and the "whore" gain the local society's approval, as well as the audience's. Mal seems heroic in standing up for Inara and agreeing to participate in the duel, but he also, once again, doesn't play completely fair. He turns the tables on his opponent while he is distracted, certainly a pragmatic action to save himself. Mal doesn't "win" on his own; he takes advantage of the distraction Inara provides. As in other episodes, he isn't a "proud" fighter. He exploits any advantage he can get. Once in control of the duel, Mal spares his opponent's life, seeing no need to eliminate the threat, although Mal has no qualms about killing those who pose a deadly threat to him or his crew.

Instead of following a consistent set of moral imperatives, Mal acts by what he feels is right at the time, although he insists that his actions are always in line with his core values, which usually differ from the Alliance's or local laws. Mal is the anti-hero who does what is right when social mores are morally wrong; he believes that taking the law into his own hands is the morally right action when the Alliance is corrupt and fails to protect many of its citizens (including River Tam, who has been held captive, tortured, and trained to be an assassin by the Alliance).

From the very first, Mal often displays contradictory traits—or what he does contradicts what he says he believes. For example, he professes to be interested only in making a living, preferably while thwarting the Alliance running the 'verse. His preferred profession is smuggling, although he has the combat skills to be even more mercenary, if he chooses. An ideal job, then, would be a way to make money while stealing from the Alliance.

In "The Train Job" (1.2), Mal agrees to a contract that seems beneficial to his crooked employer and himself.[17] Working for harsh client Adelei Niska, Mal agrees to steal the Alliance cargo on a train, only to learn that it is medicine to be delivered to a town. Mal and Zoe have trouble both in stealing the cargo first and then, after they identify the cargo, returning it without becoming incarcerated. Even when Mal believes they've done the right thing in making sure the town gets the medicine, he still must face his unhappy client, who is known for brutally dealing with anyone who crosses him.

When he doesn't receive his cargo, Niska sends two henchmen to deal with Mal. The captain and crew viciously battle Niska's men, but Mal tries to reason first with one, then the other, after their capture. The first refuses Mal's offer to return the client's money and stay out of his way in the future. When that "negotiation" doesn't work, Mal simply kills the man by dumping him into the ship's engine intake. The second henchman quickly agrees to Mal's plan, takes the money, and is allowed to leave.

Even when Mal does the "honorable" deed of ensuring that a town receives its badly needed medicine, he still is less than heroic throughout the episode. He is a willing thief, especially when he thinks that he's getting paid to steal from the Alliance. He lies in order to steal the cargo and then, when the job is botched, to get out of trouble. He kills a man, although that henchman has tried to kill him and his crew for going back on his deal with Niska. As a Western or space-age "hero," Mal seems to have a pragmatic honesty and more self-interest than willingness to help others without being paid. His primary motivation — money — takes a lower priority when his sense of "right-ness" kicks in, but he doesn't believe in absolutes like no killing, no stealing, no lying.

Although this episode was meant to be the second in the series, Fox broad-cast it first, before the pilot "Serenity" (1.1). Thus, audience's introduction to the series' "hero" comes from Mal's actions in "The Train Job." From the first moments viewers meet Captain Mal Reynolds he is a gray hero, and it takes several episodes for viewers to see the depth of Mal's loyalty to his crew and his willingness to fight for innocents.

That loyalty is shown in detail in a brutal episode, "War Stories" (1.10).[18] Zoe shares a long history of battle, and the resulting camaraderie among soldiers at arms, with Captain Mal. Although Zoe's husband, Wash, knows that she loves him (and their sexual relationship is often detailed throughout the series), he nevertheless feels inferior because he lacks the same type of combat experi-ence. Most of the time Wash remains behind in *Serenity* while Mal and Zoe take on the more dangerous field missions, but his expertise as a pilot is undis-puted. With some "war stories" of his own, Wash believes that he'll impress his wife and also have more in common with her. He might further gain status in Mal's eyes as an even more important crew member. (This character also would gain hero status with the audience, who mostly perceive Wash as a background member of the ensemble, largely less heroic because he "stays in the car.")

Therefore, Wash sabotages the shuttle Mal and Zoe plan to fly to a plan-etside business meeting. Wash proposes to go on the mission, and an upset Zoe leaves him to take her place, a plan to which Mal reluctantly agrees. Wash doesn't understand the dynamic between Zoe and Mal. He sees them bonding over past and current shared dangers and worries that Zoe argues with him while always deferring to Mal's decisions. Because he hasn't been a soldier, Wash doesn't understand that Zoe will always respect her captain's judgment and unquestioningly follow his orders. As an equal marriage partner with Wash, however, Zoe has no problem stating her ideas and sharing all her emotions.

This mission, of course, is more dangerous than anyone expects, and Wash and Mal are taken prisoner by Mal's disgruntled former client, Niska, who likes to torture those who cross him. Capturing Mal and a vulnerable crew member provides him with endless opportunities to express his displeasure over their aborted business deal.

Throughout the torture, Mal and Wash spar over who has the closer relationship with Zoe. Although Mal often is comfortable being a hero when he can fight his opponent openly, in this episode he becomes most heroic by playing mind games with Wash in order to keep the less experienced "warrior" from breaking under torture. Zoe also is heroic in planning and leading a rescue effort; she can buy one man's freedom and, of course, chooses Wash.

Mal thus becomes a sacrificial hero when he dies at the hands of his torturer, a cruelly graphic scene that doesn't leave viewers in doubt about the agony that either Wash or Mal suffers under the command of villain Niska. Even when Mal is revived, only to be tortured further, he remains stoic and determined under duress, just as an exemplary (and very traditional) hero would. For the first time, audiences see Captain Reynolds as a wartime leader protecting his comrades instead of a fly-by-night adventurer who hardly seems capable of leading strategically. In this episode Mal acts like a leader who knows how to keep up morale under horrific conditions, obviously a skill learned as a captain fighting on the wrong side of the Alliance. He doesn't give up or give in, and he ensures that Wash is released.

However, when Zoe leads yet another rescue, this time allowing Mal the opportunity to defeat his torturer one on one, the captain declines, preferring that his crew gun down the man. Mal doesn't need to be "macho" in defeating the man who captured and tortured him; he is heroic enough by expecting Zoe to save her husband and by acting as a true captain who protects his crew at whatever cost to himself. Mal doesn't believe in taking unnecessary physical punishment just to prove himself a more manly hero. He doesn't hesitate to allow himself to be rescued and doesn't feel the need to overcome his foe himself. His sense of "justice" is satisfied with Niska's death. Mal and the audience likely agree that the torturer deserves death. The captain can be merciful when it suits him, but he also can be content with vengeance when a villain threatens his crew, as well as himself.

Serenity portrays Mal similarly. He is willing to sacrifice himself if by doing so he protects his friends. He can be an avenger when his friends are slaughtered and he feels helpless to save them. He can mete out "Western justice" without blinking an eye, but he also accepts the notion of running away. He is a gray hero who may not be as complex as some others discussed in this book, but who can make audiences squirm with some of his decisions or choices. Mal Reynolds can be a charming hero as well as a callous cad, a sacrificial warrior or a cunning con man, depending on what the situation requires. Despite wearing that famous brown coat, Mal as hero is decidedly gray.

Dr. Horrible's Sing-Along Blog

During the 2007–2008 Writers' Strike, Joss Whedon provided writers and actors with a non-paying creative outlet that charmed web audiences. *TV Guide* critic Matt Roush described *Dr. Horrible* as "Whedon's stylishly scrappy, lovably cheesy and insanely tuneful return to the form for which he showed such incredible aptitude in the classic 'Once More, with Feeling' episode of *Buffy the Vampire Slayer*."[19] Word of mouth led to the short web series' increased popularity, further leading to a DVD release, Emmy nomination, and plans for a sequel.

Dr. Horrible's style certainly attracted audiences who like the absurdity of characters bursting into song while doing the laundry, and the title character initially seems like the nerd next door — awkward, self-promotional, sweet but insecure. His demeanor and appearance match audience expectations for the "boy next door" common in musical comedy or romance, and when Dr. Horrible (Neil Patrick Harris) crushes on do-gooder Penny (Felicia Day), the match seems made in musical heaven. Audiences might expect a traditional conclusion: Penny redeems Dr. Horrible and turns him from his evil ways. At first, the power-hungry scientist doesn't seem all that mad or villainous; he could very well be part of the audience laughing at the in-jokes in the web series.

Dr. Horrible is much more appealing than the story's hero, Captain Hammer (again, Nathan Fillion), a smarmy crime fighter whose heroics sometimes cause problems as much as resolve them. True to the conceit that the hero always gets the heroine, Captain Hammer seduces Penny away from her tentative romance with Billy (i.e., Dr. Horrible), yet he merely seems interested in another conquest to advance his reputation as a virile hero. Hammer knows how to manipulate the media and win fans, despite his inability to speak more than a coherent sound bite at a press conference.

Title and lead character Dr. Horrible *is* a villain, however; he never strays from his desire to take over the world and, in so doing, win a coveted spot in the Evil League of Evil. Only his superficially benign appearance lures viewers, as well as Penny and Hammer, into thinking he isn't a threat. Hammer is an ineffectual hero much more comfortable with photo ops and posing as a hero than being the real deal. When he loses in battle to Dr. Horrible, he is more concerned about wounds to his image and pride (as well as his stunning physique) than the death of his supposed "true love," Penny, or the downfall of his city to the forces of Evil. *Dr. Horrible* succeeds in presenting gray characters as increasingly savvy, competent villains or media darling gray heroes most interested in saving themselves.

Because the *Buffy* episode "Once More, with Feeling" also follows the format of a musical, *Dr. Horrible* frequently is compared with it. The opening lyrics and setting illustrate the shift from hero to villain as the most interesting character to watch and, ultimately, the most self-assured. In "Once More, with Feeling," Buffy questions whether she wants to keep her "job" as hero; she has lost touch with herself and only goes through the motions of slaying demons and vampires. Buffy can't feel much of anything; she is numb to her role as a slayer and unable to express or understand her lack of emotion. The hero is empty and on a downward spiral. Dr. Horrible also discusses feelings, but his involve falling in love and trying to win Penny's attention and affection. He is optimistic about his career aspirations as a villain, even if they so far have met with little success. His ability to do something dastardly — like freeze the world with a freeze ray — is suggested as a way to make Penny notice him romantically. In one song, Dr. Horrible wants to use terrible technology (a villainous act) simply to have the time to confess his love (a very human, possibly redemptive act).[20] Dr. Horrible's endearing inadequacy to find the right words to woo Penny is matched by the sinister undertones of the way he proposes to get her attention. His lyrics, along with his appearance and demeanor, in this scene make the villain a far more appealing character than the hero.

Captain Hammer's lyrics, in contrast, emphasize his overconfidence and sense of superiority over everyone, especially the innocents he saves. "A Man's Gotta Do" summarizes his "job" as a hero, saving the unfortunate because that is what a manly hero does— and he looks great doing it.[21] Hammer feels destined to be superior and, thus, heroic. He likes the perks of his job (e.g., media attention, groupies) far more than having to deal with the homeless or downtrodden who need to be saved.

Penny is the only true hero in this story. Only interested in funding a homeless shelter, she works tirelessly and is thrilled when Captain Hammer agrees to help her. With his high social profile and access to the press, he can offer assistance that no one else can. His motives, however, are far from pure. Penny, the pure hero, seems naïve and easily manipulated by either Hammer or Horrible, depending on the scene. For all her determination, she can't succeed in getting enough people interested in helping the homeless unless a celebrity attaches his name to the cause. She even becomes collateral damage in the show-down between Hammer and Horrible, the villain being motivated by her untimely death to become as evil as possible. Penny fails to redeem Dr. Horrible; her death tips him into the realm of serious evildoers and pushes him to succeed as a villain.

His final song, "Everything You Ever," ends the story with the rise of Evil and the defeat of Good.[22] The villains outnumber the hero, who is content to slink away and work on his self-esteem. Dr. Horrible victoriously sings a reversal of Hammer's hero lyrics. Just as Hammer feels destined to be a hero, Dr. Horrible realizes that his life's purpose is to make the world kneel before him and to instill fear in the populace. However, his conversion to a purely dark villain requires the sacrifice of all human emotion. His final lyric emphasizes his inability to feel anything, a line that dehumanizes him as much as it cements his confidence in himself to be a villain.

Whedon turns the sweet, rather "innocent" villain who can feel love into an unfeeling monster bent on dominating the world. Although Buffy ends "Once More, with Feeling" still uncertain about her future, she at least regains the ability to feel. Heroes are human, even if they are conflicted and uncertain; they have the ability to feel.

The darker ending to *Dr. Horrible's Sing-Along Blog* provides an unfeeling villain removed from humanity but confident in his career path. In this comparison, gray or pure villains are more honest, and ultimately more powerful, than heroes. Buffy retains her humanity and regains her ability to feel emotion by the end of "Once More, with Feeling," as even a gray hero must do, but she is far from confident by the end of this episode. Although *Buffy* becomes a progressively darker series over time, *Dr. Horrible* tells the entertaining story of a villain who "makes bad" and finally accepts who he is; the lead character's victory song, often an emotional conclusion to a musical, promises that Evil rules.

The popularity of *Dr. Horrible* and the entertaining, often endearing portrayal of this villain illustrate how far SF TV villains have come in the past decade and how much audiences accept the fact that heroes, in real life or on TV, may be equally self-serving and corrupt. Although Whedon's series have moments of humor and lightness, they increasingly emphasize the dark undertones of every society, from Sunnydale to Los Angeles, in space or on Earth.

7

Heroes

Hero or villain TV stories based more in fantasy than science fiction, such as Whedon's *Buffy* or *Dr. Horrible*, have always been popular, and, for generations, comic books (and later graphic novels) have furthered fantasy tales of superheroes and -villains. In 2006 Tim Kring's NBC TV series *Heroes* rode the wave of popular superhero movies and current fascination with SF TV. During its first season *Heroes* captured audiences' imagination — and high ratings (more than 14 million viewers on its first night). Its premiere garnered better ratings than any other NBC series of the previous five years.[1]

By the end of its first season, *Heroes* not only won the hearts of dedicated fans, but critics recognized the series for different types of achievements. *Heroes* won awards from the People's Choice, American Film Institute (AFI), Writers Guild of America (WGA), and NAACP, among others internationally; it received Golden Globe and Emmy nominations. The U.S. TV Critics Association named *Heroes* the Outstanding Program of the Year.[2]

The series provided a multicultural international ensemble of actors and characters determined to solve the mystery of what exactly triggered so many people's superpowers and, more important, to save the world (one cheerleader at a time). Its serial format, comic-book visual style, and interesting characters made it a mainstream, primetime SF TV series for the masses, unlike *Lost*, which, by 2006, already was becoming more difficult for casual viewers to follow.

Heroes blends the best of serialized TV with a new "look," one familiar to anyone who ever picked up a comic book. The series' themes — the nature of good and evil, love, redemption, sacrifice, loyalty — may be similar to *Lost*'s, but *Heroes*' storytelling is straightforward, its symbols and references to popular culture obvious. Its story arcs indicate the emphasis of a half or full season of episodes and often are keywords from hero literature: Genesis (obviously the first volume in the multi-chapter story "book" of modern heroes), Villains (Volume 3), Fugitives (Volume 4), and Season Four's (but Volume 5's) Redemption. *Heroes* initially made SF TV heroes even more accessible to the general viewing public, winning them millions of fans and making "hero literature" more popular to a wider audience. Even as the series declined in ratings, its vocabulary used in dialogue, allusions to Campbell's analysis of the hero, and ever darker confrontations between Good and Evil still make it one of the most important televisionary hero "texts" for this generation of audiences.

In hindsight, the TV Land Future Classic Award seems premature, given the series' later fall from ratings grace. Its first season achievements, however, not only make the first 23 episodes (and arguably many of the 2009–2010 fourth season) worth watching several times for their entertainment value, but also provide heroes and villains worthy of further study. Perhaps one of the greatest SF TV heroes ever to illustrate Campbell's hero's journey is Hiro Nakamura; his purity as a hero and desire to be a moral player in what most characters perceive as a largely immoral world separate him from much grayer, more pragmatic heroes, not to mention an increasingly powerful series' villain, Sylar.

The large ensemble cast encompasses the range of gray heroes and villains. Although some heroes (e.g., Hiro) immediately gained fan love, Sylar, the villain introduced midway through the first season, has continued to win greater attention in subsequent seasons. Week after week, characters' dialogue repeats the terms *hero, villain, monster*— but a single character may change categories frequently within and across seasons. Although *Heroes'* story arcs for the main characters often became repetitive after the first season, a return to themes like love, loyalty, redemption, and family in the fourth season brought new fans to the series. The success and popularity of the first season hasn't been duplicated, but a return to the "basics" of the hero story resonated with more viewers during the fourth season.

Heroes provides more fantasy than science, but its premise does fit within science fiction. This series explains that, during times of world crisis, more people with special abilities find their powers "switched on." Viewers and "specials" eventually learn that scientists can engineer these special abilities, but just when and how they become manifest is less clear. They seem more likely to become activated when the world needs more heroes, although not everyone with a special power wants to help save the world. Superheroes, as well as supervillains, are made; their super ability is in their genes. The moral component of the traditional hero story, however, is crucial to character development. Each "special" determines just how to use his or her ability—for Good or Evil.

In particular, Hiro Nakamura (Masi Oka) takes Campbell's hero's journey after answering the call to action. One of the consistently "best" heroes from a Judeo-Christian moral standpoint, Hiro knows exactly how a superhero should act and strives to fulfill this lofty calling. Although he doesn't always succeed and has lapses in judgment and dedication to the greater good, Hiro retains his audience popularity because he is such a "good" character.

Characters following a moral imperative aren't the only heroes, however. Politician Nathan Petrelli (Adrian Pasdar) vacillates between moral relativism and, during one story arc, religious fervor, but most often he pragmatically makes decisions regarding his superpower (the ability to fly) and the future of anyone with such a power. Because Nathan is a powerful politician, he helps set U.S. policy toward "specials." When he believes they are dangerous to national security, he wants to round them up and control them. When he becomes subjected to this policy, however, he sees it as persecution and works to change the very policy he set in motion. At times, Nathan's actions make him seem like a very gray hero indeed, even possibly villainous. Nevertheless, by the completion of his story in Season Four, the writers redeem him and give him some very traditional heroic dialogue before he dies.

Noah Bennet (Jack Coleman), although not a "special," is yet another gray character whose actions most of the time make him far from heroic. He deceives his family, including his beloved adopted daughter, Claire (Hayden Panettiere); he builds a career as a "company man" tracking down people with special abilities. For many years he does whatever his employer asks, accepting the idea that the job is necessary, even if it destroys lives. As his daughter becomes an adult and goes to university, Noah regrets his sordid past. He no longer has a family or job; his only skills involve duplicity and destruction. When he tries to make amends and work on behalf of "specials," his former prey are wary, at best, of his motives. Even Claire periodically disavows her father and works at cross purposes to him, but at heart she always loves him. As an adult in Season Four, she accepts that her father has done some terrible deeds, but she remains loyal to the man who has loved and protected her, even when it would have been easier not to do so.

These ever-shifting, frequently gray characters are typical of *Heroes*' main and seasonal characters. Each year some heroes and villains die, but others are introduced. Villains less significant (and popular) than Sylar (Zachary Quinto) come and go, usually receiving their comeuppance by the volume's finale; more heroes are recurring characters, but even their importance varies with the story arc. Of the returning heroes and villains playing key roles in the most volumes, Sylar (aka Gabriel Gray) is the most important villain, whereas Hiro Nakamura, the Petrelli brothers Nathan and Peter (Milo Ventimiglia), and Claire Bennet provide interesting variations on the development of gray SF TV heroes.

Sylar the Villain

Chief villain Sylar is visually manipulative, unlike *Lost*'s most famous "villain" (who believes he's a "good guy"), Ben Linus, who prefers word games in order to toy with someone's mind. Both intriguing villains enjoy playing mind games, but because Sylar can change his appearance, or get into others' minds to make them believe he is someone else, he doesn't need to use rhetoric to confuse or convince his victims to do what he wants. True to the nature of a comic book, visual effects (i.e., showing rather than telling) are key to the story, and so Sylar's attacks involve graphic, sometimes gruesome imagery. He may look like any other character, but the way his dark actions are illustrated on screen clearly indicate just who is behind such horrific attacks.

As with many gradually revealed monsters-turned-villains (e.g., Grendel's mother, *Torchwood*'s Selkie, *Lost*'s Smokey — discussed in other chapters), Sylar morphs from an unknown threat into one feared precisely because heroes know exactly what he is capable of. Part of his allure as a monster during the first two seasons is the legend growing up around his violent acts. First mentioned by police officer/hero Matt Parkman (Greg Grunberg) as a serial killer ("Don't Look Back," 1.2), Sylar (first played by a stunt actor instead of Zachary Quinto) appears on screen briefly in "One Giant Leap" (1.3). At first he isn't shown clearly; Sylar remains a shadowy figure wearing a coat and cap, his face hidden in darkness. He slips away after a murder, and no one knows exactly how to capture him. Even when Sylar's face is revealed and he is given a tangible form by Quinto ("Seven Minutes to Midnight," 1.8; "Homecoming," 1.9), the way he takes the special powers from other "super" characters— heroes or villains— is horrifically fascinating.

He points a finger at his victim's forehead, slicing a bloody horizontal line across the terrified face. At this point the camera often cuts away to Sylar's satisfied smirk, while the victim screams. Rumors abound that Sylar literally ingests the special talent of his dead victims; he eats their brains. Although early in Season Three ("The Second Coming," 3.1) Sylar refutes that claim, telling Claire that eating brains would be disgusting, the character's origins indicate that writers intend Sylar to be far less human than other main characters. Even when he acts more "civilized" and, through dialogue, separates himself from a cannibalistic monster, long-time fans still remember this association. His unpredictability as a killer continues to link him tangentially with being a "monster." As the character is developed throughout subsequent episodes, he becomes less traditionally monstrous in action and portrayal and more villainous as audiences, and heroes, come to understand his motives and actions.

Among Sylar's murder victims, accidental or premeditated, are a cheerleader at Claire's high school ("Homecoming," 1.9), Hiro's love interest ("Seven Minutes to Midnight," 1.8), his adoptive mother ("The Hard Part," 1.21), his biological father ("Our Father," 3.12), and Nathan Petrelli ("An Invisible Thread," 3.25; "The Fifth Stage," 4.11). Sylar litters the story with bodies and usually seems detached from remorse or emotions other than lust for power and revenge.

Only when Sylar isn't himself does he seem human. He suffers memory loss by having his memories "wiped" by Matt Parkman ("An Invisible Thread," 3.25; "Hysterical Blindness," 4.4; "Tabula Rasa," 4.5) and becomes a much more sympathetic character. He doesn't seem inherently "bad" when he doesn't know who he is and refuses to believe all the evidence police can show him. When he is a victim of others' manipulation — including having Nathan's memories implanted into his body after the politician's physical death — Sylar seems vulnerable. Nevertheless, his villainous personality becomes dominant once again in the Nathan/Sylar "shared" persona. Until he returns to his "true nature" as Sylar, the Nathan/Sylar hybrid or an amnesiac Sylar acts more like a frightened child than a hardened murderer.

Additionally, Sylar provides the series with more than just a nemesis for characters like Peter. He also forces Peter to become less gray as a hero and a better man. Of all the *Heroes* characters, Peter is the one shown in church questioning God ("Into Asylum," 3.21). He is the most caring and compassionate healer/hero. Therefore, Peter is the one tapped to illustrate the redemptive power of forgiveness.

In a pivotal Season Four episode ("The Wall," 4.17), Sylar and Peter, in reality separated by a brick wall in Matt's basement, are mentally trapped within a reality Parkman creates to keep Sylar isolated, preferably forever.[3] Sylar believes that he is really trapped in a building with no way out, but he doesn't realize that he is in a mental trap until Peter shows up in the same virtual room. Peter needs to free Sylar to help him stop a friend from inadvertently aiding another villain and thus killing thousands. Once in the room with Sylar, however, Peter discovers he also is trapped. Over the "years" the two spend imprisoned together, Sylar mellows, and Peter tentatively becomes his friend. Only when Peter gives up his anger and forgives Sylar for killing Nathan can the two find their way out of the trap. Forgiveness literally frees both Peter and Sylar. The reformed villain promises to change his ways for good, leaving Peter to question whether this time Sylar really has changed.

In the Season Four finale ("Brave New World," 4.18), Sylar claims that he is a hero and seems to covet that title. Audiences, and the series' heroes, don't trust Sylar's "conversion." His track record illustrates that his desire to become a force for good doesn't last long. This character's periodic attempts to become a hero instead of a villain raise questions for the audience: Are heroes naïve if they believe Sylar can change, or they cynical if they refuse to believe this villain can be redeemed? Can a frequently gray villain ever be accepted as anything less than Evil, even if he works for the greater good or saves the world?

Series creator Kring told *TV Guide* that, at the end of the fourth season, viewers won't be certain whether Sylar truly has repented his killer past and become a hero. Kring's vision for the next installment of the series involves "a world-changing dynamic between the characters," certainly intimating an even darker direction for the story and character development.[4]

According to Kring's series, heroes may venture into grayer territory, as Peter Petrelli and Hiro Nakamura periodically do (and Nathan Petrelli makes a semi-career out of doing). They, however, always return to goodness. Sylar, in a similar fashion as a villain, may occasionally try to be better, either because he doesn't remember who he really is or because of a trauma that forces him to reconsider his actions. When he "recovers," he becomes a villain once again.

Kring makes viewers wonder if a villain like Sylar, long noted as *the* bad guy in the series, can become a hero. It does seem far more likely that the "good guys," including grayer heroes Nathan and, at times, even Peter and Hiro, sometimes do bad things, even if they do so in the name of the greater good. Audiences find it much more difficult to believe that a villain can change and become a better person; they accept the fact that good people may sometimes make a bad decision or fail to act heroically.

Heroes start out as being very good, so they build up goodwill with the audience (and other characters). By the time the story takes them into darker territory, heroes' dark decisions or gray actions seem an anomaly, and viewers are more likely to accept (to a certain extent) horrific choices made by characters they believe are basically good. From the story's beginning, villains, on the other hand, seem to have few if any socially acceptable qualities, and the ones they have (e.g., charm, intelligence) are used to deceive others. Villains have much to overcome before viewers accept them as "good" characters.

Being an interesting or popular character may have nothing to do with his or her "goodness." Sylar is far more interesting when he threatens innocents or plots destruction, which also makes accepting him as a hero far less likely.

Traditional Hero Hiro Nakamura

Although many "good" heroes populate the series within and across seasons, two fan-favored heroes are Hiro Nakamura and Peter Petrelli. Claire Bennet (discussed in a later section) also fits this category, but Hiro and Peter already are adults at the time their special abilities become apparent. Their growth as heroes therefore isn't a coming-of-age story, as is Claire's.

Hiro is ecstatic about discovering his ability to traverse space and time. He gladly accepts the call to action, as Campbell described the initial part of the hero's journey. Hiro's journey is both physical (e.g., from Japan to the U.S.) and spiritual. More than any other character, Hiro's journey follows Campbell's stages of development.

The problem with such a pattern in the development of an SF TV hero is that only the network knows when the story will end. Even the writers can't determine if Hiro's story will be short or long, so the time spent on any one aspect of the hero's journey may be misleading in relation to overall character development. During Season One, Hiro completes almost every step of the traditional hero's journey, and his character development is most focused (and entertaining) during those episodes. For example, one of his first tests as a hero involves saving a little girl from a traffic accident. Awkward and uncertain, Hiro, with the assistance of best friend Ando, succeeds in sweeping the child from the path of an oncoming truck ("One Giant Leap," 1.3). With this act, Hiro "passes" another test along Campbell's hero's journey. In a later episode Hiro learns how to use a special weapon — a sword; he is mentored by his father, who finally accepts his son as a young hero ("Landslide," 1.22). In scenes from episodes such as these, Hiro clearly follows Campbell's well-established path for the hero's character development.

In later seasons, Hiro, already developed as a traditional hero in ways that viewers loved to see in Season One, must deviate from being a pure hero in order to have something to do within the greater story. He already completed Campbell's journey by the end of Season One. The writers' responses to this dilemma vary, but Hiro often has to "regress" after Season One so that he can return to the traditional hero's journey.

Much of this regression involves Charlie, a young waitress with whom Hiro falls in love. He fails to prevent Sylar from murdering her, and this failure makes him question his ability to be a hero/savior. When Hiro learns that he has a brain tumor (in Season Four), he decides to make amends by returning to the past to "right what once went wrong," a very *Quantum Leap* approach to problem solving and heroism.

Like *Quantum Leap*'s hero, Sam Beckett, Hiro discovers that his actions may not achieve exactly the results he envisions. Sam, however, always improves the lives of those whose timeline he changes; *Quantum Leap* is, more often than not, the story of a traditional do-good hero who sacrifices himself for the greater good and is able to make a positive impact on history (and thus the future). Hiro's *Quantum Leap*-style adventures in 2009–2010 are much darker than Sam Beckett's adventures in the 1989–1993 series, even though Hiro's story arcs typically are more uplifting than those of far grayer heroes in *Heroes*.

That some fans noticed the parallels between Hiro and Sam in Season Four becomes the focus of an in-joke during "Pass/Fail" (4.15).[5] While Hiro lies in a coma because of his brain tumor, he imagines himself as the defendant on trial for meddling with the past. As a time traveler, he should know to obey the "rules" of leaping among timelines. As a hero, he should follow the hero's code of honor, which Hiro himself has developed along his journey, based on his interpretation of successful past cultural heroes.

When Hiro defends his decision to return to the past to change events that he personally wants to change for a better outcome (often because he feels he failed to "get it right" in his childhood or youth), he explains that he was only trying to "right what once went wrong." The judge, Hiro's stern father, warns him not to invoke the opening narration of *Quantum Leap* as part of his defense. Meddling with time, which, in Hiro's case doesn't always make people's lives better, is a criminal offense. The episode's title, "Pass/Fail," provides no leeway for subjectively interpreting Hiro's actions. He either fails or succeeds as a hero, and the evidence in his trial indicates that his actions may not be as heroic as he believes.

Whereas *Quantum Leap* portrays Sam as a good-intentioned hero who succeeds in making the world a better place, *Heroes* questions Hiro's motivations as selfish and convicts him of using his special ability to further his own aims. Although Hiro never means to be a "villain," and indeed his crimes seem minimal compared to those of other villains in the series, his self-interested use of his superpower does meet part of the definition of a villain.

The comparison of such "good" heroes as Sam Beckett and Hiro Nakamura also illustrates the "graying" of SF TV series during the past few decades. Like Hiro, Sam seems naïve and idealistically (perhaps unrealistically) optimistic as a hero; he believes he can (and indeed he does) make a positive difference in the world. Post–2000 heroes usually aren't as certain of their ability to make such a difference.

After his conviction as a fallen hero, Hiro is given the choice to return to the living (i.e., not to die from his brain tumor) so that he may once again take up the role of a traditional hero or to die a gray hero and not learn from his mistakes. Being the pure hero that he usually is, Hiro, of course, decides to take the more tortuous route — to return to life and do better.

As Masi Oka noted late in Season Four, the only place for Hiro to "develop" is to become the gray hero (possibly vigilante villain) Future Hiro, first shown in Season One ("Five Years Gone," 1.20). The actor rationalized that

> if he becomes Future Hiro, there are no more stories to tell because it's hard to grow with that character.... I think that's why the writers prolonged it as much as possible, but I think if we know there's an end in sight, I think it'd be fun to just take him over the edge and turn him into Future Hiro and end it that way. The best ending for him would be to go back in time and revisit his love for Charlie over and over again and live in that infinite loop.[6]

Future Hiro initially scares new-hero Hiro so much that he vows never to become such a violent, embittered man. For Hiro simply to be destined to become a very gray hero, or even a villain, undermines this character's strength in the series and the source of his continuing popularity. Viewers want Hiro to remain "pure" as a hero—not to become as gray as other heroes, even in this series. They seem to like the idea that an "innocent" hero doesn't become jaded and cynical but retains that effervescence that was imminently appealing from the first moment Hiro appears onscreen. For Hiro to lose that innocence completely or to become Future Hiro would seem a far more disappointing result than the "graying" of other heroes in this series. The alternative, to keep Hiro completing the same tasks again and again, is unappealing, but at least Oka can find a "happy ending" for a Hiro trapped in a time loop. Viewers may not enjoy that repetition quite so much; they may find the story depressingly uncreative to allow such a beloved hero a lackluster conclusion, indicating that traditional heroes face only dead ends.

Symbolically, the death of the traditional hero (as noted in Chapter 11 about Captain Jack Harkness) occurs in part because of the nature of TV storytelling. Without the ability to determine the appropriate length of a hero's story, writers must base character development on the whims of networks and ratings. When they rely on a structure like Campbell's hero's journey, writers lack the ability to control the length of the hero's developmental arcs in a way that makes sense to the plot. Hiro Nakamura indicates that traditional heroes' stories can remain popular even in the age of dark SF TV series, but the length of the story must be carefully planned to follow Campbell's structure; when the hero's development is completed, his or her story must end.

Claire Bennet's Coming-of-Age Hero

Claire Bennet's progression from a high school cheerleader first testing her newly realized superpower to confident university student/hero in many ways parallels the coming-of-age journey of Buffy Summers. Unlike Buffy, with her coterie of close friends and a mentor/surrogate father to guide her, Claire has to find her way mostly on her own. She asks a friend to videotape a series of death-defying stunts designed to test the range of her ability to self-heal ("Genesis," 1.1). She doesn't realize until midway through the first season that she's been adopted or that her father knows about people with special abilities. Believing her life a lie and all that she counted on for support a sham, Claire lashes out by sneaking away to find out more about her biological parents and connecting with other "specials," including Peter Petrelli. Teenaged confusion and growing pains are nothing new to TV drama, in SF or another genre. Claire's inability to connect with most of her peers because she is different, or with her parents because they are covering up the truth, makes her story darker than Buffy's, at least in a comparison of the first season of their respective adventures. Nevertheless, both are attractive blonde teens who want to be normal high school students but learn they have a unique gift that allows them to help save the world.

The comparison isn't quite so strong in subsequent seasons, except that each faces greater struggles and must complete progressively more difficult tasks in the role of hero. Each survives the loss of parents. Buffy's mother dies, and surrogate father Giles forces Buffy's independence by moving away. Claire's adoptive mother and brother mysteriously disappear by Season Four, when the family splits up because of divorce and Claire moves on to university. Her biological parents die tragically, in part because they are "specials." Both Buffy and Claire briefly work in dead-end jobs and try to change their identities; they attend university but don't find the answers they seek. Both die, although at different points in their development as heroes; both return to life, changed by the experience.

Buffy, however, knows that she has been "chosen" and is special in a good way: she is her generation's vampire slayer. Her "job description" identifies her as a hero. Her confidantes, the Scoobies, help her fight Evil as well as conduct surveillance, cast spells, conduct research, or just listen to her. Buffy becomes leader/savior of an increasingly large group of friends and followers, which in time elevates her because of their estimation of her power and worth. After all, she dies and is resurrected; she becomes increasingly strong physically and emotionally as she accepts her role as slayer and all it requires her to do or be.

Claire lacks that balance and support, as well as the assurance that she is meant to be a hero. During the first season, her best friend is a young man who, many fans believe, is removed from the story prematurely because he is gradually revealed to be gay. Controversy surrounding this popular interpretation of the character led to NBC declaring midway through the season that Claire's friend Zach is not gay; he soon was written out of the series.[7] The connection between Claire and Zach is an early strength in this hero's character development, in large part because both characters are Other.

Both Claire and Zach are different from the popular kids. Although Claire is a cheerleader, usually one of the upper echelon in the high school social hierarchy, she also is one of the "common people," not as popular and generally deemed as weird as any of the geeky kids who vote her homecoming queen. Claire never has a group of closely knit friends around her, and with the departure of Zach, she mostly relies on her family for support.

Heroes typically are shown to be separate from those they lead or save, and the responsibilities of a character who acts heroically time after time change him or her so that colleagues and family see a fundamental difference between the hero and the rest of the populace. Unlike *Heroes*, which shifts emphasis among the stories of many superheroes and indicates that almost anyone might be carrying that "special" gene, the majority of traditional hero stories portray the hero as at least somewhat isolated from the rest of society, by role, choice, or both.

Although Claire is one among a large number of heroes, many she knows or to whom she is biologically related, she is far more isolated than teenaged Buffy. Post-high school, Buffy gradually becomes more isolated, but also more revered, as a slayer/leader, especially after she is "reborn" as the leader of all newly "activated" slayers. By the end of her story, Buffy has marched through all Campbell's stages of heroic development and come full circle, from accepting the call to action/heroism and learning to become a slayer to accepting her role as the leader/role model/teacher of the next generation of slayer women. After four seasons of *Heroes*, Claire has only partially completed the hero's journey, and her path has become a convoluted series of Campbell's stages taken out of order.

Claire at first tries to deny her special ability and wants only to be normal. Nevertheless, she repeatedly follows her instincts to save people, whether a man from a burning train wreck ("Genesis," 1.1), her family from the hands of a pyromaniac ("Company Man," 1.17), or other "specials" being hunted by the government ("A Clear and Present Danger," 3.14). Unlike Hiro, Claire never becomes associated with a specific weapon, and in Season Four her methods of investigating potential villains and thwarting their activities makes her much more of a militant Nancy Drew than an effective adult superhero. Claire's desire to do what is right often is thwarted by her lack of experience or long-term strategy for achieving that objective.

Even when she attends university and tries to establish a new life and identity, one free of scandal or rumor about her troubled past, she is "outed" by a new friend. Ironically, Gretchen also wants to "out" Claire sexually; a confused Claire admits she has feelings for her but doesn't do anything more than indicate her interest by holding hands. Even a brief kiss between the two causes Claire to pull back in surprise. Apparently by Season Four, NBC has no problems accepting a bisexual hero in the series and suggesting that Claire at least may want to experiment sexually with women as well as men.

In many ways, professionally and personally, Claire seems ambivalent about her life. She wants to help others, but she doesn't want to be recognized as a "special." She longs to be a normal university student, yet she goes out of her way to track down a villainous carnival manager and undermine his plans. She waffles between helping her father during a midlife crisis (e.g., divorce, loss of job, inability to make amends for past misdeeds) and rejecting him for deceiving her yet again. The way Claire is written as a hero, she is inconsistent and ambivalent far more than heroes in other coming-of-age stories. Nevertheless, writers put forth her character as one of the most important in the overall saga, and she, along with her biological uncle, Peter Petrelli, and biological father Nathan, seem destined to confront villain Sylar most often. As such, Claire becomes a continuing voice for Good, even if she seems uncertain how to battle Evil. Her uncertainty mirrors that of many similarly aged viewers who want to be "heroic" in their own lives but aren't certain how to go about that task, especially in an increasingly chaotic world.

Confrontations Between Good and Evil

During Season One, the heroes' refrain is to "Save the cheerleader; save the world." This battle cry rallies newly discovered "specials" who join forces to protect Claire Bennet from the growing power of Sylar. For his part, during the first season, Sylar literally emerges from the darkness, a shadowy figure gradually revealed to viewers and heroes. Peter and Claire first glimpse Sylar when he murders another cheerleader while trying to kill Claire. Sylar attacks Peter as he helps Claire escape, and if Peter hadn't been able to add Claire's ability to self-heal to his growing skill base, he would have died as a result of his first confrontation with this villain ("Homecoming," 1.9).

Episodes later, Claire does succumb to Sylar, who slices her forehead in order to take her power, but she doesn't die — she heals herself and becomes Sylar's enemy because of this experience, even more than because of the other atrocities he has committed. In the first season's finale ("How to Stop an Exploding Man," 1.23), the heroes gather to fight Sylar, who proves to be too strong for them, individually or collectively. The villain seems to be killed, but his body disappears when the heroes become distracted by the calamity he instigates. At the end of Season/Round One, Sylar may not have achieved a decisive victory, but he lives to fight again, and he has caused enough havoc to destroy the unity among heroes.

This pattern is repeated with varying degrees of success throughout the next three seasons and several individual story arcs. Along the way, Sylar tries to become a less gray villain or even a hero with a decidedly shady past, but a confrontation always leads to his becoming a darker villain than ever. For example, when told by Petrelli matriarch Angela that she is his mother and he is brother to Nathan and Peter ("One of Us, One of Them," 3.3), Sylar both acts out because of this past betrayal and abandonment and tries to live up to the family name. A possible future shows Sylar as a good father and brother living a very different, domestic life. Of course, in *Heroes*, some tragedy sends Sylar spiraling into villaindom again ("I Am Become Death," 3.4). In this altered future, his son is killed, and Sylar takes revenge.

In his real future, he learns that Angela Petrelli lies to him and he isn't her son. In fact, he learns that his biological father is a "special" who, Sylar later remembers, killed the boy's mother. Upon this revelation, Sylar reminds his father that the apple doesn't fall far from the tree. Dad pins Junior to the wall, but the son uses his considerable range of superpowers to free himself and then torture his father to death ("Our Father," 3.12). Convinced that being bad is in his blood, Sylar vows to become an even more fearsome villain.

Sylar confronts the Petrelli brothers, individually or united, at several points in the story. The final battle, however, results in Sylar's "victory" over Nathan. When Nathan dies, his mother refuses to let him go; as a son and as a politician, he is valuable to her and, she believes, the nation. "Mentalist" Matt Parkman fuses Nathan's memories/personality/soul within the physical body of Sylar ("An Invisible Thread," 3.25), and the two personalities duel for much of Season Four. Nathan finds that he can't exist in this hybrid environment and eventually succumbs to Sylar's power ("The Fifth Stage," 4.11).[8]

This episode makes a powerful statement about the nature of Good and Evil. In all encounters with Sylar/Evil, Good loses, temporarily or, in Nathan's case, permanently. The confrontations may succeed in Good gaining further resolve to fight Evil, but Sylar/Evil always seems to have the greater strength, most cunning escape, most devious mind, etc., in order to destroy Good or at least get away to fight again. Evil not only isn't easy to fight in *Heroes*, it may never be overcome. Whereas other villains come and go within the story, Sylar is a constant who returns, time and again, more highly motivated to remake the world as he wants it, to the detriment of heroes.

After Peter says a final farewell to Nathan, he becomes enraged at Sylar and tortures him in revenge. Of course, Sylar survives, in part because Peter can't be as Evil as he needs to be to finally rid the world of Sylar. As well, Sylar's superpowers match Peter's, and the villain is very difficult to kill. Through a scene such as this, Peter's need for revenge may seem acceptable to viewers, but the fact that healer/caregiver Peter resorts to physical torture and threatens the destruction of Sylar's physical body renders him far from heroic. Peter acts not to save or protect innocents; he merely wants revenge for personal reasons. No matter how justified he may feel by the notion that the world will be safer without Sylar, the villain poses no immediate threat at the time of his torture. Peter acts on "general purposes" and a history of Sylar's actions. Even in confrontations where the hero survives, he is tainted from his battle with Sylar.

Adult Claire's Season Four confrontation with Sylar undermines her confidence in being a Good character. Sylar makes a convincing argument to the audience, and eventually to Claire, that the two have much in common, although he never addresses the issue why Claire so far has been Good while even young Sylar caused trouble ("Pass/Fail," 4.15).[9] Both are adoptees whose biological family is "special" and whose adoptive family members aren't as supportive as they should be. Both have highly advanced special abilities that prevent them from being easily killed. Both have been hunted by the government and persecuted (or at least highly misunderstood) as Other by the general public. Sylar rattles off several similarities between the two in the hopes that Claire will join him as an ally rather than work to undermine him as an enemy.

Sylar's approach to convincing Claire of their bond as similar "specials" illustrates his successful manipulation of characters in order to get what he wants. This villain is smart and slyly devilish; he may not be as smooth or articulate a verbal manipulator as *Lost*'s Ben Linus, but he can be just as persuasive in the long run.

Sylar wants a few minutes of Claire's time so that he can convince her that they are, at heart, two of a kind. He lures Claire to a vacant classroom and tries to "educate" her about their similarities. Claire, hero that she is, refuses to listen and belligerently confronts Sylar. Her unwillingness to do what Sylar wants prompts him to try his next tactic: physical threat. He uses one of his superpowers to restrain her and warns her that a newly acquired power allows him to learn another's thoughts through intimate contact. Sylar gained this ability through a steamy consensual sexual encounter with a woman much closer to his own age. Although Claire is old enough to consent, she clearly wants nothing to do with Sylar, and his threat to "unite" with her physically and mentally isn't carried out.

Sylar then resorts to one of his favorite techniques: threatening the life of an innocent. Claire believes that Sylar has kidnapped Gretchen and runs off to find her. Her relief at finding her friend unharmed prompts Claire to let down her guard; she has a heart-to-heart with her girlfriend, only to see her morph into Sylar. The villain forces the hero to listen to him; Sylar takes the form of Claire's closest friend in order to convince her that the villain maybe isn't so bad after all and might become a better man from his association with her. By trying to persuade Claire that she can change Sylar, and that their union would be beneficial to him and, thus, the world, Sylar hopes to subvert hero Claire and, perhaps, use her considerable special abilities for his own purposes.

This little "morality play" reminds viewers that Evil can take many forms, from logical to threatening to seductive, in order to sway heroes from the path of goodness. Sylar more closely resembles a Judeo-Christian Satan figure through these scenes. He is persistent, intelligent, manipulative, falsely benign, seductive, alluring. He uses whatever tactic will work in order to make heroes doubt themselves or their cause. Although Sylar doesn't convince Claire to join forces with him, he does succeed in making her doubt herself and to be wary of anyone in whom she can confide. He "wins" in this encounter, although no one dies.

Even in an uneven serial such as *Heroes*, which is marketed more to a family or young adult audience than many other dark SF TV series, villains begin as dark characters and remain firmly shadowed in shades of gray. They never convincingly become "redeemed," even if their actions may seem to be improving their character. The many heroes become bruised or obliterated by their repeated confrontations with villains; they also become darker heroes, at times temporarily acting like the villains they choose to battle.

More than other series discussed in this book, *Heroes* uses the vocabulary of traditional hero literature: hero, villain, monster. Some characters follow Campbell's stages of the hero's development closely; others illustrate at least a few steps of the hero's journey. Although some heroes may at times act as moral pragmatists (e.g., Nathan Petrelli), they later return to religion or spirituality as their underlying moral reason for accepting the burden of remaining heroes.

No matter which hero, representing a gray shade of Goodness, confronts chief villain Sylar, representing Evil more than any other series' character, Good takes a beating. Nevertheless, heroes keep returning to the fray; they refuse to let Sylar do whatever he wants, and they actively fight (and often succeed against) lesser villains introduced each season. Sylar alone is the strongest villain and greatest representative of immorality, yet his portrayal, thanks to actor Zachary Quinto, makes him the most compelling character to watch. Evil may be reprehensible, if persistent, but it also keeps viewers interested in the story.

8

Lost

Lost has been innovative in many ways, from successfully re-introducing the serial storytelling format to primetime television (and keeping it alive for six seasons) to playing with that format by introducing flashforwards as well as flashbacks, and even flashsideways, to keep the audience guessing about when and where stories take place. It initially introduced a huge ensemble cast but then picked them off one at a time while, each season, adding dozens of new characters, some of whom would become key players. Most important for the scope of this book, *Lost* remains a hallmark among gray series by showing that every single character is gray in some way.

Hero, Nemesis, Villains, and Monster

Ostensibly the series' hero, Dr. Jack Shephard (Matthew Fox), is the "good guy." However, before long, viewers learn that even the good doctor has some dark aspects to his past, and when the story leaps ahead, Jack becomes even darker in the future. Although Jack's type of "darkness" as a hero usually hurts himself more than others, his increasingly questionable decisions and fervor in believing he is right make him seem far less heroic than the audience who watched the pilot episode would ever have believed he could become.

The man who opposes many of Jack's decisions, whether on the mysterious island or off, is a strange sort of nemesis for a "hero." John Locke (Terry O'Quinn) frequently believes that Jack is wrong, encourages other castaways to follow him instead of Jack as a group leader, and eventually goes his own way with a band of followers. He does what he can to thwart Jack's plans, at one point in Season Four even aiming a gun at Jack and vowing that he'll shoot to kill ("Through the Looking Glass," 3.23).[1] Locke, however creepy he may seem to the castaways, is a nemesis but not a true villain. He is simply a man who disagrees philosophically with Jack — and often what he stands for. Among the many questions *Lost* is good at raising is this: Does an antagonist, perhaps even a nemesis, have to be a villain?

Lost proposes that two men who are equally fervent in their beliefs, don't want to hurt others except as a last resort in aiding their "cause," and sometimes fight together but other times fight each other don't have to fulfill the roles of "hero" and "villain." They might be allies at times, but they also might become enemies, each intent on having his own way because he believes that way is the only correct path.

Jack and Locke basically oppose each other because of their different ideas about what/who rules human lives and how that belief influences every action on the island. Because of what happens on the island, these characters' lives are forever changed, even when they find a way to leave the island. It becomes a touchstone for everyone who ever lives there.

Jack initially believes the island's mysteries can be understood, but even when they are, they pose a danger to the castaways. His purpose as the castaways' leader is to find a way off the island, to save as many Oceanic 815 survivors as possible, to return his friends to their homes. Jack is a fixer, and crashing on the island is just one of many problems he tries to solve.

In contrast, Locke always believes that the island provides his salvation, and if the other castaways would just get with the program, they too could be healed from physical or spiritual ailments. Because the island quickly heals Locke's paralysis, broken leg, and gunshot wound, he believes in its power and thankfully will do whatever the island requires.

These competing interpretations of the island and its ultimate role in the castaways' lives don't lead to viewers' immediate identification of the character most likely to be the series' hero, although the audience might logically assume, based on years of television watching, that only one character can be the "hero" when two characters vehemently disagree with each other. Both Locke and Jack can't be correct in their assumptions about the island, so one man must be right. Usually the character who makes the right decision or has the correct understanding of the situation is the series' hero. *Lost*, however, doesn't work from such a standard premise. It merely expounds on characters' differences while reminding everyone — including viewers — that we must live together or die alone.

Perhaps the most important ongoing theme throughout the series revolves around the Season Two premiere episode, "Man of Science, Man of Faith."[2] The battles between Jack and Locke occur because Jack firmly believes he's a Man of Science, whereas Locke discovers his faith rewarded and encouraged on the island.

Not only as a spinal surgeon but as a pragmatic realist, Jack believes in science. Although various "miracles" that he can't explain have taken place in his life (e.g., his future wife, Sarah, makes an inexplicable recovery from a horrific car crash; "Man of Science, Man of Faith," 2.1), Jack doesn't attribute these events to spiritual or divine intervention. He understands cause-and-effect relationships in science as well as in his everyday life; if something unexplained happens, he tries to determine the cause so he can more likely predict a future outcome. He knows that he must solve problems and take responsibility for his actions; no deity is likely to save him from his flawed deeds. If Sarah can't walk as a result of a car accident, either Jack didn't do enough as her surgeon to repair her spinal injuries or the injuries were too severe for any surgeon, even one as talented and experienced as Jack, to correct, given the available technology. When Jack discovers that Sarah has regained feeling in her legs and will make a complete recovery, he doesn't immediately credit a divine being with the miracle. He assumes that he didn't completely understand the situation and acts more mystified at the effect than amazed by some divine cause or action.

Jack tries to solve everyone's problems and make the world a better place. When he is unable to mend a situation or a person, he feels personal failure. Jack assumes that if he is logical, methodical, and intelligent enough, he should be able to save everyone or at least improve a bad situation. Of course, as the story progresses, Jack learns that he can't physically save everyone and must come to grips with the fact that some problems are way beyond his comprehension. He may not be able to predict the effects from the multiple entwined causes provided by the island and its troubled inhabitants. He may not have the knowledge or skill to even nudge the future in the direction he wants by manipulating events in the castaways' past or present. On *Lost*, Jack is given the opportunity to meddle in the past as well as try to change the future with current actions; time travel and manipulation of time lines may appeal to Jack's scientific nature, but they also give his decisions more weight. *Lost* questions the amount of power even a well-educated Man of Science should wield over the lives of others.

Although John Locke's childhood was no less fraught with expectations and guilt than Jack's, Locke always believes he is "special," even if not everyone realizes it. Locke is often called a follower more than a leader because he is a Man of Faith. He wants to believe in some people (e.g., his biological father who enters his life when John is an adult) or causes (e.g., the Island) with a highly focused passion. When he becomes disillusioned with the person or cause, or if he feels he lets them down, he suffers a crisis of faith and feels extremely betrayed. Locke is a man who needs no concrete proof if he believes in a person or an entity; his faith is enough.

Viewers can easily interpret Locke's faith as a religious metaphor, but *Lost*'s writers carefully refrain from aligning this character with a specific religion. One backstory shows Locke living in a commune ("Further Instructions," 3.3)[3]; on the island, Locke asks Charlie to help him go on a spirit quest that vaguely resembles a Native American ceremony and seems to succeed in allowing Locke to be taught by his spirit guide, one of the dead castaways. The island heals and saves Locke, not only from death in the crash but by allowing him to walk ("Pilot," 1.1).[4] When he is injured, he heals remarkably quickly. When he asks for a sign to guide him, that sign appears. Although Locke does have highs and lows in his spiritual development on the island, he willingly sacrifices his life to his "cause"— the island — when he believes his death is the only way to save his beloved island ("The Life and Death of Jeremy Bentham," 5.7).[5]

Jack doesn't understand this kind of faith and often acts as if Locke is crazy or superstitious. Unlike the Man of Faith, Jack needs to see or hear proof before he believes in anything 100 percent. Although he, like other castaways, sees the dead and has some incredibly bizarre experiences on the island (e.g., time travel, interactions with the smoke monster, the "coincidence" of meeting Desmond Hume [Henry Ian Cusick] first in Los Angeles and then on the island), Jack still tries to find logical connections between happenings on the island and probable causes of these phenomena. He understands that the island is a unique place that long has been the site of strange experiments. To his scientific mind, these experiments interact with some unknown qualities of the island to create the situations he's witnessed. He may not understand the connections— yet — but he believes there's a rational explanation even for the island's weirdness.

On *Lost*, Jack Shephard is as heroic as characters come, which means he isn't always heroic. He is certainly a gray hero after the first few episodes, but perhaps, once the audience gets to know Jack, they realize that he always has been a gray character (as shown in flash-everywheres) but still manages to do what he thinks is right to fix a bad situation.

John Locke is far less heroic on a daily basis and always more self-directed, even when he becomes "chosen" to save the island from entrepreneur and former island-dweller Charles Widmore (Alan Dale) or others who would capture it and use the island's power for their own gain. Although Locke never is a true villain, he is Jack's nemesis and, as a character, seems much darker than Jack.

If fans choose one character they love to hate, they select Ben Linus (Michael Emerson). Despite Ben's protestations to the contrary and the ways in which even he is occasionally portrayed in a sympathetic light, he most often is identified as one of *Lost*'s villains. Charles Widmore also fits that category, and the two villains do battle to determine who will ultimately "win" the island. In this battle, however, Ben seems the lesser of the two evils, even if viewers know better than to trust him. At least Ben seems to have the island's best interests at heart, at least as long as his interests fall in line with the island's. Millionaire businessman and former military man Widmore acts like the type of man who would control the island for profit or prestige — or perhaps even to gain immortality. Although their agendas differ, Ben Linus and Charles Widmore are more than capable of doing whatever is required to secure the island, and neither is squeamish about killing people who get in their way.

Of course, every good SF mystery needs a monster as well as villains, and *Lost* supplies one of those, too. The smoke monster, even through Season Five, defies easy description. It encourages the castaways' superstitious fears of the unknown and apparently can't be tamed, even by those (like Ben) who understand it far better than the audience can.

Although *Lost*'s evolving ensemble cast provides plenty of examples of gray heroes or villains throughout its complex story, four characters—Jack, Locke, Ben, and Smokey — best illustrate the type of heroes, villains, and monsters common on the island during the series' six-season tenure as an innovative, unique TV series. *Lost* embodies the best of SF storytelling and helped make SF acceptable once again for primetime television, but its quality, characterization, depth of plot, and involving (and involved) mythology make it a series likely to be long remembered in television history. *Lost* is the perfect dark SF TV series for the first decade of the 2000s; it illustrates world chaos, personal confusion and lack of direction, fears about life and death, and competing philosophies leading to a leadership tug-of-war. Even its title describes the essence of gray heroes, villains, or monsters.

Jack Shephard as a Traditional Hero and a Pragmatic Gray Hero

Like Jack Shephard, viewers "awaken" amid a tropical jungle, confused by what they see and hear. Jack turns his head to see a panting dog watching him a moment before it runs off into the jungle. Getting to his feet, Jack staggers a bit. He looks dazed and bloodied, confused for a moment when he pulls a tiny bottle of liquor from his suit jacket. Birds cry out loudly, but their call suddenly sounds like a woman's scream. When Jack wanders onto a beach, he looks to the right and sees a tropical paradise — white sand, breathtakingly blue sea, clear sky. That tranquility is forever shattered, however, when his other senses begin to piece together what has recently occurred. Jack hears screams and an engine, as well as the surf. He looks to the left and sees the chaos of a plane crash — people scattered among the wrecked fuselage and other debris ("Pilot," 1.1).[6]

Like a traditional hero, Jack immediately jumps into action. He rushes from victim to victim, assessing injuries, directing mobile survivors to assist him, literally running from crisis to crisis to save as many people as possible. Often only Jack can perform triage. A young man who professes expertise with CPR nonetheless is doing it wrong; Jack intervenes to bring a woman back to life. A pregnant woman goes into labor; Jack explains to another survivor how to monitor her and time the contractions, reminding him to call Jack if the interval grows shorter. Jack finds helpers to assist him in moving one of the most seriously injured from beneath wreckage; then he ties a tourniquet around the man's mangled leg (and later performs "surgery" to save him).

In this first scene, no one else steps forward to take charge. Others may help, but Jack is clearly in charge. His is the only name introduced to audiences during this lengthy post-crash scene; through his eyes viewers see the crash and also leap into the story when Jack discovers the crash scene. The soundtrack provides a pounding drum beat to match Jack's running steps as he rushes from one accident victim to another. The entire story — point of view, dialogue, character introduction by name, and soundtrack — revolves around Jack. Although the *Lost* saga becomes much broader even during the course of the two-hour pilot episode, Jack remains a key character throughout the series, and his decisions drive much of the plot.

In Season Three's finale ("Through the Looking Glass," 3.23), for example, Jack succeeds in getting his people rescued — his objective since landing on the island.[7] He believes that, despite the many tragedies and losses dramatized during the series' first three seasons, the survivors' lives will be better off the island. If only the castaways can return home, back to their "normal" lives, they will be happier and safer. For one glorious moment the camera swirls around a triumphant Jack making a phone call to a boat offshore that can rescue the castaways. He identifies himself as a survivor of Oceanic 815 and requests help. Jack has succeeded as the leader of most of the castaways— he does what he promises to do in finding a way for them to be rescued. Jack grins and seems oh-so-relieved that this burden has been taken from his shoulders.

To celebrate this moment of the hero's triumph, the score swells, and "epic" music matches the camera angle looking up to heroic Jack. The castaways react joyfully at the realization that Jack has saved them. This scene of Jack as conquering hero reminds viewers (and the survivors) that he can be quite the traditional hero and is indeed a man to look up to; Jack has done what no one else has been able to achieve — leave the island on his own terms. The triumphant moment helps dispel the images of Jack as a darker hero who has made some dark, questionable decisions throughout three seasons of episodes leading to this point; the scene gives audiences, as well as Jack, a brief breather. *Lost*, however, is only halfway through its story, and Jack won't always seem so traditionally heroic.

For much of the series' first three seasons, Jack becomes a more pragmatic gray hero, a moral relativist whose primary objective is to save as many castaways as possible. He makes several decisions under duress based on his feelings for Kate Austen (Evangeline Lilly), a fugitive murderer who, ironically, becomes a much better person than Jack when the story moves off the island. In Los Angeles after the rescue of the Oceanic 6 (the number of castaways from the crash who eventually make it home), Kate rears another castaway's baby as her own and is exonerated for her crime ("Eggtown," 4.4). She vows to stay in the area and to be a model mother, a role she takes very seriously. On the surface, off-island Jack seems to be a good man; he sets up house with Kate and baby Aaron. For a while they succeed in creating a happy family ("Something Nice Back Home," 4.10). The lies Jack feels he had to tell about the island, however, come back to haunt him, and he begins a physical and emotional downturn, leading to a suicide attempt ("Through the Looking Glass," 3.23; "There's No Place Like Home," 4.13–14).

Even during this darkest personal hour, however, part of "traditional hero"

Jack survives. When a mother crashes while driving her son across the bridge where Jack stands poised to jump, the formerly heroic leader once again goes to help. He saves the car's occupants from a fiery death, an action captured by news media. When Jack's heroism is replayed on television, the public believes him a hero. Even when a drug-dependent Jack tries to get yet more refills on an expired prescription, the public assumes he's the hero who should be believed and the pharmacist is in error. An irate man, overhearing Jack's confrontation with the pharmacist, asks her if she doesn't know who Jack is — a hero ("Something Nice Back Home," 4.10).[8] After all, the customer saw Jack's good deed on the news. It doesn't seem to matter that a bedraggled, clearly under-the-influence Jack looks less than heroic on this day; the news has proclaimed him a hero, and the public believes.

Lost aptly illustrates the dichotomy between the reality and media hype of modern heroism. The media quickly pick up on Jack's heroic act; on-the-scene camera crews can capture the aftermath of the crash and the result of a mother and child saved from fiery death. News anchors can easily research a hero's background, especially someone like Jack, whose role as spokesperson for the Oceanic 6 gave him plenty of media attention. As well, as a prominent surgeon in a local hospital, the image of Jack as an upstanding member of the community — and a plane crash hero to boot! — makes him a media darling. *Lost* shows that the reality of a hero's life may not be as perfect as media stories initially would have the public believe.

Although in Jack's case follow-up news stories don't tear apart his life (or his heroism), as the lives of real-life heroes may ultimately play out in the press, TV audiences still see the truth beneath the media image. The man queuing behind Jack in the pharmacy might overlook the surgeon's haggard appearance or desperation in trying to get a prescription drug, but viewers know that this now is the way Jack really looks and acts. Just as other characters, including his hospital colleagues, eventually learn that Jack may have caused the accident, the audience realizes that Jack wouldn't have had to save anyone if he hadn't parked his car on the bridge where he planned to commit suicide. Even though Jack's media persona may retain the aura of a real, or even traditional, hero, the audience knows the truth and sees how far Jack has fallen as a hero since that very first scene in the pilot episode.

At times before this "incident" in Los Angeles, Jack's superficial life still seems ideal. He survives a plane crash and admirably speaks on behalf of the castaways he helped save during their ordeal ("The Beginning of the End," 4.1). He respects his dead father's memory and admirably delivers the eulogy at a memorial service ("There's No Place Like Home," 4.12). He and Kate create a home for Aaron. He resumes his role as a leading spinal surgeon at the hospital where he formerly worked. He mends fences with the mother from whom he was estranged. Yet all these "perfect" situations can't mask Jack's growing discontent with the man he has become — one who covers up the truth and leaves many friends behind on a treacherous island. He is farthest from the traditional hero introduced in the first moments of the pilot episode, but he even seems less desirable as a character, not just as a hero, once he's off the island.

At least on the island Jack's increasingly dark decisions make him a grayer hero, but he is still perceived as a heroic character, if one who often makes difficult, morally pragmatic decisions. Audiences may wonder if Jack can ever redeem himself for some less than perfect actions, but his off-island breakdown causes viewers to re-evaluate his character. Jack does nothing heroic in Los Angeles; he even loses his ability to perform surgery. He doesn't save anyone. In fact, he is in more danger than ever of losing himself. In an interview during Season Four, Matthew Fox explained that "Jack in the future [i.e., in Los Angeles] is a man marked by weakness, but Jack of the present [i.e., on the island] is strong." The previously mentioned scenes illustrate "how he made that transition."[9]

For Jack to regain any kind of hero status he must return to the island. During Season Five, after Jack and the other former island dwellers crash land once again, Jack's sense of self is reasserted, and he once again becomes a leader, even if his followers are few. He often makes decisions unpopular with his friends (and questioned by the audience), but he again tries to act heroically in his quest to save as many people as possible. By the end of Season Five, Jack endangers lives and is willing to sacrifice himself so that he can alter Time in order to "save" the Oceanic 815 passengers from the plane crash. In the series' finale, he does sacrifice himself so that a few people escape the island for good. The story ends, as it began, with Jack.

Placing Faith in a Man of Science

Although Jack Shephard always has been identified as a Man of Science in the *Lost* canon, during Season Five he seems remarkably similar to John Locke at his most zealous moments. Jack, however, places his "faith" in science, specifically the knowledge supplied by genius physicist Daniel Faraday (Jeremy Davies). Once Jack believes that the Oceanic 6 must return to the island — a conclusion drawn from his increasingly downward spiral since his "rescue" and events like Locke's death — he passionately devotes himself to convincing the former castaways to return with him. For their own reasons, not Jack's "logic" or impassioned pleas, they reluctantly agree to board Ajira 316, another doomed aircraft that crashes on the island during a window of opportunity scientifically calculated by Faraday's mother, the enigmatic Mrs. Hawking ("316," 5.6).[10] (The prevalence of real-world scientists' surnames shared with *Lost* characters isn't a coincidence.)

Jack's previous unscientific attempts to return to the island fail. He spends his weekends flying Oceanic Air to crisscross the Pacific in hopes of crashing yet again on the island. It takes Mrs. Hawking's calculations to determine exactly which airliner and flight will result in a return to the island. When Jack again relies on science, he is successful.

In a similar way, Jack believes that Faraday's planned use of a hydrogen bomb to stop a catastrophic construction disaster on the island will change the future of everyone on that island. The energy released from the bomb should counteract the energy accidentally discharged in the 1970s when a construction crew tapped into a highly volatile source of magnetic energy ("The Incident," 5.16–17).[11] The resulting "incident" changed the nature of the island, one day causing a man (Desmond Hume) stuck in an underground hatch to fail to push a button in time to avert another energy release — one that brings down Oceanic 815. Man of Science Jack believes in the logic of cause-and-effect relationships, and he knows that Faraday has studied physics to the exclusion of all else in his life. Jack's "gamble" on Faraday's theory that a strategically timed bomb blast can supersede the original "cause" of Oceanic 815's crash and, at least theoretically, allow the plane to continue unharmed to its Los Angeles destination. Jack places his "faith" in physics and Faraday's theoretical assessment of a way to break the original cause-and-effect chain of events leading to Oceanic 815's crash.

Thus, when Jack, back on the island again, has the opportunity to detonate the bomb, he takes it. His friends, among the Oceanic 815, as well as those Jack left behind on the island, think he is crazy for wanting to take such a risk with their lives. No one knows for certain just what will happen if the bomb explodes, and the odds seem just as good to the islanders that they will die in the blast as emerge unscathed in an alternate timeline. At this point in the story, Jack seems as passionate, certain of his decision, and zealous about his plan as Locke, the Man of Faith, at his most impassioned. Jack also has to take a "leap of faith" that his plan, based on Faraday's understanding of time theory, will work the way he wants. That he bases his "faith" on science doesn't make him seem any less crazy to those who question whether Jack is playing God with their lives and taking far too great a risk with his interpretation of cause and effect.

Of course, on *Lost*, nothing goes as planned, and even scientifically theorized cause-effect relationships go awry. During the botched attempt to plant and detonate the bomb, Juliet Burke (Elizabeth Mitchell), also a doctor, sacrifices herself in order to detonate the bomb. During the concluding moments of "The Incident" (5.17), the bomb goes off — leaving fans with a massive cliffhanger ending to Season Five. The screen fades to white, not black, indicating a very different "ending" to the season and this part of the *Lost* saga.

At the beginning of Season Six, Oceanic 815 flies past the island. The future has been changed — in one "reality," at least. Jack's plan seems to have worked. Oceanic 815 indeed arrives safely in Los Angeles ("LAX," 6.1). In this "reality," the former island dwellers are reunited. By the conclusion of the series, Jack is the leader who succeeds in "saving" his friends. However, the Man of Science has become a Man of Faith. Symbolically, *Lost*'s conclusion indicates that Jack's belief in science needs to be tempered by faith. *Lost* ultimately suggests that society, like Jack, should have a balanced perspective. It requires several seasons to come to this conclusion.

Modern gray heroes often rely, sometimes exclusively, on the use of science and technology to give them an edge over villains—or simply to allow them to act heroically during events that just happen. Jack expects to be heroic when he is backed up by the latest technology and scientific knowledge. When he works as a spinal surgeon early in his pre-island life, he performs exceptionally well because he relies on his knowledge and experience to get the desired result—a "saved" patient who will have a better quality of life after surgery. On the island, Jack becomes most frustrated when he lacks the scientific capability to do this job.

A Season One example ("Do No Harm," 1.20) shows Jack's zeal as a fixer when Boone Carlyle (Ian Somerhalder) is seriously injured in a fall.[12] The damage to Boone's body is too great for Jack to repair, even though he sets up a blood transfusion (using his own blood) and assesses the damage with the limited tools available to him. When these actions fail to stabilize his patient, Jack determines that Boone's crushed leg must be amputated in order to save the young man's life. He decides that parts of the plane's fuselage can be used to perform the amputation. Only the intervention of other castaways stays Jack's last-ditch effort to try to save Boone. As a healer, the surgeon wants to do all in his power to save his patient, and he becomes anxious and frustrated when he lacks the necessary technology. Jack finds it difficult to let go, or even to allow a patient to die more or less peacefully instead of subjecting him to further agony of treatment when his survival wouldn't be guaranteed.

Viewers may applaud Jack's refusal to give up and his heroic efforts to save a life, even to the point of donating his own blood. Nevertheless, Jack behaves less than logically for a "traditional" hero. He has become so accustomed to performing miraculous surgeries that he has difficulty knowing when to stop using technology in an attempt to prolong life. Jack's actions make him a grayer hero when he refuses to listen to reason and allow Boone to die when his chances of survival are realistically nil, no matter what Jack does or doesn't do. Even Boone has to tell Jack to let him go; the young man seems more heroic than his doctor in this situation because Boone refuses to use resources that may help other castaways. He knows that he is close to death and doesn't want Jack to use limited resources in further attempts to save him. Accepting the inevitability of his death, Boone's final decision is heroic. As a gray hero, Jack needs to know when and how to use science and technology to save people — or even a single person. When he believes that he can save everyone, if he only has the right tools, he becomes a darker hero.

Jack as an increasingly dark "hero" is evidenced especially during Season Three, when he goes to war against Ben Linus and the Others. Ben's group, building their own community on the previous generation's DHARMA Initiative home base and technology, certainly has more technological comforts than the castaways who still live on the beach. Ben, however, is far from generous or benevolent as one of the "haves" on the island. He likes to torture and manipulate the "have nots": the castaways. He captures three — Jack, Kate, and Sawyer — but offers special benefits to Jack because he's a spinal surgeon. Ben conveniently needs to have a tumor removed from his back, and he promises not to kill the caged castaways if Jack agrees to perform surgery ("I Do," 3.6).[13] Jack, however, plans to use his surgical skills in a way that goes against the Hippocratic oath to "first do no harm."

During surgery, Jack makes an incision in Ben's kidney sack and tells the Others that he will let Ben die if Kate and Sawyer aren't allowed to go free. Jack uses his scientific skills, aided by the Others' technology, to hold a patient hostage. Although some viewers may see Jack's action as heroic because this dire action may be the only way for him to save his friends, others in the audience may think Jack has become as bad as Ben, using torture and fear of death to manipulate people into doing what he wants. Eventually, Jack saves Ben's life, but only after he ascertains that Kate and Sawyer are out of danger.

When time travel becomes part of *Lost*'s primary plot during Season Five, Jack has yet another opportunity to save his enemy, Ben Linus. This time, caught in the 1970s on the island, Ben is just a boy, albeit one who has been shot. Young Ben has been abandoned and often abused by his father; he seems a slightly creepy yet still sympathetic "victim" of the island, just like the castaways will someday become. Because Jack knows exactly what kind of man Ben will become, he refuses to perform life-saving surgery on the boy ("Whatever Happened, Happened," 5.11).[14]

Again, some viewers may see Jack's action as only logical and part of an important cause-and-effect relationship. If Ben never grows up, he won't torture, imprison, or kill anyone in the future — and Ben does all these acts in full audience view during Seasons Three through Five. Other viewers may argue that Jack once again is playing God with lives by deciding who should or shouldn't be saved surgically. By withholding his knowledge and skills, Man of Science Jack becomes a darker "hero," even if he (and part of the audience) believes his lack of action will save people in the future. (Juliet Burke, another doctor, although not specifically a surgeon, steps in to save young Ben, who does grow up to do all the bad things Jack and the audience have seen happen.)

Jack becomes a prime illustration of a moral relativist in these episodes. He bases his decisions not on a moral imperative but on his version of logic and analysis of cause-and-effect relationships. He doesn't believe in miracles and doesn't pray for help, for example, when he performs surgery. He relies on his training, knowledge, and experience to do the job he was trained to do. He doesn't believe in divine intervention to solve problems; Jack relies on himself, often in the role of the castaways' leader, to save as many of his friends as possible. He also doesn't think that he'll be "punished" for his decisions, however dark they may be. The only "punishment" he may feel comes from achieving a less-than-desirable result from his efforts. When one of his plans fails, he feels enormous guilt and responsibility because he *should* rationally be able to figure out how to achieve a desirable outcome that allows him to save his friends or patients. As a hero, Jack's weakness is his inability to see when his "logic" isn't quite as logical as he believes, and his sometimes simple assessment of all the potential effects resulting from one changed cause may not account for all probable outcomes.

Man of Faith John Locke

John Locke is more of a nemesis than an enemy to Jack and not a true villain in the story. Actor Terry O'Quinn claims that Locke is not a hero but simply a man doing what he believes is right. O'Quinn calls Locke "a tragic figure. Not a tragic hero—just a tragic figure." Locke "never perceived anyone as an enemy unless they were trying to stop [him] from being something or doing something.... They were just an obstruction."[15] Even Ben Linus, the character the castaways and most audience members see as an important villain and certainly an enemy to the castaways/protagonists, isn't an enemy or a villain to Locke, despite the fact that Ben often manipulates and even murders him.

Locke most often goes his own way, content at times to be a follower but increasingly gaining strength as a leader, first of a few castaways and later of Richard Alpert's band of island dwellers. Locke becomes "heroic" to those who believe the island must be protected (or "saved") from outsiders; he is a believer in the island and a faithful servant to it. To those who don't believe the island is sentient or magical, however, Locke's hardcore faith without appreciable scientific evidence to back it up seems illogical or perhaps crazy, and his actions highly suspect. At best, the less faithful believe, his devotion to what he believes the island wants him to do leads to folly; at worst, castaways get killed because of Locke's misplaced ideals.

Locke's understanding of the need for sacrifice (or *a* sacrifice) illustrates a prime reason why he is a gray character, hovering somewhere between the island's hero and the castaways' villain. During Season One, Locke mentors Boone, who eagerly follows him on forays into the jungle. When Locke has prophetic visions, including one involving Boone's childhood nanny, the young man believes that Locke truly does commune with the island. He willingly climbs into a downed Beechcraft that he and Locke find further inland, a result, it seems, of following the information from Locke's visions. Unfortunately, the aircraft is precariously perched on a cliff, and Boone's weight tips the plane over the edge ("Deus Ex Machina," 1.19).[16]

Although Locke pulls Boone from the wreckage and takes him to Jack for medical attention, he also lies about what happened to Boone. Because Jack only later realizes that Boone's crushing injury couldn't have been caused by the accident the way Locke described it, the doctor loses valuable time in treating his patient. By then, Locke has retreated once more into the jungle. When Boone dies as a result of the accident, Jack (and other castaways, including Boone's sister) think of Locke as a threat to the castaway community. Locke, however, believes that the island demanded Boone as a sacrifice, almost a Biblical test of Locke's faith. When Locke then asks for a sign, he believes he receives one in the form of a light going on in the underground hatch that Boone and Locke also discovered ("Do No Harm," 1.20).[17]

By the end of Season One, Jack tells Kate that he fears they will have a "Locke problem" soon, and indeed from this point on, Locke often contests Jack's authority or offers the castaways another option to follow. Even so, Locke doesn't want to hurt others and regrets the island's required sacrifice of Boone. He sobs his frustration and grief after the young man's death, questioning the island's reason for demanding so much from Locke. When Locke receives a sign, not only after Boone's death but at other points in the story when he doesn't understand what the island wants him to do, it restores his faith and spurs him to action. Locke's time on the island is spent seeking and responding to signs from the island; he believes he has been chosen because the island recognizes why he is "special." Viewers may have a tough time disliking Locke because he earnestly tries to do what he believes is right. He seems to enjoy the power of leading followers, but even then Locke isn't a leader out for his own glory. His actions revolve around his belief in and continuing service to the island.

By Season Three, with audiences keeping track of several groups beyond the Oceanic 815 castaways, Locke has many potential followers, including some of Ben's community (aka the Others) and Richard Alpert's "hostiles," as well as a few original castaways. Locke clearly is on the side of the island; he doesn't want people from a nearby boat rescuing Jack's band of followers because the more people who know about the island, the more likely it will be exploited. Locke hopes to keep the island secret from any more people, in part to keep its magical properties intact.

To keep Jack from alerting the boat's crew to the Oceanic 815 survivors on the island, Locke shoots and kills Naomi, a woman from the boat who, conveniently, has a satellite phone with her to call the boat ("Through the Looking Glass," 3.23).[18] He successfully prevents Naomi from making that call, but Jack next becomes a threat. He challenges Locke to kill him, knowing full well that his adversary is outnumbered and, even if he should shoot, will likely be overtaken. Jack seems heroic in this scene as he stands up for his people and won't back down against Locke; getting his friends rescued is Jack's top priority, even if he needs to sacrifice himself to stop Locke from interfering with the rescue. Again, Locke not only is Jack's (and Jack's followers') nemesis in this scene, but he seems downright villainous to kill one unarmed woman and threaten a fellow castaway with death.

A moment later, however, Locke reverts to a still-dark character but one whose actions become more understandable. He lowers his gun, admitting he can't shoot Jack. Locke won't kill indiscriminately; he shoots Naomi only because the island is threatened, Locke believes, by her actions. Before he escapes again into the jungle, taking charge of Alpert's little group remaining on the island, Locke warns Jack not to leave the island. He passionately explains that the island needs to remain secret and, personifying it, doesn't want Jack to leave. Understandably, Jack thinks the heroic action is to save his friends from what so far has been a treacherous place.

In this scene, most viewers think of Jack as the hero. He overcomes villains, including Locke, in order to make that phone call, which leads to at least some castaways' rescue. Locke, on the other hand, fails to be the Island's hero. He is unable to stop Jack's action, but he is not completely defeated. He merely returns to lead people who believe in the power of the Island and in Locke as the one who can commune with It. He acts as their seer or prophet, and, as such, he will be called upon to take other actions on behalf of the Island.

At this time he doesn't know that he, like previous island leaders, will have to leave the island and sacrifice himself. As the island's "hero," however, Locke willingly agrees to do whatever it takes to protect his adopted home. From the perspective of the island lovers, Locke's actions are heroic. Whether Locke is meant to be one of *Lost*'s heroes or villains is left ambiguous. Despite the deaths he has caused, his sincerity in protecting the island makes him seem less villainous. After all, during his time on the island, Jack also shoots those who would destroy him and his friends (e.g., "The Incident," 5.16–17). Locke fires a gun fewer times than Jack does, and, at least to Locke's mind, he is justified because Naomi, like Jack, will destroy the island.

A final view of Locke at the end of the Season Three finale shows him taking his place as the leader of Alpert's "hostiles." He stands alone atop a ridge, looking down on his people, who dutifully look up to him. The camera angle tilts up, emphasizing Locke's importance and strength. Instead of looking benevolent, however, Locke wears an expression of grim satisfaction. He hardly looks like a friendly leader; instead, he seems more of a superior taskmaster eager to rule. This pose, assisted by the camera shots, portrays Locke as a gray character, perhaps a hero to the island and those who would protect it, perhaps a villain to those who only wish to leave. Viewers are left to interpret Locke in their own way; because he is enigmatic and pragmatic, even for a man of faith, he is one of *Lost*'s most intriguing characters.

The events leading to Locke as an island leader illustrate the many challenges he has had to overcome, as well as the many insecurities fueled by past relationships. Locke is not a natural leader. Flashbacks to his pre-island life often portray him as a sympathetic loser, a man who wants to have love in his life but often alienates those who would be close to him or is betrayed by those he most wants to please. Just like Jack, Locke has "daddy issues" that shape his adult life.

Abandoned as a baby, Locke later meets his biological father, who instigates a relationship with his adult son. Locke's father, however, is a con man — in fact, the same con man who wooed Sawyer's mother and inadvertently led to the murder-suicide of Sawyer's parents. Locke, however, only belatedly realizes that his father is only out to "steal" a kidney from his biological kin; once Locke gladly donates the organ, his father once again abandons him ("Deus Ex Machina," 1.19). The infuriated Locke spends a long time tracking down his father, but during their confrontation, dear old dad pushes junior out a high rise window ("The Man from Tallahassee," 3.13). The result is that Locke is paralyzed — at least until his miraculous healing on the island.

Locke's depressing experiences and continued betrayals from his father again help paint the castaway in darker shades of gray and provide him with at least a skewed rationale for fighting back. On the island, Ben Linus tries to convince Locke that he controls the lives of everyone on the island — and some people living off it. He illustrates that power by bringing Locke's father to the island, a relatively mysterious act, given that he was driving on I–10 in Florida at the time and just turns up, bound and gagged, on the island ("The Brig," 3.10).[19]

Locke is given the opportunity to kill his father as a "rite of passage" on the island. The son, however, still can't bring himself to murder his father, despite what he's done. Ben finds Locke's lack of commitment disgusting, and he humiliates Locke (talk about peer pressure!) in front of the Others. Tied to a tree, wild-eyed with fright, Locke's father hardly looks intimidating. He seems just like a scared older man, a con man caught in one of his games. Although Locke has told Ben that he wants his father dead for what he did to him, the son still doesn't have that killer instinct of a true villain. He refuses to plunge a knife into his father's chest, a move that would earn him Ben's respect, he believes, as well as show the Others that he is worthy of being their leader. Ben taunts Locke that he is weak, but, to viewers, the castaway seems more heroic to go against Ben's command, even though Locke seems less powerful to the community he wants to impress.

As with so many other *Lost* scenes in which Locke vacillates between hero and villain without truly becoming either, this ambiguously moral castaway has no qualms about his father dying prematurely — he simply can't bring himself to do the deed. He rightly calculates that the con man, who also has appropriated the moniker Tom Sawyer for some of his ruses, might be of interest to Sawyer (Josh Holloway), himself a ruthless con man. When the two con men meet each other face to face, the younger (Sawyer/James Ford) confronts the man who ruined his family and then kills him with his bare hands. Locke doesn't bloody his hands with his father's death, but he is responsible for setting up the murder. Such an action moves Locke further into villain territory and indicates a dark nature usually hidden by his "island lover" façade. Locke can kill — as shown by Naomi's death — but he only seems able to pull the trigger himself when no one is available to kill on his behalf. Locke may convince himself that he isn't really a killer by allowing James Ford/Sawyer the "honor" of avenging his family, or he may believe that his father deserves whatever happens to him. As a Man of Faith, he becomes much more comfortable with the idea that the island wants certain people (e.g., Boone, Naomi, his father) to die; after all, the island didn't save them from death. Locke, in contrast, survives an eight-story fall off-island, a plane crash, and an on-island shooting; he also is miraculously healed from these injuries and traumas.

As mentioned earlier, Locke understands the concept of sacrifice and is willing to do whatever the island demands. Acting on the faith that the island knows what is best and that its faithful believers should protect it at whatever cost, Locke ultimately sacrifices himself. During Season Five, flashbacks document Locke's exile from his beloved home. The only way to save the island, Locke comes to believe, is to leave it to return to California. There he must convince Jack to gather the Oceanic 6 so they all can return to the island. Locke seems to have no plan beyond that, but as a Man of Faith, he doesn't require a lot of explanation. He mostly operates by receiving information from guides (including Ben Linus, deceased Boone, and Jack's deceased father, Christian Shephard) or visions that show him what he should do next. Like a true Man of Faith, Locke doesn't require or expect to know everything; he doesn't need evidence, like Jack does, before he acts. Although sad to leave the island, Locke nonetheless accepts his mission to bring back the Oceanic 6.

No one who has escaped the island wants to return, however. Even an increasingly depressed and drug-dependant Jack doesn't see the need to return to the place where he felt threatened and imprisoned. Locke becomes convinced that only his death will persuade the others of his sincerity and might sway one-time leader Jack to think again about going back to the island.

Once again, however, Locke becomes a pawn, a much more sympathetic character than a "crazy" who wants everyone to return to an island they view as dangerous and inhospitable. Interrupted before he can commit suicide by hanging ("The Life and Death of Jeremy Bentham," 5.7), Locke provides information to Ben, who has tracked him off the island.[20] Once Ben finds out what he wants to know, however, he gleefully strangles Locke. Once again, another character completes a murder that Locke can't commit. Not surprisingly, Locke understands that people have to be sacrificed to a cause — whether he or Ben completes the killing, Locke understands the need for self-sacrifice and is willing to die on behalf of the island. Though normally a heroic impulse, the way in which sacrifice as a theme is portrayed through Locke's character development often seems amoral to the audience. Ironically, Locke does succeed in getting the Oceanic 6 back to the island. His death prompts Jack to reconsider Locke's argument that everyone needs to go back to the island to make right the wrong committed by their rescue.

As O'Quinn noted, Locke is a tragic character, but he never becomes truly heroic nor truly villainous. His actions may be interpreted in different ways, depending on viewers' experiences and point of view about Locke's purpose in the story. As a Man of Faith, Locke provides an interesting balance to Jack's Man of Science. As an antagonist, Locke provides Jack with a worthy opponent who argues a philosophy very different from that espoused by the castaways' primary leader. As a faithful follower of the island, Locke is both grateful for his healing and the opportunity to be special, to become a leader and an important man (i.e., not a victim).

Perhaps his ever-shifting role in the story, whether as protagonist or antagonist, leader or follower, sacrificer or sacrificed, makes Locke one of the best SF TV characters of all time. Audiences don't know what to expect from him or how his actions might affect the story. He doesn't easily fit with audience expectations about what a character should do or think; he isn't really a leader, but he is certainly a key player in the overall plot. Locke is one of the best examples of a gray character, although he isn't truly a gray hero or villain. His darkness is unfathomable to audiences, who never quite trust Locke's motives or acts but nonetheless at times see him as a highly sympathetic character.

Ben Linus as Villain

Actor Michael Emerson appreciates the meatiness of his role as Ben Linus: "I always thought that the character was going to live in the gray zone between good and bad, between vagueness and specificity."[21] Ben loves to instill fear in friends and enemies alike; he enjoys flaunting his (supposedly) insider information about the island and his command over its mysterious elements, including the smoke monster. Audiences and characters don't know whether he sincerely believes himself when he tells a castaway during Season Two that he's one of the "good guys." Ben admits that he lies all the time, and his actions in almost every episode indicate that, from a moralist perspective, he's far from good.

As with many modern villains, Ben's actions may be at least partially explained as a result of his abysmal childhood. Like Locke and Jack, Ben has major daddy issues. (As noted in Chapter 7, hero Claire Bennet and villain Sylar share similarities in background, but each responds to traumas very differently, as do Jack, Locke, and Ben. Having severe "daddy issues" may make a character more sympathetic but can't be viewed as the sole source of a character's development.) Ben's father blames his son because Ben's mother dies in premature childbirth while far from a hospital. The boy grows up on the island under the strict auspices of the DHARMA Initiative. His father blames him for his dead-end job and spends most of his time drinking and criticizing his son. He occasionally hits the boy. Young Ben's large eyes peering behind his trademark specs reveal the soul of a gentle, kind-hearted boy. He even brings an imprisoned back-from-the-future castaway food and books and begs to be taken from his abusive parent. When the castaway escapes, he does take Ben with him — only to try to kill the boy who will one day become the castaways' torturer. A seriously wounded Ben quickly learns about betrayal, and his lack of trust in the future may be a result of such dire experiences during his youth.

Ben's insistence that Locke kill his father reflects this villain's past relationship with his dad. When Ben gets the opportunity to take revenge, he relishes it. He drives his dad to a remote location, gives him a beer, and then asphyxiates him. Ben next exterminates the DHARMA Initiative and takes control of the camp as the Others' new leader ("The Man Behind the Curtain," 3.20). Because viewers get to know adult (murderous, manipulative) Ben before scenes of his family life shine a slightly more sympathetic light on him, he retains his "villain" status despite later information about his tortured past. Ben may be seen as the product of his upbringing, but this understanding doesn't mean he isn't a dark villain. He briefly may seem less gray on the hero-villain scale, but his past abuse doesn't counterbalance all the chaos and killing he instigates.

Perhaps his greatest examples of villainy involve his adopted daughter, Alex (Tania Raymonde). Sent to kill the French woman whose ship wrecked on the island, Ben as a young man discovers that the woman has recently given birth to a daughter. Unable to kill mother and child, Ben lets the mother escape but takes the baby. Later he is told to kill the child, but he can't do so. (Perhaps he associates this baby's mother, who gave birth alone in the wild, with his own mother, who died in childbirth while on a hiking trip.) Instead, Ben rears the baby as his daughter ("Dead Is Dead," 5.12).[22]

Flashbacks of Ben's memories during Alex's childhood show him pushing the little girl on a backyard swing and otherwise acting as a doting father. However, when Alex reaches her teenage years and becomes a moody adolescent, Ben reacts as a strict parent. Because women who become pregnant on the island die for an unknown reason before the baby comes to term, Ben doesn't want Alex to "date" Karl. The teenagers, however, only think that Ben is unreasonably separating them and find ways to get together. In retaliation, Ben tries to brainwash Karl and becomes distant from Alex (as mentioned in "Through the Looking Glass," 3.22–23). He gives one of her dresses to captive Kate, for example, when he tries to manipulate her into doing his bidding ("The Glass Ballerina," 3.2).

When Alex meets her biological mother and wants to live with her on the island, Ben agrees. He knows that her mother — long accustomed to living in the wild — should be able to protect her from the mercenary soldiers who have invaded the island. Even the protective mother, however, can't save her daughter. Alex is marched back to her father as a hostage, and Ben, safely ensconced within the protection of his home, refuses to surrender to the soldier holding a gun to Alex's head. Alex hysterically pleads for her father to save her, but Ben refuses, saying that she is not his daughter. The mercenary has no time to mediate this father-daughter conflict — he simply kills Alex before her horrified father's eyes ("The Shape of Things to Come," 4.9).[23]

Months later, when Ben has left and then returned to the island as part of his mission to save it from being taken over by outside forces, he is "judged" for his conduct regarding his daughter. Within an island temple, Ben meets the smoke monster, who, moments later, reappears as Alex. Ben sentimentally greets his daughter and apologizes to her, but Alex forces Ben to face the fact that, because of him, she was killed. An angry Alex doesn't forgive Ben but forces him to follow John Locke's orders, at least if he wants to live ("Dead Is Dead," 5.12).[24]

An amazed Ben is shocked that the island, via a vision of Alex, lets him live. He has become accustomed to the smoke monster's harsh judgment of those who "sin" (e.g., Mr. Eko, "The Cost of Living," 3.5). That a villain is given another chance to redeem himself is far beyond Ben's expectation.

This villain becomes humanized through the temple scene. The apparition of Alex is justifiably angry, and fans likely cheer when she pushes him around and refuses to be pacified. Nevertheless, Ben also engenders some sympathy because his memories reveal how much he loved his daughter and regrets saving himself instead of her. The act of sacrificing his daughter to save himself is villainous; his remorse and acceptance of retribution, however, make him a more sympathetic character. For a brief scene, Ben becomes a loving father whose few moments of island happiness and normalcy are the result of being Alex's dad. Such a scene doesn't dispel the dozens of scenes in which Ben plots, kills, or masterminds destruction, but it reveals a previously undisclosed gentleness and genuine ability to love. To his detriment, Ben kills even that relationship long before Alex dies. His memories are his only link with unconditional trust and love. Viewers may not empathize with Ben for long, but they at least see that he's not completely evil and, at one time, tried to be a good father.

Adult Ben seems far more manipulative and overtly villainous than most other characters. (Charles Widmore, who once lived as a violent soldier on the island and, as a mogul off-island, wants to gain control of his former home, also vies for "top villain" status.) Ben is the "everyday" villain, however, the character most often behind the destruction of the castaways viewers first got to know and love. He lies, cheats, deceives, and kills, for example, several times since his introduction during Season Two. By Season Six he is one of the main continuing characters. As the story unfolds, Ben seems more often to work to further his own power and increase his status as the island's "keeper" than to protect the island or save it from destruction. He does whatever he needs to do, including shifting his alliance among leaders on or off the island, in order to live (and lie) another day. His self-interest surpasses his interest in the island, which also makes him seem more typically villainous. Ben is pragmatic, but audiences sense that he always has a master plan, as well as Plans B, C, and D, in mind.

At the end of Season Five Ben even gets to kill "God." During his epiphany in the temple, Ben agrees to do whatever Locke tells him to do. Of course, at this point in the story, Locke is truly dead (murdered by Ben off-island), but something/someone looks like Locke and gives Ben orders. Jacob, the multi-centurion entity apparently controlling the situations in which island "visitors" find themselves, meets "Locke" and Ben in his beachside home beneath an ancient statue. As Locke commands, Ben repeatedly stabs Jacob with a knife, apparently killing him. "Locke" finishes the job by kicking Jacob's body into the fire pit.

Because Jacob seems godlike in his power over Time, as well as the lives of hapless castaways, Ben earns the dubious distinction of being able to kill the island "god"—a villainous act. However, Ben seems more sympathetic than a cold-blooded killer in this scene because he is "under the influence" of faux Locke and ignored by Jacob, the "deity" he served for most of his life. Jacob reminds Ben that he has a choice—to do what Locke asks of him or to leave. Before Ben makes up his mind, he asks Jacob why this "god" hasn't revealed himself to his long-faithful servant. Ben petulantly asks why Jacob doesn't consider him special, yet island newcomer Locke immediately gains Jacob's favor. When Ben is ignored and minimized once more, he angrily attacks Jacob and gives in to a murderous rage. As with many villains, Ben needs to feel special and wants to be the center of attention, especially to anyone of importance. Jacob, the most important being on the island, fails to praise Ben, who responds based on a lifetime of insecurity, frustration, and hatred. He is manipulated by "Locke" into fighting back, but he doesn't hold back once given the opportunity to let Jacob know just how he feels.

Of course, Jacob hardly seems like a character so easily killed, but the Season Five finale shows Ben as a willing murderer once again. That Ben has no moral objections to killing anyone (e.g., his father, Locke, Jacob) or acting in ways to get others killed (e.g., Alex) makes him a villainous character. Like *Heroes'* Sylar, Ben is a charismatic character that fans can't help but love to watch. He is so dark but often has some of the best lines. Ben's self-deprecating, sly humor highlights his wit and intelligence, but even the dark comedy of some of his dialogue further illustrates how dangerous he is. Ben clearly knows what he's doing—he (like villain Sylar) has a plan in mind, and it likely will serve only himself, no matter whose side he purports to be on.

Gray villains on modern SF TV series are often much more interesting to watch than heroes. They seem to know the score and realize that Evil is gaining more strength, on TV series as well as in real life. They know how to survive because they will do what is necessary, only not for the greater good. They look out for themselves and somehow always seem to end up on the "winning" or at least in-charge side. They are chameleons whose words can't be trusted; they will easily change their demeanor or dialogue to fit the current situation. For that reason, no matter how much audiences see of or know about these characters, they never get to know the "real" Ben (or Sylar). Gray villains are mysterious and intriguing because they continue to change while retaining their villainous nature.

Monsters

In addition to the many characters who might be labeled heroes or villains of any shade of gray, *Lost* even provides a bona fide monster. Called by fans Smokezilla, Smokey, or simply smoke monster, the island "creature" gradually becomes less monstrous and more likely to be a sentient, possibly villainous character as more is learned about it. The frightened castaways typically ascribe monster status to the dark, smoke-like cloud that mysteriously shows up at various points in the story. During Season One it brays with a frighteningly mechanical call; at times it sounds like an ancient rollercoaster winding itself up a long hill. During Season Two, when Mr. Eko (Adewale Akinuoye-Agbaje) and Charlie Pace (Dominic Monaghan) confront it, the smoke monster instead provides an electrical storm — this time of scenes from Eko's life — and the sound effects crackle with electricity.

The "monster" is friend or foe, depending upon who sees it and what his or her mental state may be during the encounter. When Locke finds himself face to face with the monster, he is unafraid, looks the creature in the eye, and finds it "beautiful." Perhaps this explains why the smoke monster later takes the form of dead Locke in order to cow Ben and kill Jacob. In Locke, the smoke monster finds an ally who is unafraid of it and willing to do whatever the island requires.

Most victims of Smokey's wrath have less enjoyable encounters. During Season Two, Mr. Eko fearlessly confronts the images of his past, as shown within the monstrous dark cloud ("The 23rd Psalm," 2.10). At this point in the story he is acting as a priest and sincerely wants to help others regain their spirituality. In contrast, he has become a less benevolent character early in Season Three. Embracing his sinful past and capability to harm others, and a personality that once made him a feared drug lord, Eko smugly confronts the smoke monster yet again ("The Cost of Living," 3.5). This time it acts more as a purveyor of cosmic justice and, finding Eko morally lacking, kills him.

The smoke monster has a history as an avenger but hardly seems an avenging "angel." When the territory it guards (e.g., hidden underground temples) seems threatened by castaways from Oceanic 815 or earlier, it drags them to its lair, sometimes maiming before killing them. When Ben "calls" the monster to help him rid the island of invaders, Smokey appears and unceremoniously wipes out mercenaries. Ben explains that he knows how to contact the monster but doesn't control it. His explanation makes the smoke cloud a true monster — uncontrollable, unpredictable. However, its appearance from within the temple during Ben's "judgment" indicates that it is far more sentient than audiences or castaways initially suspected. Whatever its true shape — whether as a human (i.e., Jacob's on-island compatriot and nemesis, first revealed during the Season Five finale) or another life form — it always seems to act as a moral barometer of acceptable behavior on or toward the island. Those who have a clear conscience and can look it in the eye fare much better than those who are proud of their immoral acts and antisocial (or anti-island) behavior.

Even when the smoke monster is revealed to be one form a humanoid shapeshifter may take, it still is an inexplicable, unique being, which makes it fit within the "monster" category. Its acts, including terrorizing and killing humans, illustrate that it is less than benevolent; the moral code it enforces may seem to be subjective at best. Perhaps Smokey, too, has a personal agenda; those who fit into its plan survive, but those who have no apparent use or, worse yet, work at cross purposes to its plan are readily eliminated.

Although nebulous and changing in form and sound, the smoke monster is a more tangible type of monstrous being than an intangible like Time. Nevertheless, Time plays such an important role during Season Five that it also becomes perceived as a monster of sorts. Time is an uncontrollable variable, as the people left behind after the Oceanic 6 are rescued can attest. They seem to bounce from era to era — or the island moves through time and space, taking its inhabitants along for a frightening ride. The uncontrollable time travel disrupts the travelers' bodies, causing mental lapses and nosebleeds. The disruption proves too much for one, who dies as a result of these abrupt shifts.

Because Time can't be controlled or "tamed," completely understood, or its shifts predicted, it fits the definition of a monster. Perhaps scientists like *Lost's* Daniel Faraday, who loses his love, mind, and life as a result of his time-travel experiments, one day will understand the nature of Time and be able to control it. After all, Faraday's calculations give Jack a strategy for changing the future and perhaps bettering the lives of Oceanic 815's passengers. Even to such scientists, however, Time currently remains an enigma. Because time travel can be deadly, or at least unpredictable, it remains a monster until it can be fully understood and manipulated.

Although the smoke monster more closely matches ancient descriptions of serpentine selkies or misshapen creatures like Grendel, *Lost* provides a modern monster that has yet to be tamed by science or technology. Science eventually explains the monsters of earlier centuries. The unexplained are revealed to be evolving life forms or natural creatures, such as sea lions, octopi, or giant eels masquerading as mermaids or sea monsters. Once they can be scientifically studied and understood, former "monsters" become only reminders of a society's uninformed superstitions.

Time, although on the verge of being scientifically understood, still escapes scientists' complete knowledge or control. The ability to change the future, or the past, often has been the province of SF, but it now is coming closer to being an explainable, interpretable, manipulable variable. Audience interest in time travel and the number of stories in which time travel plays a role (e.g., *Heroes*, *Doctor Who*, and *Torchwood* in this book alone, for example) have increased in the past decade's SF TV series. Until science makes Time a commonly understood entity, it may, in some stories such as *Lost*'s, be portrayed as a modern monster.

Lost is a notable series in many respects, not the least for its labyrinthine long-form storytelling style and intriguingly gray characters. Some seek redemption and try to find themselves, as well as save others. Some follow their own agendas and want only to gain ultimate control of their lives and the island. *Lost* details an environment that requires all three categories of characters— heroes, villains, monsters. Their interactions and conflicts illustrate the degree to which their and our societies have become lost.

9

Battlestar Galactica and *Caprica*

The original (late 1970s) and re-imagined versions of *Battlestar Galactica* are based on a simple initial story line: Humans across their solar system are attacked by Cylons, who want to exterminate humanity and nearly succeed. The survivors quickly escape their planets in any available spacecraft, and the battlestar *Galactica* guides them away from the pursuing Cylons and toward a prophesied planet, Earth. The similarity in plot between the two series ends there.

Ronald D. Moore's and David Eick's post–2000 *Battlestar Galactica* introduces a much harsher post-apocalyptic society struggling to survive as they seek a permanent home. Humans must rebuild *everything*, from the structure of their multicultural society to families to the military to social services (e.g., distribution of living space, water, food, clothing, health care, fuel). They must fight the Cylons, even or especially when they learn that the enemy may look just like them and live among them. They debate the place of religion in their society and if spirituality has any place in determining which direction they should steer their fleet. As *SFX* summarized the series, one of their Top 10 of the decade, the "flesh-and-blood protagonists, meanwhile, were usually their own worst enemies. They fought, they bickered, they had sex with the wrong people and generally made a habit of doing the wrong thing." In contrast, the "Cylons may have been the nominal villains, but they came with very human flaws and, as was gradually revealed — the capacity for acts of immense kindness."[1]

Intergenerational as well as interspecies conflict, universal themes of love and redemption, and a gradual understanding of what it means to be human are common ground for *Battlestar Galactica* (2003 pilot movie from creator Glen Larson, 2004–2009 series from re-imaginers Moore and Eick) and its spinoff prequel, *Caprica* (2009 pilot movie, 2010 — series developed by Remi Aubuchon and Moore). Set 58 years before the beginning of *Battlestar Galactica*, *Caprica* traces the creation and evolution of the Cylons. Whereas *Battlestar Galactica* is a war saga providing a timely comparison with Bush-era U.S. politics, *Caprica* is a character drama focusing on conflicts between and within two prominent families: the Graystones and the Adamas. Each series provides a plethora of gray heroes and villains, but *Battlestar Galactica* emphasizes heroism (or lack thereof) in a post-apocalyptic society facing daily challenges to survival. *Caprica*, in contrast, illustrates the sociocultural downfall of a largely complacent majority who enjoy partying all the way to doomsday.

Battlestar Galactica

Although *Battlestar Galactica*'s heroes, including lead military commander Bill Adama (James Edward Olmos) and ace pilot/guide to Earth Kara Thrace/Starbuck (Katee Sackhoff), have been featured in previous chapters (e.g., Chapter 4 about sidekicks), this chapter emphasizes some important characters initially introduced as humanity's nemeses, the Cylons.[2] The most important question in the series—What makes us human?—provides the foundation for numerous intriguing and morally ambiguous episodes, and the quest for home plays an integral role in the series' structure, including an important final season plot twist.

Perhaps because even those characters categorized as heroes, in various shades of gray, struggle with the dark elements of their personality as well as what, not just who, they are (as Kara/Starbuck does), the most intriguing aspects of this remarkable series revolve around the supposed monsters. The Cylons, perceived as a group most Other from humans, eventually splits into groups by model, and then by individual iterations of each model. Although each model is dehumanized by its numeric identifier, the individual Sixes or Eights seem very human and, once viewers get to know them, easily distinguishable by their increasingly disparate personalities.

Gaius Baltar's Caprica Six (Tricia Helfer) of the pilot episode is vastly different in experience, knowledge, and temperament from the Six (aka Head Six) of the final episode, accompanying her lover on a visit to a 21st century Earthbound metropolis. Along the way, different representations of the Six model are shown as scientists, martyrs, terrorists, religious zealots, temptresses, lovers, and mothers-to-be.

Cylon model Eight, first revealed to look like supposedly human *Galactica* pilot Sharon Valerii/Boomer (Grace Park), provides illustrations of various roles, from would-be assassin to doting mother. Eventually one of the Eights bears a half-human, half–Cylon child who becomes modern humanity's Eve. Although the series features other Cylon models, each with a distinctive appearance but with myriad personalities, the Six and Eight models are discussed in this chapter.

Through the Cylons, much more so than the humans, audiences learn more about the nature of humanity and have to redefine biological, experiential,

or spiritual definitions of just what makes each of us "human." For all its successes and critical strengths, revealing what is, isn't, or shouldn't be part of the
definition of *human* is the greatest achievement of *Battlestar Galactica* and
undoubtedly will make it an important text in SF TV and hero literature for
years to come. Its themes transcend the politically chaotic years of one U.S.
presidential administration, although certainly a sociopolitical analysis of *Battlestar Galactica* also is a worthwhile endeavor. The longer lasting exploration
of humanity, however, transcends one time or political era and can make this
series one of the most socially important SF TV series of all time. One reviewer
aptly summarized the series' long-term significance to SF TV: "Proving once
and for all that science fiction TV can have deep meanings, dark tones, apocalyptic scenarios, space battles, and robots while retaining credibility and large
audiences, *Battlestar Galactica* changed the future of sci-fi forever."[3]

THE CYLONS

The original Cylons from the 1970s series clanked a lot and replied "By
your command" to show their subservience to their leader. Imposingly tall and
broad, these gleaming silver monsters viewed the world through one horizon-
tally scanning red eye in their helmet-shaped heads, but their aim was still
deadly. They looked more like a hybrid of *Star Wars'* storm troopers (without
the humans inside the protective gear) and *Doctor Who*'s Cybermen.

When Moore and Eick re-imagined this classic monster, they immediately
illustrated the duality between the original metallic models and the sleek, sexy
human variety. In the first moments of the pilot miniseries, two Cylon Centurions clank onto the space station where a human ambassador awaits an annual
meeting with the Cylons.[4] Of course, in previous years, the Cylons never sent
a representative, so the human is suitably surprised and frightened when two
Centurions arrive and immediately stand guard. They, too, have been upgraded
from the versions with which humans (including the audience) may be familiar.
The camera provides a close-up of razor-sharp Cylon "fingers" stretching as if
eager to dismember human flesh.

After this scary introduction to the Centurions, the beautiful blonde
who saunters into the room is a relief on many levels. She is certainly much
more attractive to look at. The human ambassador stares at her, the desk photo
of his family pushed aside. She seems exceedingly human. In fact, she seems
to have achieved human perfection in body and voice. Wearing a form-fitting
red dress, symbolic of the lust/love/violence to become associated with this
Cylon model, one of the Sixes approaches until she is well within the ambassador's personal space. "Are you human?" she asks before kissing him. As she
bestows a kiss of death, the station explodes, and the Cylons' attack on humanity
begins.

This brief scene sets the tone for the coming series, a confrontation between

Cylons and humans that results in a sexual merger between the two. Many Cylons, especially the Sixes, want to learn more about what it means to be truly human; one of the Eights is mother to a half-human, half–Cylon child and faces all the dangers and prejudices of interspecies marriage (a SF TV theme and plot device going back to the original *Star Trek*'s Spock, his human mother, and his Vulcan father). Human males become "ensnared" by their love of what turn out to be Cylon females. Gaius Baltar (James Callis), a prominent, media-savvy scientist on Caprica, beds his lab assistant before and after she betrays him as a spy, as well as before and after she reveals herself as a Cylon. Both species become fascinated and repelled by each other before finally figuring out that they need each other in order to survive. The new world on which they eventually find themselves requires new ways of thinking and cooperating, or at least co-existing, and the space-traveling humans have much more in common with their former enemies than with the cavemen whose planet they ultimately share.

THE SIXES

Several examples of the Six model provide insight into the complexities of Cylons, even within a single type. As the series progresses, the personalities of the many Sixes introduced into the plot help distinguish one from another much more specifically than differences in costume or even hair color. As portrayed by Tricia Helfer, the most often seen Sixes are Baltar's companion on Caprica (the appropriately named Caprica Six) and the Cylon who inhabits his mental space during most early episodes (Head Six). During the invasion of Caprica, Baltar's lover and scientific collaborator shields the scientist's body, saving him from planetary destruction. Although Caprica Six's body dies in the blast, her "essence" is downloaded into another body, and she is resurrected. She is seen as a hero among Cylons for successfully infiltrating human defenses, leading to the destruction of the Colonies. She is also seen as Baltar's advisor or, at times, "conscience"—although no one but Baltar can see or hear her. Because a version of her is the Six within Baltar's mental space, fans often refer to her as Head Six. Fans become most familiar with Caprica Six and Head Six, with some viewers thinking of them as the same character appearing in different forms at different points in the series. Head Six, however, seems to be the immortal who, along with a "mental" version of Baltar that advises the "real" Baltar and Caprica Six at the end of their journey, is next seen visiting contemporary cosmopolitan Earth.

After the fall of the colonies, Caprica Six becomes even more loyal to Baltar, although she increasingly sees his very human flaws and is often hurt by his behavior. Her association with him makes her more "human" by forcing her to examine emotions that she may not have experienced within a community of Cylons. She loves Baltar but wants him to become a better man, and by the end of the series she has become a positive influence on him and is content to spend the rest of her (unresurrectable) life with him on a new planet. Along the way, Caprica Six loses her status as a Cylon hero because she sides with humans and opposes the Cylons' oppressive policies (including death warrants), especially during the Cylon occupation of the first human colony established after the destruction of their home worlds. She persistently pleads for cooperation between Cylons and humans and hopes at least for a peaceful co-existence. Many of her actions throughout the series (e.g., dying more than once to save Baltar, [repeatedly] saving the Cylon-human hybrid child Hera) are a direct result of her beliefs in peace and human–Cylon equality.

From the Cylon point of view, Caprica Six is a hero who quickly darkens into a villain because of her collusion with humans. From the human point of view, Caprica Six is a Cylon monster who, at best, becomes a villain from her association with the human traitor Baltar. She never becomes a hero to humans, but the few who survive to see the colonization of the new Earth grudgingly accept her presence by the end of the series.

During the final season, Caprica Six even embarks on a romantic relationship with Colonel Tigh, who, when he begins their affair, doesn't know that he also is Cylon. When Caprica Six becomes pregnant, her child initially is perceived as important because it is another hybrid child. However, when Tigh is revealed to be one of the Final Five Cylons, her child takes on even greater significance as the first purely "natural" Cylon baby. Whereas some humans fear the realization that Cylons can now breed without having to be "created" via technology — they have become as "real" as humans— Cylons also worry that they have become "human." Caprica Six miscarries, but the possibility of a Cylon baby illustrates how "human" these "monsters" have become and adds further complications to *Battlestar Galactica*'s answer to What makes us human?

Many other Six "units" play important roles at other points in the series: Shelly Godfrey ("Six Degrees of Separation," 1.7) attempts to discredit Baltar among humans; Gina Inviere ("Pegasus," 2.10; "Razor" movie) masquerades as a human onboard the *Pegasus* where she happens to fall in love with, and later kills, the battlestar's commander, Admiral Cain; and Natalie ("Six of One," 4.4; "The Ties That Bind," 4.5), who, after attempting a coup against other Cylon models, eventually collaborates with Commander Adama to escape with the Final Five Cylons in exchange for the location of the Cylon resurrection ship. Although each of these Sixes has a slightly different physical appearance, as well as great variations in personality and demeanor, they all vacillate between being heroes and villains, whether to Cylons or humans. They are complex characters that help reveal the complexity of Cylon society and make clearcut definitions of *hero*, *villain*, or *monster* much more difficult, even within this single series, much less across the spectrum of post–2000 dark SF.

THE EIGHTS

Like the Sixes, the Eights are intricately and often intimately entwined with humans throughout the series, although the first Eight to be revealed as a Cylon is, to all appearances, a human pilot serving on the *Galactica*. Sharon Valerii/Boomer is loyal to her commander and in love with a human (also later revealed as Cylon) chief mechanic, Galen Tyrol (Aaron Douglas). Sharon/Boomer believes in the backstory implanted in her so that her "sleeper" Cylon persona won't be revealed until she is "activated" as an adult. She remembers her human life before entering the military and only while on *Galactica* begins feeling strange. She doesn't understand what is happening to her and only belatedly suspects that she may be a Cylon. (*Torchwood* also explores the possibility of alien sleeper agents among humanity in one episode, but only in *Battlestar Galactica* is this theme developed through multiple episodes to build suspense and suspicion.)

When fully activated as a Cylon, Boomer betrays her human comrades quite dramatically: she attempts to assassinate Commander Adama ("Kobol's Last Gleaming," 1.13). This Sharon/Eight incarnation is killed when she attempts to protect her former lover, Tyrol, who is suspected of being Cylon for his affair with Sharon. Both have been tormented and face death because of their association, and the characters who turn out to be Cylons are much more self-sacrificing and "human" than the comrades who want to test, torture, and then execute them as enemies. Sharon dies in Tyrol's arms, proclaiming her love ("Resistance," 2.4). When the "Sharon/Boomer" persona is resurrected in a new body, she tries to live among Cylons but finds her experiences with humans difficult to forget. Like Caprica Six, she serves as an intermediary between humans and Cylons and tries to persuade Cylons to take a more conciliatory approach to their dealings with humanity. She, like Caprica Six, has loved humans and no longer wants to exterminate the species.

In fact, even Sharon's incarceration after the attempted assassination is a necessary step in developing her "humanity." In hindsight, after viewers have seen the entire story and know who becomes the Cylons' vaunted Final Five, Sharon's/Boomer's incarceration and treatment at the hands of humans is a necessary step in the "human" evolution of the Cylons. Her then-lover Galen Tyrol is angry because he believes he has been played. He can't understand how she wouldn't know she's a Cylon. The idea of a sleeper agent is abhorrent to him, and Galen the man is subsumed under the chief engineer loyal to his ship and its commander. In a series full of ironies, Galen's later discovery that he is not only Cylon but one of the Final Five upper-echelon Cylon creators makes viewers wonder just how much he subconsciously knew or how his reactions to Sharon's Cylon "awakening" might be based on his "machine" heritage.

Without her brutal treatment, this Eight might never understand the negative side of humanity and be able to protect her future offspring. Another

Eight, Sharon Agathon/Athena might never, ironically enough, have been able to form a true partnership with the very human Karl Agathon/Helo (Tahmoh Penikett). Karl doesn't keep their relationship secret, unlike Galen did out of a sense of duty and military propriety. Because of their interspecies love, their story becomes analogous to a pragmatic if tortured Romeo-and-Juliet pairing. Their love child, Hera, is the object of great concern for humans and Cylons. Sharon's and Karl's concern for their child's safety unites them, and Sharon becomes the most "normal" (to humans) of all Cylons. She becomes a working spouse and mother, and although she always knows she's Cylon, she makes no apologies for who she is. She is committed to her relationship with Karl and, because of this very personal reason, becomes an important catalyst for improving human–Cylon interactions.

Because the Eights, like all other models, share each other's thoughts and experiences, they develop a much clearer understanding of humanity (as do the Sixes). Interestingly enough, the Eights and Sixes are the only Cylons to stay with humans voluntarily and form lasting emotional love relationships with them. Fittingly, Sharon's and Karl's child, Hera, becomes the mother of modern human (hybrid) civilization.

BALTAR'S SOCIALIZATION
AND HUMANIZATION

At the beginning of the *Battlestar Galactica* saga, Gaius Baltar is a television darling as much noted for his slick celebrity as his scientific genius. He expects beautiful women to fall in love with him. He doesn't feel the need to be monogamous or to become emotionally involved with the women with whom he has sex. Baltar has such an inflated sense of self-importance that he believes he is above security protocols, inadvertently sharing scientific secrets with a Cylon spy masquerading as a human woman besotted with him. Once the Cylon attack is underway and Baltar realizes that he has betrayed humanity, he only wants to protect himself and blame others for anything to do with the attack. He looks out only for himself and will do anything to save himself physical or emotional pain. He often represents the worst of humanity with his duplicity and self-absorption.

Nevertheless, Baltar has an important role to play both in human and Cylon history. At various times in the story he plays the role of a savior/leader with knowledge about Cylons or humans, but his motivation isn't to save others. He uses his knowledge to make either side want to keep him alive. Depending on the (TV) season, he is a scientific leader, running tests to determine who is Cylon and who isn't; a political leader who worms his way into the presidency, only once again to "betray" humanity by surrendering a fledgling colony to the Cylons; a spiritual leader who preaches peace while allowing his female followers to take care of him; and even, briefly, a warrior in defense of *Galactica* during a final battle. His role encompasses science, politics, and religion; thus he is the only character to perform so many roles in so many important areas of human life. When he takes up a weapon to fight during *Galactica*'s boarding in a final battle, he even briefly experiences a "military" life first hand, although as the colonists' Vice President and President he also technically serves as a military commander in chief.

Baltar's chameleon lives, among humans and Cylons, provide him with a vast number of experiences. In one short life he is able to infiltrate almost every aspect of human existence. In these roles, however, he usually fails to act honorably or heroically unless such an action saves his life. Of all *Battlestar Galactica*'s characters, Gaius Baltar is consistently self-centered and only shows glimpses of a willingness to sacrifice himself during what he believes will be the doomed *Galactica*'s final moments.

Throughout these many roles, Baltar eventually becomes socialized to understand others and see how real society works outside his self-important bubble of influence. More importantly, he becomes humanized so that he truly feels positive emotions, including love, and not just lust, power, greed, or fear. His socialization and greater humanity result from his association with Caprica Six. She understands him, including his flaws and many weaknesses. She knows his vanity and can appeal to it. However, she also falls in love with him and wants him to be a better man. She is a muse and conscience as much as a partner, although in many episodes Head Six is no more than an intermittent presence in Baltar's mind. Only he can see and hear her, resulting in many humorous scenes when the dialogue reflects double meanings — what Baltar says to someone on the *Galactica* and what he really means in his conversation with the "invisible" Six. Baltar also relies on her to physically save his life after being "outed" as a traitor to humanity for sharing secrets that helped the Cylons begin their attack and, later, after being captured by Cylons. She is the only constant in his life.

Caprica Six/Head Six shows Baltar how and when to act and what to say. He has become vain in expecting to be the center of attention, whether as an elite scientist, temporary president, or cult-like spiritual leader. He literally *plays* many roles on the *Galactica*; he always seems to be acting. Baltar hides behind a mask so often that he has become a disingenuous person. A Cylon Six forces him to become a real person and to face his weaknesses; she also expresses her emotions to him so that he knows exactly how his words and actions affect her. Without her comments and feedback, Baltar never would've become the humbled but, ironically, stronger and better man shown on new Earth. A Cylon is the source of his emotional redemption, and, in reality, her opinion of him is ultimately all that counts in his life.

During the finale, when he and Caprica Six land on Earth and must start over, Baltar is emotionally and psychologically crushed. His celebrity and notoriety gone, he is a new colonist just like everyone else. In fact, he returns to his poor farmboy roots, an image he worked long to dispel. Caprica Six knows even this, but she comforts him with the knowledge that, because he does understand farming, he is well suited to help them survive on this new world. She doesn't leave him because he no longer is famous/infamous or the center of humanity's attention. She stays with him because she loves and believes in him, even when he thinks he is a failure.

Without Caprica Six's continuing support and guidance, Baltar wouldn't be "redeemed" for his vain follies that lead to destruction and death, and he wouldn't understand what it means to be human. That's quite an important role for a Cylon "enemy" of humanity.

IMMORTALITY AND HUMANITY

As other characters discussed in this book discover, the common denominator among the series' answer to What makes us human? ends up being simple — mortality. The *Lost* characters, such as Jacob, who "play God" with mortals can risk whatever they like because they seem to bear no long-term physical consequences of their actions. Even dead characters like Christian Shephard or Charlie Pace seem remarkably mellow in the afterlife because they don't face time constraints involving personal risk. If they don't get something right in the afterlife, they have time to try again or make amends. They don't have to worry about facing the ultimate deadline of death. An important addition to *Doctor Who*'s Tenth Doctor is his fear of his prophesied death/regeneration. This Doctor seems all the more human to audiences for it; his final words before regeneration, "I don't want to go," could be the lament of any person wishing for a little more time ("The End of Time, Part 2"). *Torchwood*'s Jack Harkness tells a colleague that he only felt truly alive when he thought that his most recent death would be final ("Cyberwoman," 1.4). *Heroes'* Sylar smirks at the silly mortal heroes who think they can stop him; he realizes that, unless someone can take away his ability to self-heal, he can outlast any of the good guys.

Similarly, the Cylons chasing humans throughout much of *Battlestar Galactica* believe that time is on their side. Multiple copies almost ensure that one model will survive (although a complete "line" has been shut down by other Cylons, viewers come to learn). More important, as long as a resurrection ship is nearby, dead Cylons' memories and personalities can be resurrected in a new body. As long as the technological possibility of resurrection is readily available, the Cylons don't fear death and can expend their bodies at will to further their cause.

They become fearful of death and truly more "human" once the resurrection ships are destroyed. Without the convenient method of "uploading" into a new body, Cylons become just as vulnerable (i.e., mortal) as humans. Of course, a model will survive, much as the human species will survive as long as individual members still exist, but Cylons increasingly see the differences in personality, experience, and motivation — as well as increasing emotion — as individual members of even one model interact directly with humans. They become unique personalities, even if the outer bodies look remarkably similar. Deciding how to live one life, whether for oneself or the group, becomes a turning point for individual Cylons, such as Caprica Six and Sharon/Athena, as well as the entire race.

Ironically, what survives beyond the lives of characters who make the journey from a far-off galaxy to the planet they call Earth, or indeed what survives for millennia of human development, are Caprica Six and Baltar. These characters initially are villains (or "monsters") and about as far from ideal humans as writers could make them. Nevertheless, whatever "deity" is behind the story — *Battlestar Galactica*'s writers never explain if they support the monotheistic Cylons, polytheistic humans, or neither — continues to monitor the progress of humanity into the 21st century. An ethereal Six and Baltar tell their real-life counterparts that their role in the journey has ended with their arrival on Earth ("Daybreak," 4.22).

In the series' epilogue, the two meander a crowded metropolis and question whether the hybrid civilization, born from humans and Cylons, will learn from civilizations long gone or choose, once again, to destroy themselves. That Caprica Six and Baltar seem to be some type of divine observers or messengers frustrated many long-time viewers, although the symbolism of the characters who ultimately "survive" and become immortal is worth analysis.

In a Pinocchio-like tale of human development, Caprica Six wants to become "a real woman" and, for all intents and purposes, becomes one. She evolves from a cyborg race to achieve the ability to procreate — with another Cylon, no less (newly revealed member of the elite Final Five Colonel Tigh). Her influence redeems Baltar and transforms him through many roles (possibly representative of several "lives") during his journey to Earth.

Baltar and Caprica Six apparently please their unseen ultimate creator so much that "he" (using the masculine pronoun these two mention when discussing their "boss") allows them to survive in some form throughout time. Like *Torchwood*'s choice of Captain Jack to represent what humanity becomes or which traits survive, *Battlestar Galactica* allows a "gray" selection of characters who have been both heroes and villains to become immortal.

Caprica

The 2009 DVD movie (later shown at film festivals and downloaded from the SyFy website) that serves as *Caprica*'s pilot episode introduces a host of characters who, on the surface, could become heroes, villains, or even, under the right circumstances, monsters.[5] The leading families— the Graystones and the Adamas— have upper-class social status, education, and charisma on their side, all traits of winners that could make them the series' heroes. On the other hand, they also share a tragedy — the loss of a daughter — from a terrorist bombing and some atypical ways of dealing with that loss. Whether their responses to senseless death and the destruction of their families provides the impetus to act heroically or simply provides them a reason for becoming self-absorbed and indifferent to the consequences of their decisions provides the starting point for the SyFy TV series in 2010.

As a prequel to *Battlestar Galactica*, *Caprica*'s new characters offer more opportunity for development because they, less than established *Battlestar Galactica* characters like Bill Adama (in *Caprica* still a young boy), aren't yet part of the *Battlestar Galactica* mythology or canon. Seeing how a devoted dad might become father to the Cylon race that attacks humans in the first moments of the *Battlestar Galactica* series should provide a modern primer of how even the best-intentioned characters can become the villains not only of a TV series, but of the whole (fictionalized) human race.

The emphasis on character drama, rather than warfare or apocalyptic drama, made *Caprica* seem a natural for the film festival circuit, including stops at the San Diego Film Festival in September and the Woodstock Film Festival in October 2009. SyFy's press release announcing this innovative marketing identified the series this way, a distinct difference from its description of *Battlestar Galactica*: "This original, standalone series will feature the passion, intrigue, political backbiting, and family conflict in an omnipotent society that is at the height of its blind power and glory ... and, unknowingly, on the brink of its fall."[6]

Because *Battlestar Galactica* maintains a faithful following among fans and TV critics, *Caprica* was highly anticipated. The press release, like much of the prequel's marketing, attempted to play up the connection with *Battlestar Galactica*'s success while distinguishing the series as a "standalone" story attractive to new audiences. Throughout 2009, especially when casting began for the regular series, further press releases enticed prospective viewers whenever a new development took place.

Once again, casting agents called on James Marsters to portray a villain, as he previously has done on *Buffy*, *Angel*, and *Torchwood*. This time SyFy described his character as "driven by moralistic and yet carnal desires, this unpredictable villain is constantly torn by his conflicting motivations," a description that easily fits previous gray villains Spike and Captain John Hart.[7] *Entertainment Weekly* prefaced Marsters' entry into the series and increased audience anticipation by publishing the first photo of Marsters as Barnaby Greely; the image, published in late January, well before Marsters' debut in March 2010, portrays this villain as intense and angry. Sitting on a well-worn leather chair in what looks to be a dirty warehouse, Greely barely restrains himself from leaping toward the camera. The article this time refers to the villain as "an enigmatic and dangerous villain in the monotheistic world."[8] Similar to charismatic villains Sylar (*Heroes*) or Ben Linus (*Lost*), Greely is a character described in the press as a series' villain. Whereas other characters, including the leads, may be ambiguously good or bad, Greely much more easily fits into the villain category. He already seems like a dark villain even before viewers get a chance to meet him.

Such a villain seems an appropriate anchor point on a scale of gray villains. *Caprica* is a dark series, given its premise. According to creator Moore, the story explains how "it's all going to end for all of these people and it's really about ... these people who didn't see it coming and how it came. How they planted the seeds of their own destruction and this society sort of had to be destroyed."⁹ The parallels with Western societies that many citizens either fear will happen within the next generation or two or what cultural critics predict will happen unless we change direction quickly make *Caprica* seem like an appropriate series to begin the second decade of the 21st century.

THE PILOT MOVIE

By repeating the *Caprica* pilot movie as the series' premiere on January 22, 2010 (a film which had been released on DVD months earlier and then shown elsewhere, including on the SyFy website), the network lost momentum already built up for the series. Hardcore fans who anticipated the premiere then had to wait yet another week for a new episode. New viewers could have caught up with the backstory via the SyFy website or DVD; showing the movie in its entirety didn't help build a core audience for the continuing series.

This disappointment and further wait for more of the *Caprica* story didn't help increase viewership when some TV critics, with the opportunity to review the first four episodes ahead of broadcast, complained that the post-pilot episodes were uneven and less focused than the well-received pilot. As an introduction to *Caprica* the series, however, the pilot movie is an intriguing story in itself, with plenty of gray heroes, villains, and potential monsters. Its first regular episodes further establish the Adamas and Graystones while clearly illustrating Otherness at every level of personal and societal relationship. The character development only muddies the waters regarding who is a hero and who is not; Zoe/avatar Zoe/Cylon becomes the most sympathetic character in the early story, but even she has monstrous moments.

FROM ENTREPRENEUR TO VILLAIN

One of the series' initial protagonists, Daniel Graystone (Eric Stoltz), loves his only child, Zoe (Alessandra Toreson), who is closer to him than to her mother, Amanda (Paula Malcomson). Whereas Zoe continually pushes her mother's buttons in rebellion, her personality and interests resemble those of her father, a computer/robotics expert working on a government defense contract. Zoe shares her father's proficiency in program design but uses it for a different aim — to improve society.

Zoe despises the violence and sexuality openly on display each night in a holographic entertainment site frequented by teenagers. This online underground offers everything for easy experimentation: a variety of sexual acts with one or many partners, a rave-like atmosphere where a human sacrifice becomes center-stage entertainment, a pulsing beat to which the frenzied partiers dance and shout, secret rooms where drugs and alcohol can be shared. Instead of participating in the nightly rituals, Zoe and her best friend Lacy Rand (Magda Apanowicz) and boyfriend Ben Stark (Avan Jogia) infiltrate the holo venue to see if they can stop or change the direction of this communal depravity. To help her mix with the crowd and possibly commit some act to stop the sacrificial deaths, Zoe creates an avatar into which she pours her memories and aspirations. When the physical Zoe dies in a terrorist bomb explosion, her avatar becomes all that is left of her personality and memories.

Zoe could've been a heroic martyr to a cause — a religious young woman planning to escape her polytheistic planet to join the monotheistic faithful on a nearby world. She may not have had the clearest idea about how to effect social change, but she uses her ability to create a life-like avatar as a starting point. Perhaps what is tragic in *Caprica* is that this wannabe hero becomes the first of the Cylons, her "mind" placed into a metallic body without her permission. Given the direction of Cylon development leading to the *Battlestar Galactica* story, Zoe is unlikely to become a series' hero; instead, she is far more likely to be perceived as either monster or villain to the future of humanity.

Zoe's father isn't a classic villain. He might even be viewed as a Caprican hero who develops innovative technology that can be used to bring the physically dead holographically back to life, and then to re-animate them within a robotic body. Audiences, however, may not take the "Caprican" view of Daniel Graystone, instead seeing him as a gray villain who commits the worst atrocity against the memory of his daughter. He turns her into the antithesis of who she was as a living young woman. By the end of the pilot movie, Graystone certainly seems more of a villain with his personal desire to keep Zoe alive at all costs— even against her holographic will.

Even without his treatment of real and holographic Zoe, Graystone is still a gray character on the basis of his business dealings. His need to keep the defense contract on his home world, instead of seeing it outsourced to another planet, may seem understandable. However, his corporate espionage to retain the contract and keep his company's technical edge moves him into ever-grayer territory. Because *Battlestar Galactica*'s fans know that the Cylons, within a few years, will evolve and wipe out most humans, Graystone's current actions in this prequel take on more sinister overtones. Audiences understand how a series of small acts can lead an ordinary man, whose previous "crime" is the enjoyment and perpetuation of his affluent lifestyle, into ultimately villainous acts.

In the pilot movie, Zoe takes after her father in using technology to "play God," but she does so for sincerely good reasons. "Zoe knew God, and God touched her heart and gave her the ability to create life itself," Lacy tells Daniel Graystone. Zoe, in effect, "played God" by creating her avatar, but this ability to create a benign avatar living in a remote holosuite seems like a divine gift, not a curse. According to Lacy, Zoe knew the difference between good and evil, right and wrong, and she instilled her morality in her avatar. Zoe only designed the avatar as a vehicle for change; she needed someone to stop depraved actions in the holographic world in which other young people experimented with all sorts of "sin." Real Zoe didn't, and probably couldn't have, realized the potential effects of creating such a "real" avatar. Like her father, she only wants to create life for personal reasons, and hers seem altruistic: to save her world. According to the pilot movie, the younger generation of Zoe, Lacy, and Ben believe in one God who shows them the difference between Good and Evil. Zoe's polytheistic parents obviously don't follow the one God, and so, it is implied, they lack this morality.

Zoe's father, however, is not a Man of Faith (as discussed in Chapter 8 about *Lost* characters); he is a scientist who demands experiential or scientific data to convince him of such an all-knowing God. "Who's to say you can't copy a soul?" Daniel asks Joseph Adama (Esai Morales), who loses both his daughter and his wife in the train blast. Daniel wants to see the proof when Joseph protests that a soul can't be copied; he just feels that's wrong but can't scientifically support his conviction that an avatar is the same as a living person. "Isn't it worth trying?" Daniel emotionally persuades Joseph. He makes a compelling argument in order to do what he wants to do and to rationalize his plan.

The rhetoric sounds "logical" to viewers as well as Joseph because Daniel first establishes the ways that the men are alike — both in their grief over the loss of their daughters and in their less-than-virtuous business practices. Then he appeals to the grieving father's emotions and makes the audience question whether they would be able to pass up the opportunity to bring dead loved ones back to life. When Daniel offers Joseph an avatar of his daughter, the wary man can't overcome his curiosity and hope, so he agrees to talk with her.

The opposing view in the fathers' moral debate is represented by Tamara Adama (Genevieve Buechner), Joseph's daughter-turned-avatar. Her reaction to the realization that she physically is dead but holographically alive further establishes the moral feud between the grieving fathers. Whereas avatar Zoe embraces her "life" and fiercely argues that she is as close to a "real" human as possible, new avatar Tamara is frightened by her "awakening" in a dark space she doesn't remember entering.

"Daddy, my heart isn't beating!" Tamara cries. "She'll adjust" (to being heartless), Daniel explains to the horrified father. Joseph admits that only the gods have power over death, but Daniel rejects that notion. The avatars aren't human; they literally lack a heart, but they seem in every other way to be "human." Perhaps Daniel also is "heartless" and less than human, for all that he is biologically real. Whether *soul* or *heart* is the definition of being human, *Caprica* suggests that biological, electrical, or chemical definitions may be lacking. What makes us human can't be proven scientifically, but, just as Joseph Adama insists, we all know what we feel makes us human.

FROM STEREOTYPICAL VILLAINY TO POTENTIAL HEROICS

The paternal protagonists in this series have the capability to be either heroes or villains. Most obviously, Daniel Graystone could be viewed as a modern Dr. Frankenstein, creating life from parts of his dead daughter. His ethics already are questionable and set in motion a series of cause-effect scenes. He orchestrates the theft of scientific secrets to turn his military robot into an expert killing machine; in so doing, he undermines a competitor and wins a government contract. He secretly creates an avatar of Joseph Adama's dead daughter, based on his own daughter Zoe's prototype avatar. He deposits Zoe's avatar into a Cylon body. If his work were aboveboard and he didn't fear some kind of censure, whether from his wife or the scientific or business communities in which he is prominent, he likely would've made his "discoveries" and ability to return to life(form) the recently dead known—for glory and profit. Daniel Graystone seems to enjoy his upscale lifestyle and will do anything to maintain it. Similarly, once he sets his mind to getting his daughter back, at whatever cost and in whatever form, he becomes extremely focused.

Yet for all his ability to "play God" and to work on avatars in his secret lair—a hidden lab in his house—Graystone doesn't seem all that villainous. He doesn't seem likely to turn Zoe into a monster who preys on society; he only wants to keep his daughter's personality alive. He isn't forcing anyone to create an avatar; in fact, he accepts Adama's horror at his daughter's avatar and, although he doesn't understand why he wouldn't want one, abides by Adama's decision not to continue this "model." Graystone is brilliant, cunning, and obsessive, but these traits could be used as easily for Good as for Evil. His motives, at least in the pilot movie, may not be pure, but they don't hurt the rest of society.

Although Graystone's prototype Cylon soldier is efficient and ruthless in a demonstration of seek-and-destroy enacted before government authorities, his work as a Caprican contractor may even make him seem heroic. The mechanical soldier is designed to protect citizens from invaders; in a war, a corps of these soldiers would be efficient protectors, killing the enemy. As well, they are mechanical and would save human soldiers' lives. By developing such a prototype, Graystone seems to be a hero of his colony—no matter that he creates the prototype as a business deal instead of for any philanthropic reason (or that he steals the information that solves a technical problem that previously stymied him). Graystone is a proficient, successful inventor and businessman. When he uses his skill and knowledge for the protection of society, he seems more of a heroic character.

Similarly, Joseph Adama can be perceived either as a potential villain or a hero, depending upon the circumstance. He has made good as an immigrant who becomes a successful attorney and can work on behalf of the innocent or wrongly accused. However, he also comes from a family whose reputation is at best shady.

Without wanting to create a "Mafia"-style stereotype, showrunner and scriptwriter Jane Espenson developed Adama's brother Sam as an "enforcer" type of character. Sam works for his "family" of businessmen, who resort to extortion and threats in order to further their business dealings or to ward off competitors. They punish those who dare go against them. Although Joseph Adama tries to stay away from this business, he occasionally is drawn in. Like others who have gone to the family for help, Adama owes his education and resulting successful career to their funding. To repay his debt, despite his misgivings, he agrees to threaten a judge into deciding in the family's favor.

Joseph Adama doesn't always give in to "Mafia" demands, but he occasionally works illegally and undermines the justice system because he feels indebted to "villains." He thus occasionally drifts into ever grayer territory and selectively determines who is sentenced and who is set free. In these scenes from the pilot movie, Adama shows the potential to become more villainous, whether as a "Mafia" pawn or as a more powerful man who uses underworld connections to get what he wants.

Ironically, the protagonists of the pilot episode are initially portrayed as gray characters with the potential to be either heroes or villains. As mentioned in earlier chapters, these protagonists are series' leads who have the capability to become anything, to work for Good or Evil, based on what viewers see from the pilot. They may become more complex and darker as the series progresses, but they start out as less than pristine heroes. Their initial characterizations further illustrate the way that SF TV series have grown progressively darker and lead characters more ambiguous as the first decade of the 2000s ended and the next decade began. *Caprica* enters the 2010s as a prime example of popular, populist dark SF TV.

CHARACTERS WITH THE GREATEST
AUDIENCE APPEAL

The strongest characters in *Caprica* should be the gray heroes/villains represented by adult characters/fathers Daniel Graystone and Joseph Adama. However, their children and children's generation are more likely to be the characters the majority of young viewers want to follow. In the pilot, however, the younger generation plays supporting roles, and the most important teen character, Zoe Graystone, is dead early in the movie.

Zoe seems less a hero, a role she may have wanted, than a victim or potential monster, given the future shown in *Battlestar Galactica*. Her best friend, Lacy, is a conflicted teen who misses her dead friends but fears to do anything against the dominant society's laws or her school's rules. She seems unlikely to become a revolutionary, despite her psychological agreement with Zoe's philosophy that the world must change. She doesn't find spiritual comfort in the religion promoted by her school and culture, but she also doesn't seem nearly as committed to her conversion to monotheism as Zoe or Ben. However, she is attracted to the possibility of a more loving family life, which she first witnesses at the home of Sister Clarice Willow (Polly Walker). The polytheistic headmistress shares her rambunctious but loving home with several husbands and wives; the plural marriage intrigues Lacy. Using the possibility of familial or sexual love to entice Lacy is one way for Sister Clarice to convert her student to polytheism ("Rebirth," 1.1).

Avatar Zoe is increasingly human, thanks to a biofeedback program that allows the avatar to feel real Zoe's emotions, including fear and pain from the bombing, in real time. "You're just a thing," Zoe's best friend Lacy cries to the avatar, who insists she is as real as the "real Zoe." "I'm not a person. I know that, but I feel like one," Zoe explains. Similar to the replicants in *Blade Runner*, who might not realize they aren't human, avatar Zoe at some level knows that her "creation" isn't typical of humans, yet she experiences everything a human teenager does. In the *Battlestar Galactica* story, the Cylons, especially the Sixes and Eights, often explain that they feel human and are as close to human as possible, although they were created by "unnatural" (to humans) methods. The Cylons are the technological children of humans, and, as *Caprica* illustrates, that parallel is much more realistic than *Battlestar Galactica* fans might've imagined.

Even the supporting characters who easily could become stereotypical villains in the black-and-white Caprican world are given shades of gray in this miniseries describing families' and societies' radical changes before their fall. Two characters, in particular, illustrate this trend toward oppositional interpretations—as villain or hero—depending on which set of cultural values introduced into the series best fits the viewers' or characters' beliefs. Their ambiguity makes them more intriguing to audiences, who want to know more about them and their backgrounds, as well as whether they will change in future episodes.

Sam Adama (Sasha Roiz) works for the "Mafia," and Zoe Graystone's boyfriend Ben is a devout monotheist eager to bring change to a polytheistic culture—to the extent of becoming a willing martyr. Both characters are depicted in straightforward style; their actions are shown as they occur, with no backstory or expectation about how they "should" behave, leaving other characters to praise or condemn these supporting characters based on these acts alone.

Although Sam has few scenes in the pilot movie, one in particular is highly descriptive. Sam the executioner sneaks into a judge's house at night, his ritualistically tattooed body gleaming in the pale light. He takes two knives and slashes the judge's throat, the blood becoming yet another red highlight within the gray-toned night scene. Sam is an efficient employee; the murder scene seems similar to the "horsehead" death scene from *The Godfather*, when another rich man refusing to capitulate to "Mafia" demands awakens in a bloody bed. Sam seems less villain or monster than a dedicated employee who is efficient at his job and knows better than to question his superiors. The murder seems less an immoral act than a business deal; the execution is merely a promised result if the judge doesn't change his course of action. The judge who withstands pressure from messenger Joseph on behalf of the "Mafia" doesn't seem like a hero; instead he comes across as a bigoted man who insults Joseph's ethnicity. Because Joseph is one of the protagonists or gray heroes in the story, anyone who insults him, such as the judge, by default seems villainous. The only difference among characters is the shades of gray of their dark deeds; no character is completely good.

Terrorist Ben "was fighting evil with all his heart," their monotheistic school headmistress tells Lacy after Ben's and Zoe's deaths. Although Ben is shown as nervous and distracted when he and Zoe board the train, Zoe interprets his anxiety as stemming from their running away to another planet. When Ben tears open his jacket to reveal bombs strapped to his chest, he looks more like a scared but determined teen than a hardened militant. To devout monotheists literally dying for change, the dominant society is the one that is evil and depraved (and surprisingly similar to our own); such a political commentary, while not quite as overt as that in *Battlestar Galactica*, still presents an interesting look at modern politics and religion.

Playing God:
Monotheists vs. Polytheists

Like *Battlestar Galactica*, especially in its early seasons, *Caprica* pits two opposing religions against each other, and that conflict becomes integral to the disintegration of the relationship between then-alive Zoe Graystone and her parents. The "terrorists" and "extremists" in this saga are the monotheists; the mainstream religion is polytheism. When Zoe embraces monotheism, she feels religiously persecuted, even at home, with parents who wouldn't understand her spiritual choices. Her religious beliefs incite her activism, which, in turn, leads her to fall in with friends who are more violent in their expression of devotion. Although Zoe herself doesn't advocate the use of violence and merely plans to run away to a planet where people share her religious beliefs, her boyfriend does. Ben sets off a bomb in a crowded commuter train, killing himself and Zoe in the process.

As a result of her friendship with this bomber and reports of her monothe-

istic conversion, Zoe is labeled a "terrorist" by the police investigating the bombing. Zoe's mother Amanda is horrified and insulted when police officers question her about her daughter's political/religious activities. Ironically, during
the first regular episode, Amanda Graystone "outs" her dead daughter as a terrorist during a memorial service for the bombing victims ("Rebirth," 1.1).[10] She
ruthlessly changes her mind about her only child when she finds the infinity
symbol, emblematic of the radicalized Soldiers of the One, within her daughter's
personal effects returned by Ben's mother. Amanda apologizes for her child's
wrongful religious belief, which led to the deaths of so many.

"We create life, and then one day we have to face who they are, what they
become, and what they do." Amanda's voice at the memorial overlays a scene
at the Graystone home when Cylon Zoe finds a shiny surface in which to view
her image. The scene becomes symbolic not only of the family's past (creation
of a monotheist), but of its present (creation of an avatar and Cylon prototype)
and humanity's future (creator of the Cylon species). Publicly, because of her
parents' high visibility and status within the community (e.g., owners of a pyramid team, entrepreneurs of Graystone Industries, prominent professionals—
he a computer/robotics designer and government contractor, she a neurosurgeon),
Zoe becomes a poster child for the monotheists. Thus, Zoe becomes Other both
publicly and privately, providing many themes for further character development. Again, her role is ambiguous enough that she could be seen either as a
hero/martyr to the monotheists or as a misguided terrorist/victim/villain by
the polytheists.

Amanda may have given birth to Zoe, but Daniel masterminds her rebirth
as Zoe/avatar and Zoe/Cylon — what Lacy refers to as the "trinity," a religious
metaphor not lost on the audience. Daniel plays God with technology; indeed,
his "religious fervor" involves his love of science and technology, and his ability
to be an innovative creator of robotic prototypes. The Cylons, however, become
a unique creation: a blend of Zoe's personality and memories, the avatar she creates, and the robotic body able to house and synthesize its own memories with
those of the avatar and dead teen. A "miracle" allows these three distinctive life
forces to become a new entity, one that surpasses Amanda's, Daniel's, or Zoe's
ability as creators. Those who "play God" with this ability to create new life aren't
inherently Good or Evil. Their creations' later actions ultimately determine
whether creators are sociopolitically viewed as heroes or villains; for creators to
be identified as cultural heroes, their creations need to become heroes.

Two promotional posters released in late 2009 in preparation for *Caprica*'s
official January 2010 series debut play up monotheistic imagery with which
viewers reared in a Judeo-Christian culture would be familiar.[11] The posters
emphasize the concept of "forbidden fruit" and the Biblical Eve taking an apple
from the tree of knowledge. Two posters representing key characters stand out:
one of the conflicting (and conflicted) fathers and one of pre–Cylon Zoe.

Daniel Graystone's temptation to "play God" is specifically emphasized in the poster in which he faces a barren tree bearing one red apple. As mentioned in Chapter 5, the red/black/white color scheme is extremely popular in recent SF TV series, including *Caprica* and its predecessor, *Battlestar Galactica*. In these posters, the colors heighten the story's dramatic elements and visually draw viewers' attention to the apple of "forbidden knowledge." The black/white/gray scheme used in the rest of the poster matches the darkness or bleakness of the grieving fathers' world but contrasts their current lives with the possibility of what that forbidden knowledge might help them achieve. The suited leads look like businessmen, but Graystone stands in the foreground, much closer to the red apple of temptation suspended from a tree in the poster's foreground. As the pilot movie reveals, he gives in to temptation to place his daughter's avatar into the body of a cyborg. Just what else he plans to do in his quest to use/abuse science and technology for his own ends undoubtedly will form the basis of the regular series' plots. The otherwise barren tree of knowledge looks almost sinister; it suspiciously bears only one fruit — that gleaming red apple. Graystone's expression gives no indication whether he will pick that fruit, but the opportunity is clearly in front of him.

A similarly themed poster shows young (pre–Cylon) Zoe coyly glancing over her shoulder at the camera. She is nude and looks knowingly seductive; a bite is out of the apple she holds before her. The avatar–Cylon hybrid Zoe is both the result of using forbidden knowledge to prolong her "life" and the source of the temptation to combine Zoe's avatar (which she brilliantly created and gave life to) with the impressive (and potentially violent) Cylon body created and programmed by Daniel Graystone. Zoe's demeanor adds a sexual overtone to this poster and foreshadows the (*Battlestar Galactica*) future of sexy, humanoid Cylons. In effect, Zoe becomes the Cylons' Eve, an appropriate metaphor for this poster.

The nature of God is an obvious theme within *Caprica*, even more so than in the early seasons of *Battlestar Galactica* when humans searched for divine guidance in their trek toward Earth and Cylons were convinced of their superiority over humans in part because of their belief in the one God. With the introduction of Zoe as the mother of all Cylons, her religious beliefs naturally become an important focus in the prequel. Because Zoe fervently believes in one God, enough to run away from home on the way to religious freedom on another planet — and unknowingly becoming a martyr to the religious cause — her ideas may form the foundation of Cylon spiritual development. "Playing God" may take on additional meaning with the increasing emphasis on religion in *Caprica*.

LIGHT AND DARK IN CHARACTER DEVELOPMENT

The judicious use of color provides a stark contrast with the grayness of most of Caprican society, and how and where that color appears emphasizes differences between the younger generation's view of their world and that of their parents. The main characters often illustrate the black-and-white dichotomies of Caprican citizens' social, religious, political, economic, and philosophical views. Within each character, too, is the capability to choose how to act, to be enlightened or to live in darkness, to work to make a better future or to enforce the status quo— or persecute others. Color versus lack of color, oppositions in black and white, as well as dark and light — these visual effects reinforce *Caprica*'s sometimes heavy-handed indications of a divided society soon to collapse.

Teenaged Zoe sees these oppositions, and the clothing and colors she wears at night, hidden in the depths of a holorave, are quite different from the school uniform she wears to conform during the day. She wears a blue dress in the holoroom, her "real" self looking at her avatar standing next to the stage for a sacrifice planned to the underworld goddess Hecate, an appropriate patron for acts committed in a dark, electronic "underground." Zoe and the avatar are connected—"She's going to help change it," Zoe says of the avatar—a prophetic statement if ever there was one. The only difference is that Zoe initially plans to change the holoraves' violence and death; instead, the avatar ends up changing the very nature of humanity. "You're going to help bring that change," she avows to her avatar in a subsequent scene. Zoe believes that change is necessary because the real and virtual Caprican worlds foster only the views and desires of the majority. According to Zoe and her friends, the resulting depravity can be correlated to Caprican culture; the world needs to accept monotheism (not polytheism), political and social equality, and less sex and violence.

Zoe the teenager and Zoe the avatar are peaceful catalysts for change, not wanting to hurt others. The holo rave is awash with color — vibrant red offset by "normal" Zoe's blue dress. During the day, she and her friends wear black-and-white school uniforms; her parents wear black-and-white tennis togs. Their home is white and spacious, sterile. The real world is black and white for Zoe; its relationships between parent and child, as well as polytheists and monotheists, are as oppositional and two-dimensional as these colors. The blue infinity symbol on her computer, flashing primary hues on her holoband, red-drenched holoworld, or multi-colored stained glass windows in the holosuite provide the only color in her otherwise drab world.

Like the Graystones, Joseph Adams (née Adama, a name to which he soon returns) favors a similar color palette. He wears a black hat and overcoat set off with a white shirt as he goes about his business day. Only his red tie foreshadows emotion in his otherwise highly structured black-and-white world.

The lack of color in the real-world scenes is broken by red highlights— the red detailing on the side of the train Zoe boards shortly before the bombing, Ben's hand resting on a red handle bar inside the train. Even the terrorist explosion that propels the action from that point on is an explosion of red fire, black debris, and white smoke. As with the preview posters, the dominant color theme in the early scenes of the pilot episode especially emphasizes a black-and-white color scheme broken by splashes of red.

This color palette continues with the regular episodes. When Amanda replays home movies, she freezes an image of Zoe as a little girl. The child wears a black dress with white polka dots. Another image frozen on the screen is Zoe as a teen shortly before her death. Her black-and-white dress is offset with tiny red highlights, but this time a gold infinity symbol is prominently pinned to the dress. The infinity pin, highlighted with splashes of red on the dress, helps indicate Zoe's "change" into an independently thinking young woman who emotionally embraces monotheism — as well as the more militant boyfriend her mother doesn't even realize she has ("Rebirth," 1.1).

Zoe also is represented by images of light in the scenes between the real girl and the ever-similar avatar she created. The real teen initially emerges from bright white backlighting when she enters the holosuite to talk with her avatar. "Nothing in here is real," avatar Zoe tells her real self about the holoworld (Pilot movie), a fact that Daniel Graystone would do well to remember when he tries to "re-create" his daughter from what she leaves behind. During Zoe's heart-to-heart with her avatar, a single candle warmly backlights the pair. Zoe brings the light, possibly to the world and definitely to her parents, taking it away with her death. She represents new knowledge and hopes that the rest of the world will "see the light" when her avatar makes a change in the depraved world.

Zoe symbolizes a candle in the dark. When the avatar finally wins over Daniel Graystone by recalling specific memories from flesh-and-blood Zoe's childhood, two candles flicker in the foreground, with Daniel standing in the background. He "sees the light" after hearing Zoe's recitation of memories. At the end of this scene he asks if he can hug his daughter. When they connect emotionally, light streams through the stained glass window in the background. It is a "religious epiphany" for Graystone.

Even this emotional family moment, however, is turned into a parental trap a moment later, a subversion of Zoe's morality and honesty into Daniel's duplicity and immorality. He captures her digital image to transfer it into another form. Little shocks of white light make avatar Zoe seem to be electro-cuted as the transfer takes place. Instead of the warm light of the candles or "sunlight" through the stained glass — Zoe's symbols of light and enlighten-ment — Daniel's are sharp, harsh, and mechanical. He uses knowledge for his own gain; avatar Zoe uses hers to inspire the world to change. Perhaps Zoe's knowledge and use of technological creativity (e.g., the creation of a realistic avatar) seem naïve, but Daniel's knowledge and appropriation of Zoe's avatar seem calculating, cold, and selfish. The uses of light, especially as symbols of enlightenment and attainment of divine knowledge, emphasize the previously mentioned oppositions.

SYMBOLIC SUBTEXT THROUGH MUSIC

Music, as well as the use of light and a black-white-red color palette (as mentioned previously), further embed symbols into the *Caprica* pilot episode. Although Zoe's musical theme is new and played most often throughout the pilot movie, *Battlestar Galactica* fans are brought into the *Caprica* story through the use of Bill Adama's (or the Adama family's) theme in both series.

Bill Adama's theme plays when young Willy (Sina Najafi) learns that the family surname has been changed from Adams. His father returns them to their proper surname and embraces his son. The father-son embrace to this musical theme will be repeated in a future generation when estranged father and son Bill and Lee Adama embrace. *Battlestar Galactica* fans are likely to recall this theme from poignant father-son moments in the war-torn series, in part because they underscore a tender side to the often harsh commander but also because such scenes provide a respite from the tension inherent in this drama.

The music of Zoe's world prior to her death is wistful and haunting, almost a dream. When her friends and family remember or discuss her after her death, the flute-based theme plays in the background. A few piano notes sound like a musical clock ticking away the seconds of her life, or the increasing time since she truly lived. The flute later gives way to a clarinet solo in the longer versions of Zoe's theme, but its purity and innocence are appropriate both to a representation of the living teen and others' memories of her. Zoe's theme becomes the *Caprica* opening music with the first regular episode.

When Zoe escapes school to meet her friend Ben so they can run away to Gemenon, the pace increases. It becomes harsh and matches Zoe's eager rush toward the train. She runs toward her future, not knowing that her "destiny" is death and rebirth as a Cylon. The drums' faster beat resonates with the war drums prevalent in *Battlestar Galactica*'s opening theme (which lacks instruments other than voices and drums). Zoe's escape is a precursor to the *Battlestar Galactica* future, an association that long-time fans can easily make.

The war drums, as well as the sound effect of the Cylon's roving eye, are familiar to *Battlestar Galactica* fans. During the *Caprica* pilot the Cylon battle prototype, a killing machine designed to track down and slaughter cute little droids, hunts against the backdrop of pounding drums. Again, connecting drums with Cylons, whether through Zoe or a killing machine, further connects *Caprica* with its parent series and foreshadows future events.

In a subsequent killer Cylon scene with a much more ruthless robot the drums accompanying the test are louder and more insistent. They match the Cylon "music" repeated in *Battlestar Galactica*. A driving drumbeat is the undercurrent for Zoe's "awakening" as a Cylon, the drum beats providing the missing heartbeat, and becoming increasingly strong and intense as the cybernetic lifeform gains sentience. The end of the pilot movie concludes with the drumbeat and the Cylon's red eye staring into the camera.

In sharp musical and thematic contrast, when Daniel Graystone tries to break the encryption on Zoe's holoworld, the music first consists of harp trills, perhaps a musical allusion to Biblical heaven, where Zoe resides. The holorave where Daniel finds himself, however, is the red-drenched "hell" that Zoe wanted to change. Its music is loud and pulsating; the sound screams sex and violence. Bringing back dead Zoe from a heavenly rest to the hellish reality of modern life seems less a boon to Zoe than to her father. Daniel is alien to this virtual world, as opposite from his real world as possible; his foray into the holorave lets him see just how little he knew his daughter. Her teenaged world is vibrant but violent, chaotic, noisy, crowded, sensual, overwhelming. His adult world is cold, controlled, colorless, silent.

Daniel is further linked with humanity's destructive future by a musical backdrop to a scene within his at-home lab. While an assistant works with the Cylon prototype, Daniel plays the piano ("Rebirth," 1.1). Long-time fans of either the 1970s *Battlestar Galactica* or the 2000-era series recognize the music as the original series' introductory theme. Although the re-imagined series only used snippets of that theme in episodes referring to the *Galactica*'s history, it paid homage to the original soundtrack and series. *Caprica* provides a similar connection among all three series, but by making Daniel the "instrument" of change, the sweet melody takes on sinister symbolism.

The contrasts in light, color, and music further dramatize the ever-widening gulf between oppositional groups and worlds. The oppositions between Zoe and her parents, the youthful world versus the adult world, the monotheistic world versus the polytheistic world, the lawful world versus the underground world make viewers, as well as characters, question what is real or even right about their existence. Each world operates under different rules, making one culture's gray hero the oppositional culture's (possibly gray) villain. Audiences must decide which culture's rules and norms will determine which characters they believe are heroes or villains.

Otherness in Caprica

In this gray series all characters introduced during the pilot movie are flawed in at least one or two ways. Questions about morality revolve around which of two proposed sets of religious beliefs characters (and viewers) should follow. In this world, Otherness takes many forms. Zoe and her friends are perceived as Other spiritually from the majority of students attending their school; however, their headmistress reveals to only a select few that she also is a monotheist. Although most students would see Zoe et al. as Other, even some school officials perceive that monotheists will become the dominant religious voice if all goes according to their plan. Being religious Other in *Caprica* at least initially separates monotheists from polytheists, with each group perceiving its opposite as Other. The monotheists, however, plan that polytheists someday will become the minority Other in their society.

Of course, one of *Battlestar Galactica*'s key determinants of Otherness is whether a character is human or Cylon, and ways to discover one's true identity provided many plot twists throughout *Battlestar Galactica*. In *Caprica*, the use of technology to create Otherness is in its infancy. Avatar Zoe's "rebirth" in a Cylon body leads to her Otherness and indicates only the first step in the development of a new "species" of technological human. It takes the *Battlestar Galactica* finale before the only human–Cylon hybrid child, Hera, becomes the model for the ideal citizen of Earth.

"Rebirth" (1.1) highlights Zoe's growing sense of Otherness from the human she once was. The trinity of Zoe/avatar Zoe/Cylon becomes enraged when treated as a "thing" and dehumanized. Lab assistants roughly load her into a casket-like crate for transfer to the Graystone home. She draws first blood when she snaps off the finger tip of the lab tech who tries to drill into her face as part of a mechanical test ("Rebirth," 1.1). A human response to the horrifying image of a drill being slowly leveled at a young woman's face is to be repulsed by the image, to want to stop the drill — or the driller. Zoe acts in self-defense and gains the audience's sympathy or even approval for her action. Yet the seeds of mistrust between Cylon and human are sown from the first moments of the first regular series episode. Humans hurt Zoe, and by extension, Cylons; they lie to them and betray them, as Zoe quickly learns from Daniel's and the lab techs' actions. Zoe/Cylon is physically abused and dehumanized by the scientists; she is merely a thing to them, whereas she feels human.

Even Lacy has trouble seeing past the mechanical exterior, despite Zoe's pleas that she hasn't really changed. "My mom called me a monster," Zoe confides to her best friend. "Well, to be honest ..." Lacy begins, but she quickly takes Zoe's hand and embraces her. The first view of this embrace shows the two teens hugging as human best friends; the next shows Lacy embracing the metallic "monster." Such scenes showing human Zoe first, then the "real" image of the Cylon, reinforce Zoe's sense of Otherness and the realization that she no longer fits within human society.

Cultural Otherness based on factors other than religion also is prevalent in *Caprica*, just as in *Battlestar Galactica*. Quite clearly the Taurons, including immigrant Joseph Adams, are perceived as culturally inferior to the Capricans. As a result, Joseph changed the family name to Adams to better blend with the locals. Adama is the honorable family name from their home world, a name to which Joseph and his son Willy return. Taurons are also associated with the "Mafia" on Caprica, and although Joseph Adama tries to distance himself from this part of his culture, he owes his prosperity to this organization's financial assistance. Joseph's brother Sam, however, is deeply involved with the "Mafia" and abides by its culture, as well as his Tauron roots, making him doubly culturally Other from mainstream Caprican society.

Cultural intolerance among Capricans apparently is common. "Dirt eater" is a mild epithet applied to attorney Joseph Adama, but throughout the pilot episode several Capricans, including teenagers, make cultural slurs to those from other planets. Gemons are perceived as religious zealots because the majority religion there is monotheism, which makes them culturally and religiously Other to Capricans.

Perhaps a surprising example of sexual Otherness is the introduction of a gay character into *Caprica*'s supporting cast. In an interview published shortly before *Caprica*'s official SyFy debut, executive producer and scriptwriter Jane Espenson revealed additional information about the series. "When creator Ronald Moore laid out his vision for *Caprica* ... he just mentioned, matter-of-factly, that one of the characters— Sam Adama (Sasha Roiz)— is gay."[12] Because *Caprica* is set within an advanced society in a different time frame from viewers' world, she believes that a term like "gay" wouldn't even be necessary: "Why do you have to have a different word for who they fall in love with? Having a different word for a same-sex relationship struck me as something this culture wouldn't have thought of since those relationships were just considered on a par and unremarkable."[13] Whereas Sam Adama may be perceived by some viewers as Other because of his sexuality, Espenson believes that he wouldn't be perceived as Other for that reason on Caprica; his sexuality is simply another aspect of his character revealed to audiences as the story and character develop.

Espenson, a *Torchwood* fan, specifically credited the groundbreaking role of Captain Jack Harkness for making Sam's sexuality less of an issue than it might have been a few years earlier on TV. Series like *Torchwood* make possible series like *Caprica*, with its ambiguous heroes and villains and open attitude toward sexuality. Espenson noted that, on *Torchwood*, the "way they own Jack's sexuality is very admirable and very much like what we're trying to do. The people around him have to be comfortable with it because he's comfortable with it. It's fantastic."[14]

Perhaps *Caprica* invites either acceptance or censure, just as *Torchwood* faced after "Children of Earth" was broadcast, because of the characters portrayed as gay. Sam, after all, is a "Mafia" executioner who also has a partner and happy home life, a close relationship with his brother, and a mentorship relationship with his nephew. The second episode illustrates both parts of his life: Under Joseph's approving eye, Sam beats Daniel Graystone; his brother later requests that Sam murder Amanda Graystone in retribution for the loss of his own wife. At home, Sam and his partner share dinner with nephew Willy. Sam is teased about being "desperately in love" with his partner ("Reins of a Waterfall," 1.2).[15] Whether Sam-the-killer is accepted as an "acceptable" gay role model may yet make him perceived as Other, even among viewers who want to see more GLBT characters on television in general. For all that he's a dark character whose actions in "Children of Earth" seemed to go too far for some fans to accept, Captain Jack is still seen as a hero by most viewers and is often called a gay icon or role model.

Nevertheless, some critics and fans felt that even omnisexual Captain Jack became simply a tortured gay character who loses his lover and is left with nothing by the end of the mini-series, whereas the heterosexual couple in *Torchwood* experience a happy ending. Concerns also arose in early 2010 when Fox announced it planned to remake *Torchwood* for U.S. audiences. If Captain Jack had become a Fox series, long-time fans feared that his sexuality would be toned down to make him "acceptable" to more conservative audiences. Espenson doesn't seem to have that concern about *Caprica*. Perhaps *Caprica*'s inclusion of Sam can be seen as an effective way of making a character's sexuality less about Otherness than just another detail about the character. In "Rebirth" (1.1), for example, Sam reminisces to Willy during an afternoon spent walking around the old "Tauron" neighborhood of his youth. Uncle Sam mentions that he used to chat up boys while Willy's father chatted up their sisters. Willy seems unfazed by this comment. With the inclusion of such scenes, featuring casual conversation between uncle and nephew, the series then might not face as much criticism that it makes the lone gay character a "villain" because of his profession.

Both *Torchwood* and *Battlestar Galactica* influence *Caprica*'s character and plot development, creating dark drama with ambiguously moral characters. Whereas the earlier series emphasize one or two main reasons why viewers—or the series' cultures—might consider characters as Other, *Caprica* introduces multiple sources of Otherness. Even a single character may be perceived as Other for more than one reason, and oppositional groups within *Caprica*'s downward spiraling civilization often perceive one another as Other. Otherness is key to many characters of any shade of gray.

10

Doctor Who

Doctor Who is the longest running SF TV show. During its early years it became renowned not just for an intriguing SF premise — a Time Lord traveling throughout all of Space and Time — but for the low-budget effects that were hardly "special," even in the 1960s. The Doctor and the monsters are two reasons why audiences keep coming back to *Doctor Who*.

The Doctor has a distinctive difference (or advantage) over other heroes in long-running stories: He can regenerate into a new body and personality. When an actor leaves the series, the Doctor regenerates into a new actor/Doctor. Before the series' first "end," seven Doctors had traveled in the TARDIS between 1963 and 1989. The Eighth Doctor was very short lived: only one U.S.–produced TV special in 1996. By 2005, a very different Doctor was needed for the post–9/11, post–London bombings world. Russell T. Davies and Julie Gardner re-imagined a *Doctor Who* suitable for children and new viewers, but updated with better effects, edgier stories, and dramatic Doctors. Christopher Eccleston's Ninth Doctor, a survivor of the Time War that culminated in the genocide of his people, and David Tennant's Tenth Doctor, a sometimes goofily likeable traveler/sometimes very dark Time Lord, brought adult audiences to the program while still attracting the target demographic. Davies' scripts gave the new *Who* a modern sensibility, which not only gave the series credibility and higher ratings, but also led the Doctor into increasingly dark territory. By the time Davies turned *Doctor Who* over to new showrunner Steven Moffat, whose Eleventh Doctor began a new era for the Whoniverse in 2010, the Tenth Doctor had been everything from a traditional hero to an increasingly gray one.[1]

Davies knows that SF TV can be powerful and life changing, especially to children, and each successive generation of children needs to be re-introduced to heroes, villains, and monsters. Children grow up very quickly, and the "child" audience continually changes. If they're going to grow up with the Doctor, he needs to be consistently smart, entertaining, and unique. The monsters also need to be updated and kept in the public eye, because children's sense of "history" is very different from that of adults. Every few years, at least, the Doctor should face returning "classic" monsters and villains. *Doctor Who* should provide new mythology for the adults who grew up with the series and know its nearly 50-year history but also tell new tales of legendary monsters and villains that then become important to the children currently watching the series.

Davies discussed his approach to writing *Doctor Who* episodes shortly before his time as series' creator and frequent writer ended with the January 1, 2010, episode "The End of Time, Part 2." Talking with *SFX* magazine, he explained that writers should "never forget where [the series is] coming from — and there's a brand new audience, never forget, because children are watching and they're a huge and powerful part of the audience, and they keep renewing." He mentioned a conversation with a six-year-old boy who recalled stories from three years earlier in the *Who* saga. "He was talking about the Emperor Dalek, and it was like a legend to him!"[2] Davies knows that children's perspective of time is vastly different from adults', but he also realizes that hero and monster stories told to children can influence them for a lifetime. A long-running series like *Doctor Who* needs to be true to its original premise but keep updating the hero and the monsters or villains he encounters to make them reflect current audiences' expectations.

Although the Doctor is always meant to be the series' hero, and indeed the character is an enduring part of SF TV history, each regeneration means that a new actor, and thus a new version of the Doctor, can take the character into different directions while fitting within the concept of one multi-lived Doctor. When asked, adults around the world who spent at least part of their life watching *Doctor Who* quickly identify "their" Doctor. (Mine, for example, was Fourth Doctor Tom Baker, although the Ninth Doctor piqued my interest in the re-imagined series, and the Tenth Doctor kept me watching.) The same "tradition" is true even for Tenth Doctor Tennant.

During a 2007 Children in Need special, the Tenth and Fifth Doctors shared a moment in which Tennant breaks character while talking to his earlier "self": "I *love* being you," he confesses, showing the Fifth Doctor his influences on the Tenth Doctor's costume and line delivery. "You were *my* Doctor," long-time *Who* fan Tennant said earnestly.[3] Yet Tennant revealed in a 2009 interview that he first followed the adventures of the highly popular Fourth Doctor and, at one time, considered him to be "my Doctor," too: "I'd grown up with and idolized [Tom Baker] for seven years, and then Peter Davison turns up and he's young and blond, and what's going on? And within two weeks he was the guy. So that's how it works. It's one of the many pieces of genius that define what makes this show special."[4] The Doctor as a character may change, but he must retain those heroic qualities that transcend individual Doctors' quirks, wardrobe, and mannerisms. This hero must easily capture long-time and new viewers' interest, meshing with previous iterations of the character, but quickly make the newly regenerated Doctor unique.

Although the re-imagined series is a breadwinner for BBC, the new *Who* still faces budget constraints. Davies understands the realities of economic hard times in the television industry and the need to work within a limited budget, even though CGI effects and improvements in storytelling technologies have come a long way since the early days of *Who*. One way that Davies could keep costs low was to write quiet scenes full of character revelations and emotional moments in less exotic locales. He could create an intriguing scene between characters "in a kitchen because they've got interesting things to say."[5]

One of the most memorable character scenes in "The End of Time, Part 1" takes place in a restaurant where Wilfrid Mott (Bernard Cribbins) and the Doctor catch up on recent changes in their lives and the latest threat to Earth.[6] Mott pleads for the Doctor to help heal his granddaughter Donna Noble (Catherine Tate), one of the Doctor's former companions. The Doctor explains to the distraught man that Donna must never remember him or she will die (a plot summary for viewers who many not have seen earlier episodes, including "Journey's End" [4.13]). The Doctor also becomes emotional. In a rare break-down, he confesses his fear of his impending regeneration, which has been fore-told (in 2009 specials "Planet of the Dead" and "The Waters of Mars"). The Doctor explains that regeneration is like death, only that a new man walks away with all his memories. In such a scene, Davies expands viewers' understanding of what regeneration entails, something never before discussed in depth. The fact that the Doctor can become frightened and tearful when thinking of death makes him more human and less Other than he seems in other scenes, even within this story arc. It also emphasizes that heroes also can be frightened but still protect innocents and strive to make the Earth a safer place.

Davies' series does have incredibly memorable "big scenes," including spaceships crashing into Big Ben ("Aliens of London," 1.4), but the writer didn't always require "expensive pictures, just good pictures."[7] Saving expensive effects for when they're most effective and knowing how to move story and character development forward during simpler, less expensive scenes has improved the overall quality of post–2005 *Who* episodes while keeping them within the BBC's budget. As a result, the series has gained acclaim and respect from critics and audiences. Davies succeeded in modernizing the Doctor as an SF TV hero suitable for children but dramatically interesting to adults as well.

As might be expected for a program initially designed for children, a strength of *Doctor Who* has always been its monsters. In particular, the Daleks (masterminded by the Doctor's long-time nemesis Davros) and the Cybermen strike fear across the universe, and several of the Doctor's audience-favored companions (e.g., Sarah Jane Smith, Rose Tyler, Captain Jack Harkness) have had more than one run-in with each. When Davies re-imagined the new *Who* with the Ninth Doctor, the Daleks were also brought back. By the end of the Tenth Doctor's life, Daleks and Cybermen are once again staples of the Whoni-verse, and their impending invasion of Earth, present or future, provides the drama for some of the recent series' most memorable episodes.

The Daleks, in particular, also become the catalyst for a "reunion" of the Doctor's companions and a way for cast members from *Torchwood* and *The*

Sarah Jane Adventures to join *Doctor Who* for a Season Three-ending extravaganza. In "The Stolen Earth" (4.12) and "Journey's End" (4.13), several companions cross the universe to help the Doctor fight a Dalek invasionary force taking over 21st century Earth. Sarah Jane, Captain Jack, Rose, Mickey Smith, Jackie Tyler, Martha Jones, and then-current companion Donna Noble pool their unique skills, knowledge, and experience during the two-parter. On Earth, Sarah Jane's son Luke; Torchwood's Gwen Cooper and Ianto Jones; Donna's grandfather Wilfrid Mott; former Prime Minister Harriet Jones; and members of UNIT (where Martha is stationed pre-invasion) forge a connection and assist the Doctor from afar.

In the battle between Good and Evil, the humans unite to fight, but they often are as barbaric, as least in theory, as the monsters who want to enslave them. They also pool their weapons and knowledge of how to use them, preferring to die themselves if, in so doing, they can also kill their enemies. On Earth, Martha literally holds the key to Earth's destruction; by using it, she can detonate a series of nuclear explosions. The Doctor is horrified that his beloved companions would agree to such destructive acts to keep humans from being conquered by Daleks.

Despite his outward passivism and refusal to carry a weapon, the Doctor, as Davros reminds him, is noted for creating "weapons" out of his companions and the others he influences during his long life. For all that the Doctor wants to be the universe's force for Good, several of his actions and influences are questionable at best.

Of the myriad ways *Doctor Who* as series or lead gray hero could be analyzed, three emphases have been chosen for this chapter: (1) the classic monsters of the series, most notably, the Daleks and Cybermen, who repeatedly challenge the Doctor; (2) the classic villain, the Master, who Davies chose to end the Tenth Doctor's story arc and force his regeneration (as well as end the Davies era of *Doctor Who*); and (3) the Doctor, who "plays god" while attempting to save humanity. Although the Master is also a staple of the long-running series, John Simm's characterization of this classic nemesis provides new insights into 21st century gray villains. Only episodes involving the Ninth and Tenth Doctors (2005–2010) are discussed because they illustrate the trend toward ever-darker SF TV heroes, villains, and monsters, even within children's programming.

Classic Who Monsters

The following brief table describes some alien monsters who, in one way or another, want to take over Earth or its people, past, present, or future during Season One (2005) of the new *Doctor Who*. Daleks, sans Davros, make two appearances. In the first, "Dalek" (1.6), the lone Dalek is as much a tragic survivor of the Time War as the Ninth Doctor, and their confrontation — each willing to wipe out the other — makes them equals in vengeance. In episodes like this, the human element, this time represented by companion Rose, brings the Doctor back from the brink of being "monstrous." She sees the common loss shared by these long-time enemies and tries to make them come to some sort of truce. Genocide, to Rose, isn't the solution, no matter how terrible either side's losses in the Time War.

Classic monsters remind long-time viewers of the link between the post–2005 *Who* and its many serials beginning in the 1960s, but Davies' series also introduces new, sometimes single-episode monsters who threaten the Doctor, Rose, or, more generally, Earth and humanity.

Table 3. Season One's Non-Human Monsters

Non-Human Monster	Action	Episode
Autons	Feed off the Earth's resources/pollutants; attack humans	"Rose" (1.1)
Gelth	Use gas lines as a source of life; inhabit bodies of dead humans; want a permanent entrance into the human world	"The Unquiet Dead" (1.3)
Slitheen	Want to destroy the Earth and sell it for scrap; kill and inhabit human bodies while on Earth	"Aliens of London" (1.4)
Dalek	Still wants to exterminate all humans; tries to take over an underground compound by killing everyone in it	"Dalek" (1.6)
Jagrefes	Uses unwitting human slaves to produce enough energy on Satellite Five to keep it alive	"The Long Game" (1.7)
Reapers	Are compelled to sterilize a wound in time (a time paradox) and, in the process, kill everyone on Earth, including the Doctor	"Father's Day" (1.8)
"Margaret," last of the Slitheen	Attempts to build a power plant set to destroy the Earth and then sell it to the highest bidder	"Boom Town" (1.11)
Emperor of the Daleks	Re-creates a Dalek army to invade Earth and exterminate all humans	"Bad Wolf" (1.12), "Parting of the Ways" (1.13)

Although recurring monsters or villains, such as Daleks and their creator Davros, are important to the series' mythology and continuing themes, even the first Davies season of *Who* includes "monsters" or "villains" who become more sympathetic characters because audiences can understand and, to a certain extent, identify with them. The lone Dalek, for example, is being held captive and tortured by a human entrepreneur determined to extract the alien's secrets, just for his own knowledge and personal gain. The Dalek is at the mercy of a merciless human. Furthermore, the Dalek, like the Doctor, loses everything in the Time War and is the (supposedly) last of its kind (a plot point negated by later episodes revealing yet more Daleks, as well as Time Lords). Although the Dalek isn't innocent, as its attempts to kill humans in order to escape illustrate, it is a more sympathetic alien in this episode than in previous or subsequent ones. It remains a monster, according to the definitions previously discussed, but it also is a gray character in this episode — not the purely, mindlessly evil that Daleks are portrayed to be in other episodes.

The human "monsters" in the following table, such as new time traveler Adam or appearance-conscious Cassandra, may go to extremes to get what they want, trampling the lives of others along the way. They may be perceived as villains rather than monsters, but their less-than-human appearance clearly marks them as extremes of physical Otherness. Their obsessions, too, seem almost mindless because the characters will do anything to achieve what they want, without considering the physical consequences to themselves. Whether audiences identify them as monsters or villains, these characters are also shown to be the product of their cultural indoctrination. They know that technological superiority and beauty can lead to success and fame, something prized by humanity across the galaxy and time. Even within a single season, the first of the series' re-imagination, *Doctor Who*'s list of monsters and villains provides a balance between recurring enemies and single-episode characters who illustrate a range of grayness.

Table 4. Season One Human "Monsters"/Villains

Human "Monster" or Villain	Action	Episode
Cassandra	Becomes so vain that she does anything to retain a sleek (i.e., bodiless), moisturized form	"The End of the World" (1.2)
Henry van Statten	Erases memories before having his employees dumped somewhere in the country when he tires of them; maintains a "collection" of alien artifacts, including a Dalek; tortures the Dalek; plans to keep the Doctor as an artifact	"Dalek" (1.6)
Adam Mitchell	Has a port installed in his forehead so he can download technological information from 200,000; plans to use this "insider information" to get rich back in the 21st century	"The Long Game" (1.7)

Purging humanity, in whatever form, often results in the creation of monsters. Adam has a port implanted in his head so he can download information about future technology. He plans to return home to 21st century Earth to exploit that knowledge. He doesn't care if his actions will change humanity's future; he only wants to make a lot of money. Although the Ninth Doctor foils his plan, Adam still reaps the consequences of his planned get-rich-quick scheme. The implant remains in his forehead, and 21st century humans likely will see Adam as a "monster" if they find out about it.

Another technology-worshipping "monster," Cassandra, may revel in her human ancestry, but she looks nothing like "normal" 21st century humans. The last of her species, her compulsion to be as slim and wrinkle-free as possible results in her being nothing more than a taut face and skin stretched across a frame, with her brain in a jar. Her demise comes when she loses the ability to transfer her essence into a younger body; her skin-only "body" is immovable and requires assistants to care for her. Cassandra's devotion to maintaining her beauty ultimately is futile, and all the terrible acts she initiates to maintain her wealth and appearance are in vain.

As discussed in Chapter 11 and mentioned in Part 1, even Captain Jack Harkness, who becomes one of the Doctor's companions and is transformed into a hero, begins as a shady character running a con during Earth's World War II. The charismatic captain seems like a "good guy" in appearance, but he inadvertently almost annihilates the human race ("The Empty Child," 1.9).

Doctor Who shows that even characters who don't seem to be all that bad, such as Adam, may become "monsters" temporarily, or their acts may inadvertently lead to others' pain or death. Although other SF series also have classic monsters, as well as very human villains, *Doctor Who* is one of the few remaining series with long-running "classic" monsters or nemeses. As such, it reminds audiences of the days of SF rubber monsters as well as the better CGI versions; it spans the history, good and bad, of SF monsters and villains.

Davros and the Daleks, 2005–2009

During yet another invasion of Earth, this time by Daleks, companion Donna Noble's grandfather, Wilfrid Mott, refuses to surrender to the Daleks rounding up humans. He witnesses the extermination of an entire family because the father/husband stands up to the invaders. "Monsters," Mott intones, slipping away so that he can fight them another time.

Moments later, however, he finds himself cornered by a lone Dalek. Armed with a paint gun, with which he plans to blind the one-eyed Dalek, Mott finally shoots when faced with capture. His weapon is ineffective, and the Dalek "blinks" away the paint. Only Rose's timely arrival saves Mott. Carrying a monster-sized futuristic weapon, Rose blasts the Dalek ("The Stolen Earth," 4.12).[8]

Only large, futuristic technology can stop the invaders, as Rose has learned since she began traveling with the Doctor. She introduces Mott to the more effective ways to fight Daleks, but she also shows that she now has no qualms about killing them. Her attitude and approach are quite different from her first encounter with a lone Dalek ("Dalek," 1.6), during which she inadvertently "bonds" with it and helps humanize it.

In "The Stolen Earth," however, the Daleks lack any human compassion. Once again the hive-minded metallic race proclaims that they "are the Masters of Earth." Despite their many incursions on Earth, and their frequent run-ins with the many Doctors, this time the Daleks seem confident of a long-awaited victory. The scene changes from one Dalek proclaiming mastery of humanity to a screen full of Daleks hovering in space to infinity.

Even within the new *Who*, Daleks return to being monstrous as a race, even if the occasional lone Dalek becomes a more sympathetic character. They gain greater prominence as mindless monsters in "Journey's End" (4.13) when their creator, Davros, becomes little more than their mascot or pawn. Of course, he still has the rhetoric of a true villain. Davros plots the destruction of reality itself, but the once-powerful creator, physically decimated by time and war, now is nothing more than a withered shell encased in a metallic box. He even "lives" in the lower levels of the Dalek base, emphasizing his decreased importance to the race he created.

Ironically, the mastermind who creates an unemotional race determined to exterminate humanity is able to wound the Doctor most deeply by appealing to his emotions. The "heart" of the passivist Doctor who refuses to carry a weapon, Davros declares, is nothing more than this: "You take ordinary people, and you fashion them into weapons. Behold your Children of Time [the Doctor's companions, fighting the Daleks] transformed into murderers."[9] Davros' referring to the Doctor's heart as singular, when Time Lords have two hearts, suggests a "hybrid" personality for the Doctor. Although he fights on behalf of the human race and most often chooses human companions, the Doctor still is "alien" or Other and may not be as kindly as his friends perceive him to be.

Davros is right: No matter how much the Doctor loves his companions and tries to protect them, because they travel with him and often become involved in conflicts, they learn how to use weapons and develop strategies to use against enemies. Instead of becoming a hospital physician, as she plans before traveling with the Doctor, Martha Jones goes to work for UNIT as a soldier. Shopgirl Rose is transformed from a feisty peacemaker (e.g., "Dalek") into a blaster-toting alien fighter working for her alternate world's version of Torchwood. Captain Jack changes from a rogue Time Agent and faux World War II officer into the head of Torchwood, with plenty of WMD at his discretion. Even the Doctor's final companion ("The End of Time"), retired veteran Wilfrid Mott (who, dialogue pointedly notes, never killed a man during his national service) takes up arms against the Daleks and becomes involved in a showdown to shoot the Master. Of course, the Doctor can't be held responsible for humans' innate capacity for violence or long cultural indoctrination about the propriety of wielding weapons, but exposure to the Doctor's adventures does seem to trigger his companions' more violent responses to encounters with aliens.

The duality of the two-hearted Doctor, half (increasingly repressed) emotional human, half determined Time Lord, can be best contrasted with a second Doctor created during "Journey's End." His cloned self has only one very human heart, and, for better or worse, that version of the Doctor is extremely passionate, in love or hate, joy or anger. The "real" Doctor values compassion and, indeed, has a habit of trying to save his nemeses Davros and the Master when they are close to death. Davros even alludes to this fact in "Journey's End," reminding the Doctor that a Dalek saved him when the Doctor failed to do so. (Also, in "Last of the Time Lords" [3.13], the Doctor holds a dying Master and encourages him to regenerate. When the Master refuses, the Doctor mourns the loss of the only other surviving Time Lord.) Perhaps Davros' greatest feat during "Journey's End" (4.13) is his ability to make the Doctor question himself — the Doctor becomes horrified that his companions would annihilate themselves or Earth, as well as the Daleks, to prevent being enslaved, and basically takes himself out of the role of humanity's savior, at least for the duration of this episode.

Although Daleks can be politically symbolic of a populace who fails to think for themselves and who, in effect, become drones working mindlessly on behalf of a distant leader, they also can represent a more general fear of technology. The Daleks, after all, are really the small, squid-like, soft aliens encased in a mass of metal; their outer form and voice bear little resemblance to who they are inside. This armor protects them and strikes fear in their enemies. What is "real" about the Daleks is hidden, and only the few aliens who have managed to look beneath the metallic exterior casing realize what the Dalek race is meant to be.

Individual Daleks may not be that difficult to kill with the right weapon, but their strength comes from their sheer numbers. The classic image of a TV screen full of Daleks, stretching to infinity, illustrates unending Evil, an unstoppable force with enough members to keep attacking long after humans inevitably are defeated. Losing humanity to technology and losing individuality to mindless conformity are two human fears well embodied by the Daleks.

The Master, 2008–2010

Throughout the almost half century of *Doctor Who*, the Master has been a continuing foe. At times during the 1970s, when working against the Third Doctor (Jon Pertwee), the Master (Roger Delgado) looked more like a Bond villain, complete with goatee and shifty dark eyes. By the Davies era, however, both the Doctor and the Master regenerated into younger men, both attractive and charismatic, who were true equals. Until the Master revealed himself ("Utopia," 3.12) and traveled from the end of the universe to Earth to re-appear as politician Harold Saxon, the Doctor believed that he was the last of the Time Lords. With the return of the Master, the Doctor tries but fails to turn his childhood comrade from the Dark Side. The Doctor believes that the incessant drumbeats the Master hears is a sign of his madness; thus, the Master really isn't responsible for all his horrible decisions. He is simply mad as a result of being unprepared but forced to look into the time vortex as a child on Gallifrey. The Doctor, for all that he abhors what the villain does and eventually creates a plan to thwart him, still has a personal connection with the Master.

When Harold Saxon becomes prime minister of Britain, one of his first acts is to execute, on primetime TV, the U.S. president. Saxon takes over the world, sending monsters (the silver-sphered Toclafane) to destroy any humans trying to resist his power grab. Torchwood is sent on a futile mission in the Himalayas, and all other alien-fighting organizations are helpless. Captain Jack is imprisoned with the Doctor and dies repeatedly for the Master's amusement. Only the Doctor's then-current companion, Martha, is able to escape and travel the world to spread a message of peace and love. She talks of the Doctor as a Christ-like savior and asks only that humanity join as one to think of him, to speak his name, as a unifying force.

After a year on Earth of creating disciples of peace, Martha allows herself to be captured. The Master finds that the combined minds of all humanity joining at once to think of the Doctor empowers his captive, who then is able to stop the Master. The Doctor even manages to return humanity to its status from a year earlier, at the time the Master took control. Only the people imprisoned with the Doctor during "the year that never was" know what happened.

In this pivotal confrontation (and story arc), the Doctor as healer/savior and the Master as destroyer/persecutor seem complete opposites, one Good, one Evil. However, the two share the same cultural upbringing and educational experiences from their lives on Gallifrey. They know the temptations associated with being a Time Lord and wielding immense power, greater than that of any other being in the universe. At times they must choose how to use this power, and most often the Doctor tries to help as many species as possible, while the Master seems intent on destroying humanity first — simply because humans are the Doctor's favorite species.

After this confrontation and the Master's supposed demise, the Doctor prefers to travel alone. Without a human influence to balance him, however, he becomes ever more like the Master — changing Time at will, determining who lives or dies, and doing only what pleases him on a whim. During the 2000s, the Master is not so much the Doctor's opposite as an illustration of the temptations and possibilities that, so far, the Doctor has chosen not to take.

The capacity to be like the Master becomes ever clearer to audiences, making the Tenth Doctor a much grayer hero.

Davies chose the Master to be the Tenth Doctor's final nemesis. The Master's regeneration requires a magical ceremony ("The End of Time, Part 1") to return his spirit to corporeal form; after all, the Doctor burns this villain's dead body on a pyre (a pagan ritual) and assumes him dead forever. The Master's ring, a magic potion, and a few well-chosen followers help resurrect the Master, although this version is more crazed than Harold Saxon. A blond, wild-eyed Master wears a dark hoodie, often pulled up to hide his face. He is a vagrant with a voracious appetite, not only for food (frequently referred to as "flesh") but power. He also has been given silly special effects powers, including the ability to shoot electrical bursts from his palms and to jump several stories high. The Master has become Supervillain.

The Doctor contrasts with this out-of-control, highly powerful maniac. Although he, too, is psychologically off-kilter and more emotional than ever, he is determined to confront the Master and stop his plan to destroy humanity (yet again). The Doctor wears a closely buttoned dark suit and looks proper and prosperous. He has a home, both within the TARDIS and on Earth; he has people who care about him. Yet he can't stop the Master from turning all humans into versions of himself. The Master succeeds in wiping out human individuality; almost every human (Wilfrid Mott and Donna Noble being the exceptions) is turned into a Master lookalike. The complete homogenization of humanity can be taken at a symbolic level (e.g., the ultimate result of globalization, citizens as "sheep" following a leader) or simply as an SF TV villain's most effective takeover scheme yet. By the end of the first part of the Tenth Doctor's last story arc, the Master/Evil has won, the Doctor/Good seems powerless, and humanity wears the face of gleeful Evil, unable to change themselves.

The Ninth and Tenth Doctors

When the new *Who* debuted in 2005, the Ninth Doctor simply appears on Earth, the familiar blue box of a TARDIS landing on an average council estate in London. He looks nothing like his predecessors: tall, thin, big eared (a running joke throughout his time as the Doctor), frequently rude and outspoken. His speech also made viewers take notice; instead of the posh London sounds of former Doctors, the Ninth Doctor has a northern accent. He wears average clothes less "costumy" than the dandified Third Doctor, long-scarved Fourth Doctor, or Victorian Eighth Doctor; his trademark becomes a battered leather jacket. The Ninth Doctor bears battle scars and seems to suffer from PTSD because of his actions during the Time War (a theme Davies further discusses in the Tenth Doctor's last episode). This Doctor is a loner who has lost everything — home, family, friends. He refuses to take part in anything "domestic," even when dragged into Rose's family. Nevertheless, he is not closed off from a human connection. At the end of the first episode, "Rose" (1.1), he gains a traveling companion unafraid to challenge, charm, and change him. She even gets him to dance ("The Doctor Dances," 1.10). Although the Ninth Doctor lives for only one TV season, he becomes transformed into a gentler, kinder, less angry survivor.

The Tenth Doctor acts far more confident from the start. He often is wild eyed in battle and excessively exuberant when an idea or a plan takes his fancy, but he clearly needs the mediation of his companions to keep him from extremes. This Doctor can be an enthusiastic tour guide who delights in showing his companions the many glorious cultures in Time and Space. More than his predecessor, he displays his knowledge of many non-human cultures and languages. This Doctor also prizes his non-violent solutions to problems, an obvious reaction to his actions as another Doctor/soldier. He becomes so fearful of losing his companions that he decides he is better off traveling alone, but his loneliness and isolation eventually bring him to the brink of megalomania. When he realizes that he can do whatever he wants as the last Time Lord, and no one else has the power to stop him, he decides that changing history or deciding who lives and who dies isn't such a bad power to have. Before he can become "Master" of the universe, however, he becomes horrified at what he's capable of doing. He doesn't want to die — and at the conclusion of "The Waters of Mars" flees Death knocking on his door — but he also runs from who he fears he has become.

The beginning of "The End of Time" even shows a determinedly carefree Doctor wearing a cowboy hat and a pink lei as he meets with the Ood, the very beings who foretell his death and force him to see what is going wrong with the universe. Before the Doctor learns that the Master is returning from death, viewers see the last moments of the "abnormal," self-absorbed Doctor who travels only for his own pursuit of pleasure. He even quips about taking the Virgin Queen's virginity on a recent trip to Earth. This uncharacteristically cavalier Doctor illustrates how out of control the story's "hero" has become. From one extreme of determining the course of history by deciding who lives or dies (e.g., "The Waters of Mars") to the other, traveling only for his own pleasure without becoming involved in life-or-death matters, the Tenth Doctor is forced to act more heroically when faced with the ultimate villain, the Master.

A late 2009 Gocompare.com poll showed that the Tenth Doctor's popularity only increased with his impending regeneration. A 2006 poll of *Doctor Who Magazine* readers showed David Tennant's Tenth Doctor (28.2 percent) being chosen favorite over Tom Baker's Fourth Doctor (26.5 percent).[10] The 2009 poll listed 45 percent of respondents choosing Tennant's Doctor as their all-time favorite. Not surprisingly, this poll also showed that more viewers (36 percent) liked Rose (Billie Piper) as the Doctor's companion, with Captain Jack (John Barrowman) coming in second with 11 percent.[11] The popularity of these characters, including child-friendlier versions of gray heroes, suggests that darker characters, whether leads or secondary characters, are becoming much more acceptable, or even expected, even in a series ostensibly written for children.

The Tenth Doctor's demise caused even actor David Tennant to shed a few tears when he read Davies' script. Tennant sees the Doctor as a traditional hero, in premise, at least, but the character's ability to regenerate allows writers and actors the chance to showcase different aspects of the title hero. At the end of every story arc, Tennant noted in 2009, "the Doctor is going to triumph over evil and be back to wandering the universe again. And the whole regeneration idea gives out this wonderful thing for the character, although the story will go on, and the Doctor will go on, this version will reach an end — will die effectively — and that allows you to take the story to emotional places that you can't quite go to when you have to continue the story."[12] Viewers did indeed become emotional about the end of the Tennant-Davies era of *Doctor Who* on January 1, 2010. In a fittingly epic battle, this Doctor helps "reset" the series for Steven Moffat's direction of the Eleventh Doctor. The Tenth Doctor regenerates, but not before leaving a legacy of epic episodes showcasing an increasingly complex gray hero who plays a variety of roles through his interactions with humanity.

The Doctor as Humanity's Healer or Mender

In the early scenes of the Tenth Doctor's final story arc ("The End of Time, Part 1"), Wilfrid Mott wanders into a church. A woman in white, who mysteriously disappears after imparting her message, sees him looking at a corner of a large stained glass window. A tiny blue TARDIS joins the more traditional religious imagery displayed in the sanctuary, and the woman explains that, centuries ago, an angel fell to Earth and a man emerged. He was known as a blessed healer.

In most *Doctor Who* Christmas specials, the Doctor is associated with some type of religious imagery (as discussed in a later section in this chapter). Yet not all explanations or symbols are meant to be spiritual. In "The End of Time," the allusion to the Doctor as a blessed physician is humorous, because the literal translation of "Doctor" and humanity's early interpretation of his arrival as a mystical event are simply wrong from the point of view of the TV audience. They know that the Doctor isn't technically a blessed physician, but his role, as illustrated through seasons of episodes, most often is to heal those companions he can help or to thwart the extermination of the human race. Perhaps he is more reasonably a "mender" than a healer; he can patch together humanity but can't heal them of what he perceives is a fatal flaw: persistent violence and the urge to destroy rather than negotiate with, understand, co-exist alongside, or even run away from those who confront them.

Although the Doctor most often is perceived as a savior/healer, in part because of his often-advanced technology and broad range of knowledge, he isn't all that successful in healing his companions' most serious injuries. He considers Jack Harkness' immortality "wrong," and the Ninth Doctor abandons the fledgling immortal without explanation on the Game Station. The Tenth Doctor tries unsuccessfully to leave Earth before Jack can catch up to him and then uses Jack's immortality as a convenience when he needs someone to fix a radiation leak; Jack can do so, and die, but the Doctor seems unconcerned about yet another one of Jack's deaths. In fact, in later episodes, Jack continues to die to help the Doctor escape or to buy time so the former companion can secretly help the Doctor again once he comes back to life out of the enemies' sight.

The Doctor explains that there's nothing he can do to "cure" Jack's immortality. He simply uses it for his own purposes and seems uncaring about "healing" Jack's many psychological or emotional scars that result from the Doctor's adventures. After being tortured by the Master for a year, for example, Jack likely needs some mental/emotional healing more than physical regeneration, yet the Doctor is unlikely to provide that type of care.

Even Donna Noble, who the Doctor saves from death by closing off her memory of her travels with him — including the time she saved the universe, remains "injured" as a result of her time with the Doctor. She returns home to live with her mother and grandfather, eventually finding a low-paying job and becoming engaged to a sweet but not terribly successful young man. As her grandfather tells the Doctor, Donna "settled," but she feels she's missing something important. She just doesn't know what.

If the physician's credo of "first do no harm" is applied to the Doctor, he might be found wanting. His companions explore the universe and gain experience, self-knowledge, and self-confidence as they see worlds and species they wouldn't otherwise have encountered, but they also pay a price. They lose their innocence, and quite often they become physically or emotionally injured as a result of their travels. Of course, they also choose to become more heroic, and heroes often sacrifice themselves in order to save others. The Doctor, however, seldom follows up to "heal" the wounds his companions suffer. When they've had enough, or when a crisis forces their separation from the Doctor, they no longer travel with him, but they, without the Doctor's intervention, must find ways to go on after their intergalactic adventures end.

The Doctor does, however, often succeed in healing worlds or intervening so that species (including humans) are saved from extinction. He often seems like a one-Time Lord crusade to protect the weak or defenseless against intergalactic bullies, but he alone often determines who lives and who dies. Seldom does he have such a joyful moment as in "The Empty Child," when one of his plans works perfectly: an alien-modified child is returned to humanity, a mother and child are reunited, and humans under the influence of aliens return to nor-mal — quite literally. They are healed of their injuries or illnesses by from-the-future nanogenes. The Ninth Doctor grins and proclaims, "Everyone lives!" Certainly this situation is a rarity, and the Doctor rejoices when it can happen.

Another irony in "The End of Time" is that the Master takes over a device designed specifically to "heal" whole worlds, a mechanical, more efficient strat-egy than what the Doctor uses. The device, appropriated from a destroyed Torchwood by a wealthy businessman and his daughter, removes imperfections and restores worlds to "health." The young woman assists her father in sup-porting the Master but has her own agenda: she wants to become immortal, and the device should help her achieve that aim. (Davies again works immor-tality, and its high price, into one of his scripts, showing yet again that becoming immortal is not the ultimate of "health" but rather a curse for humanity.) The Master "heals" Earth by turning everyone into "the Master race," removing the human imperfections of diversity in any form. To the Doctor, Earth's "cure" is worse than the affliction of "being human."

The Doctor as "God"

Because the Doctor knows so much about (and, to a certain extent, can control) Time, his actions may seem "godlike" to the less technologically advanced or younger civilizations he visits. Yet even with the Doctor's advanced experience and knowledge he still doesn't make all the right decisions. Some-times his actions seem callous as he determines who will live or die. Often he doesn't "pull the trigger" himself, so to speak, but he fails to intervene in a sit-uation that causes death. Two examples from the Ninth and Tenth Doctors clearly illustrate this point.

When the Ninth Doctor takes Rose five billion years into the future to wit-ness the glorious explosion of an uninhabited Earth ("The End of the World," 1.2), they become involved in a murder mystery.[13] The reputed "last human," Cassandra, is nothing more than a bodiless face amidst skin stretched across a frame, her brain conveniently stored in a nearby jar. She is humanity's thinnest woman, an extreme version of "one can never be too thin nor too rich." In fact, to be able to afford more operations to keep her skin beautifully young, Cas-sandra plots a hostage crisis by which she can extort money from the home planets of the dignitaries attending the "death of Earth" party. When the obser-vation station is threatened by the coming inferno, Cassandra hopes to make a killing, so to speak. Before the Doctor foils this plan, several staff and digni-taries die or are injured. Although the Doctor is able to save many, he also believes that Cassandra should pay for causing death and destruction. When the rising heat of the observation station threatens to dry out her skin to the point of popping, the Doctor doesn't intervene by changing the environment or assisting Cassandra. He doesn't kill her, per se, but he also doesn't save her. His actions determine her "punishment." Although a key theme in the Ninth Doctor's stories is "all things must end; nothing lasts forever," how and when planets or people "end" is often affected by the Doctor's decision whether to intervene.

During the final moments of "The Waters of Mars" the Tenth Doctor manages to save three members from a monstrous infection on a Mars colony, including Captain Adelaide Brooke. Earlier in the episode the Doctor confesses his admiration for the captain and tells her that her death on the Mars colony will inspire her granddaughter to leave Earth to travel the stars, beginning humanity's interstellar colonization. When the Doctor decides that he can change history to save the captain, he returns her to her home on Earth. Brooke is horrified that the Doctor might have changed the course of human development by saving her. "No one should have that much power," Brooke exclaims. "Tough," replies the Doctor. He then tells her that he previously just considered himself a survivor but has come to realize that he's the winner of all Time Lords. "That's who I am: the Time Lord victorious."[14] Brooke still has free will, however, and exercises it in brutal fashion. Off camera, after she closes the door to her house, the audience (and Doctor) hears a gunshot. The captain kills herself to preserve the timeline altered by the Doctor. He then realizes the ramifications of his actions and, while partially believing he should be stopped from "playing God," that he also doesn't want to die. Instead, he flees his responsibilities/ choices as a powerful "god" and his prophesied death.

These scenes may be difficult for children to understand. A few parents wrote to the BBC to complain that their children were confused by the dark ending to this creepy episode. The monsters created by the waters of Mars didn't frighten children, who generally like such weirdly visual monsters. The problem came with the Doctor's actions and Brooke's suicide, not typical scenes for the conclusion of a children's special. Although adults understand and more likely appreciate this dramatic character development, the target audience may not comprehend this aspect of their "hero."

As one critic blogged, "Suddenly, the Doctor saving the day is scary. And wrong. And worse, he's enjoying the godlike stuff way too much.... "The Time Lord victorious" is not the Doctor we know ... or is it? He's always been arrogant and sure of himself — is this really so different?"[15] Perhaps this "unraveling" of the Tenth Doctor is simply the Doctor as moral relativist. No "higher power" in the universe is going to be able to sanction him. He can do as he pleases; after all, he is *the* Time Lord in this episode, the "winner" of all previous conflicts. He leaves Brooke to deal with his decision in any way she chooses, although he tells her that she now is free to spend more time with her family and to enjoy the extended life he has given her.

Even when the Doctor believes that his actions free humans to make decisions for themselves or will improve their future lives, sometimes the results of his actions are very different from what he expected. Even the Doctor doesn't know how everything will turn out; he doesn't have perfect knowledge. Time will sometimes "correct" a change that the Doctor makes. The Doctor may try to "play God" at times, but he's clearly not omnipotent.

The Doctor can be fallible when he chooses who should live or die, or when to interfere in past events supposedly set in time to change the flow of events. Although only hardcore *Doctor Who* and *Torchwood* fans would appreciate a tangential connection between two of Peter Capaldi's roles, Davies brought it up in a half-joking way during a *Torchwood Declassified* segment about "Children of Earth." Capaldi first played Caecilius, a man in pre-explosive Pompeii who helps the Doctor and Donna ("The Fires of Pompeii," 4.3).[16] When the Doctor prepares to leave just before Krakatoa erupts, Donna begs him to carry just this one family to safety in the TARDIS. Although the Doctor realizes that this action will change history, he also knows that these people won't appreciably change the course of human development. They seem a "safe" change to make, and the Doctor acquiesces to Donna's plea. Capaldi later played John Frobisher, a London family man caught in negotiations with the alien 456. When the 456 demand a percentage of the world's children, Frobisher's boss, the prime minister, demands that Frobisher's children be sacrificed as two of that number. Instead of allowing the 456 to take his children, Frobisher takes their lives, as well as his wife's and his own.[17] Time may have taken thousands of years to "correct" the Doctor's action, but the family line of that ancient family from Pompeii is finally wiped from human history.[18]

The Doctor, like Rose and his other human companions, faces the choice of doing what is right versus doing what he (or Rose) wants (and then justifying the action by saying it's the right thing to do). At times the Doctor "plays god" by forgiving Rose even the destruction of Earth; he also sacrifices himself in a last-ditch effort to save the humans under his protection. Once again a church provides the setting for viewers to learn more about the Doctor and the boundaries of his power. Convinced that Rose needs to see her father's death to gain closure, the Doctor takes Rose back in recent history, where she sees her father hit by a car on the way to a friend's wedding. A traumatized Rose doesn't comfort the dying man, and she begs the Doctor to give her another chance, thus increasing the odds of a temporal paradox with too many Roses and Doctors cluttering the street. With a second chance, however, Rose saves her father from the accident. This changed timeline results in the monster-of-the-week, huge winged Reapers, arriving to eliminate the situation now "out of Time." Rose, the Doctor, and the wedding party take refuge in the church, but the tenacious Reapers attack until they can get in.

The Doctor blames Rose for the impending destruction, but he immediately embraces and forgives her once she recognizes her "sin" and asks forgiveness. He soon after steps in front of the humans he protects in the church so that the Reapers kill him rather than them. Only after the Doctor has been taken does Rose realize the enormity of her, and humanity's, loss, and the Doctor's sacrifice prompts Rose's father to correct the timeline by sacrificing himself. Although the Doctor often shows a surprising amount of forgiveness for the possibly world-ending errors made by his current or future companions (e.g., Jack Harkness in "The Empty Child"), he also wants them to understand the magnitude of the consequences when they attempt to "play god." The Doctor, with his vast knowledge and experience, is fallible enough when he uses his power over Time and Space to change lives; humans simply don't know enough to do so.

"Playing God" in the sense of loving, helping, and forgiving humanity is a positive interpretation of the Doctor's actions in these and other episodes. As the Davies era continues, the Doctor finds it increasingly difficult to be the (presumably) only Time Lord left to solve the universe's problems and to decide who should live or die if he interferes. He becomes an ever more remote "savior" or God-like figure who sets events in motion but increasingly isn't personally involved in dealing with their ramifications. For example, he turns up for almost every British Christmas invasion, but he's nowhere to be found when the 456 attempt to destroy humanity. He initially is out of touch when the universe begins winking out and Daleks begin taking over Earth (again). He wouldn't realize the Master is about to return and wreak havoc yet again if the Ood hadn't forced him to pay attention. Although the Doctor prefers humans to other species and spends an inordinate amount of time on Earth instead of traveling the cosmos, he either can't save humanity on his own (instead requiring the help of human companions) or he isn't around to help every time he's needed.

Perhaps "God," as inferred from these dark episodes and series like *Doctor Who* and *Torchwood*, isn't going to save humanity from itself or invaders. Humans can't rely on even a superior being like the Doctor to help them every time they get in trouble. They even may have historically misinterpreted the Doctor's periodic visits as divine intervention, when in reality he is merely a time traveler whose more powerful actions were perceived as "god-like" by the lesser mortals.

As a hero, then, the Doctor isn't perfect. When he takes his power over Time, in particular, too seriously or for his own purposes, he seems far less than a beneficent savior. Perhaps Davies' Ninth and Tenth Doctors serve more importantly to remind viewers that they can't delegate planet-saving to someone else; they have to be heroic, too, and rely on themselves more than an outside force that may or may not step in to guide or save them.

Religious Symbolism in Episodes

Whether the Doctor is a god or a demon, he is certainly at the center of much religious symbolism during the Davies era of *Who*dom. Two of the Tenth

Doctor's final episodes illustrate the extremes of symbolism involving the Doctor.

In the final scenes of "The Waters of Mars," a frightened crew member, transported safely back to Earth via TARDIS, asks the Doctor, "Who the hell are you?" Her question recalls previous scenes in this episode when the Doctor, wearing a red spacesuit, walks toward the camera (and Mars colonists) amid a hellish background. Flames surround his image, and he seems to walk from the fire. He decides to help the colonists flee Mars, even though he knows he'll also change the timeline and thus likely change the course of humanity. Although saving a few colonists seems to be a heroic act, the repercussions on humanity's future ultimately suggest that the Doctor is serving his own need to save someone important (i.e., Adelaide Brooke) because he has always admired her — and because he can — rather than thinking of the greater good of all humanity.

If the audience doesn't believe in a darker Doctor, they might see where even his "good" acts merely are flawed interpretations grown into legend by humans trying to find an explanation for what they've seen. They can't comprehend the "truth" of the Doctor's actions and explain what they've witnessed in a way that makes sense to them. A white-garbed woman briefly appears, angel-like, to tell Wilfrid Mott a different kind of Christmas story in a church. She describes an event on this site, now commemorated in stained glass, when a man called "the sainted physician" captured a demon who fell from the skies. This saint traveled in the blue box, an image prominently displayed in the church's stained glass window ("The End of Time, Part 1").

Davies' Christmas specials use holiday imagery, much of it Christian in origin, but turn these familiar symbols into the pawns of monsters or villains or the result of alien activity. During "The Christmas Invasion," for example, killer Santas are on the loose. "Snow" is created from the destruction of an alien-helmed Titanic ("Voyage of the Damned"). A Time Lord narrator tells the momentous tale of Earth's final days, a solemn new "Christmas story" for the ages, explained in past tense. Much like modern Christians might discuss Yule rites of their ancestors, the narrator describes Christmas 2009 as a "pagan rite to banish the cold and the dark." Of course, the Doctor, being a Time Lord, would also share this interpretation of human holiday rituals, whether sacred or secular.

Angels also become monsters in several episodes, the most famous being the stone angels in the award-winning episode "Blink" (3.10). "Voyage of the Damned" features a literal heavenly host: the gold-faced, white robed angel kiosks aboard the Titanic are called information hosts.[19] In response to their programming, they kill the ship's passengers and crew until the Doctor can gain command of them. He does so by forcing them to see the logic of obeying him. Once that problem is solved, the Doctor commands two angels to fly him to a higher location on the ship, where he can further try to stop the villain and save as many remaining passengers as possible. One scene shows the Doctor ascending on the arms of angels.

Is the Doctor a representative of Good when he fights traditional symbols associated with Christianity, such as angels? Or is he really an outcast working on his own behalf, or for an even darker force, because he fights traditional symbols of Christianity, such as angels? "Morality" doesn't seem to have much to do with the Doctor's actions or success; he determines what is right and when he has gone too far, and he deals with the consequences either way. By using religious imagery in these stories, Davies gives viewers a different perspective on the role of religion in humanity's history and the "validity" of sacred "hero" stories involving religious sites, such as churches. Whether the Doctor is good or not depends on his actions' outcomes on all of Time; there is no inherent Good or Evil. The Doctor does try to save as many people as possible, but not so much because of a moral rationale as because he genuinely likes humanity, despite the species' many flaws. The Doctor acts without a moral imperative, and, according to the Christmas episodes in particular, the Doctor's decisions and actions are only given a (sometimes wildly incorrect) moral interpretation based on their sociocultural values.

The Human-Doctor Hybrid, or Doctor as Other

The "hybrid" creation, usually involving the ameliorating influence of humanity on another species in the Whoniverse, further illustrates the grayness of modern heroes and villains. Humans aren't exclusively good or evil, but they can positively influence other species. The best part of humanity—compassion, intelligence, kindness—can offset the worst qualities in an alien species. If humans could focus on these positive, often peaceful qualities, they could make the dark side of humanity (e.g., violence, unbridled desire for power) less dominant.

In a powerful episode in the first season, "Dalek" (1.6), even the unemotional, inhuman Daleks have to deal with the imperfections of the human race in their desire to become "perfect" (i.e., free of all traces of emotion and any connection to their sworn enemy). Trying to survive after the rest of the Daleks are annihilated during the Time War, a lone, tortured Dalek on Earth uses Rose's DNA to heal itself when she reaches out to comfort it. However, with this infusion of human DNA the Dalek in effect becomes partly human and feels emotion, a horrific result for an alien that prides itself on lack of emotion and adherence to the group will.

In the later episodes "Bad Wolf" (1.12) and "The Parting of the Ways" (1.13), the Daleks' Emperor admits that he merged unwanted humans with the remaining Daleks; in this way he creates a vast hybrid–Dalek army designed to exterminate humans. The Daleks used human DNA to survive, but this part of their evolution eventually confuses and helps destroy them because they now, to their mind, are flawed. Only the "machine" qualities of the Daleks, symbolized by their metallic outer bodies, are prized — after all, they are efficient, emotionless, and relentless, qualities often missing in humans. The Daleks thus hate what they have become and seek to destroy the human race that helped them survive extinction.

Similarly, the half-human/half–Doctor character created during the "Stolen Earth" (4.12)/"Journey's End" (4.13) story arc is unsuitable to take his place in the Doctor's world. This hybrid suffers from the anger and violence the Tenth Doctor realizes plagued his Ninth self, qualities that the subsequent Doctor hoped to have purged from himself. He doesn't want to be that Time Lord anymore, but he also knows that the very human Rose can "socialize" this hybrid, just as she did with the Ninth Doctor. The hybrid, because of his human half, has no qualms about expressing his feelings for Rose. In a "happy ending" of sorts, Rose kisses the hybrid "Doctor" who will stay with her throughout their human lifetimes. Rose ends up with the type of Doctor she has always wanted, but the real Doctor knows that the hybrid version isn't suitable for the world the Tenth Doctor inhabits.

Another hybrid resulting from this story arc is the "Doctor Donna." Like Rose, Donna takes on the power of the TARDIS in order to save the universe. Unlike with Rose, however, that power can't be completely removed, resulting in a flawed hybrid. Donna's memory of her time with the Doctor, including her heroic role as universal savior, is erased. If she regains her missing memories her head might literally explode. Therefore, the confident, powerful Doctor Donna reverts to being a frustrated, often belligerent woman stuck in a dead-end life.

The Doctor Donna hybrid is only subsumed beneath an average, human existence. When the Master turns all humans into versions of himself, Donna is the only "human" left on Earth who hasn't been changed ("The End of Time, Part 1"). Although she doesn't know it yet, she is special, an improved person who still has the capacity to fight evil instead of being turned into a villain's pawn.

Half-human/half-alien hybrids may suffer because of their human flaws, but their human half also can provide some peace-inducing or heroic qualities not found in a "pure" species. As Doctor Donna gleefully tells the Doctor during "Journey's End": "You were just a Time Lord. You lacked just that little bit of gut instinct that comes from planet Earth." The combination of knowledge/experience gained by the long-lived Time Lord needs to be balanced with positive human emotions or instincts (e.g., love, compassion, intuition) to create a full-fledged hero.

The Transition Between Davies' and
Moffat's Who Eras

Davies ended the Tenth Doctor's saga with "The End of Time" specials shown on Christmas 2009 and New Year 2010. The Tenth Doctor's regeneration episode takes themes illustrated in the Ninth Doctor's regeneration episode ("The Parting of the Ways," 1.13) but makes them darker. When Eccleston's Ninth Doctor regenerates after saving Rose, the "death" scene is quite short and simply bittersweet as the Doctor realizes that he won't be able to show his companion all the wonders of the galaxy as he had hoped. His final words provide the closure for this Doctor's adventures: both he and Rose were "fantastic." Tennant's Tenth Doctor, however, rages against death and questions whether he wants to save a companion if that action will result in his regeneration. Both regeneration episodes require the Doctor to sacrifice himself in order to save a companion, but the Tenth Doctor is far from a willing sacrifice.

Final companion Wilfrid requires saving from being enclosed in what will be a radiation-flooded chamber. He gives the Doctor an "out" as a hero/savior, telling him that he's an old man who has lived a full life. In a reference to the earlier "Waters of Mars" episode, the Doctor even complains that Wilfrid isn't anyone special or important, unlike Mars colonist Adelaide Brooke, the historically significant commander the Doctor saves at the end of the previous special. However, the Ninth and, to a certain extent, Tenth Doctors previously valued the lives of "little" people precisely for their ordinary lives. The Doctor once relished the everyday celebrations and joys that make living a human life worthwhile. During "The End of Time," however, the Tenth Doctor agonizes over giving up this wonderful incarnation simply to save one mortal old man who, to his knowledge, will never be "significant" in the course of Time. "I could do so much more — and this is what I get. It's not fair!" the Doctor exclaims, acting more like a child having a tantrum than an ancient Time Lord ("The End of Time, Part 2").[20]

This action is quite unlike the heroic Doctor in whom fans, especially children, want to believe. He is very much the gray hero when he contemplates, however briefly, walking away from an endangered companion in order to keep his own life, when viewers and the Doctor know that he technically will live past another regeneration. The Tenth Doctor will cease to exist, but "the Doctor" will survive. By valuing his own life more than a companion's, the Tenth Doctor seems much more human but far less heroic.

Sighing "I've lived too long," the Tenth Doctor soon resigns himself to his fate, thus fulfilling the prophesy of dying after hearing four knocks on a door — Wilfrid knocking on the chamber to ask to be freed. Fulfilling such a prophesy, especially given the Biblical resonance of the first part's narration, elevates the Doctor's heroic status as the focal point of an epic tale.

As the Doctor walks toward his companion, and thus the camera, he seems much more like the hero fans expect. He walks calmly and confidently toward the audience as the sentimental music swells to an emotional crescendo. A close-up of the Doctor as he speaks his most heroic line — "It's my honor" — restores him to his "pure" hero status and allows him to be "redeemed" as a hero. Once he frees Wilfrid and walks willingly into an adjacent chamber that then is flooded with radiation, the self-sacrificing savior completes his heroic deed. The strings-heavy music pulses and reaches an emotional high point before quickly fading away, signaling the Doctor's final sacrifice and imminent death.

Unlike the Ninth Doctor's immediate willingness to save Rose, the Tenth Doctor takes a few minutes to consider his choice — save himself or save another — and the consequences of both options, for himself and the universe. His decision thus is given more weight, even if it makes his character a far grayer hero than he has been in previous incarnations. Although heroes act without hope of reward, the Tenth Doctor is granted a "final wish" of sorts. He has changed the lives of his companions, but they also have been the most important part of the Tenth Doctor's life. By being allowed to say goodbye to them, and to perform one final act of kindness for each, he provides himself and the audience closure with characters and story lines established during the Davies era.

Not surprisingly, "love" is the theme of these final farewells, but the Doctor doesn't express his love in words or isn't the love object in these scenes. He helps his companions either find the love they're looking for or to hang onto their loved ones just a little longer. He doesn't change the past so that lost lovers are returned, but he affects the current time line, according to established Davies canon in *Doctor Who* and spinoffs *The Sarah Jane Adventures* and *Torchwood*.

Although the Tenth Doctor's regeneration scene is the last official glimpse of the Tenth Doctor, the final scene Tennant filmed as this character appears in the earlier broadcast wedding episode of *The Sarah Jane Adventures*.[21] This farewell to the Doctor is far less angst-ridden, as appropriate for his more traditional role as hero/savior in the even more child-friendly spinoff. This "finale" also mirrors the Fourth Doctor's farewell to Sarah Jane (Elisabeth Sladen) in "The Hand of Fear" serial (14.4N) in 1976.

"Will I see you again?" Sarah Jane asks, and the Doctor expresses his hope that they will someday meet again (and, indeed, Davies allows the Doctor to wave goodbye in "The End of Time"). The Tenth Doctor asks her to remember him, and Sarah Jane quite appropriately replies, "You'll never be forgotten." These prophetic words provide a kinder, gentler send-off to the Tenth Doctor and the Davies era. More than any previous Doctor, Tennant's Tenth takes the character into ever-darker themes as he questions whether he wants to be a hero and what kind of Time Lord he should be. The Tenth Doctor thus serves as a socioculturally important bridge between the turbulent first decade of the

21st century, with a Doctor well suited for that time period, and the new decade and incoming Steven Moffat era of *Doctor Who*, beginning with the Eleventh Doctor (Matt Smith).

Interestingly enough, just as Davies' "Children of Earth" decimates Torchwood's "home," the writer/creator also destroys the interior of the TARDIS during the final moments of "The End of Time." Support beams tumble and fires erupt around the console as the newly regenerated Eleventh Doctor discovers what he looks like. Out of control, the TARDIS free falls toward Earth — the Eleventh Doctor begins by symbolically descending to Earth, his home and past in flames, where he can begin a new life on his favorite planet. The death of one hero leads to the birth of the next, and, in this case, the "older generation" of Doctor passes the torch to the youngest incarnation ever, effectively transferring the duties of "hero" to the next generation.

11

Torchwood

Although series like *Battlestar Galactica* regularly received accolades in television magazines and at academic popular culture conventions for its gritty realism and thinly disguised Bush-era plot points, *Torchwood* didn't get much positive notice until 2009, when "Children of Earth" debuted. Despite its controversy and some fans' outrage at the way the lead hero, Jack Harkness, and the Janto (i.e., Jack Harkness/Ianto Jones) love relationship turned out by the end of Day Five, the series received global critical attention and much praise. *TV Guide* critic Matt Roush listed "Children of Earth" among his Top 10 TV series of 2009, an achievement echoed by other U.K. and U.S. critics in newspapers and magazines worldwide.

In his brief rationale for the choice, Roush used phrases and descriptors like "quite simply the most terrifying thing I've seen in years," "epic dark fantasy," "riveting," "ruthless," and "thriller," before praising Season Three as the one that "shocks our system while breaking our hearts."[1] Other critics agreed, calling "Children of Earth" "deeper, scarier, and vastly more thrilling."[2] The Pittsburgh *Post-Gazette* not only included it in the year's Top 10 but reminded readers that "[s]ci-fi at its best forces viewers to ask tough questions while considering their own humanity, something this British import did without blinking."[3] A quartet of U.K. critics voiced many long-time fans' critique: "The five-part story was creepy and intriguing and the change of format worked well but did they have to kill off Ianto?"[4]

Even "Ianto" actor Gareth David-Lloyd finds much to like about "Children of Earth." When asked if the miniseries might help establish a new standard for SF TV, he replied:

> I hope it sets the mold really for the rest of the *Torchwood* series and for drama and SF generally. Having those five hours of story, with every hour ending with a cliffhanger, you get time to develop character, story. In 45 minutes [the usual time for an episode] you have to tell a whole story, and it never seemed like enough time to me. [CoE] is a five-hour film, with brilliant character development. It allowed you to go back into Ianto's past and see those scenes. It allowed you to go into Jack's past. It allowed a huge five-hour story arc for Ianto and Jack's relationship to develop and end. It just gives [the story] so much more scope. You can spend more money on it. You can spend what you would've spent in 13 episodes and get the quality,

239

rather than the quantity. If *Torchwood* comes back, I'd like it to do two of those a year. People would get 10 hours of *Torchwood* a year, get two great set-piece storylines.[5]

In many ways, "Children of Earth" is powerful entertainment that both attracted new fans to the series and repelled long-time viewers. Its themes provoked discussion not only about the series but about the nature and role of SF within drama. Its characterization takes the hero story into dark depths. In the scope of this book, it defines the gray hero and gray SF TV series.

Of all the series analyzed in this book, *Torchwood* is one of the most controversial, largely because of "Children of Earth." The series' hero, Jack Harkness, is the epitome of a gray hero. He may set the standard, or break the mold, of new SF TV "heroes" who speed up the paradigm shift from morality-based traditional heroes to moral relativists. Captain Jack still looks for "redemption" and bears the weight of grief and guilt by the end of "Children of Earth," but because he is faced with the darkest of choices, and *Torchwood* mercilessly illustrates the consequences of his actions, Jack Harkness is perhaps *the* pivotal gray hero of early 21st century SF TV.

One of the most impressive aspects of studying *Torchwood* as a source of modern SF TV heroes is its many texts, which present different aspects of Jack as everything from a lovable, redeemable hero-in-waiting (in *Doctor Who* episodes introducing Jack as a character) to a decidedly gray hero (in many TV episodes and novels) to an anachronistic hero, one sometimes illustrated in very traditional ways (with clothing choices, including that famous World War II–era coat). With so many texts presented for different audiences via multiple media, *Torchwood* gains further significance as an SF text worth not only a memorable place in popular culture but also one worth academic analysis in a study both of SF and hero literature.

Torchwood offers a group of misfits who somehow work together to help protect the world — or at least Cardiff, Wales—from monsters and villains, extraterrestrial and human. Across the first three seasons, Torchwood operatives include Suzie Costello, Owen Harper, Toshiko Sato, Ianto Jones, and Gwen Cooper. By the end of Season Three, only Gwen, in addition to Jack, survives. *Torchwood*, with its high death toll and ability to shock fans with the unexpected deaths of beloved characters, symbolizes a chaotic, violent modern world at its most extreme. Frequently filmed on dark streets, in storms, within abandoned warehouses, or within the subterranean base (the Hub), the scenes' darkness mirrors modern fears about what lurks just beyond human sight or what may attack without provocation. *Torchwood* episodes seldom have a happy ending; even the successes require someone's sacrifice or loss.

Although, in particular, Owen (Burn Gorman), Tosh (Naoko Mori), Ianto, and Gwen (Eve Myles) are heroic characters in their own right, clearly the standout character is Jack Harkness. As the series' lead and one of the few continuing characters, Captain Jack best represents the evolution of the gray hero and perhaps the death of the traditional SF TV hero.

The Beginnings of Captain Jack Harkness: From Con Man to Hero

A comment from a magazine interview is exceptionally telling about viewers' and critics' perception of Captain Jack Harkness: "It's practically a given that everyone who talks about either [actor John] Barrowman or Captain Jack eventually uses the word *hero*. 'A cheeky hero,' [Executive producer Julie] Gardner says, laughing, 'most definitely.'"[6] Audiences may enjoy Jack's playfulness, fall in love with his good looks, admire his ability to seduce anyone, or respect his desire to do anything to protect humanity, but he's not the type of hero viewers could or would become. He's larger than life, as is appropriate for a mortal time traveler who becomes an immortal hero.

One of the biggest shifts toward ever-grayer heroes occurred in the development of this character, first introduced in *Doctor Who* during the Ninth Doctor's tenure ("The Empty Child," 1.9).[7] After saving Rose during the Blitz, Captain Jack proceeds to charm both her and the Doctor. He loves high-tech gadgets and showing off how to use them. He isn't yet a hero in this early story arc; instead, he's a con man and former Time Agent who must have displeased his former employers so much that they erased two years of his memory. A self-angry Jack confesses to his new friends, "I'm a con man; that's who I am" ("The Empty Child," 1.9), and tries to defend his actions before the Doctor, who doesn't trust him nearly as readily as Rose does. Jack has no illusions about who he is, but after seeing the Doctor and Rose trying to help others throughout this story arc, he begins to feel that he's not as worthy and should be more easily expendable. Jack completely turns around from his previous self-centered, save-himself attitude.

A few seasons later Jack's former partner from the Time Agency, Captain John Hart (played with gleeful abandon by *Buffy* and *Angel* alum James Marsters), turns up in *Torchwood*'s Season Two ("Kiss Kiss, Bang Bang," 2.1).[8] When the Captains interact, audiences realize just why Jack once told the Doctor and Rose that he's not sure exactly what kind of man he was or what terrible things he may have done during the missing two years from his memory. Captain John happily confesses that he's spent the intervening time away from his former partner in a series of rehabs: alcohol, drug, and murder. None, apparently, seemed to take. From this background, pieced together from various episodes of *Doctor Who* and *Torchwood*, audiences learn that Jack likely wasn't heroic before he met the Doctor. Nevertheless, the "hero" from whom Jack learns the most is also called "the oncoming storm," and the 2000s-era Ninth and Tenth Doctors often make dark decisions themselves.

At least from his travels with the Doctor, Jack attempts to do the right thing to save as many people as possible, even at his own peril (and before he becomes immortal). Jack has a moral epiphany when, during "The Empty

Child" (1.9) and "The Doctor Dances" (1.10), he admits that his con during London's blitz is brilliant but possibly dangerous. He realizes the unintentional consequences of his self-centered con game when he hears the plaintive cries of its first victim, a child. Jack's defense — "I didn't know" — sounds lame even to himself. To make amends, and thus become a redeemed character worthy of being called a hero, Jack ends this story arc by taking a soon-to-be-detonated bomb away from London, even if he won't be able to escape the blast. At the last minute, of course, the Doctor and Rose save Jack, who then becomes a companion traveling in the TARDIS during the next series of adventures.

During one crucial battle against the Doctor's long-time enemy, the monstrous Daleks, Jack sacrifices himself in a last-ditch effort to save Earth ("The Parting of the Ways," 1.13).[9] His sacrifice is "rewarded" when he inadvertently is made immortal. Evil (the Daleks) is destroyed, and Good (Jack) is saved, this time eternally. Jack, however, frequently considers the "gift" of immortality more of a curse, and it colors his role as a hero from this point on.

Torchwood's Captain Jack

By the time Jack "joins" Torchwood (after a be-forever-tortured-and-studied or join-us-to-track/destroy-aliens choice), he is very much a gray character once again, and not always heroic. As an immortal stuck on Earth without his time-traveling technology, he bides his time waiting for the Doctor's return and works for Torchwood in the meantime. Jack dies again and again, sometimes by his own hand, sometimes in fights or during torture, but he can't stay dead. When Jack eventually becomes the leader of the secretive Torchwood Three in Cardiff, he becomes more heroic, although he is very much a gray hero with often questionable morals, according to 21st century Western values. Jack is a pragmatic leader who has a blind spot for the actions of those he loves, rationalizing their behavior if it suits his mood or purpose. Many themes begun during Jack's early character development in *Doctor Who* episodes continue throughout *Torchwood*.

According to Barrowman, Torchwood answers "to no one but themselves. Jack's the leader and the glue — he keeps everyone together. He's the hero, although I don't think he'd call himself a hero, he'd just call himself a man who does the job because it needs doing." In *Torchwood*'s early episodes, the actor explains, Jack is "a little bit darker and angrier [than in *Doctor Who*].... He doesn't always consider other people's feelings, with his priority the good of the world."[10]

In *Torchwood*, Jack is the kind of leader who orders employee Ianto Jones to execute his half-converted cyberwoman girlfriend but, a few scenes later, ensures that Ianto not only survives the cyberwoman's attack ("Cyberwoman," 1.4) but continues working for Torchwood. This change of heart is meant to illustrate Jack's compassion and his understanding that Ianto was acting out of love for his girlfriend-turned-monster. Jack's superior knowledge of this particular alien threat overrides Ianto's emotional involvement, yet audiences also see that Jack's emotions guide his actions regarding his team.

In some episodes Jack's forgiveness and compassion for his team become almost spiritual. When Jack and Tosh are lost in 1940s-era London ("Captain Jack Harkness," 1.12), Owen decides to open the Rift to retrieve them, despite Jack's orders not to do so.[11] Tempted to retrieve his own love lost to the Rift, as well as to bring back his Captain and Tosh, Owen succeeds in opening the Rift and not only retrieves his friends, but begins a chain of events that unleash a monster. The Biblically horrific Abaddon (although the victim of bad CGI that minimizes his apocalyptic threat) destroys Cardiff in his wake and is bent on bringing about the end of the world ("End of Days," 1.13).[12] Abaddon seeks power, and Jack sacrifices himself by providing the monster with an unlimited abundance of life-giving power — Jack's gift/curse as an immortal. Abaddon is destroyed when he can't handle such power, but Jack's life force also is depleted.

Even Jack's ability to survive death seems tested in the aftermath of his sacrifice. He stays dead for approximately three days (another Biblical allusion). His "Mary Magdalene," Gwen (a "fallen woman" who has an affair with co-worker Owen while she lives with boyfriend Rhys), remains at his Torchwood tomb, refusing to believe he won't rise from the dead. He rewards her faith by returning to life with a big smile just for her and then returns to his adoring team.[13] Tosh receives a hug; Ianto a tender kiss; but Owen is gifted with Jack's forgiveness. As Owen weeps in his arms, remorseful for going against "nature"— and Jack — by opening the Rift and unwittingly unleashing evil on Earth, Jack simply holds him and gently offers absolution: "I forgive you."

Jack as hero isn't always so forgiving, however. Although frequently willing to be a sacrifice because he knows he's immortal (while also hoping that one death might be permanent), he is further motivated by guilt. He has never forgiven himself for letting go of his little brother's hand during a planetary invasion of his homeworld. Jack searches but is unable to find Gray, and he lives with this torment throughout his centuries-long adult life. John Hart manages to "rescue" Gray in hopes of winning Jack's and Gray's undying gratitude, only to be used by the vengeful little-brother-grown-to-tortured-man ("Exit Wounds," 1.13). Whereas Jack's abandonment (e.g., on Earth) and torture (e.g., at the hands of Torchwood, among others) make him more self-doubting and humbled, Gray's years of torture only motivate him to destroy his brother, the one he holds responsible for his abandonment and torture. Gray thus becomes as much unpredictable monster as a villain out for revenge against Jack.

In a (failed) attempt to save Cardiff and his team, Jack agrees to let Gray bury him alive, resulting in a series of awakenings and deaths that lasts for 2000 years. Again, Jack's "return" to the world to try to save it provides a spiritual metaphor, which may seem odd for a gray hero, especially one created by an atheist. Jack is far from a perfect savior, and his actions during Season One often portray him as ruthless and, according to ultra-conservative Western mores, sinful, especially because of his sexual exploits and omnisexuality. During Season Two, however, Jack's recurring roles as sacrifice and savior elevate him as a still-gray but possibly-redeemed hero.

Even after 2000 years of torment, Jack is unable to permanently destroy Gray. He freezes him, in the same way that other people out of their time or former Torchwood employees have been preserved to be revived some time in the future. Gray, in essence, is suspended between life and death, much as Jack was suspended in the grave ("Exit Wounds," 2.13). Jack's hope is that someday Gray may be revived and redeemed. Jack again serves as the judge in determining what should be done with aliens. His words and actions determine who will be saved and who killed.

Jack isn't always a compassionate hero. During the first two seasons of *Torchwood* he gruesomely dispatches Tosh's alien lover, who attempts to take over Torchwood and the minds of its employees ("Greeks Bearing Gifts," 1.7); tortures a woman who doesn't know she's harboring an alien inside her ("Sleeper," 2.2); destroys Adam, who "lives" by becoming part of the faux memories he places in Torchwood's minds ("Adam," 2.5); and, even in the pilot episode ("Everything Changes," 1.1), allows the resuscitation of a murder victim only so that Torchwood can study the alien technology used to temporarily revive him. Solving crimes isn't Torchwood's business, as Jack tells Gwen early in their association. Torchwood studies aliens and tries to give humanity a helping hand in surviving against potential alien threats. That Jack may himself be perceived as such an alien threat doesn't seem to enter his mind.

Nevertheless, Jack often does show compassion — when it suits his mood or reminds him that he also has suffered similarly. When an alien is being used as a neverending supply of meat by an entrepreneurial human businessman, Jack wants not only to break up the butcher's ring but to save the alien ("Meat," 2.4). However, the vivisection has traumatized the whale-like creature for so long that Owen instead euthanizes it to stop its pain. Jack genuinely mourns the alien, tied down and endlessly tortured for human pleasure; undoubtedly he feels kinship with the creature after his torture by early Torchwood (and perhaps his future imprisonment and torture by the Master in later *Doctor Who* episodes ["The Sound of Drums," 3.12; "The Last of the Time Lords," 3.13] is foreshadowed as well).

Jack at times is willing to sacrifice himself for only one person, especially if the situation reminds Jack of one he has endured. In the aptly named "Out of Time" (1.10), Jack allows an accidental time traveler who can't acclimate himself into a new century to commit suicide. Instead of intervening to stop the man from committing what to some audience members would be a mortal sin, Jack sits in the front seat of a borrowed car and holds the man's hand as he, and presumably Jack, succumb to carbon monoxide poisoning. Jack's sacrifice again seems coupled with guilt — he must give one of his many lives as penance for not being able to offer the man a new life worth living. Perhaps Jack even lives vicariously through this man's death; after all, his immortality stops him from such a convenient way out of being displaced from all he once knew or wanted.

As these many examples illustrate, Jack Harkness is a conflicted man who may not have been meant to be Torchwood's (or any organization's) leader because of his extremely long, troubled past. He does the best he can, but his "management" skills are subject to his current emotional state and spur-of-the-moment decisions in crises. Jack improvises, charms, or cons his way through life, but he also harbors regrets, guilt, and uncertainties about his worth. The many layers of Jack's personality are as deep and mysterious as the Hub he chooses for his home and workplace. Perhaps he keeps forgiving his colleagues and brother for their many dark secrets, human frailties, and poor decisions because he is just as flawed as they and would like someone to forgive him or make everything all right. Yet Jack seems to have given up expectations of any "happy ending," instead becoming determined to do what he can but knowing his best efforts will never be enough.

Jack's public persona is much more gung-ho hero, and this side of his personality is what he shares with outsiders, government leaders, threatening aliens, and his colleagues out on a mission. His exuberance and commanding confidence belay any deeply hidden self-doubt. To the outside world, Jack is that larger-than-life hero who can save the world in the nick of time.

Jack frequently makes a grand, heroic entrance to blast aliens threatening Cardiff, humanity in general, or members of his team. Frequently he looks the part of a classically grand hero making a bold entrance to save the day. For all that Jack is an increasingly gray hero, he has moments during the first two seasons in which he is portrayed as a classic hero arriving in the nick of time to save the day.

His arrival in Season Two's first episode provides a typical Jack-as-hero rescue. At this point in the series Jack has been missing for several months (traveling with the Doctor in a series of *Who* episodes, culminating with "The Last of the Time Lords," 3.13). During Jack's absence, the Torchwood team has pulled together without their Captain, although they aren't quite as effective without him.

In the first few moments of "Kiss Kiss, Bang Bang" (2.1), a blowfish holds a family hostage, and Torchwood attempts to rescue the family.[14] Owen tends the wounded father, Tosh takes tech readings, and Gwen protects the hysterical mother. Ianto stands frozen, unsure whether to take a shot as the alien taunting him holds a weapon to the daughter's head. Suddenly a shot splatters the alien and frees the hostage. Ianto looks puzzled, because he hasn't fired the gun. The camera then pans to show Jack, weapon in hand, smirk on his face, RAF greatcoat flowing behind him. "So, kids, did you miss me?" he asks. Moments later he receives a holographic message from Time Agent John Hart. Knowing that Hart is bad news, and probably wanting a more private reunion with his former partner, Jack bounds into Torchwood's SUV and leaves his team behind as quickly as he burst in to save them.

In response, Ianto simply hails a taxi to go after Jack. The team expresses both their frustration and their admiration for the newly returned Captain as they trail him. They dislike Jack's ability to make such grand entrances to save the day, and themselves, but, as Ianto puts it, Torchwood "is a lot more fun with him."

This grand entrance not only sparks audience interest in the new series of episodes, it re-establishes Jack as Torchwood's leader and Earth's savior, roles that become increasingly difficult for him in subsequent episodes. In contrast, during Season One, Jack acts as the standard SF hero who can do what his team can't. During "Countrycide" (1.4), for example, Gwen is shot by a frightened young man hoping to defend himself against cannibals. Owen is more effective as a doctor than a fighter. Tosh and Ianto are captured by the cannibals, and although Ianto desperately tries to provide a diversion so that Tosh can escape, the pair only end up battered and next in line as dinner. To save the town, as well as his colleagues, Jack drives into the cabin where his team and other captives are being held and captures the cannibals' leader. His dramatic arrival is typical "hero" behavior appropriate for the larger-than-life Captain Jack.

In such scenes Jack can be idealized as the classic TV hero found in genres such as the Western, as well as SF. He is a loner who shows up in the nick of time and knows exactly what to do. He is superior to his enemies and knows how to destroy them, which he doesn't hesitate to do if they threaten innocents, especially those he loves. At times he is shown standing on the roof of one of Cardiff's tallest buildings, surveying his domain while the most symbolic item in his costume, his long military coat, flows behind him. He is symbolically and visually elevated as a heroic protector surveying his domain.

Although Jack is often considered a traditional hero along the lines of a Christ-like savior (although many Christians would dispute Jack as anything like Christ), Barrowman thinks of Jack as the mythic Prometheus, the god who brings light to humanity and sacrifices himself on their behalf, but then angers authority (in the form of all-powerful god Zeus) enough to warrant eternal punishment. Barrowman explains that, over the course of three seasons, Jack becomes "a twenty-first century Prometheus, and in 'Children of Earth' the allusions and connections are even stronger. Both Prometheus and Jack are cunning, smart, and immortal."[15]

Plot and costume devices portray Captain Jack as the ideal classic hero, with allusions to important cultural myths going back centuries. Whereas some mythic characters, whether from classic literature or recent SF TV series, represent a single type of hero or fail to grow after their initial development, Jack evolves. His hero's journey takes him into dark territory but then allows him some redemption or retreat back toward the expected actions or traits of classic heroes. Many of his actions, especially during Season Two, change him from either the hardline hero who must make often tragically difficult decisions or the truly gray hero whose decisions may be based as much on his desires as on logic or the need to save humanity. Jack increasingly becomes more of a troubled modern hero who questions himself and the rightness of his actions; he becomes at times the despondent loner who feels isolated from his team. His immortality and role as Torchwood's leader force him to live separately from everyone else in the universe; his experience can never be truly understood, even by the extremely long-lived Doctor. Jack becomes more of a troubled, brooding hero in later episodes, which is appropriate for the increasingly apocalyptic dangers introduced into the plot.

Perhaps the best example of Season Two Jack as a more troubled modern hero, albeit one good enough to warrant some spiritual allusions to the forgiving, self-sacrificing, resurrected Christ, comes from a comparison of Jack with John Hart. Not coincidentally, the two share the same initials and a similar past as partners in the Time Agency. Through Hart's immediate familiarity with Jack and his certainty that the two will fall right back into a highly sexualized attraction (which they do, brawling and bloodying each other before that first exuberant reunion kiss), audiences better understand just what kind of man Jack — going by another, if unknown-to-us name — was before his association with the Doctor and his eventual leadership of Torchwood Three.

Hart is just as charismatic as he is sociopathically dangerous — which is to say extreme in both cases. He clearly does what he pleases, although he often suffers because of his whims — such as stealing a gem from the woman he seduces and then kills, only to become ensnared in her deadly trap, or locating and freeing the long-imprisoned Gray, only to be used as the former captive's pawn in his quest for violent vengeance against Jack. Hart is careless with his life and the lives of those around him; he is self-centered and hedonistic, gluttonous for power and casual in his use of murder, sex, and betrayal to get what he desires. He is quite possibly what Jack once was or would have become had he not been "redeemed" by the Doctor's influence and his own sobering experiences on Earth. As a villain, Hart even pushes Harkness to yet another death. Symbolically, Good (Jack) is temporarily overcome by Evil (Hart), only to return yet again to defeat the villain.

Like the oppositional Good and Evil, Jack has been bound (quite literally, in a five-year time loop) to Hart, and although he wants to get his former partner out of his current life as soon as possible, Jack still recognizes the strength of their former relationship. Even in the aftermath of the Gray debacle, Hart still loves Harkness and seems rather miffed (never a good sign regarding such a volatile personality) that Jack isn't willing to metaphorically and physically embrace his former lover. Jack has moved on and outgrown the purely self-directed lifestyle represented by Hart; he has backed away from narcissistic villainy and self-absorbed action in favor of a more restrained, outer-directed responsibility for others. Emotionally, however, Jack still tends to favor extremes. He either withdraws from his friends and lovers because the idea of losing them is too painful to risk further involvement, or he takes extreme measures—and displays wildly shifting passionate emotions—in order to save or protect those he loves.

A *Newsday* review of the Season Two opener described *Torchwood*'s "intense human drama" and commented specifically on Captain Jack as a busy but ambivalent "swashbuckling hero":

> Poor Jack, drowning his sorrows in physicality and space-age CSI-ing, all because he "can't die." ... Captain Jack has planted himself in the evocatively filmed metropolis of Cardiff, Wales, giving up his galactic con job to take a more adult approach to his unending days.... [Later in the article, Jack's "lusty" approach to life is discussed.] Jack's no-boundaries lust actually moves his every relationship beyond the physical to a distinctly spiritual connection. Because Jack doesn't make distinctions of gender or race or anything else ... he's everybody's soul mate.... His lust is for life itself—and death, too—which means he doesn't rule anything out. He's fearless and feisty.[16]

Jack isn't a completely stable, ideal hero, even by the end of Season Two, but he clearly has moved a long way from his time as John Hart's partner. Audiences get the feeling that their current relationship of opposites attracting differs from their previous one of kindred spirits out of control, a very different, but intriguing, look into Jack Harkness' past.

By Season Three, Torchwood is down to three members: Jack, Ianto, and Gwen. To cover up an old agreement with aliens, the British government issues a death warrant specifically for Jack and Torchwood. Philosophically and pragmatically, Jack tries to take a higher road and, as a good soldier (evidenced by his fondness for World War II–era garb and history as a soldier in numerous Earth-bound and interplanetary battles), do his duty for Queen and country, at whatever cost to himself. Only when his duty conflicts with what he believes is right does Jack rebel and become, once more, a "criminal" by going against a government trying to wipe out Torchwood (and thus the forces of Good). The plotline in "Children of Earth" takes Jack into a new level of darkness as he decides he must go even further against society's laws and moral conventions (e.g., stealing from citizens and blackmailing the government are wrong) in order to right a devastating wrong.

Jack becomes the gray hero who must sacrifice those he loves in order to protect the rest of humanity. He expects no thanks but instead knows the government has marked him for death — or, worse yet, eternal captivity and torture. Jack believes he must act as the hero (although he feels decidedly unheroic) who must act outside the law in order to protect civilization. The world has become so chaotic that the government, while publicly seeming to act in the best interests of its citizens, instead is ultimately leading civilization toward its destruction. In an attempt to solve the current Earth-threatening crisis, as well as redeem himself for his past "sins," Jack jumps into the fray and faces increasingly gray moral areas.

This time, however, even his best efforts and long-lived insights fail him. He saves the world once again, but his personal world is demolished and his sense of self destroyed. Although Gwen tries to reassure Jack that his actions have saved millions, time and again he realizes that he grew to like being his friends,' and the world's, savior — he felt infallible. Jack as the all-knowing hero who swoops in to save the day is gone. In his wake is a broken man who must live with the consequences of his inability to save everyone. That he is immortal and may face similar devastating results over and over makes him a tragic character, whether long-time fans believe he is still heroic or fallen too far in the darkness to be easily redeemed.

By the end of Season Three, Jack Harkness has been portrayed as every type of hero in varying shades of gray. His ability to morph among heroic "types" isn't just a question of questionable writing or a poorly defined canon; it illustrates the gray hero in all his glory. Jack's heroism at times may be smug and self-congratulatory, but it also can be sacrificial and mournful. Although his loneliness may make audiences empathize with him, they can never share his experiences.

Characters like Ianto and Gwen, with their human emotions and frailties, are much more relatable to audiences because they are common heroes who share with the audience the same hopes for a good life during impossibly difficult times. Jack is removed from the common experience, as is the Doctor, but his sheer charisma makes him a likable and imminently watchable character — because of or despite the shade of gray coloring a particular episode or interpretation of Jack as hero.

Children as Catalysts: Jack's Ever Grayer Heroism

Ironically, most of Jack's epiphanies, in *Doctor Who* and *Torchwood*, come at the expense of children, just like the transformation occurring during "The Empty Child" (1.9). When a child is hurt, lost, or killed, he typically responds with guilt and self-loathing, which motivate him to change his character. This pattern is developed most notably through the following episodes:

• "Small Worlds" (1.5)[17] — Jack fears the fairies attacking Cardiff's citizens as they claim their Chosen One, a little girl named Jasmine. When Jack realizes that he can't protect those he loves, much less all of the city's citizens, against this ancient force, he agrees to give up the child. She may live forever with the fairies, and she wants to go with them, but Gwen, in particular, has a difficult time forgiving Jack for letting the girl go. Beginning with this episode, Jack's decisions involving children make him a grayer hero and present a side to his character that even his closest friends have trouble understanding. As Barrowman noted in the commentary accompanying the "Children of Earth" DVD, if Jack is faced with a decision to sacrifice one person in order to save many, he always will choose to sacrifice the one.[18] The fact that Jasmine, although a child, wants to accompany the fairies, and indeed is shown as a smiling winged being of light in the episode's final close-up, makes her loss less devastating than if she had simply been handed over. Of course, the question whether children can make such informed decisions, as well as the impact of Jasmine's loss on her distraught mother, may help viewers rationalize Jack's decision, but they don't make it any easier to accept.

• "From Out of the Rain" (2.10)[19]— Although Jack doesn't save the lone child who survives the arrival of the Night Visitors (Ianto does that), the good Captain is shown cradling the young boy whose stolen soul is returned to him. The child awakens, much to Jack's joy. In fact, without Jack's knowledge of how to return the bottled soul to the child before his physical body dies, no one attacked by the alien visitors would have survived. Ianto berates himself for not being able to save more people, although the way his actions are shown on screen — he heroically catches the open bottle tossed by the villain and manages to cap it with his hands before all the stolen souls "spill" — clearly illustrate that he did well to save the boy. Jack, much more than Ianto, recognizes that being able to save one victim is cause for celebration. Certainly the loss of the others is regrettable, but the emphasis is on the sole survivor, a blond boy who, in hindsight, turns out to look a lot like Jack's then-unrevealed grandson, Stephen.

• "Children of Earth" (3.3)[20]— In the 1960s a much darker Captain Jack hands over twelve children to the monstrous 456 as part of a bargain to gain the antidote to a virus. Another character explains that Jack is the ideal soldier to present the children to the aliens because he doesn't care about others and displays no emotions over such an order. In his defense, at that point Jack doesn't have any reason to believe the 456 will someday return and that the "trade" would be nothing more than a one-off.

• "Children of Earth" (3.1)[21]— Jack's daughter, Alice Carter, echoes the sentiment of her father's 1960s superior. She refuses to let her father spend much time with his grandson and fears him as a dangerous man. Her mother apparently felt the same way; when Alice attempts to run away with Stephen before governmental agents can capture them, she reminds her son of the "game" his grandmother taught him — to be silent, no matter what happens. Stephen recalls that his grandmother told him that someday he'd need that skill. Jack's own family apparently regards him as dangerous at best and as monstrous at worst — an uncontrollable, unpredictable force that could endanger their lives.

• "Children of Earth" (3.5)[22]— To save the rest of humanity, more generally, from the returned 456, and, more immediately, to free ten percent of the world's children from being taken by the aliens, Jack faces a terrible decision: sacrifice the nearest child in order to force the 456 to depart Earth or watch as the child-exchange takes place.[23] Once again Jack chooses to sacrifice one to save many. This time, however, the child has no choice and, trustingly, follows orders without knowing that he goes to his death. Jack's actions may be heroic in the sense that he does save the world, but at great personal cost. Stephen Carter's lack of choice, much less ability to consent to being a sacrifice, makes Jack seem far less heroic in this latest example. He isn't alone in considering a child expendable, and, if anything, the tears streaming down Jack's face as he watches his grandson die indicate the depth of his emotion and the extent to which he has become a broken man. The British government in particular, as well as the rest of the world's leaders, agree that the children they plan to hand over to the 456 are "units," and several times throughout "Children of Earth" children are portrayed as little soldiers, apparently on the front lines of modern social warfare. Throughout the miniseries Stephen frequently is dressed in uniform, whether a school uniform or military-style camouflaged clothing. Jack more than once refers to Stephen as "soldier," a term of endearment made more ironic given Jack's long military history. For Jack, being a soldier, at whatever age, may entail personal sacrifice in the name of duty. The aliens provide even more damning evidence of humanity's inhumane treatment of children. As the 456 explain, hundreds of children die daily of abuse or neglect, while the world looks the other way. How much worse is humanity for directly, knowingly sacrificing children to aliens than to ignore their deaths from violence or starvation? Compared to the world's governing authorities, Jack is very human and at least mourns that whom he sacrifices.

Of course, Jack is meant to be the lead hero of *Torchwood* and at least a visiting secondary hero on *Doctor Who*, where he periodically returns to assist the Doctor in fighting even greater villains or monsters than those who fall through Cardiff's Rift in space and time or are home-grown evildoers out to wreak havoc. During *Torchwood*'s first three seasons Jack frequently puts himself in danger and would rather die himself than risk his friends. Many episodes, however, also show Jack's playful, loving, or even boyish qualities—he's not always a dark hero or a guilt-ridden leader.

Traditional heroes often become role models or mentors for the next generation. True to that aim, long-lived Jack instills in his Torchwood colleagues a purpose or mission: to protect their city, nation, world, or universe at whatever cost to themselves. His interactions with the next generation of children nevertheless indicate that he is far from being the ideal mentor; the role of children within *Torchwood* also marks Jack as a dangerous man to be feared instead of trusted at face value.

Jack as Other

The most important elements that mark Captain Jack Harkness as a gray hero are his leadership of a secret agency even above the government (generally a fear-inducing concern for most citizens), his status as a human "alien" from another planet and an immortal who makes life-or-death decisions for an entire world, and, last but certainly not least for more conservative audiences, his omnisexuality and (at least initially) lack of culturally shared values with citizens of the 21st century. Jack as a 51st century hero displaced into a rather socially backward world becomes an acceptable hero whose better qualities (e.g., loyalty, non-judgmental love, capacity for forgiveness) offset those aspects of his characterization that might otherwise be too difficult for some audience members to accept. Jack's perspectives offer unique insights on relationships and real-world issues facing audiences who follow Jack's adventures not only on TV, but through a variety of other media.

One reason for Captain Jack's enduring popularity in the early 2000s, not only in the U.K. but internationally, is the amazing amount of publicity actor John Barrowman (as Captain Jack or in his other roles as TV presenter, stage actor, and singer) receives in the press. He even was called a "national treasure" by *The Times*.[24] Glasgow-born, U.S.–reared Barrowman is perceived by fans to be an international "hero," both for his most famous (to date) role as Captain Jack and for being an out actor. Although an actor's sexual orientation shouldn't be the basis of whether he is deemed "suitable" for a role, heroic or not, Barrowman's high profile and openness about his personal life bring an important element to fans' appreciation for Barrowman's casting as Captain Jack; at least a part of *Torchwood*'s audience tunes in to see Barrowman in a high profile TV role as much as to follow *Torchwood*'s adventures. The fact that Jack is open about his relationships, and *Torchwood* emphasized the Janto relationship, especially in Season Three, are reasons for the series' and characters' popularity. (See Chapter 3 for a complete discussion of Jack's sexuality and Otherness.) *Torchwood* in many ways celebrates Otherness, and fans who themselves feel or are perceived to be Other gravitate to the series.

Jack as the Anachronistic Hero

Jack was originally envisioned as a boy from a humble background who makes good. He tells the Doctor that he was plucked from a backwater planet to be a poster boy for the Time Agency ("The Last of the Time Lords," 3.13). As Barrowman writes in *I Am What I Am*, Jack's costume beneath that trademarked greatcoat was designed to reflect Jack's rural beginnings. Series creator Russell T. Davies wanted Jack's *Torchwood* outfit to be different from his *Doctor Who* wardrobe. Jack's eventual costume of white or blue shirt, braces, belt, and boots represents an Earthly "fashion trend in the thirties and forties, and it projected an image of Jack as a kind of Midwestern farm boy."[25] Like other famous space captains before him (including Captain Kirk, from Iowa's farmland, and Captain Picard, with a childhood home among French vineyards), Captain Jack's roots are very much middle class and heartland, although his home is on distant Boeshane rather than Earth.

With this background, Jack initially looks like a benign, expected type of SF TV hero. He is "one of us," an average person who becomes greater than his origins might have indicated he would be. As *Torchwood* progresses, and as Jack's immortality stretches his life experiences far beyond any other human's possible lifespan, Jack becomes far more Other than "one of us." Even typical life experiences, such as falling in love or getting married, take on unique significance because of his immortality. Jack may have more opportunities for different types of love relationships, but he also faces loss more often. He will always outlive a partner or a child, whether his family and friends survive to old age or die young because of their association with him.

Jack's immortality and increasing Otherness over time make his typical human experiences seem quaint. He may have truly loved wife Lucia Moretti, and want to be reconciled with daughter Alice Carter and grandson Stephen, but these relationships, one way or another, are merely moments within an eternal lifespan. Jack promises a dying Ianto that he'll remember him, but after billions of years will he be able to? Jack's desire to be typically human may be as anachronistic and antiquated as his *Torchwood* wardrobe.

Even Jack's name is both a lie and an anachronism. The power of a name is crucial in hero stories. Traditional heroes often reveal their true lineage or rise to leadership because of noble heritage. Family names, as well as names bestowed during battle or heroic deeds, indicate the hero's significance. Ironically, audiences— not to mention Jack's family and friends— don't know or use his real name. His Torchwood colleagues are stunned to learn that his current moniker comes from a deceased World War II American pilot who heroically dies during a mission ("Captain Jack Harkness," 1.12). Jack tries to honor the deceased by living up to the man whose name he takes.

That Jack is known by the name of a World War II officer isn't surprising. Jack seems most comfortable donning the role of war hero. His personal tastes reflect the 1940s, whether in music, clothing, or books. His preferred weapon is a Webley instead of space tech. His living space is reminiscent of a military barracks, functionally spartan. He only feels adequately dressed when wearing his typical "costume," including braces, work shirt, boots, and long coat, all from a bygone era. He knows how to blend in with 1940s wartime society and would seem at home there if forced to live in that time frame again.

For all that he tells stories of his sexual exploits across the galaxy, Jack is also a former con man who knows how to spin a yarn. In the 20th and 21st centuries on Earth he seems quaintly monogamous when he's in love. He flirts, but he's not shown acting on sexual desires with more than one partner at a time. Even in the potential love triangle with Gwen and Ianto, Jack consistently reminds Gwen to maintain her normal outside–Torchwood life with Rhys. Although the Captain may love Gwen and under other circumstances act on their "best friend" relationship, he becomes devoted to Ianto and, by Season Three, is clearly a one-man man.

As a heroic character, Jack's methods of dealing with villains and monsters also reflect a 1940s sensibility. His leadership style places him in charge as the final decision maker. All blame for a less than successful mission returns to him, but success is shared among those in his command. He demands the final say, although his colleagues increasingly prove themselves capable of handling crises. Although personally he seems to rely more often on Ianto and willingly gives up his authority, especially in their personal life, when on the job Jack expects to be the boss.

As Ianto states when Jack asks how he should have handled the invading 456 in the 1960s, "The Jack I know would've stood up to them" ("Children of Earth," 3.4).[26] When Jack, accompanied by ever-loyal Ianto, does just that, he sounds just like a traditional hero. He confronts the 456 first with rhetoric and then with bullets. He states the rightness of his cause and vows to lead humanity into battle, if that's what it takes. However, his traditionally heroic demeanor and rhetoric are woefully inadequate for the modern monster/villain. The 456 don't discuss options, negotiate, or offer their own retaliatory rhetoric. They simply seal a building and use chemical warfare to kill everyone, including Jack. Only the fact that he is immortal allows him to survive the attack.

Traditional heroes don't give up, even when faced with overwhelming odds. Going against audience expectations for a traditional hero, a post–Ianto Jack instead encourages Gwen to surrender and accepts being imprisoned. He doesn't volunteer to help the government try to avert the looming crisis, but he does agree to try when his daughter still believes in him and convinces authorities that Jack will be able to help. To her devastation, the way that Jack succeeds in getting rid of the 456 is more horrific than she could have ever imagined.

As a result, Jack abandons Earth, presumably for good. Although he may return in Season Four under the name Jack Harkness or as another incarnation, the "traditional hero" has become such an anachronism against foes like the 456 that he must die. A hero like Jack — using rhetoric, traditional weapons, and confidence in his ability to know and do what is right — no longer seems adequate against foes that will use any weapon at any time, without warning. Villains and monsters, as represented by the 456 as well as the world's governments, have more power, money, status, and technological superiority to overcome any would-be traditional heroes, like Jack.

Symbolically, "Children of Earth" highlights the "death" of this traditional style of hero by once more showing how anachronistic he is to current expectations for what a hero is or should be. Once again dressed in his anachronistic long coat and standing atop a hill, highlighted against the night sky, Jack stands alone. Traditional literary heroes often die while standing atop a hill, and the "death" of "Jack Harkness" appropriately follows this pattern. Instead of vowing to make amends for what he sees are his "sins" leading to the deaths of his family and friends, Jack chooses to leave Earth because the memories of his life on this planet are too much to bear. He runs away instead of staying to fight the good fight; he abandons his role as hero. The conclusion to "Children of Earth" seems to be Davies' political statement that heroes like Jack, no matter how beloved or how mythic in origin, are inadequate against current villains and monsters. For this reason alone, "Children of Earth" may achieve long-lasting significance in SF TV history as one of the darkest series to come along, a chilling reflection of societal fears and political issues facing humanity in the early 21st century.

Hero Development and Intertextuality

As mentioned at the beginning of this chapter, *Torchwood* is also note-worthy because the heroic adventures of Captain Jack take place beyond TV episodes. Although *Doctor Who* also provides a magazine, novels for different ages of audiences (e.g., hardbacks for older readers, paperbacks and graphic novels for younger readers), yearbooks, and audiobooks, even this venerable series has trouble keeping up with *Torchwood*'s marketing. Most recent SF TV series, including *Buffy, Angel, Lost, Battlestar Galactica,* and *Heroes,* are well represented with products in the marketplace, but the number of story-related texts is greater for *Torchwood.*

For a recent series with relatively few episodes (compared to a long-running series like *Doctor Who*), *Torchwood* benefits from rich intertextuality. By early 2010 the series spawned more than a dozen hardback novels; a *Torchwood* fan magazine, including the special "Selkie" comic; four original radio plays; an official BBC website featuring additional content like the Captain's Blog; and original audiobooks. The stories develop different aspects of characters, and Jack in particular provides a wealth of opportunities for stories in any location or timeline.

The BBC's *Doctor Who* franchise also helps *Torchwood* characters achieve a higher level of public acceptance and become part of the *Who* franchise's mass marketing. When *Torchwood* became a hit on BBC America, U.S. fans clamored for the licensing of additional merchandise that was already available in the U.K. Beginning with novels, worldwide audiences learn even more about Torch-wood's adventures, but other storytelling media help build up the images of Captain Jack (and, by extension, the Torchwood team) as modern heroes.

In addition to the story-based "texts" in various media formats, Captain

Jack's exploits have been celebrated with soundtrack CDs, posters, and action figures of the principal cast and even Captain John Hart, a character who memorably appears in two episodes during Season Two. As well, *Torchwood* conventions sprang up around the U.K. and Ireland, with more general SF conventions in the U.S. or special events like Chicago's Torchsong and Orlando's Hurricane Who providing plenty of opportunities for fans to meet cast members.

These media allow Captain Jack to become a long-lasting SF hero who may continue to achieve far more than cult status. His stories, and thus his role as a gray hero, are becoming an important part of popular culture, not just popular SF TV culture. Although *Torchwood* likely won't achieve the same longevity in popular imagination as a *Star Trek* or a *Doctor Who*, the series already has gained enough of a following — and enough merchandising in multiple media — to make the character long remembered as an SF icon.

As Neil Perryman explained in *Convergence: The International Journal of Research Into New Media Technologies*, the ways these SF stories are told through multiple media is worthy of academic study as much as the characters who become popular through such massive media exposure. According to Perryman, the BBC uses *Doctor Who*

> to trial a plethora of new technologies, including: mini-episodes on mobile phones, podcast commentaries, interactive red-button adventures, video blogs, companion programming, and "fake" metatextual websites. In 2006 the BBC launched two spin-off series, *Torchwood* (aimed at an exclusively adult audience) and *The Sarah Jane Smith Adventures* (for 11- to 15-year-olds), and what was once regarded as an embarrassment to the Corporation now spans the media landscape as a multi-format colossus.[27]

Part of the rationale behind *Torchwood*'s move from BBC3 to BBC2 to BBC1 was its growing popularity. Even when *Torchwood* someday fails to survive ratings wars, Captain Jack may live on in the *Doctor Who* series as an occasional visitor/assistant hero to future Doctors. Thus, his presence in additional novels, audiobooks, and DVDs is highly likely.

Not only are there different "adult" and "child-friendly" versions of Captain Jack on TV, but his heroic persona changes depending on the target audience for additional stories told in different media. The following sections illustrate the way that Jack's heroism or, conversely, his darker side and potential as a "monster" are developed in comics, novels, audio books, and even music, which also serve to embed the character within current and future popular culture.

BBC Radio Broadcast/CD
of "Lost Souls"

On Big Bang Day in 2008, when the CERN particle accelerator was being used for the first time to split atoms and attempt to create black matter, BBC

Radio celebrated the event with a series of radio dramas. The *Torchwood* cast, with special guest Freema (Martha Jones) Agyeman, presented basically a one-hour episode for radio entitled "Lost Souls." Although some fans criticized the "science" involved in the plot, the characterizations of Captain Jack, Gwen, Ianto, and Martha closely resembled those from TV. The episode, set after the end of *Torchwood*'s Season Two, allowed the remaining Torchwood team members to grieve for Tosh and Owen. Thus, the episode provides closure for fans wondering how the survivors would handle their friends' deaths; it also gave fans a little more *Torchwood* during a long hiatus between Seasons Two and Three.

In this dramatization, Captain Jack is very much the leader trying to protect his remaining team while not hovering over them every moment. His outer persona is as boisterous as ever, telling wild tales about exploits on past worlds and flirting with an engaged Martha. Yet when Martha gets him alone for a few minutes and asks how he's doing, he opens up to her more than he would to the team members he tries to protect. "Death follows me," he reminds her. "I have to protect Gwen and Ianto."[28] Jack the protector, denying his own grief in order to remain strong for his friends (whom he regularly sends into danger), is the strongest element in this episode. Once again Jack plays the stoic hero, subsuming his own grief and guilt in order to try to be the "perfect" leader.

Even so, and likely because the short drama with few characters demands the participation of all cast members, "Lost Souls" presents Jack, Gwen, and Ianto as a unified team. Together they chase Weevils, travel to CERN, and help solve the mystery. Martha, with her own secret agency (UNIT) credentials, gets Torchwood onto the secure CERN site by introducing Ianto as the Ambassador of Wales and Gwen as his wife. As a joke, leader Jack is relegated to being Ianto's assistant.

This set-up is only a façade. Jack gets the best lines, everything from explaining the particle accelerator to Ianto and Gwen (and listeners) to finding a way to save both the CERN experiment and people's lives from an alien who infiltrated the test site. He is the informed, creative thinker who does what scientists can't do and thus, once again, saves the day. However, even in this brief radio drama he reveals his inner concerns and fears that he's inadequate in protecting his surviving team members.

Gwen also has a heroic moment in thwarting the alien's attempt to enter her mind and saving the stricken Ianto, but she is clearly a secondary hero compared to Jack. In this episode poor Ianto is mere support and a bit of comic relief, with his dry delivery of typically "Ianto" witticisms.

The adventure itself isn't as important to the series' mythology as the significance of *Torchwood* being included in the BBC's special broadcasts. The radio drama further establishes *Torchwood* as a valuable *mainstream* part of BBC programming, not an SF niche program or specialized "cult" drama. Placing *Torchwood* among the series of special broadcasts, which were highly promoted in the U.K., made the general public more aware of the characters and series, and attempted to introduce them to a wider audience. By making the dramatization available on CD worldwide, this special *Torchwood* episode gained a greater following among TV fans living outside the U.K. who otherwise would have missed the next "episode" in the continuing saga. The family-friendly nature of the broadcast presents the basic elements of the characters without resorting to a particularly violent or sexy plot. Both violence (e.g., an alien taking over human bodies and rendering them translucent) and sex (e.g., Jack recalling a memorable flight crew on an interplanetary jaunt) are implied from the dialogue, but the radio/CD episode is generally free of any "adult" content.

2009 RADIO DRAMAS

The July 2009 BBC Radio broadcasts of "Asylum," "Golden Age," and "The Dead Line" gave *Torchwood* fans new adventures enacted by cast members John Barrowman, Eve Myles, and Gareth David-Lloyd. The strategically timed broadcasts increased interest in the third TV season, which debuted a few days later. Most notably, the plots added tidbits about Jack's past and philosophy. He once had a relationship with an operative at a Torchwood institute in India and relives some of the Empire's glory moments from earlier in the 20th century. Surprisingly, Jack also seems rather intolerant of alien immigrants, even ones who aren't a threat to natives. Perhaps Jack forgets that, although he's human, he also is an immigrant.

More insightful is Jack's overconfidence in his ability to solve problems, as evidenced in "The Dead Line."[29] Although he realizes that answering a mysteriously disconnected phone may cause him to face the same coma-like state as others who have done so, Jack unhesitatingly answers the phone and, not surprisingly, falls into a coma. Although the plot allowed Barrowman to be part of the radio play even though his schedule precluded full participation in the story, the result is that Jack seems woefully unconcerned about the consequences of his leap-first, think-later action. This plot device weakens him as a hero in this episode. The story does, however, lead to Gwen and Ianto doing more to solve the mystery and save Jack. Once again, Ianto's love leads to Jack's recovery. Ianto's monologue to the comatose Jack also foreshadows his upcoming death in "Children of Earth."

After each broadcast the plays remained on the BBC Radio website for download. Within a few weeks, CDs of the radio plays provided yet another level of merchandise for *Torchwood* fans and ensured that these stories, like DVD editions of TV episodes, would last as part of Jack's continuing adventures. Because these radio plays in 2008–2009 come from and were broadcast by the BBC, they are also canon, unlike other texts not directly produced by the network.

The Torchwood Comic "Selkie"

Torchwood magazine, in which the "Selkie" comic was published, is a mass-produced fan magazine from Titan, the publisher of similar TV-series magazines about *Doctor Who*, *Lost*, and *Heroes*. An issue typically features interviews with cast or crew, production updates, analyses of episodes, and fiction, such as this comic. The magazine's information fits within the existing canon instead of expanding it with additional content.

As expected, the heroics of the lead characters are most likely to be the basis of interview questions or stories, and although "adult" themes, such as violence or sex in upcoming episodes, are discussed, the magazine's language and style are suited to a teen or older audience. The magazine helps increase international interest in the series by keeping the *Torchwood* name in front of the public, which is especially important during long hiatuses between seasons. It also provides a place where new stories further emphasize the positive heroic qualities of lead characters.

In spring 2009, *Torchwood* magazine introduced "Selkie," a comic featuring Jack Harkness. With a story by John Barrowman and his sister Carole E. Barrowman (who co-authored her brother's two autobiographies), and drawn by artists Tommy Lee Edwards and Trevor Goring, the comic focuses on Jack, sans Torchwood.[30] As John Barrowman explained in an interview just before the comic's publication, "I'd always wanted to do something that put Jack in Scotland and [Carole's] original story was set on an island off the Orkneys. Plus we'd already agreed to tell a story that showed a side of Jack and a part of his history that hadn't been explored too much in other media.... I wanted to give fans something original about Jack." Barrowman wanted to emphasize "Jack's compassion ... maybe his guilt."[31]

In this story, Jack's past once again haunts him, this time during an encounter with a mythic Scottish creature, the Selkie. Although the story moves quickly (in only 15 pages, roughly the size of a regular comic book), Jack's personality consistently and clearly meshes with his heroic TV characterization. Called to help Torchwood Two in Glasgow, Jack discovers that he knows the story's "monster" better than he expected and must make amends for his past decisions that are now affecting a seaside community.[32] The story provides a plausible reason for Jack to work alone in Scotland, but it also gives non–Scottish fans a bit of cultural insight into the Barrowmans' homeland.

In "Selkie," Jack once saved an alien from a dying world, bringing her to Earth, where she becomes known as a mythic sea creature. Years later the Selkie preys upon abusive men, murdering them as a way to protect the community's battered women. Jack's past good deed — saving the alien — ultimately leads to a series of murders. When he discovers the connection between the Selkie and the deaths, Jack tries to make amends. He faces yet another no-win scenario: kill the Selkie and spare the community from additional deaths-by-alien (thus executing a murderer for her crimes) or spare the alien Selkie and let the murders continue. Jack no longer has the option of sending the alien somewhere else in time or space, and the way the story is told indicates that the Selkie, if left alone, is unlikely to stop "protecting" abused women.

Although the dialogue is necessarily limited in a comic, the carefully chosen words convey Jack's heroic sense of responsibility to everyone/everything affected by his past actions. Carole Barrowman, a reviewer and essayist for a number of U.S. newspapers, typically writes short stories or novels, but in "Selkie" she "had to rid the story of most of its exposition and let the captions, dialogue and the images carry the narrative forward." Her script provided directions to artist Tommy Lee Edwards "about what elements would be presented visually and which ones would be best presented as dialogue or captions." The art and prose needed to make Jack's "moral dilemma ... clear — despite saving the Selkie in the past, he was going to have to kill her/it in the end."[33]

The dramatic art well illustrates *Torchwood*'s TV darkness by setting scenes at night and along stormy shores; deep browns and blue-grays highlight the dark past that shadows Captain Jack. The comic-book character looks like TV Jack, too, in wardrobe, physicality, and expression. As befitting the hero of the tale, Jack's face is drawn in close up in several panels so that readers can clearly see how his past decisions affect him emotionally. One panel even replicates the TV series' frequently used lighting effect of having half of Jack's face in light, half in shadow; the drawing emphasizes Jack's "dark side," which shades everything he does. Even with the best intentions or desire to save as many people as possible, Jack always must contend with darkness in some form.

Although the comic can only sketch the complexity of this gray hero, even new *Torchwood* fans who haven't yet seen all the episodes would understand the basic elements that establish Jack as a hero. The undercurrent of Jack's past lets even new readers know that this character is much more complex than can be illustrated in a few panels and, indeed, is more complex than most SF TV heroes.

Jack's complexity as a hero interests author Carole Barrowman:

> I don't think [series' creator Russell T. Davies] ever imagined Jack to be "traditional." I liked that Jack was confronting the world with a different, more complicated perspective, and I do think the heroes of the 21st century are going to be this complicated and this shifting between the light and the dark and all the grey areas in between. I've always seen Jack as a kind of rebel angel in the vein of John Milton, the fallen hero, the ex-angel, if you will. I can already see that same sensibility emerging in some of the ways the heroes in other television shows are being imagined.[34]

Captain Jack's future adventures in stories told outside TV episodes can and should continue his development as a complex hero by revealing darker aspects of the character not previously shown onscreen.

"Selkie"'s success and the publicity surrounding the comic's publication suggest an audience eager for more stories written by series insiders. Even though other comics within *Torchwood* magazine continue the exploits of the team in their original Hub, the most anticipated stories come from the actors and authors closely affiliated with the characters. In November 2009, Gareth David-Lloyd revealed that he had been asked to submit a story to be illustrated by Pia Guerra. When asked about the story, David-Lloyd hinted that different aspects of Ianto, such as "a mischievous and maybe jealous side of him, come out. Maybe he creates a little problem."[35] The story, set after the end of Season Two episodes but before "Children of Earth," may provide readers with greater insight into Ianto's relationship with Jack and more backstory exploring Ianto's past. Because those closely involved with the TV series are creating additional texts, fans are more likely to interpret these stories as canon. Stories like "Selkie," for example, thus become more significant to fans and their understanding of a series' heroes.

PRINT AND AUDIO NOVELS

Following closely in the mold of the *Doctor Who* novels for young adults/adults, the *Torchwood* series of hardbacks provides print "episodes" that are not considered canon but are significant texts to fans because they bear the BBC logo. Captain Jack is featured in several *Doctor Who* novels about the Ninth and Tenth Doctors and Rose. Just as his character further expanded between 2005 and 2009 from a series of *Doctor Who* episodes into *Torchwood*'s lead, the *Who* novels track his maturation from charming rogue into bona fide hero. The *Torchwood* novels then explore Jack's role as Torchwood's leader.

Most novels follow the format of the TV series, with each member of the Torchwood team given an important task to complete. Although "adult" language seeps into some novels, the tone is most often suited to a general readership. Nothing is too explicit in these novels, but the plots don't shy away from the adult themes and relationships depicted on TV. Novels like *The House That Jack Built*, in which the mysterious happenings take place in a Cardiff house that Jack used to own, emphasize expected aspects of Jack's personality.[36] Although his relationship with Ianto isn't well developed at this point in the Torchwood timeline, Jack's previous relationships are explained, as is his knowledge of an alien living in Cardiff who may be able to assist in his investigation. Jack's contacts, his long life in Cardiff, and his memories of his house and former lovers create yet more layers to the character.

The original audionovel *The Sin Eaters*, like "Children of Earth," compares the Gwen/Rhys dynamic with that of Jack/Ianto.[37] Both Rhys and Ianto loyally support their partners but are heroes in their own right, and "couple" moments provide listeners with further insights into the personal relationships that sustain these heroes and help them do their jobs. In the novels and audiobooks, Jack, alone or ably assisted by his colleagues, always saves the day.

In part, these novels and audiobooks provide interesting additional texts in assembling a complete picture of Jack as hero because they represent different authors' interpretations of the character. *The House That Jack Built* constructs part of Jack's turn-of-the-20th-century Cardiff past by making his former home the site of gruesome deaths and "demonic" possession. Two long-dead lovers haunt him, and the flashbacks indicate what Jack's personal life was like more than a hundred years before the current timeline. Gareth David-Lloyd reads *The Sin Eaters*, which makes the story even more interesting to fans of the Jack-Ianto relationship. A few scenes describe Ianto's ingenuity at uncovering technology that Jack has successfully hidden for many years; their interactions also state Jack's need for Ianto's loving support. The characters' interactions in this story are more playful and indicative of an established "couple" relationship than in other texts. Similarly, Rhys' intelligence and willingness to assist in Gwen's investigations of the supernatural or extraterrestrial are emphasized, and Rhys (Kai Owen) truly seems to be Gwen's equal. Although not all fans may read, listen to, or watch every *Torchwood*-related text, the sheer number of multimedia stories available to audiences helps ensure the longevity in popular culture of Captain Jack and other Torchwood heroes.

The Barrowman siblings plan to write their own novel, set in a post–"Children of Earth" time frame. Carole Barrowman describes Jack's character in their story as follows:

> In our novel I think Jack is much closer to being the Jack of "Children of Earth." He'll have a sense of humor—maybe a love interest or two—but he's going to be struggling with what he did in "Children of Earth."[38]

A novel exploring Jack's evolution in light of "Children of Earth" would help develop him as a gray hero, especially for adults who follow the series and expect far-reaching consequences from "Children of Earth." *Torchwood* fans sometimes complain that new TV episodes seldom deal with the fallout from tragedies in previous episodes.

Although, for example, Gwen says hello to a wrinkled photo of Tosh and Owen when she arrives in the Hub ("Children of Earth," 3.1), only veiled references indicate that the team is less than complete. Jack comments that they "need a doctor" when watching prospective employee Dr. Patanjali pace Roald Dahl Plass looking for Torchwood, but the plots generally move quickly into new crises or adventures instead of dwelling on the past. Even Jack's year on the *Valiant*, in which he is tortured and killed many times while being unable to free himself, help the Doctor, or save the Earth, is glossed over with a few lines during "Kiss Kiss Bang Bang" (2.1) (e.g., Jack's comments that "I had a lot of time to think" and "I died over and over"). The ramifications of these tragedies to Jack's psyche and character development fail to be explored in depth in subsequent episodes. The Barrowmans' novel may give readers and fans of the TV series some much-needed insights into the ways that Jack's guilt, remorse, and pain over a continuing series of losses change him as a gray hero.

JACK'S MUSICAL THEMES

The arrival of a soundtrack CD in 2008 showcased the variety of personal themes (for Jack, Gwen and Rhys, Tosh, and Owen) that support and help develop onscreen characterization throughout *Torchwood*'s first two seasons. In particular, the musical themes representing Captain Jack provide some interesting insights. Even when these themes are heard out of context (as only CD music instead of as another layer to the story being shown onscreen), the tempo, choice of instruments, and emotional undercurrents provided by the music reveal a great deal about this pivotal *Torchwood* character.

The hauntingly beautiful "Jack's Love Theme" provides insight into Jack's emotional nature and indicates why Jack reacts so passionately (sometimes in extreme ways) when confronted with death or loss.[39] This theme begins with strings and a gentle piano setting a much slower pace than other cuts on the CD. The song intensifies as it progresses, but the pace is never rushed. The theme is lush with strings, always poignant and wistful, yet with an underlying strength. Timpani rolling softly into the background introduces a harsher section that ends with the drum's final beat, like a door closing musically.

Fans of the series may recognize this theme from the episode "Captain Jack Harkness" (1.12), in which Jack meets and falls in love with the hero whose name he took as his own. With this plot, and through this love theme, audiences/listeners perceive that the "love theme" not only represents Jack's love for the Captain but also his love of self in wanting to honor the real Jack Harkness by becoming a better person, a better leader. The "Captain Jack" audiences have come to know is, they and Jack are reminded, only an "impostor" whose real name is never revealed. Jack's true identity is subsumed beneath his duty, but occasional glimpses into his emotions and inner self provide audiences with a better understanding of who this hero— going by whatever name — really is.

After this brief break in the theme, a pause like the fading of a memory, the strings return. However, the love theme ends abruptly, as if the song has been ended too soon; a definitive ending, or at least a fade-out, is expected but not delivered. Perhaps this lack of a definitive musical ending implies that Jack's love song isn't yet finished, or perhaps it indicates that his love is too often thwarted before a "happy ending" can be achieved.

A male hero, especially one who looks as all–American athletic as Captain Jack, rarely has such a poignant love theme. In fact, stereotypically "macho" heroes wouldn't have *any* love theme. Jack's sexuality, a gray area of acceptance for many viewers, is embraced through this musical theme and indicates that, as much as Captain Jack fits into the traditional mold of a stalwart loner/hero who sacrifices much to save others, he is also atypical in the depth of emotion portrayed as an integral motivating factor for this hero's actions.

In contrast, "Captain Jack's Theme" can best be described as *driven*.[40] It is repetitive, sometimes harsh, and always edgy. Any softer themes layered into the insistent phrasing are deeply buried. This theme is action music, sometimes with a futuristic feel, and the same theme is repeated in different keys and with different countermelodies. A brief bridge provides more traditional "hero" music — lots of strings providing a lush "savior-arriving" respite before the next series of repeated, driving beats. A second bridge is heralded by cymbals, providing a quick rest in the "action" before the determined forward progression begins again. The last section of this cut is less harsh, perhaps more "dedicated" — the pace is less frantic and the theme played more smoothly, with less emphasis on the beat. Nevertheless, the overall feel is one of purpose and grim determination. Again, this theme has an indeterminate ending appropriate for Jack's immortality and as-yet-incomplete TV story.

The contrasting themes separate Jack-the-hero's outer and inner personas. Although the driving, determined, rhythmic, repetitive action theme highlights Jack's determination to do his duty as a protector, the "Captain Jack" theme is more difficult to listen to because it's so repetitive. It never seems to end, just to present the same sequence of notes in a slightly different way. Fans might understand Jack better, however, through this non-traditional theme for a TV hero.

The immortal Jack, potentially faced with millennia of planets/people to save and duties to perform, would likely see his life as a repeated sequence of actions, albeit in different times and places. The pace is relentless, as is much of *Torchwood*'s plot pace, and at the end it's hard to remember much beyond the driving beat. Perhaps this is an appropriate, if less melodic, musical interpretation of Jack's daily life. "Jack's Love Theme" (with a noticeable lack of "Captain" in this title) indicates just what the hero might be sacrificing personally in order to be that driven action hero. In the love theme, Jack's longing and understanding of what it means to be a true hero (as well as heroic qualities he feels he may lack) provide an intriguing counterpoint to the character's outer persona — and the type of hero "traditionally" portrayed as alien fighter and planet savior. The extremes of Jack's character, and what they infer about his role as hero, are well represented with these two musical themes.

In "Children of Earth," Jack's action theme returns within other tracks. The separate "Children of Earth" CD provides a chronologically organized soundtrack of all five days/episodes. When Jack leads the charge against the 456, a few bars of his theme accompany his stern-faced march into Thames House. Other themes from the previous soundtrack, including a few bars of Owen's or Tosh's theme, also emphasize Jack's guilt over their deaths. Changes to Jack's character incorporate musical themes from the original soundtrack CD and reflect his growing sorrow and feelings of inadequacy as a hero. "I Can Run Forever" is a poignant, beautiful — and epic — ending to the miniseries and Jack as audiences know him from three seasons of *Torchwood*.[41] Music, as yet another text, reveals more details about Jack's emotions and psyche, and tracks the many changes in character.

Surprisingly, even a monster/villain like Gray, Jack's brother who destroys so much in his search for vengeance, has two songs on the original soundtrack CD. The theme is the same in each, but the ways the theme is introduced in "Gray's Theme" and "Memories of Gray" indicate as much about Jack as his younger brother. "Gray's Theme" is sung (without words) by a strong, hauntingly beautiful female voice, much like a strong maternal or at least familial influence on the characters. As in most emotion-inducing melodies (in both *Torchwood* and *Doctor Who*), strings play a prominent part in expressing deep, unspoken feelings. This time the melody creates the impression of a sad but strong emotional river running through memory; it is relentless but not harsh. Strings gain volume and power as the theme continues. Near the end of the song a minor key is introduced as part of a more sinister melody, typical of a villain's theme to show what Gray has become. Again, percussion becomes a more important part of the background before the song's quiet end.

This melody can represent young Gray longing for his mother and home, as well as for a loving past long gone—certainly elements that the boy must have felt upon first being separated from his family. However, the theme also indicates Jack's sad memories of his long-gone family and the guilt associated with his final memories of his father and brother.

"Memories of Gray" continues this theme, but this time female voices harmonize with more instruments, primarily strings. The darker undercurrent in this piece provides a mournful "memory" of the earlier piece. Cymbals and the use of minor chords indicate the turmoil in Gray's and Jack's lives as a result of Gray's abduction by enemies and subsequent captivity and torture. "Memories of Gray" reflects not only the memories of a lost boy and the guilt of the older brother who failed to protect him but of the Gray who might've been, the illusion of Gray that Jack holds onto, even after seeing his brother's maddened wrath.

That Gray's theme becomes featured twice on a CD summarizing two seasons of music indicates the importance of this character. Although Gray's destructive acts and disregard for human life mark him as a villain, the reasons behind his actions also make him less than a "monster." Like his name, his musical theme humanizes him as a gray character, more villain than hero, certainly, but not a complete monster that audiences can't understand.

The Complexity of Captain Jack

With the success of "Children of Earth," *Torchwood* was eventually renewed for yet more episodes. As well, more novels and magazine fiction confirm that, despite Season Three's less than hopeful ending, Captain Jack will return. How the character continues to evolve largely is up to the series' creators and BBC/Starz, but Jack Harkness' place within SF TV is assured. Seldom has such a gray hero been so popular, and even when Jack seems to have moved beyond accept-able boundaries as a hero, audiences still want to know what happens next.

What makes Jack such an interesting character to analyze is his ability to reflect the quickly changing social climate in the early 2000s and audiences' expectations for different types of characters. When real-life heroes and villains are difficult to discern or seem to "change" from one side to the other based on information leaked to news media or revealed after a crisis, TV heroes are more likely to follow suit. Audiences are more accepting of chameleon-like heroes who can't fight today's villains or monsters without resorting to their less-than-moral tactics. Gray heroes may be perceived as more savvy simply because they understand that the rules have changed.

Whereas Jack marching into Thames House to confront the 456 without a weapon of mass destruction or alien-killing backup plan seems naïve and senseless in today's political climate, audiences may still want Jack to represent and uphold more traditional (i.e., moral) values like sanctity of all life or the equal significance of a single life to the worth of millions. The character's con-tinuing success may be based on Jack's ability to save the world by occasionally doing dark deeds but then seeking "redemption" for such acts, a moral balancing act designed to please at least most of the audience some of the time. As *Torch-wood* continues in its many texts, Jack Harkness has the potential to be one of the few SF TV heroes who truly reflects the moral ambiguities of the 2000s and sets the standard for acceptable but increasingly dark heroes.

Appendices — Introduction

The appendices should help you refer to each series' episodes, which often are discussed not only within the main chapter about that series but as examples in Part One. Appendix 1 provides background information about each series (in alphabetical order), including years broadcast, and in the final column, indicates which leading characters are discussed in the present work. Appendix 2 indicates a few elements in pivotal episodes worth further study; the series are listed in the order in which they are discussed in Part Two.

Although scenes in these series' episodes are highlighted as examples in previous chapters, you should see an entire episode to better understand the context surrounding dialogue or action. In addition, by analyzing an episode for specific details, such as lighting, costuming, setting, use of music or sound effects, and so on, you can better understand these stylistic elements' effectiveness in developing gray heroes, villains, or monsters. If you are using this book as a textbook for a "heroes," media, or popular culture course, you may use these tables to select TV episodes that will further an understanding of individual characters or the series as a whole.

The science fiction television series analyzed throughout the book comprise far too many viewing hours to discuss within the confines of one course. In my classes I have found it helpful to concentrate on one or two series, selecting pivotal episodes that illustrate key moments in character development or plot, *or* choosing to follow one hero or villain in the story and then discussing episodes that best illustrate the ways that character has been developed through dialogue, plot development, and stylistic elements. When my students analyze *Lost*'s Jack Shephard as a gray hero, for example, the required "texts" include the pilot episode, "White Rabbit," "Man of Science, Man of Faith," and "Through the Looking Glass." A discussion of *Heroes*' Hiro Nakamura might emphasize his development as one of Campbell's heroes on a developmental journey, best illustrated with Season One episodes.

Many useful examples of the development of heroes, villains, and monsters can be gleaned from other episodes, but the in-text references to the following episodes should guide you to a deeper understanding of these characters and series and their importance within hero literature.

Appendix 1:
Series Background
Information

Angel (1999–2004) WB TV (US), Chum TV (Can), Sky One (UK); *Created by* David Greenwalt and Joss Whedon; *Production Companies:* Kuzui Enterprises, Sandollar Television, 20th Century–Fox Television; *Characters Discussed:* Angel, Spike.

Battlestar Galactica (1978–1979; 2004–2009) ABC (US); Sci-Fi (U.S.), Chum TV (Can), Sky One (UK); *Created by* Glen A. Larson; Ronald Moore and David Eick; *Production Companies:* Glen A. Larson Productions, Universal TV; BSkyB, NBC Universal TV, Universal Media Studios; *Characters Discussed:* Bill Adama, Lee Adama, Kara Thrace.

Buffy the Vampire Slayer (1997–2003) WB TV and UPN (US), Sky One (UK); *Created by* Joss Whedon; *Production Companies:* 20th Century–Fox Television, Kuzui Enterprises, Sandollar Television; Buffy, Spike, Angel, Willow.

Caprica (2009 (DVD), 2010–) Sci-Fi (US), Sky One (UK); *Created by* Remi Aubuchon and Ronald D. Moore; *Production Companies:* David Eick Productions, NBC Universal Television; *Characters Discussed:* Graystone family, Adama family, Zoe.

Doctor Who (1963–1989; 1996; 2005–) BBC (1963–1989), often PBS stations in U.S. during this time; Fox (U.S., 1996 movie); BBC (2005–), Sci-Fi (US, 2005–2009), BBC America (2009–); *Created by* Sydney Newman; Re-imagined by Russell T. Davies and Julie Gardner (2005–early 2010), Steven Moffat as showrunner beginning in 2010; *Production Companies:* BBC as the primary producer throughout; BBC, BBC Worldwide, Fox, and Universal co-produced the 1996 movie. *Characters Discussed:* Ninth Doctor, Tenth Doctor, Rose Tyler, Captain Jack Harkness, Donna Noble, Wilfrid Mott, The Master, Davros, Daleks, Cybermen.

Firefly (2002–2003) Fox Network, Sci-Fi (UK); *Created by* Joss Whedon; *Production Companies:* 20th Century–Fox Television, Fox Television Network; Mal Reynolds, Inara Serra, Zoe Washburne.

Heroes (2006–)NBC (US), CanWest (Can), sci-Fi and BBC (UK); *Created by* Tim Kring; *Production Companies:* NBC Universal Television, Tailwind Productions, Universal Media Studios (UMS); *Characters Discussed:* Hiro Nakamura, Ando Masahashi, Claire Bennet, Noah Bennet, Peter Petrelli, Nathan Petrelli, Sylar.

Lost (2004–2010) ABC (US), CTV (Can), E4 and SkyOne (UK); *Created by* J.J. Abrams, Jeffrey Lieber, and Damon Lindelof; *Production Companies:* ABC Studios, Touchstone Television, Bad Robot, Grass Skirt Productions; *Characters Discussed:* Jack Shephard, John Locke, Ben Linus, Kate Austen, Smoke Monster.

Torchwood (2006–2009) BBC Worldwide, BBC, BBC America; *Created by* Russell T. Davies; *Production Companies:* BBC Wales, Canadian Broadcasting Corporation (CBC); *Characters Discussed:* Jack Harkness, Gwen Cooper, Ianto Jones.

Appendix 2:
Important Series
Episodes

The episode or movie titles placed in **bold** are pivotal episodes within a series or a study of heroes, villains, and monsters. Each episode has been described in more detail within chapters.

Buffy the Vampire Slayer

Episode & Number	Some Reasons for Watching It
"Fool for Love" 5.7	The relationship between Spike and Buffy deepens. Spike's villainous past contrasts his current concern for Buffy, illustrating him as a gray villain.
"Once More with Feeling" 6.7	Buffy: The Musical, a prime reason to watch this episode. A disillusioned Buffy questions her "job" as a hero, and Buffy's relationship with Spike changes yet again.
"Seeing Red" 6.19	Tara's death also kills an important GLBT groundbreaking couple and leads to Willow's transformation into a much darker character.
"Grave" 6.22	Willow illustrates how former heroes/sidekicks can fall from grace. In contrast, Spike becomes "redeemed" when he regains his soul.

Angel

Episode & Number	Some Reasons for Watching It
"That Old Gang of Mine" 3.3	Questions whether Angel is a monster or a hero come into play in the episode's dramatic conclusion.
"Not Fade Away" 5.22	The series' finale illustrates how much Angel has developed as a hero and a leader as he and his colleagues face the ultimate Big Bad.

Firefly

Episode & Number	Some Reasons for Watching It
"The Train Job" 1.1	Although not the first episode filmed, it was the first shown on TV and provides an interesting introduction to the series' gray hero Mal Reynolds. This episode illustrates the gray hero within both the Western and SF space genres.
"Shindig" 1.6	Mal and Inara act heroically in part to save each other, although Mal remains a gray (and sometimes socially insensitive) hero.
"War Stories" 1.9	Mal becomes a sacrificial hero/leader in this more graphically violent episode that provides insights into popular definitions of *hero* and reasons why that role is attractive to people like Wash.
"Serenity" 1.11	In the official pilot episode (shown much later in the series), Simon and River first come aboard *Serenity*. In hindsight, this episode reveals Whedon's planned introduction of gray hero Mal.
Serenity (movie)	Mal, as well as several crew members, are heroes in this movie. The Alliance and its minions are revealed as monsters, prompting Mal's transformation into a different type of hero by the story's end.

Dr. Horrible's Sing-Along Blog

Episode & Number	Some Reasons for Watching It
DVD or online episode	This short webisode/DVD "episode" portrays the villain as the story's protagonist, the questionable "hero" as a failure, and the rise of Evil as inevitable.

Heroes

Episode & Number	Some Reasons for Watching It
"Genesis" 1.1	The world needs (super)heroes, and characters like Hiro answer Campbell's call to action. Not all people developing superpowers want others to know about them. In this and the next few episodes, Hiro's journey should be emphasized in a study of a traditional hero.
"Don't Look Back" 1.2	Hiro travels to New York and begins to understand his potential role in averting a crisis. In response to Ando's lack of understanding about his newly revealed power, Hiro begins to develop a list of rules for heroes.
"One Giant Leap" 1.3	Hiro not only convinces Ando that his power is real, but he faces his first test as a superhero—to save the life of a young girl.

(Heroes, continued)

Episode & Number	Some Reasons for Watching It
"Seven Minutes to Midnight" 1.8	Sylar becomes more than a shadowy presence as he kills Hiro's true love. This episode, in hindsight, is pivotal to understanding Hiro's later desire to go back in time to change the past.
"Homecoming" 1.9	Peter faces his own death as he confronts Sylar in an effort to save Claire. This episode further illustrates Sylar as the series villain but also highlights Peter's desire to be a true hero.
"Company Man" 1.17	Noah Bennet is a company man, usually portrayed as a villain. In this episode he reveals shades of gray in his personal and professional life.
"The Hard Part" 1.21	This episode begins to set up the first season finale's confrontation between Good and Evil by bringing together several heroes in New York.
"Landslide" 1.22	Another one of Campbell's stages of the hero's journey is achieved when Hiro learns to use a sword. He also realizes that, as a hero, he might need to kill the villain Sylar.
"How to Stop an Exploding Man" 1.23	In the first season's finale, Nathan becomes a more traditional hero, and characters like Peter and Hiro discover that they may not be able to overcome the villain (Sylar) as easily as they thought.
"The Second Coming" 3.1	Sylar seeks Claire in order to gain her healing ability. This episode illustrates yet another encounter between Claire (hero, Good) and Sylar (villain, Evil). In a study of Sylar or Claire, this episode may be useful.
"One of Us, One of Them" 3.3	Although this episode is not pivotal to the character development of Hiro or Peter, each has scenes that might be helpful to a continuing understanding of the ways they question their ability to remain heroes.
"I Am Become Death" 3.4	Just as Future Hiro frightens himself, a future vision of Claire hunting her uncle and hero Peter indicates how even this young hero may become a very gray character.
"Our Father" 3.12	Claire travels back in time to see how she became the adopted daughter of company man and gray character Noah. In a study of Hiro's use of time travel (which climaxes in this hero's actions being judged at a crucial point in Season Five), this episode may become more important.
"A Clear and Present Danger" 3.14	Heroes and villains become ever grayer. Politician Nathan implements a plan to capture everyone with a superpower, which forces "heroes" Claire and Peter to react as vigilantes or fugitives. Sylar tries to

(*Heroes,* continued)

Episode & Number	Some Reasons for Watching It
	find his biological parents in order to understand who he is. This fourth season opener illustrates the possibilities open to characters who must decide who they want to be in the future.
"Into Asylum" 3.21	An important, if brief, scene shows Peter questioning God and doubting his role as a hero. In a study of Peter as a hero, this scene is well worth a closer look.
"I Am Sylar" 3.24	Heroes and villains may not be as clearcut as originally portrayed. In this episode, Hiro attempts to break into a government facility, Nathan questions his policy of rounding up people with special abilities, and Sylar still is unsure who or what he should be.
"An Invisible Thread" 3.25	As a season finale, this episode is not as strong as previous episodes. Nevertheless, Hiro's understanding that the return of his superpower entails consequences, and Sylar's plan to shapeshift as the president, provide some pivotal moments in key characters' development.
"Hysterical Blindness" 4.4	Sylar awakens with no memories and is literally a "blank slate." He may choose whether to be a hero or a villain, free of any preconception or memory of past deeds. Another (albeit one-season) villain, Samuel, is introduced in this episode.
"Tabula Rasa" 4.5	Sylar again is an important focus of this episode, as Samuel tries to guide him into the type of man he should be if he wants to help people with special abilities achieve their true place in society. The persuasive nature of "evil" is illustrated through Samuel's rhetoric in several episodes.
"Once Upon a Time in Texas" 4.8	Hiro becomes a grayer hero as he attempts to change the past. Definitions of "white hat" and "black hat" characters are illustrated during a confrontation between Hiro and Sylar.
"The Fifth Stage" 4.12	Nathan, who survives only as a "personality" subsumed within Sylar's subconscious, decides he no longer has the strength to be a hero. Nathan's final death grieves Peter so much that he becomes a much grayer character. The rhetoric and implications of Nathan's and Peter's choices are worth a closer analysis in regards to Nathan's death scene.
"Pass/Fail" 4.16	Claire and Hiro come to grips with what is expected of them if they are to remain heroes. Sylar illustrates the strategies a villain may employ in trying to convince a hero to change sides. Hiro goes on trial for his life, and his past actions as a "hero" are scrutinized.

(Heroes, continued)

Episode & Number	Some Reasons for Watching It
"The Wall" 4.18	Peter illustrates the power of forgiveness as a quality of a true hero. Sylar begins a transformation from a villain into a hero.
"Brave New World" 4.19	The fourth season finale questions whether villains can be "redeemed" as heroes and how the world might be changed for the better.

Lost

Episode & Number	Some Reasons for Watching It
Pilot 1.1	Jack illustrates the nature of a traditional hero trying to save others in the aftermath of a plane crash.
"White Rabbit" 1.5	Jack questions his ability to be a hero/leader. In a study of Jack as hero, this episode provides important background information, as well as a turning point in the development of Jack as an island leader.
"Deus Ex Machina" 1.19	The role of the "man of faith" is further explored when Locke follows signs. By the end of the episode he may be perceived as a much grayer character.
"Do No Harm" 1.20	Jack fails as a "fixer" of impossible situations and becomes more of a gray hero. Locke seems ever more like a gray villain.
"Man of Science, Man of Faith" 2.1	This episode further illustrates Jack's and Locke's differences in philosophy and approach to life. "Man of Science" Jack is often pitted against "Man of Faith" Locke, and these opposing points of view become a major theme throughout the series.
"The 23rd Psalm" 2.10	Eko is a possibly redeemed former villain whose influence on Charlie helps him return to his religious faith. A study of additional gray heroes, villains, and even monsters (e.g., the Smoke Monster evident in this episode) within this large cast should include this episode, especially for the character development of Eko and Charlie.
"Live Together, Die Alone" 2.23	Another important theme revolves around Jack's line at the end of this episode: "We must live together or we will surely die alone." The importance of a community working together is emphasized.
"The Glass Ballerina" 3.2	Sun is revealed to have a grayer past, making her a much more complex character. Held captive by the Others, Jack learns that he may be able to leave the island, but by doing so he won't fulfill his goal to return all his friends back home.

(*Lost,* continued)

Episode & Number	Some Reasons for Watching It
"Further Instructions" 3.3	Locke's backstory provides a rationale for his on-island behavior and furthers his role as a "Man of Faith." In a study of Locke, this is an important episode.
"The Cost of Living" 3.5	Eko again faces his past as a villain and makes choices that ultimately condemn him to death. Once again the Smoke Monster plays an important role in the story. This episode emphasizes Eko's shift back and forth between hero and villain.
"I Do" 3.6	Kate also has a murky past, and her actions, even when motivated by love for her husband, make her a gray character. In a study of Kate, this is a pivotal episode.
"The Man from Tallahassee" 3.13	Locke deals with his father, who betrayed him several times in the past. He struggles with his desire for vengeance and his aversion to killing the man he holds responsible for all that has gone wrong in his life. A study of Locke should include this episode. Also, Ben as a gray villain who can easily manipulate Locke is another important character to study.
"The Brig" 3.19	Sawyer, often portrayed as a gray villain, commits an act of revenge that may negate his more recent "good" acts. In a study of Sawyer or Locke, scenes involving the death of Anthony Cooper/Tom Sawyer are crucial to an analysis of these characters.
"The Man Behind the Curtain" 3.20	Ben, often seen as one of the most villainous characters in the series, is given a more sympathetic backstory. In a study of Ben as a gray villain who proclaims himself a hero, this backstory is important.
"Through the Looking Glass" 3.22–.23	The third season finale (and the end to the first half of the series) allows Jack another important success as a traditional hero. Locke's actions portray him as a gray villain. Even other characters, including Charlie, have moments of great heroism in this two-part episode.
"The Beginning of the End" 4.1	The results of Jack's "heroic actions" to bring his friends home initiate the beginning of a serious decline in his hero status. In this episode Jack's life as one of the Oceanic 6 begins to spiral out of control.
"Eggtown" 4.4	Jack's further deterioration as a hero and his changed relationship with post–island Kate are important parts of his character development. However, in a study of Kate as a gray villain-turned-parent/potential hero, this episode provides interesting insights into her "redemption."

(*Lost,* continued)

Episode & Number	Some Reasons for Watching It
"The Shape of Things to Come" 4.9	A pivotal scene affecting Ben's character development as a villain (possibly seeking forgiveness by Season Five) involves the death of his daughter. Because this scene is crucial to an understanding of Ben as a gray villain, this backstory episode should be studied.
"Something Nice Back Home" 4.10	Jack's life continues its downward spiral in revealing "flashforward" scenes in this episode. His change from a hero to gray hero to potential gray villain continues in the off-island scenes.
"There's No Place Like Home" 4.12–.13	Almost every character reaches a pivotal moment in the Season Four finale. Depending upon which characters are being studied as heroes or villains, the episode may be important because it illustrates changes in the lives of several major characters, including Jack and Locke. The main plot involves the return of the Oceanic 6 to the island to which they vowed never to return.
"316" 5.6	The reasons why the Oceanic 6 decide to return to the island are revealed. Although this episode isn't pivotal to a study of heroes or villains, it does provide more backstory about individual characters who board Ajira 316.
"The Life and Death of Jeremy Bentham" 5.7	In a study of Locke or Ben, this episode is crucial. Locke is willing to sacrifice himself in order to protect the island. Ben commits a villainous act which leads to repercussions in Season Six.
"Whatever Happened, Happened" 5.11	As a gray hero returned to the island, surgeon Jack refuses to operate on the boy who will become future villain Ben. This episode is also important in a study of Kate as a more likely hero now that she is back on the island.
"Dead Is Dead" 5.12	A study of Ben must include this episode, in which he is illustrated as a manipulative gray character, most often perceived as villainous, as well as a penitent father mourning the loss of his daughter. The nature of the Smoke Monster is further revealed.
"The Incident" 5.16–.17	How far is each character willing to go in order to change the past and, they hope, improve the future? The Season Five finale illustrates the best and worst of several main characters, including Jack, Kate, Sawyer, and Juliet.
"LAX" 6.1	The beginning of the final season provides an alternate view of what the lives of several main characters would be if Oceanic 815 doesn't crash. On the island,

(Lost, continued*)*

Episode & Number	Some Reasons for Watching It
	Jack, Kate, Locke (who soon is called "Evil Incarnate"), Sawyer, and Ben also deal with the ramifications of changing the past. The Season Six episodes further character development and indicate just where the lengthy journeys of these characters will end.

Battlestar Galactica

Episode & Number	Some Reasons for Watching It
Pilot Movie	The introductions to Bill Adama, Starbuck/Kara Thrace, and Caprica Six/Cylons are an especially important starting point for the development of these characters, who unexpectedly shift between heroism and villainy throughout the series.
"Six Degrees of Separation" 1.7	A study of Baltar and Caprica Six/Head Six requires an analysis of this episode, which explores Baltar's role in the annihilation of the human home worlds.
"Kobol's Last Gleaming" 1.12–.13	The first season's finale reveals what, with hindsight, become pivotal moments in the lives of several characters, including Sharon, Baltar, Bill and Lee Adama, and Laura. The question What makes us human? is an important theme in this episode.
"Resistance" 2.4	Tyrol has a difficult time understanding how Sharon/Boomer didn't know she is a Cylon. Sharon is perceived as a monster in this episode.
"Pegasus" 2.10	Should enemy prisoners be treated humanely, even if they're not human? Admiral Cain's answer differs from Adama's. The Cylons, including another Six, Gina, seem more human than the "monster" in command of the fleet. This episode should be watched in conjunction with the movie *Razor.*
"Six of One" 4.2	Starbuck/Kara believes she knows the way to Earth, but no one believes her. She threatens the president and loses Adama's confidence in her. In an interesting sidestory scene, Baltar explains that Cylons have feelings. Several characters seem to be shifting on the "gray" scale.
"The Ties That Bind" 4.3	Politics among Cylons is just as divisive and polarizing as it is among humans. A comparison of human desire for power with that of Cylons is an interesting approach to a study of this episode.
"Sine Qua Non" 4.8	Laura is taken hostage onboard a Cylon ship, creating more mistrust between humans and Cylons trying to learn the true nature of visions and prophesy.

(*Battlestar Galactica,* continued)

Episode & Number	Some Reasons for Watching It
"Sometimes a Great Notion" 4.11	On a decimated Earth, Starbuck finds her body and wonders what she is, because she obviously isn't still human. The Cylons see evidence of their former civilization and wonder if they are more closely related to humans than they thought. A study of Starbuck/Kara requires this pivotal revelation about her death and apparent afterlife.
"Blood on the Scales" 4.14	Who is friend or enemy is questioned in this dramatic episode involving mutiny on the *Galactica.* A once-loyal soldier plots against his commander because of decisions being made about the Cylons. As humans and Cylons work together to try to save both societies, some humans question why they should cooperate with the enemies who almost wiped out humanity.
"Someone to Watch Over Me" 4.17	Tyrol and Sharon, both Cylons who have been "outed" among humans, make a sort of peace with each other and consider the life they might have had together. A study of Starbuck/Kara should include this episode, in which she comes to terms with her role as a visionary, as well as a "dead" human.
"Daybreak" 4.19–4.20	The series' finale, just like its pilot, should be viewed for closure, even if many intervening episodes have been skipped. By the end of the story, Baltar and Six have evolved beyond either human or Cylon; human heroes, including Bill Adama and Starbuck, realize their "jobs" are now over. This episode provides a final word on the nature of humans and Cylons.
Razor Movie	Although this TV movie was broadcast partway through Season Four, it is a stand-alone story explaining what happened onboard the *Pegasus.* Commander Cain's relationship with the Cylons and her brutal "human nature" are emphasized in this movie, which should be paired with "Pegasus" for a case study into human–Cylon relationships and the human tendency to become "monstrous" when abusing power.

Caprica

Episode & Number	Some Reasons for Watching It
Pilot DVD/Movie	This movie/first episode can stand alone as an introduction to the thematic question What makes us human? The rise of technology, humans' proclivity to "play God," and the birth of the "monstrous"

(*Caprica*, continued)

Episode & Number	Some Reasons for Watching It
"Rebirth" 1.1	Cylon race provide plenty of discussion topics raised in previous chapters. Differing perspectives of the same character illustrate the grayness of each protagonist. In this episode the Cylon/ avatar/ "soul" of Zoe gain sympathy because her outer form is perceived as a metallic monster. The nature of human or technological "monsters" is further explored.
"Reins of a Waterfall" 1.2	Sam as Other is a highlight of this episode. Although he is a gray villain based on societal perceptions of his profession, Sam also can be perceived as a familial "hero" and role model.

Doctor Who

Episode & Number	Some Reasons for Watching It
NINTH DOCTOR	
"Rose" 1.1	Rose begins her travels with the Doctor after overcoming the first alien monsters she meets. This first episode of Russell T. Davies' re-imagined series introduces the Ninth Doctor as a less than perfect hero.
"The End of the World" 1.2	The last human tries to wipe out other species watching future Earth's destruction. As in most episodes, the Doctor and Rose face a human or an alien "monster" (in this case, Cassandra) that reveals something about humanity.
"The Unquiet Dead" 1.3	During a "zombie" episode, the Doctor and Rose discover aliens trying to survive on Earth, but their actions create the living dead.
"Aliens of London" 1.4	The Doctor returns Rose home for a visit, and she realizes how Other she has become to her family. How "alien" is acceptable? The Doctor, an alien, helps save humanity from other visiting aliens.
"Dalek" 1.6	Daleks are a traditional *Doctor Who* monster, and this episode should be studied for that reason alone. However, both the Doctor and the Dalek are the lone survivors of an interplanetary war. Both seem equally sympathetic, as well as horrific, based on their dialogue and actions in this episode.
"The Long Game" 1.7	Humanity has managed to stifle its growth by its complacence and lack of desire to think critically. Again the Doctor and Rose thwart the plan of an alien monster out to help humanity destroy itself.
"Father's Day" 1.8	Rose "plays God" by changing the past. Saving one

(Doctor Who, continued*)*

Episode & Number	Some Reasons for Watching It
	person leads to consequences she never imagined (a theme repeated in "The Parting of the Ways").
"The Empty Child" 1.9	This episode is notable because it introduces Captain Jack Harkness, later the lead of *Torchwood.* As a gray villain who finds a way to be redeemed, Jack becomes an intriguing character. A study of Jack Harkness should include this episode, as well as the next, which ends this short story arc.
"The Doctor Dances" 1.10	The Doctor seems more "human" by the conclusion of this episode, which also features important character development for future gray hero Jack Harkness.
"Boom Town" 1.11	The Doctor, Jack, and Rose visit Earth, where they apprehend a murderous alien. However, they have difficulty becoming the alien's executioners.
"Bad Wolf" 1.12	Mindless TV game shows and reality programs take on deadly consequences. This episode provides some additional background information about the Doctor, Rose, and Jack, but it is more of a general entertainment than an exemplary episode.
"The Parting of the Ways" 1.13	This episode is important to a study of the Doctor, Rose, or Jack. It also ends the Ninth Doctor's series of episodes. Rose "plays God" and makes Jack immortal. The Ninth Doctor faces death very differently from the Tenth, which could provide an interesting comparison of the "heroic" qualities of different iterations of the same character.
TENTH DOCTOR "The Christmas Invasion" 2.0	The Tenth Doctor is introduced as a different type of "hero" than his predecessor. While the Doctor is incapacitated, Rose must act more heroic.
"School Reunion" 2.3	This episode is important only in that it re-introduces Sarah Jane Smith, one of the Doctor's former companions, and illustrates how heroes may have difficulty returning to a "normal" life.
"Doomsday" 2.13	This episode pits classic monsters the Daleks and Cybermen against the Doctor and humanity. This episode is pivotal in a study of Rose as a sidekick and sometimes hero.
"Blink" 3.10	An award-winning episode, "Blink" allows a guest character to become heroic. The "monster" in this episode is especially frightening.
"Utopia" 3.11	This episode and the following two are important in a study of the Master as the Doctor's nemesis and series villain. The episode also involves Jack Harkness; a

(Doctor Who, continued*)*

Episode & Number	Some Reasons for Watching It
	study of Jack as a gray hero might include this story arc.
"The Sound of Drums" 3.12	The Master becomes the political master of Earth in this part of the story arc. His cruelty shows how a human-looking "alien" can terrorize humanity. The Doctor, strangely enough, is powerless in this episode.
"Last of the Time Lords" 3.13	Jack as a tortured/sacrificial hero, Martha as one of the Doctor's "disciples," and the Doctor as a messianic hero are key roles in this episode. The Doctor's display of mercy toward an enemy is also noteworthy in a study of this character.
"Voyage of the Damned" 4.0	The Doctor acts as a more traditional hero in this episode.
"The Fires of Pompeii" 4.2	Should the past be changed in order to save people? The Doctor "plays God" by deciding who survives Pompeii.
"The Stolen Earth" 4.12	This episode and the next are notable for a study of sidekick characters. The story arc brings together many of the Doctor's former companions, including Rose and Jack.
"Journey's End" 4.13	This episode should be a companion piece to the previous episode in a study of sidekick characters and the Doctor's lasting (and very gray) influence on them.
"Planet of the Dead" 2009 special	The Doctor first learns that his time is limited and must decide whether to face "destiny" or try to avoid death.
"The Waters of Mars" 2009 special	In one of the darkest episodes, the Doctor "plays God" to save human scientists colonizing Mars, but in doing so he changes the future. He relishes his power over Time and considers himself a "god." This episode is important to a study of the Doctor as a gray hero or possibly even a gray villain.
"The End of Time" 2009–2010 special	The Doctor faces the Master again, but, more important to a character study, in the second part of this two-parter the Doctor must decide whether to sacrifice himself in order to save his companion. This death scene is very different from that of the Ninth Doctor. The episode also marks the finale of the Davies era.

Torchwood

Episode & Number	Some Reasons for Watching It
"Everything Changes" 1.1	This pilot episode introduces Torchwood as a gray setting for equally gray "heroes" who often perform

(*Torchwood*, continued)

Episode & Number	Some Reasons for Watching It
	illegal or possibly immoral acts as part of their jobs. The setting and character introductions define the very nature of a gray SF TV series.
"Cyberwoman" 1.4	Although the special effects make this episode almost laughable in places, the nature of the story and its depiction of Otherness and "monsters" make it thematically worth studying. Jack is portrayed as either a hero or a villain, depending on various team members' perceptions of his actions.
"Small Worlds" 1.5	In a study of Jack as a gray hero, this episode provides details about the immortal's past lives, as well as his ability to hand over a child to aliens in order to protect the rest of humanity.
"Countrycide" 1.6	Cannibals represent how monstrous humans can be toward each other.
"Greeks Bearing Gifts" 1.7	Same-sex lovers as acceptable Other are a sidestory in this otherwise typical Jack-defeats-aliens story.
"They Keep Killing Suzie" 1.8	Former Torchwood employee Suzie, who died in the pilot episode, provides bleak insights into the nature of life after death.
"Out of Time" 1.10	Jack sacrifices himself and questions his ability to make everything all right for three lost time travelers.
"Captain Jack Harkness" 1.12	This award-winning episode is important both to a study of Jack as a gray hero and of Otherness. Jack becomes trapped in the 1940s, where he meets and loves the man whose name he takes for his own.
"End of Days" 1.13	Jack takes on a very bad CGI version of the Biblical Abaddon, but the plot emphasizes his role as a sacrificial (perhaps messianic) hero.
"Kiss Kiss, Bang Bang" 2.1	Jack's past, in which he perhaps was a gray villain, illustrates how much he has tried instead to become a hero as the head of Torchwood. This episode is important to a study of Jack as, alternately, a swashbuckling, sympathetic, or tragic hero.
"Sleeper" 2.2	Similar to stories from *Battlestar Galactica* and *Lost*, in which "heroes" must decide whether to torture potential enemies, this episode illustrates how far Jack is willing to go to save the most lives. Whether he or the sleeper alien terrorist is the true "monster" is open for discussion.
"Meat" 2.4	Once again, humans are more monstrous than the marooned alien "whale" being tortured as a source of meat.
"Adam" 2.5	What makes us human? is again explored, this time

(Torchwood, continued)

Episode & Number	Some Reasons for Watching It
	through memories. Jack's and Ianto's memories make them question who they really are and what they will become if they can't trust their memories.
"Reset" 2.6	Martha goes undercover to help reveal a villain's plot; however, Owen becomes a sacrificial hero when he saves Martha's life.
"Dead Man Walking" 2.7	Jack finds a way to bring Owen back to life, but he becomes a "dead man walking" rather than truly living. Jack's desire to save his team may be heroic, but the extent to which he'll go to defeat death makes him a gray hero at best.
"A Day in the Death" 2.8	The answer to What makes us human? is provided from an analysis of "walking dead man" Owen's post–death life.
"From Out of the Rain" 2.10	Although in most ways a typical Torchwood vs. Monsters episode, it might be included in a study of Ianto simply because he has difficulty dealing with his inability to "save" souls imprisoned by the aliens.
"Fragments" 2.12	Backstories for each team member provide a baseline to illustrate how their jobs at Torchwood have changed them.
"Exit Wounds" 2.13	Jack's past, in the form of series villain Gray, haunts him and decimates his team and city.
"Children of Earth" 3.1–.5	This very dark miniseries is the highest quality *Torchwood* series of episodes, but it sparked controversy among fans and critics. Jack becomes a very gray character, to the point that some viewers question whether he is a hero or a villain/monster. Although the 456 are the alien monsters of the miniseries, they are not nearly as monstrous as the humans in charge of world governments. This miniseries is crucial to a study of Jack Harkness, Otherness, and monsters of all types.

Chapter Notes

Introduction

1. "21st Century Sci-Fi: The Top 10s," *SFX*, Special *SFX* Collector Edition, *41*(Winter 2009), p. 4.

2. "Top 20 Heroes and Villains According to *Entertainment Weekly*," *Central POP*, March 28, 2009, http://centralpop.wordpress.com/2009/03/28/1034/.

3. Jeff Jensen, "Heroes and Villains These Days. Why So Many? And Why So Dark?" *Entertainment Weekly*, March 26, 2009, http://popwatch.ew.com/2009/03/page/9/.

Chapter 1

1. Joseph Campbell, *The Hero with a Thousand Faces, Third Edition* (Novato, CA: New World Library, 2008). Variations on Campbell's criteria have been popularized and interpreted for specific needs through such sites as "The Hero's Journey: Summary of the Steps," Maricopa Community College, http://www.mcli.dist.maricopa.edu/smc/journey/ref summary.html; "Joseph Campbell's 12 Stages in the Hero's Journey," A Psychotherapy Group in the Village in New York City, http://www.am-psychotherapists-new-york-city.com/Joseph-Campbell.html; and "Campbell's 'Hero's Journey' Monomyth," Changing Minds.org, http://changingminds.org/disciplines/storytelling/plots/hero_journey/hero_journey.htm. A *Star Wars*–themed interpretation can be found at http://www.moongadget.com/origins/myth.html.

2. "Cast and Creators of *Heroes* Speak!" *MovieWeb*, September 19, 2006, http://www.movieweb.com/news/NENmlNPSXqoZSN.

3. FitzRoy Richard Somerset Raglan, *The Hero: A Study in Tradition, Myth, and Drama* (New Haven, CT: Greenwood Press Reprint, 1975). Lord Raglan's scale, summarized from *The Hero*, 1936, is also listed at http://missy.reimer.com/library/scale.html.

4. Bradley Thompson and David Weddle,

"Sometimes a Great Notion," *Battlestar Galactica*, SciFi, January 16, 2009 (U.S. airdate).

5. Russell T. Davies, "Children of Earth: Day Five," *Torchwood*, BBCOne, July 10, 2009.

6. J.R.R. Tolkien (Trans.), *Sir Gawain and the Green Knight* (New York: Random House, 1975).

7. Susan Mackey-Kallis, *The Hero and the Perennial Journey Home in Film* (Philadelphia: University of Pennsylvania Press, 2001).

8. J.J. Abrams (director), *Star Trek*, Paramount Pictures, 2009.

9. Although discussed on many fan and SF websites, one of the best discussions of character development in the original *Star Trek* series is David Gerrold's *The Complete Story of One of Star Trek's Favorite Episodes: "The Trouble with Tribbles"* (New York: Ballantine, 1973).

10. This photo has been used on several fan and TV web sites: http://www.daveexmachina.com/gfx/2009/twcoe.jpg; http://www.daemons-tv.com/wp-content/uploads/2009/07/torchwood_childrenofearth2–520x345.jpg; http://www.tvworthwatching.com/werts/torchwood%20coe.jpg; and so on. It was frequently published in promotional articles for "Children of Earth."

11. Russell T. Davies famously discussed Ianto Jones' death in an interview with *Entertainment Weekly*'s Michael Ausiello: "Torchwood Boss to Angry Fans: Go Watch 'Supernatural,'" *EW.com*, July 24, 2009, http://ausiellofiles.ew.com/2009/07/24/backlash-shmacklash-thats-torchwood-creator-russell-t-davies-reaction-to-the-outcry-over-the-death-of-gareth-david-lloyds/. He also discusses the decision to kill off Ianto in the *Torchwood* "Children of Earth" DVD commentary.

12. Russell T. Davies, "Children of Earth: Day Five," *Torchwood*, BBCOne, July 10, 2009.

13. J.J. Abrams and Damon Lindelof, "Pilot," *Lost*, ABC, September 22, 2004.

14. David S. Goyer and Brannon Braga, "No More Good Days," *FlashForward*, ABC, September 24, 2009.

15. Carlton Cuse and Damon Lindelof, "Through the Looking Glass," *Lost*, ABC, May 23, 2007.

16. Christian Taylor, "White Rabbit," *Lost*, ABC, October 13, 2004.

Chapter 2

1. Ironically, *Dr. Horrible*, with a villain as lead character, gave Joss Whedon his first Emmy win.

2. Joss Whedon, Jed Whedon, Zach Whedon, and Maurissa Tancharoen, *Dr. Horrible's Sing-Along Blog*, July 15–20, 2008, http://www.drhorrible.com.

3. Russell T. Davies, "Everything Changes," *Torchwood*, BBC, October 22, 2006.

4. James Moran, "Sleeper," *Torchwood*, BBC, January 22, 2008.

5. *Torchwood*'s opening narration for Seasons One and Two likely comes from series co-creator Russell T. Davies, who also wrote part or all of each season's first episode.

6. Brian K. Vaughan and Drew Goddard, "The Shape of Things to Come," *Lost*, ABC, April 24, 2008.

7. Ibid.

8. Carlton Cuse and Damon Lindelof, "Live Together, Die Alone," *Lost*, ABC, May 24, 2006.

9. J.R.R. Tolkien, *The Hobbit* (London: Allen & Unwin, 1937).

10. *Merlin*, BBC, 2008–

11. Russell T. Davies, "Rose," *Doctor Who*, BBC, March 26, 2005.

12. Mark Gatiss, "The Unquiet Dead," *Doctor Who*, BBC, April 9, 2005.

13. Rob Shearman, Q&A session, October 30, 2009, Hurricane Who convention, Orlando, Florida.

14. Robert Shearman, "Dalek," *Doctor Who*, BBC, April 30, 2005.

15. "Radio Free Skaro—#123 Shearman After Dark," February 14, 2009, http://www.radiofreeskaro.com/2009/02/14/radio-free-skaro-123-shearman-after-dark/.

16. Russell T. Davies, "The End of the World," *Doctor Who*, BBC, April 2, 2005.

17. Russell T. Davies, "The Long Game," *Doctor Who*, BBC One, May 7, 2005.

18. Carlton Cuse and Damon Lindelof, "The 23rd Psalm," *Lost*, ABC, January 11, 2006.

19. Alison Schapker and Monica Owusu-Breen, "The Cost of Living," *Lost*, ABC, November 1, 2006.

20. Chris Chibnall, "Cyberwoman," *Torchwood*, BBC, November 5, 2006.

21. Douglas Petrie, "Fool for Love," *Buffy the Vampire Slayer*, WB, November 14, 2000.

22. Steven DeKnight, "Seeing Red," *Buffy the Vampire Slayer*, UPN, May 7, 2002.

23. David Fury, "Grave," *Buffy the Vampire Slayer*, UPN, May 21, 2002.

24. J.C. Wilsher, "Reset," *Torchwood*, BBC, February 13, 2008.

25. Matt Jones, "Dead Man Walking," *Torchwood*, BBC, February 13, 2008.

26. Joseph Lidster, "A Day in the Death," *Torchwood*, BBC, February 27, 2008.

27. Catherine Tregenna, "Adam," *Torchwood*, BBC, February 20, 2008.

28. Tim Kring and Aron Eli Coleite, "The Hard Part," *Heroes*, NBC, May 7, 2007.

29. Tim Kring and Aron Eli Coleite, "I Am Become Death," *Heroes*, NBC, October 6, 2008.

30. Ambience 327, "Future Sylar—How Did He Become 'Betty Crocker'?" *Superhiro.org*, October 8, 2008. http://www.superhiro.org/future-sylar-how-did-he-become-betty-crocker-vt3410.html.

31. Joe Pokaski, "Hysterical Blindness," *Heroes*, NBC, October 12, 2009.

32. "Top Ten Villains," *Torchwood Magazine*, Issue 18, November 2009.

33. Chris Chibnall, "Exit Wounds," *Torchwood*, BBC, April 4, 2008.

Chapter 3

1. Jeff Jensen, "Heroes and Villains These Days. Why So Many? And Why So Dark?" *Entertainment Weekly*, March 26, 2009, http://popwatch.ew.com/2009/03/page/9/.

2. Aron Eli Coleite and Aury Wallington, "Once Upon a Time in Texas," *Heroes*, NBC, November 2, 2009.

3. "Remembering Gene Roddenberry," *Star Trek.com News*, October 24, 2003, http://www.startrek.com/startrek/view/news/article/3289.html.

4. John Barrowman and Carole E. Barrowman, *I Am What I Am* (London: Michael O'Mara Books), p. 147.

5. Bryan Fuller, "Company Man," *Heroes*, NBC, February 26, 2007.

6. *Spider-Man*, Dir. Sam Raimi, Columbia Pictures, 2002.

7. Lincoln Geraghty, *Living with* Star Trek: *American Culture and the* Star Trek *Universe* (London: Tauris, 2007), p. 88.

8. Russell T. Davies, "Children of Earth: Day Five," *Torchwood*, BBC, July 10, 2009.

9. Paul Cornell, "Father's Day," *Doctor Who*, BBC, May 14, 2005.

10. Russell T. Davies, "The Parting of the Ways," *Doctor Who*, BBC, June 18, 2005.

11. Karen Price, "Prime-Time Slot for New Torchwood: Cardiff-Based Sci-fi Series Moves to BBC1 for Its Third Series," *South Wales Echo*, August 14, 2008, p. 6.

12. Ibid.

13. "Action Man!" *Torchwood*, 12 (Winter 2008), p. 17.

14. Michael Jensen, "Torchwood's John Barrowman: 'I Love Captain Jack, What He Stands For, What He Represents,'" *AfterElton*, July 15, 2009, http://www.afterelton.com/people/2009/7/john-barrowman?page=0%2C3.

15. Darren Scott, "Jack's Back: Interview with John Barrowman and Gareth David-Lloyd," *Gay Times*, June 2009, p. 36.

16. Michael Jensen, "Torchwood's John Barrowman: 'I Love Captain Jack, What He Stands For, What He Represents,'" AfterElton, July 15, 2009, http://www.afterelton.com/people/2009/7/john-barrowman?page=0%2C3.

17. Neil Wilkes, "Live: 'Torchwood' Panel at Comic-Con," *Digital Spy*, July 26, 2009, http://www.digitalspy.com/tv/a167433/live-torchwood-panel-at-comic-con.html.

18. Gareth David-Lloyd, personal interview, November 1, 2009.

19. Carole E. Barrowman, personal email, September 21, 2009.

20. Nichelle Nichols has relayed this story many times at Star Trek conventions. One site listing the story is http://www.startrek.com/startrek/view/series/TOS/cast/69077.html.

21. Russell T. Davies, "The Christmas Invasion," *Doctor Who*, BBC, December 25, 2005.

22. Daniel Schorn, "The Quest for Immortality," *60 Minutes*, CBS, January 1, 2006, http://www.cbsnews.com/stories/2005/12/28/60minutes/main1168852.shtml.

23. Damon Lindelof and Carlton Cuse, "The Incident," *Lost*, ABC, May 13, 2009.

24. Jeph Loeb, "One Giant Leap," *Heroes*, NBC, October 9, 2006.

25. Adam Armus and Kay Foster, "I Am Sylar," *Heroes*, NBC, April 20, 2009.

26. Joyce Millman, "The Frontiers of Immortality," *Obit*, March 4, 2008, http://www.obit-mag.com/viewmedia.php/prmMID/4919.

27. Bradley Thompson and David Weddie, "Sometimes a Great Notion," *Battlestar Galactica*, SciFi, January 16, 2009.

28. Ben Scarlato, "Immortality and Death in Battlestar Galactica," *Ethical Technology*, Institute for Ethics and Emerging Technologies, January 18, 2009, http://ieet.org/index.php/IEET/more/scarlato20090118/.

29. Ronald D. Moore, "Daybreak," *Battlestar Galactica*, SciFi, March 13 and March 20, 2009.

Chapter 4

1. "Top 7 Science Fiction Sidekicks," *The World in a Satin Bag*, July 19, 2009, http://wisb.blogspot.com/2009/07/top-7-science-fiction-sidekicks-in-film.html.

2. Frankie Marchiony, "I'd Hang Out with You: TV's Top 10 Sidekicks," *Examiner.com*, June 25, 2009, http://www.examiner.com/x-15322-Long-Island-Television-Examiner~y2009m6d25-Id-hang-out-with-you-TVs-top-10-sidekicks.

3. Susan Young, "Top 10 New TV Sidekicks," October 15, 2008, http://www.film.com/tv/house/story/top-10-new-tv-sidekicks/23588592.

4. Lolly Wycherley, "Sci Fi Sidekicks—A Thing of the Past?" *Sci Fi Channel UK*, July 28, 2009, http://www.scifi.co.uk/blog/author/lolly_wycherley/.

5. Chris Chibnall, "Cyberwoman," *Torchwood*, BBC, November 5, 2006.

6. Gareth David-Lloyd, personal interview, Orlando, Florida, November 1, 2009.

7. Ibid.

8. Gareth David-Lloyd, class discussion, Embry-Riddle Aeronautical University, Daytona Beach, Florida, November 2, 2009.

9. Gareth David-Lloyd, Q&A session, Hurricane Who Party, Orlando, Florida, February 26, 2009.

10. Emily Lambert, "Tea? Coffee? Muffin?" *Western Mail* (Cardiff), October 28, 2006, p. 17.

11. Simon Hugo, "Earning His Stripes," *Torchwood*, 14 (April-May 2009), p. 20.

12. Catherine Tregenna, "Adam," *Torchwood*, BBC, February 13, 2008.

13. Catherine Tregenna, "Captain Jack Harkness," *Torchwood*, BBC, December 17, 2006.

14. Gareth David-Lloyd, personal interview, Orlando, Florida, November 1, 2009.

15. Michael Angeli, "Blood on the Scales," *Battlestar Galactica*, Sci-Fi, February 6, 2009.

16. Mary McDonnell, Dragon Con panel, September 5, 2009.

17. Michael Taylor, "Sine Qua Non," *Battlestar Galactica*, Sci-Fi, May 27, 2008.

18. Ronald D. Moore, "Daybreak," *Battlestar Galactica*, Sci-Fi, March 20, 2009.

19. "Interview: Starbuck Steps It Up," *CanWest MediaWorks Publications. Dose.ca*, February 6, 2009, http://www.dose.ca/tv/story.html?id=8a74aed8-54e2-4140-804f-363ca4d8d0f7.

20. Ronald D. Moore and Christopher Eric James, "Night 1," *Battlestar Galactica*, pilot miniseries, Sci-Fi, December 8, 2003.

21. Ronald D. Moore, "Daybreak," *Battlestar Galactica*, Sci-Fi, March 20, 2009.

22. Russell T. Davies, "The Parting of the Ways," *Doctor Who*, BBC, June 18, 2005.

23. Russell T. Davies, "The Christmas Invasion," *Doctor Who*, BBC, December 25, 2005.

24. Russell T. Davies, "Doomsday," *Doctor Who*, BBC, July 8, 2006.

25. Russell T. Davies, "The Stolen Earth," *Doctor Who*, BBC, June 28, 2008.

26. David Tennant, *Doctor Who Confidential*,

12 (4); *Doctor Who: The Complete Series 4*, DVD, 2008.
27. Russell T. Davies, "The End of Time, Part 2," *Doctor Who*, BBC, January 1, 2010.
28. Russell T. Davies, "Journey's End," *Doctor Who*, BBC, July 5, 2008.
29. Murray Gold, "Rose's Theme," *Doctor Who Original Television Soundtrack*, CD, BBC, 2006.
30. Ben Foster, "Ianto Jones" and "The Ballad of Ianto Jones," *Torchwood, Children of Earth Original Television Soundtrack*, CD, BBC, 2009.
31. Russell T. Davies, "Children of Earth: Day Five," *Torchwood*, BBC, July 10, 2009.

Chapter 5

1. *Star Trek*, Paramount, 2009, dir. J.J. Abrams, written by Roberto Orci and Alex Kurtzman.
2. "Children of Earth: Days One Through Five," *Torchwood*, BBC, July 6–10, 2009.
3. David S. Goyer and Brannon Braga, "No More Good Days," *FlashForward*, ABC, September 24, 2009.
4. James Moran and Russell T. Davies, "Children of Earth: Day Three," *Torchwood*, BBC, July 8, 2009.
5. Carole E. Barrowman, writer, Tommy Lee Edwards and Trevor Goring, artists, "The Selkie: A Captain Jack Tale," *Torchwood*, 14 (April–May 2009), pp. 61–75.
6. Remi Aubuchon and Ronald D. Moore, "Pilot," *Caprica*, SciFi, April 21, 2009, June 2009 DVD release.
7. Russell T. Davies, "Children of Earth: Day Five," *Torchwood*, BBC, July 10, 2009.
8. James Moran and Russell T. Davies, "Children of Earth: Day Three," *Torchwood*, BBC, July 8, 2009.
9. *Star Trek: Wrath of Khan*, director Nicholas Meyer, Paramount, 1982.
10. Russell T. Davies, "Boom Town," *Doctor Who*, BBC, June 4, 2005.
11. Tim Kring and Jesse Alexander, "Landslide," *Heroes*, NBC, May 14, 2007.
12. Russell T. Davies, "Children of Earth: Day One," *Torchwood*, BBC, July 6, 2009.
13. Lewis Wallace, "Review: *Caprica* Spins Religion, Race Into Worthy *Galactica* Prequel," *Wired*, April 20, 2009.
14. Ronald D. Moore, *Caprica*, DVD, SciFi, 2009.

Part Two. Introduction

1. Margaret Atwood, "The Queen of Quinkdom," *The New York Review of Books*, 49 (14), September 26, 2002, http://www.nybooks.com/articles/15677.

Chapter 6

1. Laura Davis, "Chart Reveals Who the True Masters of Science Fiction Were This Decade," io9, *Science Overmind*, December 25, 2009, http://io9.com/5434005/chart-reveals-who-the-true-masters-of-science-fiction-were-this-decade.
2. "Good Reads," Quotes by Joss Whedon, http://www.goodreads.com/author/quotes/18015.Joss_Whedon.
3. Joss Whedon, "Once More, with Feeling," *Buffy the Vampire Slayer*, UPN, November 6, 2001.
4. Joss Whedon, lyrics, and Christophe Beck, music, "Going Through the Motions," in "Once More, with Feeling," *Buffy the Vampire Slayer*, UPN, November 6, 2001.
5. Tim Minear, "That Old Gang of Mine," *Angel*, WB, October 8, 2001.
6. "Angel," *SFX*, Top 10 TV Series of the Decade, *SFX* Special Collector Edition 41, 2009, pp. 12–13.
7. Jeffrey Bell and Joss Whedon, "Not Fade Away," *Angel*, WB, May 19, 2004.
8. "Firefly," *SFX*, Top 10 TV Series of the Decade, *SFX* Special Collector Edition 41, 2009, 16–17.
9. "Serenity," *SFX*, Top 10 Films of the Decade, *SFX* Special Collector Edition 41, 2009, pp. 60–61.
10. Zach Oat, "*Castle*: Nathan Fillion Flashes Back to his *Firefly* Days," The Telefile, *Television Without Pity*, October 27, 2009, http://www.television withoutpity.com/telefile/2009/10/castle-nathan-fillion-flashes.php.
11. "Gone Too Soon: The Decade's Top 10 Canceled TV Series," *PressDemocrat.com*, December 19, 2009, http://tv.blogs.pressdemocrat.com/12014/gone-too-soon-the-decades-top-10-canceled-tv-series/.
12. Will Allen, "Who Wouldn't Want to Be Han Solo?" *South Bend Tribune*, December 14, 2009, http://www.southbendtribune.com/article/20091214/BLOGS33/912149976.
13. Joss Whedon, "Serenity," *Firefly*, Fox, December 20, 2002.
14. John Crook, "Just Down-to-Earth Folks: 'Firefly' Shuns Sci-Fi Clichés for a Space Adventure with More Realistic Characters," *Chicago Tribune*, September 15, 2002, p. 3.
15. Joss Whedon (director), *Serenity*, Universal Pictures, 2005.
16. Jane Espenson, "Shindig," *Firefly*, Fox, November 1, 2002.
17. Joss Whedon and Tim Minear, "The Train Job," *Firefly*, Fox, September 20, 2002.
18. Cheryl Cain, "War Stories," *Firefly*, Fox, December 6, 2002.
19. Matt Roush, "Exclusive: First Look at Joss Whedon's 'Dr. Horrible,'" *TV Guide*, June

30, 2008, http://www.tvguide.com/roush/exclu sive-look-joss-9886.aspx.

20. Joss Whedon, lyrics and music, "Freeze Ray," *Dr. Horrible's Sing-Along Blog.*

21. Jed Whedon, lyrics and music, "A Man's Gotta Do," *Dr. Horrible's Sing-Along Blog.*

22. Joss Whedon, lyrics and music, and Jed Whedon, bridge, "Everything You Ever," *Dr. Horrible's Sing-Along Blog.*

Chapter 7

1. "'Heroes' Debut Paces NBC's Second Monday Win of the New Season," NBC Press release published by the *Futon Critic*, September 26, 2006, http://www.thefutoncritic.com/news. aspx?id=20060926nbc03.

2. *"Heroes," NBC Official Website,* http:// www.nbc.com/heroes/about/.

3. Adam Armus and Kay Foster, "The Wall," *Heroes*, NBC, February 1, 2010.

4. Michael Logan, "Unstrung *Heroes*," *TV Guide*, February 8–14, 2010, p. 40.

5. Oliver Grigsby, "Pass/Fail," *Heroes*, NBC, January 18, 2010.

6. "Masi Oka Discusses Possibilities of Hiro Finding Charlie," *TV Guide* quotation republished on *Heroes Spoilers*, January 24, 2010, http://heroesspoilers-odi.blogspot.com/2010/ 01/masi-oka-discusses-possibilities-of.html.

7. Brian Juergens, "'Heroes' Straightens Up Its Gay Character," *AfterElton.com*, December 11, 2006, http://www.afterelton.com/TV/2006/ 12/heroes.html.

8. Tim Kring, "The Fifth Stage," *Heroes*, NBC, November 30, 2009.

9. Oliver Grigsby, "Pass/Fail," *Heroes*, NBC, January 18, 2010.

Chapter 8

1. Carlton Cuse and Damon Lindelof, "Through the Looking Glass," *Lost*, ABC, May 23, 2007.

2. Damon Lindelof, "Man of Science, Man of Faith," *Lost*, ABC, September 21, 2005.

3. Carlton Cuse and Elizabeth Sarnoff, "Further Instructions," *Lost*, ABC, October 18, 2006.

4. J.J. Abrams and Damon Lindelof, "Pilot," *Lost*, ABC, September 22, 2004.

5. Carlton Cuse and Damon Lindelof, "The Life and Death of Jeremy Bentham," *Lost*, ABC, February 25, 2009.

6. J.J. Abrams and Damon Lindelof, "Pilot," *Lost*, ABC, September 22, 2004.

7. Carlton Cuse and Damon Lindelof, "Through the Looking Glass," *Lost*, ABC, May 23, 2007.

8. Edward Kitsis and Adam Horowitz, "Something Nice Back Home," *Lost*, ABC, May 1, 2008.

9. Jeff Jensen, "'Lost': Secrets of the Set," *Entertainment Weekly*, April 10, 2008, http://www.ew.com/ew/article/0,,201904 15_4,00.html.

10. Damon Lindelof and Carlton Cuse, "316," *Lost*, ABC, February 18, 2009.

11. Damon Lindelof and Carlton Cuse, "The Incident," *Lost*, ABC, May 13, 2009.

12. Janet Tamaro, "Do No Harm," *Lost*, ABC, April 6, 2005.

13. Damon Lindelof and Carlton Cuse, "I Do," *Lost*, ABC, November 8, 2006.

14. Carlton Cuse and Damon Lindelof, "Whatever Happened, Happened," *Lost*, ABC, April 1, 2009.

15. "The Return of Lost," *Entertainment Weekly*, January 15, 2010, pp. 42–43.

16. Carlton Cuse and Damon Lindelof, "Deus Ex Machina," *Lost*, ABC, March 20, 2005.

17. Janet Tamaro, "Do No Harm," *Lost*, ABC, April 6, 2005.

18. Carlton Cuse and Damon Lindelof, "Through the Looking Glass," *Lost*, ABC, May 23, 2007.

19. Damon Lindelof and Carlton Cuse, "The Brig," *Lost*, ABC, May 2, 2007.

20. Carlton Cuse and Damon Lindelof, "The Life and Death of Jeremy Bentham," *Lost*, ABC, February 25, 2009.

21. "The Return of Lost," *Entertainment Weekly*, January 15, 2010, p. 43.

22. Brian K. Vaughan and Elizabeth Sarnoff, "Dead Is Dead," *Lost*, ABC, April 8, 2009.

23. Brian K. Vaughan and Drew Goddard, "The Shape of Things to Come," *Lost*, ABC, April 24, 2008.

24. Brian K. Vaughan and Elizabeth Sarnoff, "Dead Is Dead," *Lost*, ABC, April 8, 2009.

Chapter 9

1. "Battlestar Galactica," *SFX*, Top 10 TV Series of the Decade, *SFX* Special Collector Edition 41, 2009, pp. 22–23.

2. In this chapter, characters who have a pilot call sign and a name, and are referred to by both names in the series, are designated first with their real name and then with the call sign, as in Kara/Starbuck or Sharon/Boomer.

3. Kyle Brady, "The Best of 2009's Tech and Entertainment," *True/Slant*, December 26, 2009, http://trueslant.com/kylebrady/2009/12/ 26/the-best-of-2009s-tech-and-entertainment/.

4. Ronald D. Moore, *Battlestar Galactica*, SciFi, December 8–9, 2003.

5. Remi Aubuchon and Ronald D. Moore, *Caprica*, pilot movie, Sci-Fi, 2009. This pilot

movie, first released on DVD in 2009 and later shown as the premiere two-hour "episode" of *Caprica* on SyFy in 2010, is the reference for the majority of scenes and character analyzed in this chapter. Individual early episodes, such as "Rebirth," are separately noted. Otherwise, the reference is to the pilot movie.

6. Robert Seidman, "SyFy Launches First Phase of Innovative *Caprica* Marketing," September 30, 2009, http://tvbythenumbers.com/2009/09/30/syfy-launches-first-phase-of-innovative-caprica-marketing/29069.

7. "TV Buzz: James Marsters stars in 'Caprica,'" *Newsday*, August 21, 2009, http://www.newsday.com/entertainment/tv/tv-buzz-james-marsters-stars-in-caprica-1.1385461.

8. "First Image of Marsters in Caprica," *HDR, The Head Room*, January 22, 2010, http://www.thehdroom.com/news/First_Image_of_James_Marsters_in_Caprica/6240.

9. James Rundle, "Caprica: The Beginning of the End," *SciFi Now*, 35, 2009, p. 37.

10. Mark Verheiden, "Rebirth," *Caprica*, SyFy, January 29, 2010.

11. SyFy released six promotional posters and encouraged fans to vote for their favorite on the SyFy website. Two posters prominently feature apple imagery and were among the most widely distributed posters on the web. Not surprisingly, the nude Zoe poster has been viewed most often and copied to fans' websites. The six posters were announced in October 2009: "New Caprica Posters," *Caprica TV.net*, October 1, 2009, http://www.capricatv.net/2009/10/new-caprica-posters.html.

12. Glenn Diaz, "Jane Espenson Talks about Gay Character, Sexuality on Caprica," *Buddy TV*, January 21, 2010, http://www.buddytv.com/articles/caprica/jane-espenson-talks-about-gay-33920.aspx.

13. Ibid.

14. Michael Jensen, "Caprica's Jane Espenson: 'It's Time for Sexuality to Be Incidental,'" *AfterElton.com*, January 20, 2010, http://www.afterelton.com/people/2010/01/jane-espenson?page=0%2C3.

15. Remi Aubuchon and Ronald D. Moore, "Reins of a Waterfall," *Caprica*, SyFy, February 5, 2010.

Chapter 10

1. In mid–January 2010, *The Hollywood Reporter* announced that Davies would be writing scripts for a proposed new *Torchwood* series for the U.S. Fox network. (Fox declined the series, however. It later was picked up by cable network Starz. The fate of any other Davies-helmed series is unknown.) In the same article, *Doctor Who* fans learned a more frightening prospect:

the possibility of an Americanized Doctor. Jane Tranter, who moved from BBC-U.K. to BBC offices in the U.S. with BBC Worldwide, is now a vice president of programming; alarmed fans immediately homed in on the *Reporter*'s line that "Tranter might try to reboot *Doctor Who* for U.S. audiences." With such a prospect, the newest new *Who*, helmed by the writers and creators of the ever-darkening SF plots of "Waters of Mars" and "Children of Earth," might introduce a very dark hero indeed. (James Hibberd, "Fox Developing New Version of 'Torchwood,'" *The Hollywood Reporter*, January 19, 2010, http://www.hollywoodreporter.com/hr/content_display/news/e3id183d5e80b48e57c2e6102a3f94da557.)

2. "The Tao of Russell," *SFX* Collector Special Edition 41, Winter 2009, p. 35.

3. Steven Moffat, "Time Crash: Children in Need Special," *Doctor Who*, BBC, 2007.

4. Sarah Lucy May, "The Ten Commandments," *SFX*, Winter 2009, p. 42.

5. "The Tao of Russell," *SFX* Collector Special Edition 41, Winter 2009, p. 31.

6. Russell T. Davies, "The End of Time, Part 1," *Doctor Who*, BBC, December 25, 2009.

7. "The Tao of Russell," *SFX* Collector Special Edition 41, Winter 2009, p. 35.

8. Russell T. Davies, "The Stolen Earth," *Doctor Who*, BBC, June 28, 2008.

9. Russell T. Davies, "Journey's End," *Doctor Who*, BBC, June 21, 2008.

10. "David Tennant Named 'Best Doctor Who,'" *BBC News*, December 6, 2006, http://news.bbc.co.uk/2/hi/6211584.stm.

11. David Bentley, "Viewers Would Prefer Ewan McGregor Over Matt Smith as the Next Doctor Who," *The Geek Files*, December 23, 2009, http://blogs.coventrytelegraph.net/thegeekfiles/2009/12/viewers-would-prefer-ewan-macg.html.

12. Jeff Renaud, "He's the Doctor," *Geek*, September 2009, p. 45.

13. Russell T. Davies, "The End of the World," *Doctor Who*, BBC, April 2, 2005.

14. Russell T. Davies and Phil Ford, "The Waters of Mars," *Doctor Who*, BBC, November 15, 2009.

15. "'Doctor Who' Blogging: 'The Waters of Mars,'" *FlickFilospher.com*, December 24, 2009, http://www.flickfilosopher.com/blog/2009/12/122409doctor_who_blogging_the_waters.html.

16. James Moran, "The Fires of Pompeii," *Doctor Who*, BBC, April 12, 2008.

17. Russell T. Davies, "Children of Earth, Day Five," *Torchwood*, BBC, July 9, 2009.

18. "John Frobisher," Doctor Who Wiki, citing Russell T. Davies' comment in a *Torchwood Declassified*.

19. Russell T. Davies, "Voyage of the

Damned," *Doctor Who*, BBC, December 25, 2007.

20. Russell T. Davies, "The End of Time, Part 2," *Doctor Who*, BBC, January 1, 2010.

21. Gareth Roberts, "The Wedding of Sarah Jane Smith, Part 2," *The Sarah Jane Adventures*, BBC, October 30, 2009.

Chapter 11

1. Matt Roush, "Matt Roush's Top 10," *TV Guide*, December 21, 2009–January 3, 2010, p. 27.

2. Alan Sepinwall, "Best of 2009 in TV — Sepinwall on TV," *The Star-Ledger*, December 22, 2009, http://www.nj.com/entertainment/tv/index.ssf/2009/12/best_of_2009_in_tv_-_sepinwall.html.

3. "The Best Series of 2009," *Pittsburgh Post-Gazette*, Republished in the *Victorville Daily Press*, December 21, 2009, http://www.vvdailypress.com/entertainment/pain-16318-residual-series.html.

4. Doug Lambert, Ian Westhead, Helen Jones, and Mike Watkins, "2009 in Television: Gems," *ATV Network News*, December 8, 2009, http://www.atvnewsnetwork.co.uk/today/index.php/atv-today/1884-2009-in-television-gems.

5. Gareth David-Lloyd, class discussion, Embry-Riddle Aeronautical University, Daytona Beach, Florida, November 2, 2009.

6. Shana Naomi Krochmal, "Interview with John Barrowman," *Out*, p. 101.

7. Steven Moffat, "The Empty Child," *Doctor Who*, BBC, May 21, 2005.

8. Chris Chibnall, "Kiss Kiss, Bang Bang," *Torchwood*, BBC, January 16, 2008.

9. Russell T. Davies, "The Parting of the Ways," *Doctor Who*, BBC, June 18, 2005.

10. Steve Pratt, "Television — All Right Jack," *Northern Echo* (Darlington), October 19, 2006, p. 3.

11. Catherine Tregenna, "Captain Jack Harkness," *Torchwood*, BBC, January 1, 2007.

12. Chris Chibnall, "End of Days," *Torchwood*, BBC, January 1, 2007.

13. In "Children of Earth, Day Two," Jack completes a similar Biblical-themed resurrection. Although the government thinks that entombing him in cement will keep him dead, Jack is freed from his tomb, once again leading to a smiling reunion with his followers.

14. Chris Chibnall, "Kiss Kiss, Bang Bang," *Torchwood*, BBC, January 16, 2008.

15. John Barrowman and Carole E. Barrowman, *I Am What I Am* (London: Michael O'-Mara Books, 2009), p. 197.

16. Diane Werts, "Review: You Could Call It ... Lust in Space," *Newsday*, January 25, 2008, p. B29.

17. Peter J. Hammond, "Small Worlds," *Torchwood*, BBC, November 12, 2006.

18. John Barrowman, "Children of Earth," *Torchwood*, DVD commentary, 2009.

19. Peter J. Hammond, "From Out of the Rain," *Torchwood*, March 12, 2008.

20. Russell T. Davies and James Moran, "Children of Earth: Day Three," *Torchwood*, BBC, July 8, 2009.

21. Russell T. Davies, "Children of Earth: Day One," *Torchwood*, BBC, July 6, 2009.

22. Russell T. Davies, "Children of Earth: Day Five," *Torchwood*, BBC, July 10, 2009.

23. As a writer and fan, I question whether the scriptwriters of Day Five had to provide an either/or dilemma: kill Jack's grandson or kill more children, or possibly all of humanity. It seems that a more creative solution, not just a *deus ex machina* ending, might have been used to make Jack seem less monstrous. However, if "Day Five's" conclusion is interpreted as a political statement instead of simply an entertainment decision, the script becomes more acceptable to more *Torchwood* fans. This decision, after all, turns Jack into the last of the traditional heroes and indicates that such heroes no longer are viable both, either in real life or in entertainment (except perhaps escapist fantasy).

24. Several websites refer to *The Times* dubbing Barrowman a "National Treasure." One such site is the *MyPlay* biography at http://myplay.com/artists/john-barrowman/bio.

25. John Barrowman and Carole E. Barrowman, *I Am What I Am* (London: Michael O'-Mara Books, 2009), p. 40.

26. John Fay, "Children of Earth: Day Four," *Torchwood*, BBC, July 9, 2009.

27. Neil Perryman, "Doctor Who and the Convergence of Media: A Case Study in 'Transmedia Storytelling,'" *Convergence: The International Journal of Research into New Media Technologies*, 14 (1), 2008, pp. 21–39.

28. Joseph Lidster, "Lost Souls," *Torchwood*, BBC Radio, September 10, 2008.

29. Phil Ford, "The Dead Line," *Torchwood*, BBC Radio, July 3, 2009.

30. The autobiographies (cited fully in the Bibliography) are entitled *Anything Goes* and *I Am What I Am*.

31. Iron Dude, "Interview with John Barrowman," *Hero Spy*, February 17, 2009, http://herospy.com/2009/john-barrowman-interview/.

32. Carole E. Barrowman, writer, Tommy Lee Edwards and Trevor Goring, artists, "The Selkie: A Captain Jack Tale," *Torchwood*, 14 (April-May 2009), pp. 61–75.

33. Carole E. Barrowman, personal email, September 21, 2009.

34. Ibid.

35. Gareth David-Lloyd, personal interview, November 1, 2009.

36. Guy Adams, *The House That Jack Built* (London: BBC Books, 2009).

37. Brian Minchin, *The Sin Eaters* (London: BBC, 2009).

38. Carole E. Barrowman, personal email, September 21, 2009.

39. Ben Foster, "Jack's Love Theme," *Torch-wood Original Soundtrack Recording*, CD, Silva America, 2008.

40. Ibid.

41. Ben Foster, "I Can Run Forever," *Torch-wood: Children of Earth Soundtrack*, CD, Silva America, 2009.

Bibliography

"Action Man!" *Torchwood*, 12 (Winter 2008), p. 17.

Adams, Guy. *The House That Jack Built.* London: BBC Books, 2009.

Allen, Will. "Who Wouldn't Want to Be Han Solo?" *South Bend Tribune*, December 14, 2009, http://www.southbendtribune.com/article/20091214/BLOGS33/912149976.

Ambience 327. "Future Sylar — How Did He Become 'Betty Crocker?'" *Superhiro.org*, October 8, 2008, http://www.superhiro.org/future-sylar-how-did-he-become-betty-crocker-vt3410.html.

"Angel." *SFX*, Top 10 TV Series of the Decade. *SFX* Special Collector Edition 41, 2009, pp. 12–13.

Ausiello, Michael. "Torchwood Boss to Angry Fans: Go Watch 'Supernatural.'" *Entertainment Weekly*, EW.com, July 24, 2009, http://ausiellofiles.ew.com/2009/07/24/backlash-shmacklash-thats-torchwood-creator-russell-t-davies-reaction-to-the-outcry-over-the-death-of-gareth-david-lloyds/.

Barrowman, Carole E. Personal email, September 21, 2009.

Barrowman, Carole E., writer, and Tommy Lee Edwards and Trevor Goring, artists. "The Selkie: A Captain Jack Tale," *Torchwood*, 14 (April-May 2009), pp. 61–75.

Barrowman, John. *Torchwood*. "Children of Earth." DVD commentary, 2009.

"Barrowman, John." *MyPlay*, http://myplay.com/artists/john-barrowman/bio.

Barrowman, John, and Carole E. Barrowman. *Anything Goes.* London: Michael O'Mara Books, 2008.

_____. *I Am What I Am.* London: Michael O'Mara Books, 2009.

"Battlestar Galactica." *SFX*, Top 10 TV Series of the Decade, *SFX* Special Collector Edition 41, 2009, pp. 22–23.

Bentley, David. "Viewers Would Prefer Ewan McGregor Over Matt Smith as the Next Doctor Who." *The Geek Files*, December 23, 2009, http://blogs.coventrytelegraph.net/ thegeekfiles/2009/12/viewers-would-prefer-ewan-macg.html.

"The Best Series of 2009." *Pittsburgh Post-Gazette*, republished in the *Victorville Daily Press*, December 21, 2009, http://www.vvdailypress.com/entertainment/pain-16318-residual-series.html.

Brady, Kyle. "The Best of 2009's Tech and Entertainment." *True/Slant*, December 26, 2009, http://trueslant.com/kylebrady/2009/12/26/the-best-of-2009s-tech-and-entertainment/.

Campbell, Joseph. *The Hero with a Thousand Faces*, Third Edition. Novato, CA: New World Library, 2008.

"Campbell's 'Hero's Journey' Monomyth." *Changing Minds.org*, http://changing-minds.org/disciplines/storytelling/plots/hero_journey/hero_journey.htm.

"Cast and Creators of *Heroes* Speak!" *MovieWeb*, September 19, 2006, http://www.movieweb.com/news/ NENmlNPS XqoZSN.

Crook, John. "Just Down-to-Earth Folks: 'Firefly' Shuns Sci-Fi Clichés for a Space Adventure with More Realistic Characters," *Chicago Tribune*, September 15, 2002, p. 3.

"David Tennant Named 'Best Doctor Who.'" *BBC News.* December 6, 2006, http://news.bbc.co.uk/2/hi/6211584.stm.

David-Lloyd, Gareth. Class discussion, Embry-Riddle Aeronautical University, Daytona Beach, Florida, November 2, 2009.

_____. Personal interview, Orlando, Florida, November 1, 2009.

_____. Q&A session, Hurricane Who Party, Orlando, Florida, February 26, 2009.

Davis, Laura. "Chart Reveals Who the True Masters of Science Fiction Were This Decade." io9, *Science Overmind*, December 25, 2009, http://io9.com/5434005/chart-reveals-who-the-true-masters-of-science-fiction-were-this-decade.

Diaz, Glenn. "Jane Espenson Talks about Gay Character, Sexuality on Caprica." *Buddy TV*, January 21, 2010, http://www.buddytv.com/articles/caprica/jane-espenson-talks-about-gay-33920.aspx.

"'Doctor Who' Blogging: 'The Waters of Mars.'" *FlickFilospher.com*, December 24, 2009, http://www.flickfilosopher.com/blog/2009/12/122409doctor_who_blogging_the_waters.html.

"Firefly." *SFX*, Top 10 TV Series of the Decade, *SFX* Special Collector Edition 41, 2009, p. 17.

"First Image of Marsters in Caprica." *HDR, the Head Room*, January 22, 2010, http://www.thehdroom.com/news/First_Image_of_James_Marsters_in_Caprica/6240.

Foster, Ben. "The Ballad of Ianto Jones," *Torchwood, Children of Earth Original Television Soundtrack*. CD. BBC, 2009.

_____. "Captain Jack's Theme," *Torchwood Original Soundtrack Recording*. CD. Silva America, 2008.

_____. "I Can Run Forever," *Torchwood: Children of Earth Soundtrack*. CD. Silva America, 2009.

Geraghty, Lincoln. *Living with Star Trek: American Culture and the Star Trek Universe*. London: Tauris, 2007.

Gerrold, David. *The Complete Story of One of Star Trek's Favorite Episodes: "The Trouble with Tribbles."* New York: Ballantine, 1973.

Gold, Murray. "Rose's Theme," *Doctor Who Original Television Soundtrack*. CD. BBC, 2006.

"Gone Too Soon: The Decade's Top 10 Canceled TV Series." *PressDemocrat.com*, December 19, 2009, http://tv.blogs.pressdemocrat.com/12014/gone-too-soon-the-decades-top-10-canceled-tv-series/.

"Good Reads." Quotes by Joss Whedon, http://www.goodreads.com/author/quotes/18015.Joss_Whedon.

"The Hero's Journey: Summary of the Steps." Maricopa Community College, http://www.mcli.dist.maricopa.edu/smc/journey/ref summary.html.

Heroes. NBC Official Website. http://www.nbc.com/heroes/about/.

"Heroes' Debut Paces NBC's Second Monday Win of the New Season." NBC Press release published by the *Futon Critic*, September 26, 2006, http://www.thefutoncritic.com/news.aspx?id=20060926nbc03.

Hibberd, James. "Fox Developing New Version of 'Torchwood.'" *The Hollywood Reporter*. January 19, 2010. http://www.hollywoodreporter.com/hr/ content_display/news/e3id183d5e80b48e57c2e6102a3f94da557

Hugo, Simon. "Earning His Stripes." *Torchwood*, 14 (April–May 2009), p. 20.

"Interview: Starbuck Steps It Up." CanWest MediaWorks Publications, Dose.ca, February 6, 2009, http://www.dose.ca/tv/story.html?id=8a74aed8-54e2-4140-804f-363ca4d8d0f7.

Iron Dude. "Interview with John Barrowman." *Hero Spy*, February 17, 2009, http://herospy.com/2009/john-barrowman-interview/.

Jensen, Jeff. "Heroes and Villains These Days. Why So Many? And Why So Dark?" *Entertainment Weekly*, March 26, 2009, http://popwatch.ew.com/2009/03/page/9/.

_____. "'Lost': Secrets of the Set." *Entertainment Weekly*, April 10, 2008, http://www.ew.com/ew/article/0,,20190415_4,00.html.

Jensen, Michael. "Caprica's Jane Espenson: 'It's Time for Sexuality to Be Incidental.'" *AfterElton.com*, January 20, 2010, http://www.afterelton.com/people/2010/01/jane-espenson?page=0%2C3.

Jensen, Michael. "Torchwood's John Barrowman: 'I Love Captain Jack, What He Stands for, What He Represents." *AfterElton.com*, July 15, 2009, http://www.afterelton.com/people/2009/7/john-barrowman?page=0%2C3.

"John Frobisher." Doctor Who Wiki, citing Russell T. Davies' comment in a *Torchwood Declassified*.

"Joseph Campbell's 12 Stages in the Hero's Journey." *A Psychotherapy Group in the Village in New York City*, http://www.am-psychotherapists-new-york-city.com/Joseph-Campbell.html.

Juergens, Brian. "'Heroes' Straightens Up Its Gay Character." *AfterElton.com*, December 11, 2006, http://www.afterelton.com/TV/2006/12/heroes.html.

Krochmal, Shana Naomi. "Interview with John Barrowman." *Out*, pp. 100–105.

Lambert, Doug, Ian Westhead, Helen Jones, and Mike Watkins. "2009 in Television:

Gems." *ATV Network News*, December 8, 2009, http://www.atvnewsnetwork.co.uk/today/index.php/atv-today/1884-2009-in-television-gems.

Lambert, Emily. "Tea? Coffee? Muffin?" *Western Mail* (Cardiff), October 28, 2006, p. 17.

Logan, Michael. "Unstrung Heroes." *TV Guide*, February 8–14, 2010, p. 40.

Mackey Kallis, Susan. *The Hero and the Perennial Journey Home in Film*. Philadelphia: University of Pennsylvania Press, 2001.

Marchiony, Frankie. "I'd Hang Out with You: TV's Top 10 Sidekicks." *Examiner.com*, June 25, 2009, http://www.examiner.com/x-15322-Long-Island-Television-Examiner~y2009m6d25-Id-hang-out-with-you-TVs-top-10-sidekicks.

"Masi Oka Discusses Possibilities of Hiro Finding Charlie." *TV Guide* quotation republished *Heroes Spoilers*, January 24, 2010, http://heroesspoilers-odi.blogspot.com/2010/01/masi-oka-discusses-possibilities-of.html.

May, Sarah Lucy. "The Ten Commandments." *SFX*, Winter 2009, pp. 38–42.

McDonnell, Mary. Dragon Con panel, September 5, 2009.

Merlin. BBC, 2008–

Millman, Joyce. "The Frontiers of Immortality." *Obit*, March 4, 2008, http://www.obit-mag.com/viewmedia.php/prmMID/4919.

Minchin, Brian. *The Sin Eaters*. London: BBC, 2009.

Moore, Ronald D. *Caprica*. DVD. SciFi, 2009.

"New Caprica Posters." *Caprica TV.net*, October 1, 2009, http://www.capricatv.net/2009/10/new-caprica-posters.html.

Oat, Zach. "*Castle*: Nathan Fillion Flashes Back to His *Firefly* Days." The Telefile, *Television Without Pity*, October 27, 2009, http://www.televisionwithoutpity.com/telefile/2009/10/castle-nathan-fillion-flashes.php.

Perryman, Neil. "Doctor Who and the Convergence of Media: A Case Study in 'Transmedia Storytelling.'" *Convergence: The International Journal of Research Into New Media Technologies*, 14 (1), 2008, pp. 21–39.

Pratt, Steve. "Television — All Right Jack." *Northern Echo* (Darlington), October 19, 2006, p. 3.

Price, Karen. "Prime-Time Slot for New Torchwood: Cardiff-Based Sci-fi Series Moves to BBC1 for Its Third Series." *South Wales Echo*, August 14, 2008, p. 6.

"Radio Free Skaro—#123 Shearman After Dark." February 14, 2009, http://www.radiofreeskaro.com/2009/02/14/radio-free-skaro-123-shearman-after-dark/.

Raglan, FitzRoy Richard Somerset. *The Hero: A Study in Tradition, Myth, and Drama*. New Haven, CT: Greenwood Press Reprint, 1975.

"Remembering Gene Roddenberry." *Star Trek.com News*, October 24, 2003, http://www.startrek.com/startrek/view/news/article/3289.html.

Renaud, Jeff. "He's the Doctor." *Geek*, September 2009, pp. 44–45.

"The Return of *Lost*." *Entertainment Weekly*, January 15, 2010, p. 43.

Roush, Matt. "Exclusive: First Look at Joss Whedon's 'Dr. Horrible.'" *TV Guide*, June 30, 2008, http://www.tvguide.com/roush/exclusive-look-joss-9886.aspx.

_____. "Matt Roush's Top 10." *TV Guide*, December 21, 2009–January 3, 2010, pp. 26–27.

Rundle, James. "Caprica: The Beginning of the End." *SciFi Now*, 35, 2009, pp. 36–40.

Scarlato, Ben. "Immortality and Death in Battlestar Galactica." Ethical Technology, *Institute for Ethics and Emerging Technologies*, January 18, 2009, http://ieet.org/index.php/IEET/more/scarlato20090118/.

Scott, Darren. "Jack's Back." *Gay Times*, June 2009, p. 36.

Seidman, Robert. "SyFy Launches First Phase of Innovative *Caprica* Marketing." September 30, 2009, http://tvbythenumbers.com/2009/09/30/syfy-launches-first-phase-of-innovative-caprica-marketing/29069.

Sepinwall, Alan. "Best of 2009 in TV — Sepinwall on TV." *The Star-Ledger*, December 22, 2009, http://www.nj.com/entertainment/tv/index.ssf/2009/12/best_of_2009_in_tv_-_sepinwall.html.

Serenity. Joss Joss (director). Universal Pictures, 2005.

"Serenity." *SFX*, Top 10 Films of the Decade, *SFX* Special Collector Edition 41, 2009, pp. 60–61.

Shearman, Rob. Q&A session, Hurricane Who convention, October 30, 2009, Orlando, Florida.

Spider-Man. Sam Raimi (director). Columbia Pictures, 2002.

Star Trek. J.J. Abrams (director). Paramount, 2009.

Star Trek: Wrath of Khan. Nicholas Meyer (director). Paramount, 1982.

"The Tao of Russell." *SFX* Collector Special Edition 41, Winter 2009, pp. 28–36.

Tennant, David. "Doctor Who Confidential." 12 (4). *Doctor Who*. The Complete Series 4. DVD. 2008.

Tolkien, J.R.R. *The Hobbit*. London: Allen & Unwin, 1937.

Tolkien, J.R.R. (Trans.). *Sir Gawain and the Green Knight*. New York: Random House, 1975.

"Top 7 Science Fiction Sidekicks." *The World in a Satin Bag*, July 19, 2009, http://wisb.blogspot.com/2009/07/top-7-science-fiction-sidekicks-in-film.html.

"Top Ten Villains." *Torchwood Magazine*, 18, November 2009.

"TV Buzz: James Marsters Stars in 'Caprica.'" *Newsday*, August 21, 2009, http://www.newsday.com/entertainment/tv/tv-buzz-james-marsters-stars-in-caprica-1.1385461.

Wallace, Lewis. "Review: *Caprica* Spins Religion, Race Into Worthy *Galactica* Prequel." *Wired*, April 20, 2009.

Werts, Diane. "Review: You Could Call It ... Lust in Space." *Newsday*, January 25, 2008, p. B29.

Whedon, Jed, lyrics and music. "A Man's Gotta Do." *Dr. Horrible's Sing-Along Blog*.

Whedon, Joss, lyrics and music. "Freeze Ray." *Dr. Horrible's Sing-Along Blog*.

Whedon, Joss, lyrics, and Christophe Beck, music. "Going Through the Motions," in "Once More, with Feeling," *Buffy the Vampire Slayer*, UPN, November 6, 2001.

Whedon, Joss, lyrics and music, and Jed Whedon, bridge. "Everything You Ever." *Dr. Horrible's Sing-Along Blog*.

Whedon, Joss, Jed Whedon, Zack Whedon, and Maurissa Tanchareon. *Dr. Horrible's Sing-Along Blog*, July 15–20, 2008, http://www.drhorrible.com.

Wilkes, Neil. "Live: 'Torchwood' Panel at Comic-Con." *Digital Spy*, July 26, 2009, http://www.digitalspy.com/tv/a167433/live-torchwood-panel-at-comic-con.html.

Wycherley, Lolly. "Sci Fi Sidekicks—A Thing of the Past?" July 28, 2009, *Sci Fi Channel UK*, http://www.scifi.co.uk/blog/author/lolly_wycherley/.

Young, Susan. "Top 10 New TV Sidekicks." October 15, 2008, http://www.film.com/tv/house/story/top-10-new-tv-sidekicks/23588592.

Authors of
Episodes Discussed

Abrams, J.J., and Damon Lindelof. "Pilot." *Lost*. ABC. September 22, 2004.

Angeli, Michael. "Blood on the Scales." *Battlestar Galactica*. SciFi. February 6, 2009.

Armus, Adam, and Kay Foster. "I Am Sylar." *Heroes*. NBC. April 20, 2009.

_____. "The Wall." *Heroes*. NBC. February 1, 2010.

Aubuchon, Remi, and Ronald D. Moore. *Caprica*. "Pilot." DVD. June 2009.

_____. "Reins of a Waterfall." *Caprica*. SyFy. February 5, 2010.

Bell, Jeffrey, and Joss Whedon. "Not Fade Away." *Angel*. WB. May 19, 2004.

Cain, Cheryl. "War Stories." *Firefly*. Fox. December 6, 2002.

Chibnall, Chris. "Cyberwoman." *Torchwood*. BBC. November 5, 2006.

_____. "End of Days." *Torchwood*. BBC. January 1, 2007.

_____. "Exit Wounds." *Torchwood*. BBC Two. April 4, 2008.

_____. "Kiss Kiss, Bang Bang." *Torchwood*. BBC. January 16, 2008.

Coleite, Aron Eli, and Aury Wallington. "Once Upon a Time in Texas." *Heroes*. NBC. November 2, 2009.

Cornell, Paul. "Father's Day." *Doctor Who*. BBC. May 14, 2005.

Cuse, Carlton, and Damon Lindelof. "Deus Ex Machina." *Lost*. ABC. March 20, 2005.

_____. "Further Instructions." *Lost*. ABC. October 18, 2006.

_____. "The Life and Death of Jeremy Bentham." *Lost*. ABC. February 25, 2009.

_____. "Live Together, Die Alone." *Lost*. ABC. May 24, 2006.

_____. "Through the Looking Glass." *Lost*. ABC. May 23, 2007.

_____. "The 23rd Psalm." *Lost*. ABC. January 11, 2006.

_____. "Whatever Happened, Happened." *Lost*. ABC. April 1, 2009.

Davies, Russell T. "Boom Town." *Doctor Who*. BBC. June 4, 2005.

_____. "Children of Earth, Day Five." *Torchwood*. BBC. July 10, 2009.

_____. "The Christmas Invasion." *Doctor Who*. BBC. December 25, 2005.

_____. "Doomsday." *Doctor Who*. BBC. July 8, 2006.

_____. "The End of the World." *Doctor Who*. BBC. April 2, 2005.

_____. "The End of Time, Part 1." *Doctor Who*. BBC. December 25, 2009.

_____. "The End of Time, Part 2." *Doctor Who*. BBC. January 1, 2010.

_____. "Everything Changes." *Torchwood*. BBC. October 22, 2006.

_____. "Journey's End." *Doctor Who*. BBC. June 21, 2008.

_____. "The Long Game." *Doctor Who*. BBC. May 7, 2005.

_____. "The Parting of the Ways." *Doctor Who*. BBC. June 18, 2005.

_____. "Rose." *Doctor Who*. BBC. March 26, 2005.

_____. "The Stolen Earth." *Doctor Who*. BBC. June 28, 2008.

_____. "Voyage of the Damned." *Doctor Who*. BBC. December 25, 2007.

Davies, Russell T., and Phil Ford. "The Waters of Mars." *Doctor Who*. BBC. November 15, 2009.

_____, and James Moran. "Children of Earth: Day Three." *Torchwood*. BBC. July 8, 2009.

DeKnight, Steven. "Seeing Red." *Buffy the Vampire Slayer*. UPN. May 7, 2002.

Espenson, Jane. "Shindig." *Firefly.* Fox. November 1, 2002.

Fay, John. "Children of Earth: Day Four." *Torchwood.* BBC. July 9, 2009.

Ford, Phil. "The Dead Line." *Torchwood.* BBC Radio. July 3, 2009.

Fuller, Bryan. *Heroes.* "Company Man." NBC. February 26, 2007.

Fury, David. "Grave." *Buffy the Vampire Slayer.* UPN. May 21, 2002.

Gatiss, Mark. "The Unquiet Dead." *Doctor Who.* BBC. April 9, 2005.

Goyer, David S., and Brannon Braga. "No More Good Days." *FlashForward.* ABC. September 24, 2009.

Grigsby, Oliver. "Pass/Fail." *Heroes.* NBC. January 18, 2010.

Hammond, Peter J. "From Out of the Rain." *Torchwood.* BBC. March 12, 2008.

_____. "Small Worlds." *Torchwood.* BBC. November 12, 2006.

Jones, Matt. "Dead Man Walking." *Torchwood.* BBC. February 13, 2008.

Kitsis, Edward, and Adam Horowitz. "Something Nice Back Home." *Lost.* ABC. May 1, 2008.

Kring, Tim. "The Fifth Stage." *Heroes.* NBC. November 30, 2009.

_____. "An Invisible Thread." *Heroes.* NBC. April 27, 2009.

Kring, Tim, and Jesse Alexander. "Landslide." *Heroes.* NBC. May 14, 2007.

Kring, Tim, and Aron Eli Coleite. "The Hard Part." *Heroes.* NBC. May 7, 2007.

_____. "I Am Become Death." *Heroes.* NBC. October 6, 2008.

Lidster, Joseph. "A Day in the Death." *Torchwood.* BBC. February 27, 2008.

_____. "Lost Souls." *Torchwood.* BBC Radio. September 10, 2008.

Lindelof, Damon. "Man of Science, Man of Faith." *Lost.* ABC. September 21, 2005.

Lindelof, Damon, and Carlton Cuse. "The Brig." *Lost.* ABC. May 2, 2007.

_____. "I Do." *Lost.* ABC. November 8, 2006.

_____. "The Incident." *Lost.* ABC. May 13, 2009.

_____. "316." *Lost.* ABC. February 18, 2009.

Loeb, Jeph. "One Giant Leap." *Heroes.* NBC. October 9, 2006.

Minear, Tim. "That Old Gang of Mine." *Angel.* WB. October 8, 2001.

Moffat, Steven. "The Empty Child." *Doctor Who.* BBC. May 21, 2005.

_____. "Time Crash: Children in Need Special." *Doctor Who.* BBC. 2007.

Moore, Ronald D. "Daybreak." *Battlestar Galactica.* SciFi. March 13 and March 20, 2009.

Moore, Ronald D., and Christopher Eric James. "Night 1." *Battlestar Galactica* pilot miniseries. Sci-Fi. December 8, 2003.

Moran, James. "The Fires of Pompeii." *Doctor Who.* BBC. April 12, 2008.

_____. "Sleeper." *Torchwood.* BBC. January 22, 2008.

Petrie, Douglas. "Fool for Love." *Buffy the Vampire Slayer.* WB. November 14, 2000.

Pokaski, Joe. "Hysterical Blindness." *Heroes.* NBC. October 12, 2009.

Roberts, Gareth. "The Wedding of Sarah Jane Smith, Part 2." *The Sarah Jane Adventures.* BBC. October 30, 2009.

Schapker, Alison, and Monica Owusu-Breen. "The Cost of Living." *Lost.* ABC. November 1, 2006.

Schorn, Daniel. "The Quest for Immortality." *60 Minutes.* CBS. January 1, 2006. http://www.cbsnews.com/stories/2005/12/28/60minutes/main1168852.shtml.

Shearman, Robert. "Dalek." *Doctor Who.* BBC. April 30, 2005.

Tamaro, Janet. "Do No Harm." *Lost.* ABC. April 6, 2005.

Taylor, Christian. "White Rabbit." *Lost.* ABC. October 13, 2004.

Taylor, Michael. "Sine Qua Non." *Battlestar Galactica.* Sci-Fi. May 27, 2008.

Thompson, Bradley, and David Weddie. "Sometimes a Great Notion." *Battlestar Galactica.* SciFi. January 16, 2009.

Tregenna, Catherine. "Adam." *Torchwood.* BBC. February 20, 2008.

_____. "Captain Jack Harkness." *Torchwood.* BBC. January 1, 2007.

Vaughan, Brian K., and Goddard Drew. "The Shape of Things to Come." *Lost.* ABC. April 24, 2008.

Vaughan, Brian K., and Elizabeth Sarnoff. "Dead Is Dead." *Lost.* ABC. April 8, 2009.

Verheiden, Mark. "Rebirth." *Caprica.* SyFy. January 29, 2010.

Whedon, Joss. "Once More, with Feeling." *Buffy the Vampire Slayer.* UPN. November 6, 2001.

_____. "Serenity." *Firefly.* Fox. December 20, 2002.

Whedon, Joss, and Tim Minear. "The Train Job." *Firefly.* Fox. September 20, 2002.

Wilsher, J.C. "Reset." *Torchwood.* BBC. February 13, 2008.

Index